ROUTLEDGE LIBRARY EDITIONS: ACCOUNTING HISTORY

Volume 28

HISTORY OF PUBLIC ACCOUNTING IN THE UNITED STATES

T0382746

HISTORY OF PUBLIC ACCOUNTING IN THE UNITED STATES

JAMES DON EDWARDS

LONDON AND NEW YORK

First published in 1988 by Garland Publishing, Inc.

This edition first published in 2021
by Routledge
2 Park Square, Milton Park, Abingdon, Oxon OX14 4RN

and by Routledge
52 Vanderbilt Avenue, New York, NY 10017

Routledge is an imprint of the Taylor & Francis Group, an informa business

British Library Cataloguing in Publication Data
A catalogue record for this book is available from the British Library

ISBN: 978-0-367-33564-9 (Set)
ISBN: 978-1-00-304636-3 (Set) (ebk)
ISBN: 978-0-367-53517-9 (Volume 28) (hbk)
ISBN: 978-0-367-53522-3 (Volume 28) (pbk)
ISBN: 978-1-00-308232-3 (Volume 28) (ebk)

Publisher's Note
The publisher has gone to great lengths to ensure the quality of this reprint but
points out that some imperfections in the original copies may be apparent.

Disclaimer
The publisher has made every effort to trace copyright holders and would welcome
correspondence from those they have been unable to trace.

History of Public Accounting in the United States

JAMES DON EDWARDS

GARLAND PUBLISHING, INC.

NEW YORK & LONDON 1988

For a list of Garland's publications in accounting,
see the final pages of this volume.

Reprinted by permission of the author and Michigan State University
Press, and reproduced from a copy in the American Institute of Certified
Public Accountants.

Library of Congress Cataloging in Publication Data

■ ■

Edwards, James Don.
History of public accounting in the United States / James Don
Edwards.
p. cm. — (Foundations of accounting) (Classics series /
Academy of Accounting Historians)
Originally published: East Lansing : Bureau of Business and
Economic Research. Graduate School of Business Administration,
Michigan State University, 1960. (MSU business studies)
Bibliography: p.
Includes index.
ISBN 0-8240-6136-5 (alk. paper)
1. Accounting—United States—History. 2. Accounting—Stan-
·dards—United States—History. 3. Accounting—Law and legisla-
tion—United States—History. 4. Accountants—Legal status, laws,
etc.—United States—History. I. Title. II. Series. III. Series:
Classics series (New York, N. Y.)
HF5616.U5E3 1988
657'.61'0973—dc 19   88-16037

Design by Renata Gomes

The volumes in this series are printed on
acid-free 250-year-life paper.

Printed in the United States of America

HISTORY OF PUBLIC ACCOUNTING
IN THE UNITED STATES

MSU Business Studies

ELECTRONICS IN BUSINESS

Gardner M. Jones

EXPLORATIONS IN RETAILING

Stanley C. Hollander

ELEMENTARY MATHEMATICS OF LINEAR
PROGRAMMING AND GAME THEORY

Edward G. Bennion

MARGINAL ASPECTS OF MANAGEMENT PRACTICES

Frederic N. Firestone

HISTORY OF PUBLIC ACCOUNTING IN THE
UNITED STATES

James Don Edwards

MSU BUSINESS STUDIES 1960

HISTORY OF

PUBLIC ACCOUNTING

in the United States

JAMES DON EDWARDS

PROFESSOR AND HEAD, DEPARTMENT OF ACCOUNTING
AND FINANCIAL ADMINISTRATION
MICHIGAN STATE UNIVERSITY

Bureau of Business and Economic Research

Graduate School of Business Administration

Michigan State University, East Lansing

Library of Congress Catalog Number: 66-63369

Dedicated to my wife, Clara

Foreword

There has long been a need for a book such as this—a readable, reasonably concise history of the accounting profession from its beginnings to the present day. Most certified public accountants have only vague conceptions of where their profession came from, how it developed, how its standards have evolved, what social, economic and legal forces have shaped it. Yet it is important that professional men should understand these things. The past is a guide to the future. If one knows the reasons why things are as they are, he can better foresee how they are likely to be in the years ahead.

Professor Edwards, in his laudable determination to keep this book down to manageable size, has had to make difficult choices of inclusion, exclusion, and emphasis. Many readers will doubtless disagree with the manner in which he has dealt with one subject or another. Indeed, I would treat some of the sections, dealing with events in which I have participated, quite differently from the way in which he has dealt with them. But this is not to say that he is wrong. Any view of history is partly subjective. Professor Edwards has kept close to the published record, and his own opinions and interpretations have been kept to a minimum.

The result is a series of dramatic highlights, illustrative of the multifarious problems besetting a young profession which has been catapulted into prominence by the economic and social forces of the twentieth century. The author does not attempt exhaustive analysis of each area of professional activity, nor does he claim to have described every event which might be considered significant. But he has set out the milestones, clearly marking out the course of professional growth.

This book, in my opinion, will be fascinating and rewarding reading, both for C.P.A.'s who have lived through some of the events described, and for C.P.A.'s and students who up to now have had no knowledge of them. I move a vote of thanks to Don Edwards for the pioneering work he has done in producing this *modern* history of public accounting in the United States.

John L. Carey
Executive Director
American Institute
of Certified Public Accountants

Preface

The purpose of this book is to fill a vacuum in the literature of public accounting, one of the more recent professions to attain the status of international recognition. The designation *Certified Public Accountant* was first used in New York state in 1896 and now has legal standing in all fifty states; international recognition is implicit in the acceptability of the public accountant's professional services anywhere in the world.

The business historian, the professional man, and the student entering the field should all know something of its growth in the United States. This study covers the significant historical developments in public accounting; it emphasizes the growth of a profession rather than the evolution of a body of subject matter. My first intention was to make a comprehensive study of all aspects of the accounting profession, but that huge task was soon discarded in favor of this more limited undertaking.

No attempt is made to present the history on a state-by-state basis. Rather, the unifying principle has been to select those national and international developments through which the prestige and professional standing of the C.P.A. have been augmented. The material is organized chronologically, from the European antecedents of American accounting practices through the evolution of the educational, legal and organizational aspects of the profession. Some of these developments are so recent that their judicious interpretation cannot yet be undertaken. The respect with which the professional opinion of the certified public accountant is viewed by government officials, businesses, banking and financial institutions, and the general public may be one of the important bases of our system of enterprise. The fact that most government agencies as well as the stock exchanges and financial institutions require an expression of opinion by a certified public accountant on the financial position of business firms is an indication of the magnitude of that individual's responsibility to the public.

My inquiry into professional history was first begun under the direction of Dr. C. Aubrey Smith of the University of Texas. I am grateful to Professor Smith for stimulating my interest in the subject. The manuscript has since been completely revised and brought up through the decade of the 1950's. Some of the material of the original research project was also used in preparation of articles which have appeared in *The Accounting Review, Accounting Research* (Cambridge University), and *The Business History Review* (Harvard University).

I am appreciative of the assistance given by Miss Katherine Michaelsen, Librarian, the American Institute of Certified Public Accountants, in locating books and periodicals for use in this study. I have also drawn on the libraries of the University of Michigan, Michigan State University, and the University of Texas.

I am indebted also to Dean Alfred S. Seelye, Dean of the Graduate School of Business Administration, Michigan State University, for encouraging the completion of the manuscript and to Dr. Anne C. Garrison and Mrs. Esther B. Waite for their constructive editorial criticisms.

Several public accountants provided details of the early development of the profession in which they played a part. The late Mr. Norman Webster, formerly Chairman of the History Committee of the American Institute, was helpful in referring me to information not generally available to the public, especially that having to do with early developments in the field of public accounting. The late Mr. Ernest Reckitt of Chicago, who was issued New York Certified Public Accountant Certificate Number 60, discussed with me the problems of writing the history of public accounting in the United States. Many of the present members of the profession gave me data on the national and international growth of their firms and about their mergers.

Mr. C. W. DeMond, partner, Price, Waterhouse and Company, was helpful in furnishing early audit certificates issued in the first two decades of this century.

I am especially appreciative of the interested comments and advice given me by Mr. John L. Carey, Executive Director of the American Institute of Certified Public Accountants.

James Don Edwards
September 21, 1960
East Lansing, Michigan

Contents

Contents

CHAPTER I

Introduction

The profession of independent Certified Public Accountant was first given legal recognition in 1896 in the state of New York. Prior to the passage of this legislation, public accountants had practiced for some time in various sections of the United States; indeed, their earliest activities antedated the American Revolution. Their first national organization, the American Association of Public Accountants, was formed in 1886.

Since its beginning, the profession of public accountancy has made a significant contribution to financial confidence in American business. Reliance on independent audits of financial statements has by now become an integral factor in public trust in business enterprise. Since this is so, it is surprising that no contemporary history of public accounting in the United States has been written hitherto. There are four books in the general area: Richard Brown's *A History of Accounting and Accountants* (Edinburgh and London, 1905), Wilmer L. Green's *History and Survey of Accounting* (New York, 1930), A. C. Littleton's *Accounting Evolution to 1900*, issued by the American Institute Publishing Company in 1933, and Arthur H. Woolf's *A Short History of Accountants and Accounting* (London, 1912). In addition, a few state societies have brought out histories of their organization on the occasion of their golden anniversaries: an example of such a book is *The New York State Society of Certified Public Accountants' Fiftieth Anniversary*, published in 1947. There have also been histories of individual public accountancy firms, such as C. W. DeMond's *Price, Waterhouse and Company in America*, which appeared in 1951.

While these books are useful in their kind, it is obvious that there is a gap in accounting literature. The present work is designed to fill this; it is addressed to accountants, business historians, and professional students. As the profession is now sixty-four years old, from the legal point of view, the potential audience is a large one; the various states have issued in excess of 65,000 C.P.A. certificates,

and the American Institute of Certified Public Accountants has a
membership of 35,000. This sizeable body of professional men
should have available to them an historical study of the national
growth of their discipline.

Throughout this book I have emphasized the importance of the
increase in dignity of the profession in the eye of the public, and
stressed the profession's own growing recognition of the necessity
for educational standards. These trends are clearly evident in the
factual records. My emphasis is less on interpretation of events
than on the events themselyes. It is of paramount importance that
the facts of accountancy history be assembled, that they be set in
order and presented in the proper matrix of contemporary economic
life. I have not attempted to evaluate economic influences on the
development of the profession, but rather to describe its growth, indicating the highlights and pointing out its special problems.

It will be obvious to the reader of these chapters that the role
of the Certified Public Accountant has changed a great deal in the
last sixty years. While one of his functions, that of independent
audit, has remained the primary one, expansion into the field of
federal income tax, estate and gift tax planning as well as the area
of management services has added to both the responsibilities and
the prestige of the public accountancy profession.

A word about the general plan of organization will be useful to
the reader. The material is developed chronologically, not on a
topical basis. Either approach has its advantages as well as its serious
deficiencies, but a choice of method had to be made. In view of
the complexities of the profession's history, organization on a time
basis seemed to present less difficulty to the reader. Accordingly,
the account opens with the historical background: the antecedents
of American public accounting in England and Scotland.

There follows a discussion of individual, legal and institutional
definitions of the public accounting function, some historical and
some contemporary. These data are given at length, as they provide
a valuable indication of the extent and complexity of the accountant's activities. It will be apparent that no "ideal" definition exists,
but a survey of the whole spectrum of definitions indicates the broad
social environment in which the profession operates, and suggests
the complications of its history.

In the chronological treatment that is then resumed, the period of
emergence of public accounting in the United States is considered

to cover the years 1748 to 1895, spanning the time from the earliest ascertainable date for the performance of any of the profession's functions in the Colonies to the year prior to the enactment of the first C.P.A. law. This chapter also contains a discussion of the functions of professional organizations and the development of accountancy education during these years.

The period 1896-1913 forms the next natural division of our chronology. It terminates in the last year before World War I, the same year in which the federal income tax was enacted. The salient topics in this chapter are C.P.A. legislation, the C.P.A. examination, and expansion in the functions of the profession.

The war and postwar years, ending in 1928 just before the onset of the Great Depression, make up the period treated in the next chapter. During this era the profession's functions increased greatly, in part as a result of the work brought about by cost-plus contracts. The augmented responsibilities of the Certified Public Accountant, including that of the auditing function, led to the establishment by the Federal Reserve Board of minimum standards for professional audits. It was this same period that brought the American Institute into real national prominence.

Influences of the depression, and the establishment of reporting standards of certified statements, receive most attention in the account of the years 1928 to 1950. The McKesson and Robbins case was influential at this time, the Securities and Exchange Commission was established, and the American Institute issued its first extension of audit procedures. The jurisdictional conflict between Certified Public Accountants and lawyers was a growing problem.

1950-1960 is recognized as the period in which the Certified Public Accountant has been acclaimed as a professional man on a par with other professional men such as lawyers and doctors. In this decade much attention was paid to the accountant's educational and experiential standards. The lawyer-accountant conflict continued; a joint commission was set up by the American Bar Association and the American Institute of Certified Public Accountants with a view to establishing principles and defining functions. National accounting firms became international in scope and operations, a development that reveals worldwide recognition of the work of the Certified Public Accountant. Likewise, during this period, auditing and accounting standards continued to receive the attention of the accountancy profession: the Institute established an Accounting

Principles Board and a Professional Development Department. The obviously short-view character of our estimate of such recent events makes the decade of the Fifties an extremely difficult one to evaluate. At so close a range one can scarcely hope to see the forest, but I have tried to record faithfully the nature and number of the individual trees.

The chronological account surveyed above is supplemented by two appendices. Appendix A gives the complete text of the first C.P.A. examination, while Appendix B records state C.P.A. certificates issued by year from 1896 to 1958.

The responsibility for the limitations of this book, as regards both omission and commission, is wholly my own. It is my hope that this factual account will serve as the basis for further study of the economic impact of the independent Certified Public Accountant upon the development of American business.

CHAPTER II

The Antecedents of American Public Accounting

In early times keeping records was associated with governmental administration and distribution of contributed capital and gain to joint adventurers in the Old World. Commercial record keeping seems to have been more vigorous and to have developed into double-entry bookkeeping and then into the analysis of proprietorship. Double-entry bookkeeping reached Great Britain from northern Italy in about the fifteenth century. In the late Renaissance it was also flourishing in Holland, and commercial contacts between that country and England also influenced practices in the latter country. Although it was introduced in London about 1550, it did not become well known for fully another century.

Just as customs, common law, and commercial practice came to the United States from England and Scotland, so did the practice of accountancy, either through books or through the accountants themselves. Direct links with countries other than England and Scotland are not very clear. This chapter describes the development of accounting in the antecedent countries during the eighteenth and nineteenth centuries.

PROFESSIONAL FUNCTIONS

Investigations and Audits

It was in 1720 that the first major recognition of a public accountant was given to Charles Snell, one of the outstanding English accountants of the eighteenth century,[1] who had written "Observations Made Upon Examining the Books of Sawbridge and Company."[2] This company was one of the subsidiaries of the South Sea

---

[1] H. C. Bentley, *A Brief Treatise on the History and Development of Accounting* (Boston: Bentley School of Accounting and Finance, 1929), p. 30.

[2] "A History of the Accounting Profession," *The Accountant*, XXI (April, 1895), 375.

Company which Snell was engaged to investigate. The implications
in the *Accountant* article lead one to believe that the report was issued early in 1721. The report apparently conformed to the standards of that day. Snell was known in London as a "Writing Master
and Accountant."[3]

Snell's report was undertaken at the request of a special committee
of Parliament. He had been appointed by this committee to conduct
an investigation of the records of the South Sea Company, a public
organization, and more particularly its subsidiary, the Sawbridge
Company. It had failed, as had many other companies after the burst-
ing of the South Sea Bubble in December, 1720.[4] Snell's report,
according to Bentley, was the first ever rendered by a public accountant.[5]

The South Sea Bubble was the collapse of a series of financial
projects which originated with the incorporation of the South Sea
Company in 1711 and ended nine years later in general disaster.

The plan was for the English government to sell certain trading
monopolies to a company in return for a sum of money to be devoted
to the reduction of the national debt. The company, founded in
1711, was granted a monopoly of the British trade with South America and the Pacific islands, the riches of which were confidently
believed to be unlimited.

As the promoters were mostly wealthy and respected merchants,
the public bought readily.[6] Soon the company began to retire the
government annuities for life, payments the government had agreed
to pay, with a small amount of stock issued at a high premium.
Previously, public purchases of stock had caused it to appreciate
greatly in value. The selling price increased over 250 percent during
the first three months of 1720. By the middle of the year the stock
had risen in price from £128 to £1,000. By this time the extraordinary success of the South Sea Company had many imitators, and
the result was a wild mania of speculation, with the inevitable end—
a crash.

The stock of the South Sea Company reached £1,000 in July; in
August the fall in price began; in September, just after the insiders

---

[3]"A Hundred Years of Accountancy," *The Accountant*, XXVII (January, 1901), 38.
[4]H. C. Bentley, *A Brief Treatise on the History and Development of Accounting*, p. 30.
[5]"A History of the Accountancy Profession," *The Accountant*, XXI (April, 1895), 375.
[6]*Cambridge Modern History* (New York: The Macmillan Company, 1908), V, 445.

sold out, quotations plummeted. Instead of everyone being a buyer, everyone became a seller. As a result, the price shortly fell to £175, while the stock of many smaller companies became worthless.[7]

Parliament was called together on December 8, 1720, and at once both houses proceeded to investigate the affairs of the company, the lower house soon entrusting this task to a Committee of Secrecy. The committee reported in February, 1721, on the activities of this company and its subsidiaries.

While there appears to be no actual authentication for other audit reports covering many of the bankruptcies of this period, it is safe to assume that many such reports were made.

By the turn of the nineteenth century the evolution of the accounting profession had reached the point where the functions of the practitioner could be enumerated. Some of these functions were:

Agent for houses in England and Scotland connected with bankruptcies in Glasgow.

The winding up of dissolved partnership concerns and the adjusting of partner's accounts.

The keeping and balancing of all account-books belonging to merchants, shopkeepers, etc.ᵎ . . .

The examining and adjusting of all disputed accounts and account books.[8]

The Company Clause Consolidation Act of 1845 made provisions for the audit of the accounts of companies regulated by act of Parliament. This act provided that railroads appoint auditors and that they call in outside accountants to assist them. It seems significant that the references to "Accountants and Agents" or "Commercial Accountants" whose duties were not very clear were no longer made.[9]

In 1868, the 1845 act was amended. The regulated railroads were now required to submit audited financial statements to the Board of Trade and stockholders. The auditor did not have to be

⁷*Ibid.*, VI, 530.

⁸Richard Brown, *A History of Accounting and Accountants* (Edinburgh and London: T. C. and E. C. Jack, 1905), p. 201.

⁹*Ibid.*, p. 318.

a stockholder but he did have to follow a prescribed form in preparing the balance sheet and revenue statement. Some authorities consider these acts a major factor in establishing the public accounting profession. Thus, during the "Railroad Mania" of the '40's, the public accounting profession in England gained major recognition.[10]

The Companies Act of 1862 offered new fields of lucrative employment for accountants and no doubt did much to attract many ambitious young men to seek their fortunes in the profession.[11] The cause for this can be found in Table A of the act of 1862.

The accounting clause of the 1862 act reads:

> No dividends should be payable except out of the profits arising from the business of the company. The directors should cause true accounts to be kept and once a year should make out a balance-sheet and statement of income and expenditures and present it at the meeting of the stockholders.[12]

Once a year, at least, the accounts of the company should be examined and the corrections of the balance sheet verified by one or more auditors, usually already members of the company at the time of their first appointment in general meeting.[13] The act set forth the form of report which was to be used by the auditor after he had examined the accounts and related vouchers to determine whether the balance sheet, in his opinion, fairly reflected the state of the company's affairs.

The main purpose of the Companies Acts was to establish a certain degree of public control through making public the circumstances of company formation, and to establish some check on the directors' responsibilities in managing the company's affairs. Another was to protect the stockholders by requiring a committee of stockholders to audit the records and financial statements of the directors.[14]

---

[10]A. C. Littleton, *Accounting Evolution to 1900* (New York: American Institute Publishing Co., Inc., 1933), p. 302.

[11]"Accountants in England from the Nineteenth Century," *The Accountant*, XLVI (January, 1912), 261.

[12]Wiley Daniel Rich, *Legal Responsibilities and Rights of the Public Accountant* (New York: American Institute Publishing Co., Inc., 1935), p. 236.

[13]Mary E. Murphy, "The Profession of Accountancy in England: The Public, the Government, the Profession," *The Accounting Review*, XV (September, 1940), 323.

[14]A. C. Littleton, *Accounting Evolution to 1900*, p. 293.

Because many unqualified accountants began to give advice to these obligatory auditing committees, professional accountants decided to seek some way of excluding such persons. In 1879, some English practitioners decided to introduce a bill into Parliament for the incorporation of the Institute of Chartered Accountants of England, setting forth the functions performed by the accounting profession. Before action could be taken on the bill a petition was substituted stating:

> That profession is a numerous one and their functions are of great and increasing importance in respect to their employment in the capacities of . . . also in the auditing of accounts of public companies and of partnership and otherwise.[15]

The charter of the Institute of Chartered Accountants in England and Wales, granted May 11, 1880, provided that the applicants must take an examination in auditing, this examination to be an application of theory to actual cases. This section of the examination probably arose out of the provisions in the Companies Acts requiring that audits be made, and out of the desire of professional accountants to insure that advisers to corporations should be qualified to give advice.

Early Court Decisions Affecting Auditors

The first important English court case on the duties of an auditor was the *Leeds Estate Building and Investment Company* vs. *Shepherd,* rendered by Justice Sterling in 1887. This case extended the auditor's duties to inquiry into the soundness, not merely the mathematical accuracy, of the figures included on the balance sheet.

The articles of incorporation of the Leeds Estate Building Company provided that the manager and the directors were entitled to a bonus based on the amount of profits available for dividends. It was therefore to the interest of the directors and manager to report a large profit. They accomplished this by overstating the assets. The balance sheet and profit and loss statements were certified by

---

15"History of Accountants and Accounting," *The Accountant*, XLVI (January, 1912), 261.

the accountant without question after being presented to him by the directors, even though the auditor was elected by the stockholders. Dividends were illegally paid out of capital. After the company went into liquidation, an action for damages was brought against the auditor and the directors. The auditor maintained that he was a servant of the directors of the company, but the judge rendered the following opinion:

> It was in my opinion the duty of the auditor not to confine himself merely to the task of verifying the arithmetical accuracy of the balance-sheet, but to inquire into its substantial accuracy, and to ascertain that it contained the particulars specified in the articles of association (and consequently a proper income and expenditure account), and was properly drawn up, so as to contain a true and correct representation of the state of the company's affairs.[16]

In the Leeds case the decision made it clear that the auditor was to check the records of the company from which the statements were taken to satisfy himself that they reflect the operations of the business. It was the auditor's responsibility to do more than just certify the statements as to arithmetical accuracy.

Another prominent case concerning the definition of duties of the public accountant with respect to a proper reflection of the values of assets in the balance sheet was the London and General Bank case in 1895.

The bank was organized for the purpose of making loans to a group of building companies, known as the Balfour group. The profits for the company consisted of the interest and commissions from the loans and services to the builders.

For several years during the operations of the bank the major portion of this capital had been advanced to four members of the Balfour group on securities which were inadequately secured and difficult of realization. The auditor of the bank, in his report to the directors, repeatedly called the directors' attention to the precarious financial condition of the bank. The auditor's report had been in the form of a memorandum written on the balance sheet with a statement that the balance sheet exhibited a correct view of

---

[16]Wiley Daniel Rich, *Legal Responsibilities and Rights of the Public Accountant*, p. 17.

the position of the bank. But in 1891 the report called the directors' attention to the financial condition of the bank and ended, "We cannot conclude without expressing our opinion unhesitatingly that no dividend should be paid this year."[17] The manager persuaded the auditor to exclude this statement from his report.

The bank then proceeded to pay a dividend because the report certified by the auditor was no different from those that had previously been given. These dividends were in fact paid out of capital, not profits. The stockholders considered that the auditor was guilty of misfeasance and took action against him.

The following are excerpts from the opinion of the court:

. . . an auditor has nothing to do with the prudence or imprudence of making loans with or without security. . . . His business is to ascertain and state the true financial position of the company at the time of the audit, and duty is confined to that. . . . An auditor, however, is not bound to do more than exercise reasonabie care and skill in making inquiries and investigations. He is not an insurer; he does not even guarantee that his balance sheet is accurate according to the books of the company. . . . Such I take to be the duty of the auditor; he must be honest—i. e., he must not certify what he does not believe to be true, and he must take reasonable care and skill before he believes that what he certifies is true. . . . Under these circumstances I am compelled to hold that Mr. Theobald failed to discharge his duty to the shareholder with respect to the balance sheet and certificate of February, 1892.[18]

In the General Bank case the auditor certified statements without taking exception or including a qualification in his report. The court held this to be negligence in the performance of his duty and established the principle that the auditor should only certify what he has reason to believe to be true.

Another major case in which the English courts defined the duties of an auditor was the Kingston Cotton Mill Company case. This case will be discussed in a later chapter, but briefly the case pertained to the overstatement of inventories by the managers. It was the decision of the court that the auditor had no reason to suspect

---

[17]Arthur W. Hanson, *Problems in Auditing* (New York: McGraw-Hill Book Company, Inc., 1935), p. 53.

[18]Wiley Daniel Rich, *Legal Responsibilities and Rights of the Public Accountant*, p. 26.

the dishonesty of the manager, who certified the amount of stock-in-trade. The auditor clearly stated that he got the figures from the manager. Furthermore, the auditor, in the absence of suspicion of dishonesty, had no duty to check the figures on the value of inventory as given by a competent officer of the business.[19]

FUNCTIONS OF THE PUBLIC ACCOUNTANT
AND LAWS AFFECTING HIM

The first major recognition given the public accounting profession in cases involving dissolutions was in respect to the Sawbridge Company in 1720, already mentioned. An accountant, Charles Snell, made an investigation into the company's books at the request of Parliament. Thus it is evident that at an early date accountants were consulted in cases of bankruptcy.[20]

A great commercial crisis occurred in Glasgow in 1777 as the result of the previous year's revolt in the North American colonies, with which part of the world the trade of the city was closely identified. The crisis afforded considerable business for the accountants in Glasgow. Then came the bankruptcies of 1793, when more than twenty banking companies failed. Accountants were commissioned to settle the affairs of these banks and liquidate their liabilities. One of them, Walter E. Maclone of Cathkin, Scotland, Merchant and Accountant, was employed to settle some of the most important bankruptcies which occurred during these crises.[21]

Brown catalogs the functions performed by these early accounts as follows:

Factor and trustee on sequestrated estates.

Trustee or factor for trustee of creditors acting under trust deeds.

Factor for trustees acting for the heirs of persons deceased.

Factor for gentlemen residing in the country for the management of heritable or other property.

Agent for houses in England and Scotland connected with bankruptcies in Glasgow.

---

[19]*Ibid.*, p. 34.

[20]"A History of the Accountancy Profession," *The Accountant*, XXI (April, 1895), 375.

[21]Norman E. Webster, "Public Accounting in the United States," in *Fiftieth Anniversary Celebration* (New York: American Institute Publishing Co., 1937), p. 102.

The winding up of dissolved partnership concerns and the adjusting of partners' accounts.

The keeping and balancing of all account-books belonging to merchants, shopkeepers, etc.

The making up of statements, reports, and memorials on account-books or disputed accounts and claims for the purpose of laying before arbiters, courts, or counsel.

The examining and adjusting of all disputed accounts and account-books.

The looking after and recovering old debts and dividends from bankrupt estates.

And all other departments of the Accountant's business.[22]

These functions seem to include almost all phases of accounting operations. It is obvious that the accountant and lawyer had some overlapping functions.

In the historic petition submitted to Queen Victoria in 1854, there were several sections giving further information on the functions of the accountant in cases of dissolution. An excerpt from the petition stated that the accountant was expected to have "an intimate acquaintance with the law of Scotland, and more especially with those branches of it which have relation to the law of merchant, to insolvency and bankruptcy. . . ."[23]

The first major legislation in cases of bankruptcy which affected the accountant's work was in 1849. Passing the final hearing in the bankruptcy court was contingent upon a favorable report by the official assignee as to the accuracy of the accounts. It was not irregular then for accountants to be employed to insure correctness of the statements. In the statements it was necessary to show the court why the business was insolvent. Therefore, a statement of affairs was finally used to give the court the required information.[24] Section 92 of the Companies Act of 1862 created the position of official liquidator "for the purpose of conducting the proceedings in winding-up a company," and in most cases a professional accountant was appointed as liquidator. When one reflects that during the twenty-two years following the passing of the act (that is, from 1862 to 1884) no fewer than 13,820 companies disappeared from the

---

[22]Richard Brown, *A History of Accounting and Accountants*, p. 202.

[23]*Ibid.*, p. 208.

[24]A. C. Littleton, *Accounting Evolution to 1900* (New York: American Institute Publishing Co., Inc., 1933), p. 280.

register, it is easy to understand why the Companies Act of 1862 is spoken of as "the Accountant's friend."[25] This is further seen in the following quotation from the original act which reveals how this act affected the public accountancy profession:

> Upon the conclusion of the examination the Inspectors shall report their opinion to the Board of Trade: Such report shall be written or printed, as the Board of Trade directs.
> . . . All expenses of and incidental to any such examination as aforesaid shall be defrayed by the members upon whose application the Inspectors were appointed, unless the Board of Trade shall direct the same to be paid out of the assets of the Company, which it is hereby authorized to do.[26]

The few years which followed passage of the act saw the failure and collapse of many large joint-stock undertakings, notably that of Overend, Gurney and Company, Ltd., and in 1866 several banks, among them the Commercial Bank of India, the European Bank, the Bank of London, and Agra and Materman's Bank. The cost of these liquidations must have been enormous and produced, no doubt, a rich harvest for the liquidators. In addition to their work as liquidators, accountants were employed to audit the accounts of the various companies which came into existence during the second and third quarters of the nineteenth century.[27]

The Bankruptcy Act of 1869, in abolishing the Official Assignees in Bankruptcy and providing for the appointment of trustees to distribute the debtor's estate, also brought grist to the accountant's mill, as these positions were largely filled by professional accountants.[28] Creditors were given complete control if the majority of them agreed on a plan. The creditors then proceeded to engage bookkeepers to handle the customary liquidation.

Not everybody was pleased with the accountants' work. In 1875 Mr. Justice Quain stated from the bench: "The whole affairs in bankruptcy have been handed over to an ignorant set of men called

---

[25]"Accountants in England from the Nineteenth Century," *The Accountant*, XLVI (January, 1912), 261.

[26]*Statutes of the United Kingdom of Great Britain & Ireland, Passed in the 25th and 26th Years of the Reign of Her Majesty, Queen Victoria* (London: G. E. Eyre and William Spottiswoode, 1862), p. 448.

[27]Richard Brown, *A History of Accounting and Accountants*, p. 326.

[28]*The Public General Statutes, Passed in the 32nd and 33rd Years of the Reign of Her Majesty, Queen Victoria* (London: G. E. Eyre and William Spottiswoode, 1869), p. 696.

accountants, which was one of the greatest abuses ever introduced into law." This sweeping remark was, in the main, quite unjustified, although it must be confessed that the opportunities offered by the Bankruptcy Act of 1869, election of receivers by creditors, attracted many persons who "styled themselves 'accountants,' but who possessed no qualification for their work, and who preyed in most unscrupulous fashion on the unfortunate who fell into their hands."[29]

The procedure in bankruptcy of electing the receiver, as regulated under the act of 1869, was altered by the act of 1883, by which receivers were appointed to administer bankrupt estates under the control of the Board of Trade, and trustees, in practice, were elected by the creditors in the case of large estates.[30]

The public accounting profession in England received additional impetus from the bankruptcy acts during the third quarter of the nineteenth century. It seems that adverse business conditions had much effect on the development of public accounting, just as did prosperity.

A further reflection on the accountants' function in such matters as bankruptcies is found in the charter of incorporation of the English societies in 1879. The following statement pertains to accountants' acting as receivers: ". . . and of receiving under decrees and of trustees in bankruptcies or arrangements with creditors and in various positions of trust under courts of Justice."[31]

The apprentice working toward his final examination to be admitted to the profession in England and Ireland had to pass an examination in bankruptcy, company, and arbitration law. Thus the Chartered Accountant of either of these countries had to have a thorough education in the field of bankruptcy before being admitted to practice in his own name.

PROFESSIONAL STATUS

Combination Vocations

Charles Snell, who wrote the report for the Special Committee in Parliament in 1721, was known as Writing Master and Accountant.

---

[29]"History of Accountants and Accountancy," *The Accountant*, XLVI (January, 1912), 261.

[30]"A Hundred Years of Accountancy," *The Accountant*, XXVII (June, 1901), 39.

[31]"History of Accountants and Accountancy," *The Accountant*, XLVI (January, 1912), 261.

It would seem that the inclusion of the "writing master" portion of his title would mean that he performed functions other than those of an accountant. Probably because of the high degree of illiteracy at that time he wrote letters and rendered other literary services for individuals.[32]

In Edinburgh the accounting profession was more clearly associated with the profession of law. For many years the accountant's work was carried on in the solicitors' offices.[33]

There are instances of members of the Society of Writers to the Signet practicing as accountants because of the overlapping of their functions of that day. After the middle of the nineteenth century, accountants were employed to do more and more public accounting work in the form of audits and the handling of bankruptcy cases, and the profession became distinctly separated from that of the solicitor.

The petition to Queen Victoria in 1854 for the formation of a Society listed the accomplishments of the accountant:

. . . the business of accountant, . . . not merely thorough knowledge of these departments of business which fall within the province of the Actuary, but an intimate acquaintance with the law of Scotland, . . . That in the extrication of those numerous suits before the court of Session, which involve directly and indirectly matters of accounting, an accountant is almost invariably employed by the court to aid in eliciting the trust: That such investigations are manifestly quite unsuited to such a tribunal as a Jury, yet cannot be prosecuted by the court itself without professional assistance on which it may rely, and the accountant, to whom in any case of this description a remit is made by the court, performs in substance all the more material functions which the Petitioners understand to be performed in England by the Masters in Chancery: That accountants are also largely employed in Judicial Remits in cases which are peculiar to the practice of Scotland, as for instance, in Rankings and Sales, in processes of Court of Reckoning, Multiple poinding, and others of a similar description: That they are also most commonly selected to be Trustees on Sequestrated Estates, and under Voluntary Trusts, and in these capacities they have duties to perform, not only of the highest responsibility, and involving large pecuniary interests, but which require, in those who undertake them, great experience in business, very considerable knowledge of.

---

[32]"A History of the Accountancy Profession," *The Accountant*, XXI (April, 1895), 375.

[33]A. C. Littleton, *Directory of Early American Public Accountants* (Urbana, Illinois: The University of Illinois, 1942), p. 7.

law, and other qualifications which can only be attained by a liberal education. . . .[34]

Even in this early stage of the development of the profession there were differences existing between the accountancy profession and the legal profession. In the latter part of the nineteenth century the Institute of England and Wales was concerned on several occasions with instances of solicitors' encroaching on the functions of accountants. One case specifically called to the Institute's attention involves two London solicitors acting as auditors of the Law Union Assurance Company. The following statement was made in regard to this case:

> We are not, of course, in a position to judge of the fitness of these gentlemen to perform the responsible duties of their office; but we have little hesitation in saying that the qualifications of the average solicitor for such an appointment would be even less than those of the average amateur, who was once considered sufficiently enlightened to undertake the audit of insurance companies accounts, but whose place is now being rapidly taken by properly qualified accountants, whose services cannot fail to prove of some use to the companies for whom they act.[35]

In the commercial city of Glasgow the function of accountant was confounded with that of merchant. The accounting profession then seems to have had its origin as a distinct calling in commercial circles, and it was not out of the ordinary for a man to be designated Merchant and Accountant. When individuals advertised themselves as "Accountants and Agents" the duties which they performed do not seem to be clearly those of professional accountants.[36]

When the original draft of the Institute in Scotland was drawn, some of those present were not accountants. In fact a provision was made so that those who had formerly practiced as accountants, but who at the time acted as managers of life insurance companies,

[34]Richard Brown, *A History of Accounting and Accountants*, p. 208.

[35]"Solicitors Acting as Accountants," *The Accountant*, XVII (October, 1891), 709.

[36]Norman E. Webster, "Accountancy in the United States," in *Fiftieth Anniversary Celebration*, p. 102.

might be members.[37] Evidently these were men who had retired from the accountancy profession and had accepted positions in business.

It was not until about the last quarter of the eighteenth century that accountants looked upon accountancy as an occupation sufficient to engage their full attention and time. At the same time public accountants were beginning to receive recognition by the public. By 1787, directories of various cities and towns were including the title "Accountant." In the British Universal Directory of 1790 there are five accountants advertised as Writing Master and Accountant, two as Accountants and Agents, one as Commercial Accountant, and the remaining one simply as Accountant. But the Post Office Directory in London of that year included only one person's name under the title of Accountant. In 1799 eleven accountants are included in Holden's Triennial Directory, and from that time the number appears to increase steadily, with twenty-four names in the 1811 edition and seventy-three in 1825.[38] The duties of these men as professional accountants are not clear, but it seems that professional accountancy, as understood today, existed in some form.

The first Directory of Edinburgh, published in 1773, contains the names of seven persons who were designated as accountants. The following year there were seventeen persons under the same heading. The earliest separate list of accountants in Edinburgh is contained in *The British Almanack and Universal Scots Register for 1805*. There are seventeen names of accountants listed. A similar Glasgow directory appeared for the first time in 1783, and contained the names of six accountants.[39]

The first professional accountant in Scotland seems to have been George Watson in 1676. In acting for several corporations, he was known for the "diligence, faithfulness, and integrity with which he conducted his business."[40] Watson was peculiarly suited for this work, since he was taken into a large mercantile business after completing his education as an accountant and cashier. When he left

[37]Arthur Lowes Dickinson, "Profession of the Public Accountant," *The Accountant*, XXXII (May, 1905), 650.

[38]"A Hundred Years of Accountancy," *The Accountant*, XXVII (January, 1901), 37.

[39]A. C. Littleton, *Directory of Early American Public Accountants* (Urbana, Illinois: The University of Illinois, 1942), p. 7.

[40]Richard Brown, *A History of Accounting and Accountants*, p. 184.

the business after twenty years, he was employed by the corporations mentioned above.[41]

Early Professional Organizations

In a discussion of the modern profession of accounting, Scotland should occupy the place of priority for in no other country in the world did it become so highly developed or so important relative to other professions. The Chartered Accountant originated in Scotland, and there also can be found the oldest societies of public accountants in existence.[42]

The first step towards formation of a Society of Accountants in Edinburgh took place on January 17, 1853, when Alexandria Weir Robertson issued the following circular to fourteen practicing accountants:

Several gentlemen connected with our profession have resolved to bring about some definite arrangements for uniting the professional accountants in Edinburgh, and should you be favourable thereto I have requested your attendance in my chambers here on Thursday next, the 20th Inst., at 2 o'clock.[43]

In response to this invitation, seven gentlemen assembled. At the second meeting there were six more, and a proof of the constitution was considered and amended.

When the third meeting was held on January 31, 1853, forty-seven attended. Archibald Borthwick explained to those in attendance that the ultimate object of the organization was to apply for a charter of incorporation conferring on the group or institute the usual powers and privileges. The institute was to consist of ordinary members (gentlemen practicing as accountants in Edinburgh) and honorary members (gentlemen who formerly practiced as accountants but now were acting as managers of life insurance companies and held appointments from the courts).[44]

---

[41]*Ibid.*

[42]Arthur H. Woolf, *A Short History of Accountants and Accounting* (London: Gee and Company, 1912), p. 164.

[43]Richard Brown, *A History of Accounting and Accountants*, p. 203.

[44]Arthur Lowes Dickinson, "Profession of the Public Accountant," *The Accountant*, XXXII (May, 1905), 650.

The annual meeting of the institute was held February 1, 1854; President James Brown and the Council announced that, in their opinion, the time had arrived to make application for incorporation by royal charter. In May, 1854, the Council approved a draft of a petition, which was signed after being approved by fifty-four members, and was sent to the queen. The petition stated:

That the profession of Accountants, to which the Petitioners belong, is of longstanding and great respectability, and has of late grown into very considerable importance: That the business of Accountants, as practiced in Edinburgh, is varied and extensive, embracing all matters of account, and requiring for its proper execution, not merely thorough knowledge of these departments of business which fall within the province of the Actuary, but an intimate acquaintance with the law of Scotland, and more especially with those branches of it which have relation to the law of merchant, to insolvency and bankruptcy, and to all rights connected with property: That in the extrication of those numerous suits before the Court of Sessions, which involve directly and indirectly matters of accounting, an accountant is almost invariably employed by the court to aid in eliciting the trust: That such investigations are manifestly quite unsuited to such a tribunal as a Jury, yet cannot be prosecuted by the court itself without professional assistance on which it may rely, and the accountant, to whom in any case of this description a remit is made by the court, performs in substance all the more material functions which the Petitioners understand to be performed in England by the Masters in Chancery: That Accountants are also largely employed in Judicial Remits in cases which are peculiar to the practice of Scotland, as for instance, in Ranking and Sales, in processes of Court and Reckoning, Multiple poinding, and others of a similar description: That they are also most commonly selected to be Trustees on Sequestrated Estates, and under Voluntary Trusts, and in these capacities they have duties to perform, not only of the highest responsibility, and involving large pecuniary interests, but which require, in those who undertake them, great experience in business, very considerable knowledge of law, and other qualifications which can only be attained by a liberal education: That in these circumstances, the Petitioners were induced to form themselves into a Society called the Institute of Accountants of Edinburgh, with a view to unite into one body those at present practicing the profession, and to promote the objects which, as members of the same profession, they entertain in common; and that the Petitioners conceive that it would tend to secure in the members of their profession the qualifications which are essential to the proper performance of its duties, and would consequently conduce much to the benefit of the public if the Petitioners who form the present body of practicing accountants in Edinburgh were united into a body corporate and politic, having a common seal, with power to make rules and by-laws for the qualification and admission of members, and otherwise.[45]

The Royal Warrant for the incorporation of the institute under the name of the Society of Accountants in Edinburgh was granted by Her Majesty's Court of St. James on October 23, 1854, and signed by Lord Palmerston at the Queen's command.[46]

The Edinburgh Society was soon emulated by the accountants in Glasgow, who petitioned the crown on July 6, 1854, for the grant of a royal charter. A royal warrant was given on March 15, 1855, for the incorporation of the petitioners "and such other persons as might be admitted as members, into one body politic and corporate" under the name of The Institute of Accountants and Actuaries in Glasgow.[47] The charter contained a provision for the appointment of a Board of Examiners

for the purpose of regulating and conducting such examinations of entrance and others as the corporations might from time to time direct, and in such manner as they may appoint in furtherance of the objects of the Societies, and that the course of education to be pursued and the amount of general and professional acquirement to be exacted from entrants should be such as the corporations should from time to time fix.[48]

In 1867 the Society of Accountants in Aberdeen was incorporated by royal charter, along the lines of the other two Scottish societies.

In the interest of uniform instruction in accounting, the three societies in Scotland decided that the rules for admission and the standards of the examination should be the same, as well as the apprenticeship service period and the terms of membership. With these ideas in view, the societies entered into a joint agreement to constitute a General Examining Board. This action led to their unification, and to the adoption of the name of Chartered Accountant for their members.[49] It took some time for the title to signify to the public a professional accountant performing the functions of a

---

[45]Richard Brown, *A History of Accounting and Accountants*, p. 208.
[46]*Ibid.*
[47]Arthur H. Woolf, *A Short History of Accountants and Accountancy*, p. 165.
[48]*Ibid.*
[49]*Ibid.*

public accountant. But the significance of the name Chartered Accountant grew in importance as the profession acquired the confidence of the people of Scotland.[50]

It seems worthy of note that these societies neither sought nor obtained any privileges or monopoly of the accounting profession; the crown charters simply conferred upon them a right to hold property and execute deeds in the name of the society for the benefit of the profession.

Having thus secured for accountants public recognition as a distinct profession, these societies steadily pursued their declared policy of raising the educational standards and position of the profession and of insuring that everyone becoming a member of a chartered society should possess the qualification for those duties which had come to be identified as the special work of the accounting profession.

It was not until some twenty-six years after the Chartered Accountants came into existence in Scotland in 1854 that some English accountants secured their charter of incorporation. The first attempt to organize the profession in England was made in Liverpool. The Incorporated Society of Liverpool Accountants was organized on January 25, 1870. In the same year, on November 29, the Institute of Accountants was established in London.[51] These societies appear to have been founded, following passage of the Bankruptcy Act of 1869, in an effort to protect the profession from those unqualified men who had taken advantage of the inadequacy of previous laws in calling themselves accountants, and had brought the profession into bad repute.

Three similar societies were formed in rapid succession: the Manchester Institute of Accountants, formed on February 6, 1871; the Society of Accountants in England, formed on January 11, 1873; and the Sheffield Institute of Accountants, formed on March 14, 1877. Like the London Society, these all had as their purpose to promote the profession and up-grade the membership.[52]

In the next several years the profession grew by leaps and bounds. On November 29, 1879, an advertisement was inserted in the *London*

[50]Richard Brown, "Recent Proposed Legislation Relating to the Profession," *The Accountant*, XX (July, 1894), 669.

[51]"History of Accountants and Accountancy," *The Accountant*, XLVI (January, 1912), 6.

[52]"Some Notes on the Profession of Accountancy," *The Accountant*, XXII (October, 1896), 843.

Gazette by the Council of the Institute of Accountants stating that they intended to apply to Parliament for leave to introduce a bill for the incorporation of the Institute. A conference between representatives of the various English societies was held, and a bill was drawn up for presentation to Parliament in 1879, but eventually a petition for a charter of incorporation was substituted. The petition stated:

> That the profession is a numerous one and their functions are of great and increasing importance in respect to their employment in the capacities of liquidators in the winding up of companies and of receiving under decrees and of trustees in bankruptcies or arrangements with creditors and in various positions of trust under courts of Justice as also in the auditing of accounts of public companies and of partnership and otherwise.[53]

The formal grant of the charter was made May 11, 1880, incorporating the existing societies into one group for united action. It was named the Institute of Chartered Accountants in England and Wales. Adequate provision was made for admittance of other persons for membership provided they possessed certain qualifications.[54] Various other societies have arisen in England. The most outstanding of these is the Society of Incorporated Accountants and Auditors, which was incorporated December 29, 1885, under a license from the Board of Trade. Membership was extended on application during the early years of its existence. At least until 1902 no examination was required, but the new rules of that year required examinations similar to those of the Institute of Chartered Accountants in England and Wales.[55] Even so, this society has grown to considerable size. In the words of Waterhouse, the President of the English Institute, it is "a body framed on principles similar to the Institute, and having in the public estimation the reputation of having placed their members on a higher level than those who are outside their number."[56]

---

[53]"History of Accountants and Accountancy," *The Accountant*, XLVI (January, 1912), 259.

[54]Arthur L. Dickinson, "Profession of the Public Accountant," *The Accountant*, XXXII (May, 1905), 651.

[55]*Ibid.*, p. 652.

[56]Richard Brown, "Recent Proposed Legislation Relating to the Profession," *The Accountant*, XX (July, 1894), 670.

The Institute of Chartered Accountants in Ireland was incorporated by royal charter on May 14, 1888, with thirty-one members, mostly practicing accountants in Dublin, Belfast, and Cork.[57] The conditions for membership included a preliminary examination in general education, five years' service "under articles" with a practising Chartered Accountant, and an intermediate examination.

Professional Standards

The institute that was formed in Edinburgh in 1853 admitted active practitioners and honorary members. This practice was followed until examinations were established for selection of new members.

The stinging criticism by Judge Quain in 1875 that the settlement of bankruptcies had been "handed over to an ignorant set of men called accountants" was combatted by the professional organizations that had been and were to be formed. Once recognition was given through government charters, the organizations followed a declared policy of improving the educational standards of the profession. Self-policing was carried further in that the members of the public accounting profession were required to abide by strict rules of ethical conduct.

The charter of the institute in England provided that those who had been in continuous practice as a public accountant for five years from January 1, 1879, were to be admitted as Fellow Chartered Accountants (F.C.A.), and everyone who had prior to the date of this charter been for three years in public practice or for five years employed as a public account-clerk was to be admitted as Associate Chartered Accountant of the Institute (A.C.A.).[58] After the initial registration it was necessary for the aspirant to membership to be apprenticed to a member of one or the other of the Associations of Chartered Accountants for a term of five years. The apprenticeship was considered to be so important that members were offered premiums varying from $250 to $2,500 for the privilege of working in their office: the "articled clerk," as he was called, received no salary during this term of apprenticeship.[59]

---

[57]Richard Brown, *A History of Accounting and Accountants*, p. 250.

[58]Richard Brown, "Recent Proposed Legislation Relating to the Profession," *The Accountant*, XX (July, 1894), 669.

[59]T. Savage Smith, "The Education of Accountants: What They Ought to Learn, and How They Are to Learn It," *The Accountant*, XX (December, 1894), 202.

During the early years of the Society of Accountants and Auditors no examination was required. The applicant could be admitted to membership if his application was approved by the members. This situation was corrected in 1902 with the setting up of an examination similar to the one given by the institute of Chartered Accountants in England and Wales.

Training in England and Scotland

In 1676 George Watson, having served an apprenticeship to a merchant, was sent from England to Holland "for his further improvement in merchandising, and particularly for his learning bookkeeping, which then was a very rare accomplishment."[60] Even though Watson was called an accountant he did not spend all his time at this pursuit. As has been mentioned, men did not devote their entire time and energy to the accountancy profession until the latter part of the eighteenth century.

The Edinburgh society had a provision in the charter which made the educational requirements a matter for the society to determine.

The societies attached special importance to practical experience, but formal education was also desired. Apprentices were required to attend university law classes. In fact one of the conditions of membership was "that such University teaching as bear on the duties of an accountant should be taken advantage of."[61]

A Chartered Accountant's Students' Society was formed in Edinburgh in 1886. Each winter a series of lectures and discussions on professional subjects was given for the education of members and apprentices.

A resolution was passed by the council of the institute in England at a meeting on July 12, 1893, establishing a centralized library which would be adequate to meet the needs of the profession. The librarian was to keep the library open until 8 o'clock in the evening for the benefit of those wanting to use it. As one accountant wrote,

In view of the great advantages and facilities now offered to practitioners as well as students, it is only reasonable that the profession should look in

---

[60]Richard Brown, *A History of Accounting and Accountants*, p. 183.

[61]Richard Brown, "Recent Proposed Legislation Relating to the Profession," *The Accountant*, XX, (July, 1894), 669.

return, not only for a warm appreciation of the liberality shown in the action of the Council, but also for a marked improvement in the position occupied by London students in the pass-lists on the Institute Examinations.[62]

When the Edinburgh society obtained its royal charter, one of the provisions called for the appointment of a board of examiners. The purpose of this board was to give such examinations as were felt necessary in furtherance of the objectives of the society and to determine those eligible for admission.[63] In providing for examinations the Edinburgh society was following the precedent set by the University of Milan, about a hundred years before, that only its graduates could be recognized as practicing accountants, and then only after passing an examination.

The three societies in Scotland set up uniform admission requirements, including standard examinations, and established a general board of examiners. One of the conditions of membership was "That the diligence and acquirements of the apprentice should be tested by examination."[64]

The examinations were divided into three parts. The preliminary section embraced the normal educational subjects, the intermediate section covered advanced mathematics and professional knowledge; the third was a final examination covering law, actuarial science, political economy, and four papers on the general business of an accountant, embracing bookkeeping and all forms of accounts, auditing, bankruptcies, trusts, factorships, apportionments, administration and liquidation of companies, and judicial and private references, remits and profits.[65]

Before being articled to a member of the Institute of Chartered Accountants of England, the candidate was required to pass a preliminary examination on general education; an intermediate examination in bookkeeping and accounts, auditing and liquidation; and a final examination in these subjects with the addition of bankruptcy, company, mercantile, and arbitration law. The device of the institute's seal, Justice, and the motto *Recte numerare*, also show that the aims of the profession were such as to require that all candidates

---

[62]"The Library of the Institute," *The Accountant*, XIX (December, 1893), 956.
[63]Arthur H. Woolf, *A Short History of Accountants and Accounting*, p. 165.
[64]*Ibid.*, p. 165.
[65]Richard Brown, *A History of Accounting and Accountants*, p. 215.

for membership be high principled as well as able to pass the exam ination.[66] The announced objectives of the institute were stated to be:

The elevation of the profession of Public Accountants as a whole, and the promotion of their efficiency and unselfishness, by compelling the observance of strict rules of conduct as a condition of membership, and by setting up a high standard of professional and general education and knowledge.[67]

In 1894 one author considered the following significant in the preparation of examinations and in preparing for them:

There was plenty that could be learned from text books for the legal subjects of the examinations, but the more important and the more difficult are those of Bookkeeping, Accounts, and Auditing. It was felt that in these areas, theory held but practical experience was important and whenever possible the theory should be tested by comparison to actual cases. The courses of lectures on bookkeeping and the legal subjects associated with the Student Society were very useful in preparing for this examination.[68]

The conditions for membership in the Irish institute included a preliminary examination in general education, an intermediate examination in bookkeeping, auditing, executorship accounts, liquidation, bankruptcy, company, partnership, arbitration law science—which was approximately what was covered in the examination given by the English institute.

The united societies of Scotland placed special importance on practical experience which the apprentice received in the office of an accountant. This has been an essential requirement for admission into any of the societies. The condition of membership was usually stated in words such as these:

---

[66]T. Savage Smith, "The Education of Accountants: What They Ought to Learn and How They Are to Learn It," *The Accountant*, XX (December, 1894), 202.

[67]C. W. Haskins, "History of Accountancy," *The Accountant*, XXVII (June, 1901), 699.

[68]T. Savage Smith, "The Education of Accountants: What They Ought to Learn and How They Are to Learn It," *The Accountant*, XX (December, 1894), 204.

That a full term of apprenticeship, under conditions potent to the society, should be served with a master whom the Society knew to be in a position to impart a thorough practical knowledge of the profession.[69]

The following was what an accountant should have learned before becoming a Chartered Accountant in 1894:

With the preliminary examination passed and the apprenticeship arranged, it would seem worthwhile to look into the duties of an articled clerk in an office. In the first few months, the student should learn the methods adopted by his principal for the regulation and management of the office, beginning even with the smallest details in the waiting room. He should know the stationery arrangements, the registration of the boxes or parcels of clients' papers, and should generally make himself acquainted with all office rules. This is a time for gathering methodical information which will always be useful. Next there is usually much to be learned at this early time in writing legibly and neatly, and in the equal ruling of double lines.

The first two years should be very busy ones, but definite examination reading may be left until the third year. The knowledge obtained now is not to be found mentioned in the syllabus of the examinations. "Readiness" and "Tact" are the points to be aimed at. Public Accountants are continually in personal contact with their clients, with the gentlemen of other professions and with practical businessmen of great experience. It is necessary, therefore, that the student should make himself somewhat acquainted with the ways in which the general business world is going around him. He should visit the Law Courts at the time of assizes, go to various Government Offices, banks and such like places as opportunity offers, and so get a knowledge of the red-tape formalities attending the transaction of their business. He should attend public meetings of all kinds: company, bankruptcy, ratepayers, political, debating, literary, and in fact, gatherings of all sorts. There will be much to notice; the arrangements for holding the meeting, the practice usually used at each kind of opening, the selection of speakers, the forms of the resolutions, and how they are brought before the meeting.[70]

The accountant in ordinary business life meets men of all classes and varied circumstances. He must study character and learn to be quite at ease, and with his mind clear at all times with anybody. He will learn to be always refined and courteous, and then he will be able to mix with all groups.

---

[69]Richard Brown, "Recent Proposed Legislation Relating to the Profession," *The Accountant*, XX (July, 1894), 669.

[70]T. Savage Smith, "The Education of Accountants: What They Ought to Learn and How They Are to Learn It," *The Accountant*, XX (December, 1894), 202.

Politeness is not to be kept for most profitable clients only. It has yet to be learned by many professional men that firmness is possible without violent verbal expression.

Honorary work on committees or as secretary is good education and experience for a young member of the profession. There is scope for individual effort, and if the office is taken up with energy and genuine interest the labor will be more than repaid by the pleasure afforded to say nothing of the value of the experience.

Completeness in office work is deserving of remark. While a "junior" the student will often be set to do some small piece of work; such as a portion of an audit or some small investigation. But before starting on any such work, it is well for him to ask his "senior" to explain the object of the work, so that he may clearly appreciate what is wanted. After a short explanation as to the reason why, gives interest to the employment and the work will be more trustworthy.

After the apprentice takes the intermediate examination, the following two years the work of the student is of a more advanced nature, and gives increased facilities for observing the mode of dealing practically with many important matters. He will, as a senior, learn to apportion work among his staff in a way to secure thoroughness and celerity. He will be preparing Profit and Loss Accounts and Balance Sheets, and then endeavor to state the facts in the clearest manner possible.[71]

The long apprenticeship and the types of work carried out by the student during his term would not seem to be very attractive to any young men except the very serious and determined. To say the least, it would appear that the apprenticeship period made it rather difficult to obtain a Chartered Accountant's certificate. But once the certificate was issued, the name of "accountant" with or without a qualifying prefix of "public" or "professional" was generally replaced by the more specific title of Chartered Accountant.[72]

Society Activities

Once the societies were established it is of interest to examine their policies as expressed by the kinds of services they performed for their members and for the profession. One society, it has been noted, scheduled annual lecture series on professional subjects.

---

[71]*Ibid.*, p. 204.
[72]"Public Accountant's Work," *The Accountant*, XVII (June, 1891), 585.

In 1896 the three Scottish societies began the publication of an annual Directory of Scottish Chartered Accountants, and since 1897 they have issued *The Accountants' Magazine,* a monthly journal, which is the authoritative publication of accountancy in Scotland.[73]

The Accountant, a newspaper, was established in 1847 after the formation of the Societies of Accountants in England. This paper was at first published monthly, but after a few months it became a weekly, in which form it is still being issued. It circulates widely throughout the world.[74]

In 1893, a library was established in London by the Institute. This library was opened in a further effort to make available to the student and the practioner accounting information and reference publications.

The societies became active in jurisdictional disputes, which have arisen frequently in the history of accountancy. Mention of one is made in the late nineteenth century, when a complaint was brought to the attention of the Institute that solicitors were performing the functions of an auditor. The qualifications of these men to perform an audit were immediately questioned by the profession.

SUMMARY

After a study of the development of the profession in England, Ireland, and Scotland, it is readily apparent that the profession in the United States has a rich inheritance of European tradition. The profession in these countries received its beginning in the field of auditing. By the middle of the nineteenth century provisions had been made for the audit of companies regulated by Parliament. Accountants gained additional recognition when the Companies Act of 1862 was passed, stating that capital must be separated from profits and that the companies' books must be audited regularly. Another act which further enhanced the standing of the profession was the Bankruptcy Act of 1869. The court decisions based on these acts further defined the responsibilities of the auditor.

During the third quarter of the nineteenth century the profession in England, Scotland, and Wales was organized on a national level.

[73]Wilmer L. Green, *A History and Survey of Accounting* (Brooklyn, New York: Standard Text Press, 1930), p. 200.

[74]"A History of the Accountancy Profession," *The Accountant,* XXI (April, 1895), 376.

The societies established in these countries were functioning and furthering the profession by improved educational standards. The major activities of the public accountant were in the fields of auditing, bankruptcies, receiverships, and as a business consultant on these and other matters. But now attention must be given to the subject of public accounting in the United States.

CHAPTER III

Definitions of American Public Accounting

Public accounting has developed rapidly in the United States, being—from a legal point of view—only sixty-four years old. Since 1896, when the first legal recognition was given the profession, approximately seventy thousand certified public accountant certificates have been issued by examination, waiver and reciprocity. Of these, about sixty thousand were issued as the result of official (formal) examinations. About thirty-five thousand certified public accountants are now practicing in this country. The remainer of those now living are in business and industry, government, teaching, or have retired from active practice.

In addition, there are probably several times as many noncertified as certified public accountants. The noncertified public accountant is licensed in those states which have enacted regulatory legislation affecting public accountants. In other states the noncertified public accountant practices as does the certified public accountant but does not have a license from the State Board of Accountancy.

The certified public accountant is subject to stricter regulation. After meeting certain requirements of age, education, and experience, and after passing the examination of the State Board of Accountancy, he is licensed to practice in the state where he lives or maintains a public accountancy office. The requirements vary considerably in different states.

In some states waiver certificates were issued immediately after the enactment of the original C.P.A. law to those accountants in practice who met the requirements set down by the State Board. These waiver certificates were issued to those accountants who were practicing as public accountants prior to the enactment of the law so that they would not be deprived of their means of making their livelihood. Reciprocity certificates may be given to those practicing in a state other than the state in which they are licensed provided they comply with the reciprocity clause of the law of that state.

Even though professional examinations have been given for public accountants since 1896, professional accountancy is older; its antecedents in this country go back some seventy or eighty years. Standard examinations for admission to the profession were established in 1917 by the American Institute. In 1924, the last state and territory passed laws providing for the licensing of certified public accountants.

DEFINITION AND DISCUSSION OF TERMS

In order that the reader may understand what the profession of public accountancy encompasses, some discussion of definitions will be useful.

Record keeping is the maintenance of any written evidence of past transactions, not necessarily kept on the basis of a common denominator or coordinated in any manner.

Bookkeeping is a method of classifying financial transactions in accordance with a system, recording these facts in terms of money as a common denominator, and arranging the data in an orderly manner in the books and accounts of the business, where they are readily available for analysis.

Although the recording of financial data, as in bookkeeping, is a separate and distinct function and is one of the phases or branches of accounting, accounting proper begins after the routine transactions have been recorded. The art of accounting begins where bookkeeping leaves off; its purpose is explanatory. Accounting draws upon the financial data recorded in the bookkeeping process to interpret the condition of the business enterprise. *Accounting,* then, is the process of recording, classifying, analyzing, presenting, interpreting, and reviewing financial information based on a common denominator, money. Normally, the responsibility for performing these functions is management's and the ultimate results are the representations of management.

In 1940, the Committee on Terminology of the American Institute of Accountants defined accounting as

the art of recording, classifying, and summarizing in a significant manner, and in terms of money, transactions and events which are, in part at least, of a financial character, and the results thereof.[1]

---

[1] Committee on Terminology, *Accounting Research Bulletin No. 7* (New York: American Institute Publishing Co., Inc., 1940), p. 59.

This definition was criticized by many members of the profession because it was not broad enough.[2] As a result, in its research bulletin published the next year, the committee added the following words to the definition: ". . . of a financial character, and interpreting the results thereof."[3] In its final form, the committee's definition appeared as follows:

Accounting is the art of recording, classifying and summarizing in a significant manner, and in terms of money, transactions and events which are, in part at least, of a financial character, and interpreting the results thereof.[4]

The terms *public accountant* and *public accounting* must also be defined. In 1886, before accounting had any legal recognition, *The Office*, a business periodical, gave the following definition of public accountant:

The functions of the expert accountant are, perhaps, less understood by the business community at large than it would be well to have them. They may be summed up under several heads; planning and remodeling books so as to adapt them to special requirements; second, auditing books and verifying the balance sheets; third, adjusting and closing books and accounts which are in a tangle. Under the first head the expert occupies a commanding position as compared with the ordinary bookkeeper, from the fact that he has wide and varied experience, and accordingly can do more than even an equally competent man who has been restricted to ordinary lines of practice. Under the second head, the expert's systematic training is a continuous safeguard against errors and frauds, and a satisfaction as well to those in charge of the cash as to those interested in the profits. Under the third head, the expert sees that all questions of depreciation, renewals, drawbacks, doubtful debts and other contingencies are duly considered, while under the fourth head his trained and practical skill finds clues in a mass of confusion, and soon determines the shortest way out.[5]

After the passage of the first certified public accountant law, in New York, there was new reason to define the term because as far

---

[2]*Ibid.*, p. 61.
[3]*Ibid.*, *No. 9* (1941), p. 81.
[4]*loc. cit.*, p. 81.
[5]Norman Webster, "The Meaning of 'Public Accountant'," *The Accounting Review*, XIX (October, 1944), 366.

as it is known this law included the term "Certified Public Accountant" for the first time in any statute.

The definition in the 1896 law was as follows:

The public practice of accountancy within the meaning of this article is defined as follows: A person engages in the practice of accountancy who, holding himself out to the public as an accountant, in consideration of compensation received, or to be received by him, offers to perform or does perform, for other persons, services which involve the auditing or verification of financial transactions, books, accounts, or records, or the preparation, verification or certification of financial accounting and related statements intended for publication or for the purpose of obtaining credit, or who, holding himself out to the public as an accountant, renders professional services or assistance in or about any or all matters of principle or detail relating to accounting procedure or the recording, presentation or certification of financial facts or data.[6]

The Public Accountant, a publication of the Pennsylvania Institute of Certified Public Accountants, carried an editorial in its issue of January 15, 1900, under the title "What Is a Public Accountant?" Answers from some twenty-nine accountants from eight cities were cited. Some of the replies are of interest here.

A public accountant is one engaged professionally in the practice of accountancy; the term accountancy being understood to cover all forms of investigations of accounts for the determination of financial conditions, detection of frauds or prevention thereof, or for whatever purpose data obtained from the accountants may be required.

—William M. Lybrand, Philadelphia.

A public accountant is a man fearless and unprejudiced, with the ability to look at both sides of a question; one who will not allow his honest opinions to be changed by client or adverse party; who dictates and is never dictated to; who places his devotion to his profession above the opportunities for gain by questionable means.

—Robert H. Montgomery, Philadelphia.

---

[6]*Accountancy Law-Reporter* (New York: Commerce Clearing House, 1941), p. 4,003.

. . . A professional accountant, whose services are available to the public for a
fee or per diem remuneration, as may be arranged. To be successful he must be
honest, diplomatic, fearless, versatile, indefatigable, experienced, perspicacious
and skilled in his craft.

—George Wilkinson, Chicago.

One who is expert in accounts and so entirely familiar with the science of
bookkeeping that he can readily apply the principles of that science to the requirements of any business by the most practical and direct methods. One who
is fitted by education and experience to examine accounts.

—Francis E. Beck, San Francisco.

The public accountant is the consulting physician of finance and commerce.
He understands the anatomy and physiology of business and the rules of health
of corporations, partnerships and individual enterprises. He diagnoses abnormal
conditions, and suggests approved remedies. His study and interest is the soundness of the world of affairs.

—Charles W. Haskins, New York.

The ideal public accountant is he who, without trenching on existing authority, systematically examines the accounts and methods of business of the institution in which his patron is interested; renders an intelligible certified report
of its financial condition; and, if necessary, suggests a safer or more economical
method of accounting.

—Elijah W. Sells, New York.[7]

A list of definitions of public accounting would not be complete
without considering some of those found in the present statutes of
some of our states. The following definitions are presented in the
order in which the laws were passed.

Illinois Law

Except as provided in Sections 10, 11 and 12, a person, either individually, or
as a member of a partnership or an officer of a corporation shall be deemed to
be in a practice as a public accountant, within the meaning and extent of this
Act:

---

[7]Norman Webster, "The Meaning of Public Accountant," *The Accounting Review*, XIX (October,
1944), 366.

(a) Who, except as an employee of a public accountant, holds himself out to the public in any manner as one skilled in the knowledge, science and practice of accounting, and as qualified and ready to render professional service therein as a public accountant for compensation; or

(b) Who maintains an office for the transaction of business as a public accountant; or

(c) Who offers to prospective clients to perform for compensation, or who does perform on behalf of clients for compensation, professional services that involve or require an audit, examination, verification, investigation or review of financial transactions and accounting records; or

(d) Who prepares or certifies for clients reports on audits or examination of books or records of account, balance sheets, and other financial, accounting and related schedules, exhibits, statements, or reports which are to be filed with a court of law or equity or with any other governmental agency, or for any other purpose; or

(e) Who, in general or as an incident to such work, renders professional assistance to clients for compensation in any or all matters relating to accounting procedure and to the recording, presentation and certification of financial facts or data.[8]

Georgia Law

For the purpose of this law a public accountant shall be defined as a person, firm or corporation having an established place of business and offering to perform for the general public any and all general accounting services.[9]

Vermont Law

A person who is a citizen of the United States or who has duly declared his intention of becoming such citizen, who is a resident of the state, who is over the age of twenty-one years, of good moral character and a graduate of a high school with a four-year course or has an equivalent education, who has had two years' experience in public accounting, or such experience in general accounting as the board may determine as equivalent to such two-year experience and who has received from the state board of accountancy a certificate of his qualifications to practice as an expert public accountant, shall be styled and known as a certified public accountant.[10]

---

[8]*Accountancy Law Reporter*, p. 2,108.
[9]*Ibid.*, p. 1,908.
[10]*Ibid.*, p. 5,304.

North Carolina Law

A person is engaged in the public practice of accountancy who holds himself out to the public as an accountant and in consideration of compensation received or to be received offers to perform or does perform, for other persons, services which involve the auditing or verification of financial transactions, books, accounts, or records, or the preparation, verification or certification of financial accounting for publication, or renders in or about any and all matters of principle or detail relating to accounting procedure and systems or the recording, presentation or certification and the interpretation of such service through statements and reports.[11]

Wisconsin Law

A person shall be deemed to be in practice as a public accountant, within the meaning and intent of this chapter:

(1) Who holds himself out to the public in any manner as one skilled in the knowledge, science and practice of accounting, and as qualified and ready to render professional services therein as a public accountant for compensation; or

(2) Who maintains an office for the transaction of business as a public accountant, or who, except as an employee of a public accountant, practices accounting, as distinguished from bookkeeping, for more than one employer; or

(3) Who offers to prospective clients to perform for compensation, or who does perform on behalf of clients for compensation, professional services that involve or require an audit or certificates of financial transactions and accounting records; or

(4) Who prepares or certifies for clients reports of audits, balance sheets, and other financial, accounting, and related schedules, exhibits, statements or reports which are to be used for publication or for credit purposes, or are to be filed with a court of law or with any other governmental agency, or for any other purpose; or

(5) Who, in general or as an incident to such work, renders professional assistance to clients for compensation in any or all matters relating to accounting procedure and the recording, presentation and certification of financial facts.

(6) Every member of a partnership and every officer and director of a corporation who, in such capacity, does any of the things enumerated in subsection (1) to (5) of this section, shall be declared to be in practice as a public accountant.[12]

---

[11]*Ibid.*, p. 4,103.

[12]*Ibid.*, p. 5,703.

Iowa Law

The term accountant includes all persons engaged in the practice of accounting, within the meaning and intent of this chapter, who, holding themselves out to the public as qualified practitioners, and maintaining an office for this purpose, either in their own names, or as office managers and/or as managing officers of assumed name, association or corporation perform for compensation, on behalf of more than one client, a service which requires the audit or verification of financial transactions and accounting records, the preparation, verification and certification of financial, accounting, and related statements for publication or for credit purposes; and/or who in general and incidental to such work, renders professional assistance in any and all matters of principle and detail concerning accounting procedure and the recording, presentation and certification of financial facts.[13]

Texas Law

A person engages in the practice of public accountancy within the meaning of this act who, holds himself out to the public as a public accountant, in consideration of compensation received or to be received by him, offers to perform or does perform, for other persons, services which involve the auditing or examination of financial transactions, books, accounts, or records, or the preparation of, or the reporting over his signature on financial, accounting, and related statements.[14]

Alabama Law

Any citizen of the United States, residing or having a place for the regular transactions of business in the State of Alabama, being over the age of twenty-one years, of good moral character, and who shall have received from the state board of public accountants as hereinafter provided, shall be styled or known as a certified public accountant, and it shall be unlawful for any other person or persons to assume such title or use any letters, abbreviation or words to indicate that such a one using same is a certified public accountant.[15]

District of Columbia Law

For the purpose of this chapter a public accountant is hereby defined as a person skilled in the knowledge and science of accounting, who holds himself

---

[13]*Ibid.*, p. 2,304.
[14]*Ibid.*, p. 5,103.
[15]*Ibid.*, p. 1,101.

out to the public as a practicing accountant for compensation, and who maintains an office for the transaction of business as such, whose time during the regular business hours of the day is devoted to the practice of accounting as a professional public accountant.[16]

Tennessee Law

. . . for the purpose of this Act the term public "accounting" shall mean: Holding oneself out to the public in any manner as being one skilled in the knowledge and science of accounting and performing the work of an accountant for more than one employer on a fee basis, or otherwise, in any of the following services; auditing, devising or installing accounting systems; making examinations or investigations on matters relating to accounting; compiling tax returns; advising taxpayers in connection with their rights and liabilities under such federal and state taxing statutes as entail or are based on accounting procedure; representing taxpayers before governmental departments of the State or the United States in matters pertaining to taxes; preparing financial statements, schedules, reports, and exhibits for publications, credit purposes, use in courts of law and equity or other purposes. Provided nothing contained herein shall be construed to prohibit attorneys in the course of their legal practice from performing any of the above enumerated services.[17]

The Committee on Terminology defined *public accounting* as:

The practice of this art [accounting] by men whose services are available to the public for compensation. It may consist in the performance of original work, in the examination and revision of the original work of others (auditing), or in rendering of collateral services for which a knowledge of the art and experience in its practice create a special fitness.[18]

These definitions are cited at such great length to illustrate how the statutes of states differ. The Texas law defines public accounting in terms of the auditing function entirely, whereas the Georgia law defines it in terms of the performance of any and all general accounting services for the public. Just what is meant by the term

---

[16]*Ibid.*, p. 1,703.
[17]*Ibid.*, p. 5,004.
[18]Committee on Terminology, *Accounting Research Bulletin No. 7*, p. 59.

"general accounting services" is not clear. But most of the laws of the several states emphasize the auditing phase of public accounting and the verification of financial statements. The prime exception to this restrictive definition is the one given in the Tennessee law. Here the definition extends the functions of a public accountant to include the preparation of income tax returns and the rights of the accountant to represent his client in such matters. This definition seems to be much wider in its scope than any included in other state laws.

Public accounting, then, for purposes of this study, will mean the performance of accounting services for several clients on a fee basis, including such functions as auditing (verifying), installation and revision of accounting systems, preparation of income tax returns (when related to accounting procedures), and representing clients before governmental agencies on tax matters related to accounting. The major distinction between accounting and public accounting is that the public accountant performs these services for several clients whereas in commercial or industrial accounting the services are performed for one employer.

In some states there are "Public Accountant" provisions in the accounting law. These usually permit the public accountant, not certified, to perform all of the functions of a certified public accountant except verifying financial statements. Then, too, the governmental agencies do not permit some "P.A.s" to represent their clients on tax questions or in other related accounting matters which may come before an administrative agency, without an examination. On the other hand, the certified public accountant has the right to practice public accounting in his own name after having been given a license to practice by the State Board of Accountancy.

CHAPTER IV

The Emergence of Public Accounting in the United States, 1748-1895

Most of the histories of accounting begin with Assyria and Babylonia, leap to Italy in the days of the well-known Renaissance tutor, Pacioli, then hurry across Europe to devote their remaining space to the origin and growth of public accountancy in Great Britain. By the time the histories have covered the period from the South Sea Bubble to the organization of the British societies during the third quarter of the nineteenth century, the authors have exhausted their space, and give but little thought to the United States. The present work follows a different scheme, devoting its attention to this country. This chapter is the first of several which trace the course of accounting in the United States down to recent times.

The story of the accountants who blazed the trails for the accounting profession in our country can only be deduced from brief, infrequent references. Many of these early accountants had their training in England.

This chapter is devoted to what may be considered the ancient history of the American profession. The date 1895 was chosen to close this period, as marking the end of an era lacking in legal recognition for the profession. Though several accounting firms had already been formed, there is no record of a professional attempt to have the practice of public accountancy recognized on a national level.

EARLY AMERICAN ACCOUNTANTS

British Accountants in the United States

Richard Brown of Edinburgh, in his *History of Accounting and Accountants*, published in 1905, leads one to believe that British accountants had visited the United States before the American Revolution.

> A great commercial crisis visited Glasgow in 1777 as the result of the revolt in the previous year of the North American Colonies, with which part of the world the trade of the city was closely identified.
> Mr. Walter Ewing Macloe of Cathkin who was designated in the earliest issue of the Glasgow directory as "Merchant and Accountant" was, we are told, from the esteem and confidence in which he was held, employed to wind up some of the largest and most important of the bankruptcies which occurred in that unfortunate year.[1]

This reference stimulates the imagination, for the extensive trade with the American colonies that had been directed out of Glasgow and other British cities called for visits to be made to this country to check on investments. It is known that James Ewing Macloe, son of Walter Ewing Macloe, acquired possessions in the West Indies, and one wonders if some of the Britishers who may have come for specific accountancy engagements did not remain here and establish themselves to serve American business firms of Philadelphia, Boston, New York, and Charleston. If so, it may be inferred that a few Americans availed themselves of the abilities and experience of these visitors. No definite dates have been determined for the earliest visits by Scottish accountants to the colonies on behalf of British traders, or for the later permanent migration of British accountants to this country.

The public accounting engagements in the American colonies during the eighteenth century were doubtless performed in one or more of the commercial towns on the Atlantic seaboard during one of the commercial crises, and they were probably connected with some of the principal businessmen of that time.[2]

Functions of Early American Public Accountants

Some early references to men performing the functions of public

---

[1]Norman E. Webster, "Public Accountancy in the United States," in *Fiftieth Anniversary Celebration* (New York: The American Institute of Accountants, 1937), p. 102.
[2]*Ibid.*, p. 103.

accountants in the United States have been found, the earliest being dated 1748. In that year Benjamin Franklin sold his interest in the firm of Franklin and Hall, a printing company, to David Hall for £ 18,000. The money was to be paid to Franklin in eighteen annual installments amounting to £ 1,000 each, subject to a final accounting for the contributions and withdrawals of the partners. This period expired in 1766 when Franklin was in London as colonial representative. He asked James Parker, who had been his partner in New York for several years, to act as his representative in the final settlement with Hall. Parker made an inventory and valuation of the equipment and materials and presented a report which he entitled "State of your Accounts with Mr.. Hall."

There is no proof that James Parker was in practice as a public accountant. Nevertheless, this may have been the first public accounting engagement in the American Colonies. This report is on deposit in the library of Columbia University.[3]

On January 11, 1786, there appeared *The New York Directory*, the first such volume issued for that city. The publisher, Shepard Kollock, advertised it as showing national, state and municipal officers, ministers, bank officers, Columbia College professors, physicians, lawyers, tradesmen, etc. One of the announcements in the directory reads as follows:

David Franks Conveyance and Accountant No. 66 Broadway begs leave to return his sincere thanks to his friends and the public and hopes the cheapness of the following will continue him their favors.[4]

Then follows the advertiser's charges for drawing a release, a bond, and a power of attorney, but fees for services as an accountant were not stated.

A similar reference to a public accountant is found in an advertisement which appeared in the *New Jersey Journal* of Wednesday, July 8, 1795, printed and published by the same Shepard Kollock at Elizabethtown, New Jersey. The advertisement reads:

---

[3] *Ibid.*, p. 104.
[4] *Ibid.*, p. 105.

Notice

A conveyancing office and office of intelligence will be opened by the subscriber on Monday next, in the brick house of William Shute, Esq., formerly
occupied by Cortland Van Ansdaler; where writings of every kind will be done
on moderate terms; also, farmers and tradesmen's books posted with accuracy
and dispatch, and those who do not understand the method of keeping their
books will be shown the form.

Benjamin Thowson

Elizabethtown, April 21, 1795.[5]

The public practice of accountancy seems to have been combined
most commonly with teaching and writing on the subject of bookkeeping. The advertisements also indicate that some individuals
were performing the duties of accountants and lawyers at the same
time.

The following display advertisement indicates the functions performed by the public accountants in the United States during the
last half of the nineteenth century.

1851

Practical bookkeeper and accountant. Opposite the Court House. Books
opened, closed, posted. Bills and accounts made out. Bookkeeping in all its
varied branches taught individually or in classes.[6]

According to this advertisement the accountant did some systems
work but was primarily a bookkeeper and probably resorted to
teaching to supplement his income.

The New York City directories give the name of James A. Bennett for the following years:

1818-1820, Accountant, 48 Fulton Street
1821-1822, Accountant, 12th Avenue

[5]"Early Days of Accountancy," *The Journal of Accountancy*, XVI (October, 1913), 311.

[6]A. C. Littleton, *Directory of Early American Public Accountants* (Urbana, Illinois: The University
of Illinois, 1942), p. 19.

1823   Not given
1824-1829, Teacher in Bookkeeping, 97 John Street
1830-1831, Teacher in Bookkeeping, 39 Arcade
1833-1835, Teacher in Bookkeeping, 73 John Street[7]

Among those who were included in the directories was Benjamin F. Foster, of Boston, who was listed as a teacher in 1834 and as an accountant in 1835-1837.

The file of directories covers most years of the two decades 1850-1869. For New York, volumes for nineteen of the twenty years have been found; for Philadelphia, the volumes for nineteen years are included; for Chicago, all directories are available. Fifty-eight of a possible sixty annual directories give a fair sample of the number of accountants holding themselves out to clients. For New York in each of three years (1850, 1852, 1856) there were fourteen names listed; in eight other years there were seven, eight, or nine names; and in eight other years there were three, four, or five names. The number of public accountants listed in city directories during the following years in New York were: twelve in 1870, eleven in 1871, sixteen in 1872, eleven in 1873, eighteen in 1874, twenty-two in 1875, twenty-four in 1876, twenty in 1877, twenty-four in 1878, forty-one in 1879, and thirty-one in 1880.[8]

The Philadelphia directories of this period showed twenty-three names in 1869, twelve in 1860, ten in 1862, four in 1850, and for other scattered years three with three names, one with five, and two with seven names. Chicago lagged far behind. In 1854, only eight names appeared in the directory; only two were listed in the 1865 directory, and there appeared only one each in the directories for eight other years before 1870.[9]

Probably the first person to call himself a public accountant in Pennsylvania was John W. Francis, who opened an office in Philadelphia in 1869. Some years later Charles Nixon Vallum opened his office as an accountant in 1875 also in Philadelphia. He sent out an attractive card, handwritten and reproduced photographically,

---

[7]H. C. Bentley, *A Brief Treatise on the History and Development of Accounting* (Boston: Bentley School of Accounting and Finance, 1929), p. 27.

[8]A. C. Littleton, *Directory of Early American Public Accountants*, p. 12.

[9]*Ibid.*, p. 13.

explaining briefly just what he was prepared to do for the public.[10]
The announcement was as follows:

1875

Prepared to make statements for executors, examine corporations, partnerships, individual books and accounts of every description, open and close books, to attend to any and every kind of bookkeeping. Books posted monthly and trial balance taken at a trifling cost. Plans furnished for books for special purposes.[11]

John Heins, who was later to play a primary role in the organization of the American Association of Public Accountants, began to practice as a public accountant in downtown Philadelphia in 1877.

Another one of these advertisements which indicates the widening scope of the accountant's functions appeared thirty-six years after the 1851 display:

1887

H........ F........, public accountant and auditor, examines and reports on individuals, partnerships, corporation accounts, investigates and adjusts disputed accounts, acts as assignee or receiver, designs new books to meet special requirements. Books posted and balance sheets rendered, accounts audited, expert work for the courts, scientifically and faithfully performed.[12]

The advertiser seemed to perform a much wider variety of functions than thirty years earlier. The emphasis in 1887 was on auditing business records and issuing reports, whereas in 1851 the accountant or bookkeeper was concerned with the more routine matters of posting and closing accounts. In the advertisement of that year the advertiser offered clerical help in drawing up statements for his clients. The accountant in the later instance was available for work of a professional nature.

---

[10]George Wilkinson, "Organization of the Profession in Pennsylvania," *The Journal of Accountancy,* XLIV (September, 1927), 162.

[11]A. C. Littleton, *Directory of Early American Public Accountants,* p. 19.

[12]*Ibid.,* p. 20.

During the early 1890's the railroad companies in the United States were having financial difficulties. When The Norfolk and Western Railway had a receiver appointed by a federal court, Price, Waterhouse and Company, through its agent and predecessor, Jones & Caesar, was engaged to make a detailed examination of the company's accounts. This was the first of several railroad engagements undertaken by this firm.

Several other audits prior to amalgamation were brought to the firm of Jones & Caesar during the last decade of the nineteenth century.[13] These mergers continued even though the Sherman Anti-Trust Act had been passed in 1890.

During this period engagements such as those by Jones & Caesar, later Price, Waterhouse and Company, helped establish the profession. It was not yet a frequent occurrence for accountants to be called in regularly for auditing engagements. In the engagements incident to mergers the accountants would audit the books of all the enterprises to be consolidated. In addition they assisted in determining the basis for recording the assets and equities of the companies.

Formation of Accounting Firms

A natural development from practice as individuals was the association of two or more accountants in partnership. Accountants probably formed partnerships in imitation of other professions such as medicine and law, or following the precedent set by British accountants. Some years later it was required by law that accountants form partnerships rather than corporations so that the accountant's liability would not be limited.

The firm of Veysey and Veysey was established in New York in 1866. The senior partner, William H. Veysey, was an Englishman who never foreswore allegiance to Queen Victoria. His oldest son, Walter H. P. Veysey, was associated with him.[14] Prior to 1880 this firm had several assistants who were to become leaders in the development of the profession. Among them were James N. Kell, later the

---

[13]C. W. DeMond, *Price, Waterhouse and Company in America* (New York: The Comet Press, Inc., 1951), p. 5.

[14]George Wilkinson, "Organization of the Profession in Pennsylvania," *The Journal of Accountancy*, XLIV (September, 1927), 162.

treasurer of the New York State Society of Certified Public Accountants, and George Wilkinson, subsequently active in setting up the national organizations.

In Cincinnati a firm was listed under the caption of Accountants Bureau in the 1876 directory. The firm was composed of Nelson, Shepard and Cooke, who were listed as Expert Accountants.[15]

Barrow, Wade, Guthrie and Company, one of the earliest national firms, if not the oldest which no longer exists, was established in October, 1883, in New York. From its earliest days engagements were taken in different sections of the United States. As far as can be determined the accounting firms prior to this date were local in their operations. Guthrie had come to this country while acting in the capacity of receiver of a certain bankrupt financial concern in England. His mission was to inquire into the value and status of certain property and assets in the United States, as representative of the firm of Thomas, Wade, Guthrie and Company, Chartered Accountants, of London and Manchester, England. During his stay here it became evident to this trained accountant that there was an opportunity to establish a firm in this country. He joined with John Wylie Barrow, of New York, an actuary, who, as the American partner. checked the branch statements of insurance companies before forwarding them to England.

Prior to Barrow's death in 1886, the firm took in another partner, Oscar E. Morton. But when Guthrie returned to this country with James T. Anyon, whom he had employed to work in the New York office, he was faced with a lawsuit brought by the resident partner. After the suit was settled in Barrow's favor, Anyon assumed the duties of the firm here and became outstanding in the development of public accountancy.[16]

All the names of the partners in James Yalden and Company are not known, but James Yalden was listed in the 1883 New York telephone directory; in 1891 he was listed under Yalden, Brooks and Donnelly, and in 1893 under Yalden, Brooks and Walker. Security offerings in the *New York Times* showed that accounts were certified in 1890 by Deloitte, Dever, Griffiths and Company and by Price, Waterhouse and Company.

[15]Norman E. Webster, "Public Accountancy in the United States," in *Fiftieth Anniversary Celebration*, p. 107.

[16]James T. Anyon, "Early Days of American Accountancy," *The Journal of Accountancy*, XXXIX (January, 1925), 2.

Samuel Lowell Price, of Price, Waterhouse and Company, was a moving spirit in the formation of the Institute of Accountants in London in 1870. He was active in this organization until it was absorbed by the Institute of Chartered Accountants in England and Wales, incorporated in 1880. All three partners, Price, Waterhouse and Holyland, were Fellows of the Institute of Accountants.

Work in the United States was undertaken by the firm as early as 1873, and thereafter visits to this country were made with increasing frequency.[17] During the next decade there was considerable activity in the conversion of privately owned businesses into public companies, and a report on earnings, signed by some well known accountant, became an indispensable part of the prospectus advertising the offer to the public. During this period London financiers were seeking opportunities for investment of funds abroad, and as a result the undertakings by the firm, particularly in America, were increasing. With the amalgamation of a group of American breweries into the Bartholomay Brewing Company of Rochester, New York, audits were made of the accounts of the constituent companies. Sheath and Fowler, and members of the staff of Price, Waterhouse and Company were sent to the United States to carry out the work involved in the merger proceedings.

The period during which these representatives of English public accounting firms came to audit the accounts of American breweries was the beginning of a new era of expansion in American business enterprise. But the great value to the profession of the work referred from London lay in the opportunity for training Americans taken on the staff, many of whom had practically no previous experience in public accounting.

The firm name of Jones, Caesar and Company was used; this was one of the first American public accounting firms. The first American office of Price, Waterhouse and Company was opened under the latter name in New York in September, 1890. The Chicago office was opened in February, 1892.

In 1893 the first of the midwestern firms, Stuart and Young, was opened by Arthur Young in Chicago.

Then came the founding of Haskins and Sells on March 4, 1895, in New York. The two founding partners, Charles Waldo Haskins and Elijah Watt Sells, had met while serving on a committee which

---

[17]C. W. DeMond, *Price, Waterhouse and Company in America*, p. 5.

was investigating the operations of the Executive Department at Washington after the panic of 1893.[18]

A note in *The Accountant,* in 1899, states that two of the best known firms of English chartered accountants opened branch offices in Chicago in the year 1891 and transferred their Western business to them.[19] Unfortunately the names of these firms were not given in the announcement, but Jones and Caesar were operating in the United States as agents of Price, Waterhouse and Company of England and had several accounts in the Chicago area, including the stockyards. Jones first came to this country in 1891 and established an office in Chicago; therefore this might have been one of the offices mentioned as branch offices of an English firm of Chartered Accountants.

PROFESSIONAL ORGANIZATIONS

Institute of Accountants and Bookkeepers

Just as it was natural to form partnerships, it was also a natural move for an occupational group to form an organization for social as well as professional benefits. The first accounting organization in the United States was the Institute of Accountants and Bookkeepers of the City of New York, incorporated July 28, 1882. The name was shortened to the Institute of Accountants on June 23, 1886. Its objects and purposes, as stated in its certificates of incorporation, were

the evaluation of the profession and the intellectual advancement and improvement of its members:

1st, By the discussion in its councils of technical knowledge and commercial practice;

2nd, By aiding its members in the performance of their professional and social responsibilities.[20]

---

[18]Charles W. Haskins and E. W. Sells, *The First Fifty Years, 1895-1945* (New York: privately printed, 1947), p. 5.

[19]"The Public Accountant in Chicago," *The Accountant,* XXV (April, 1899), 395.

[20]Norman E. Webster, "Early Movements for Accountancy Education," *The Journal of Accountancy,* LXXI (May, 1941), 443.

Although the Institute of Accountants and Bookkeepers was active during twenty-five years or more, very few records of its activities remain except its charter, its bylaws, a few notices, and some news items in the accounting journals of that period. These records show that its membership included a considerable number of accountants in public practice, and that for its highest class of membership applicants were required to pass examinations which were described as severe. Its aims, at least during the first decade of its life, appear to have been almost wholly devoted to education for accountancy and the provision of accounting literature. So far as is known, this was the earliest effort to provide educational opportunities for the profession in America.[21]

American Association of Public Accountants

After the organization of accounting firms and the establishment of collegiate schools of business, it became clear to a few men of vision that the profession then known as "expert accounting" was a profession essential to the proper conduct of business. Those men who claimed to be experts in "matters of accounts" were few in number, had no means of increasing their number or maintaining high standards of practice for their own benefit and for that of the public, nor did they have any legal status or means of controlling the profession. It was not until 1886 that the first steps were taken to organize accountancy on a professional basis.

As has been noted, James T. Anyon arrived in New York City from London in October, 1886, to enter the firm of Barrow, Wade, Guthrie and Company. After the death of Barrow, Anyon turned his attention to an inquiry into the standing of the profession of accounting in New York. Anyon made the following statement:

I had left on the other side a profession full of vitality, one that was looked upon as an essential element of business life, and so recognized in every section of business activity. It need therefore not be a matter for surprise when I say that it was natural I should expect in this great and progressive country to find relatively the same conditions in the respect named as existed in the country I had left. A general survey of the situation, however, soon made the fact apparent

---

[21]*Ibid.*, p. 443.

that these conditions existed here only to a very limited extent, that public accounting was in its infancy and that it was little known or understood as a distinct profession.[22]

It was in early December, 1886, that Edwin Guthrie, F.C.A., of Manchester, England, who was visiting the city of New York on the business of his firm, accepted John Heins' invitation to visit Philadelphia. Heins was one of the most prominent accountants in Philadelphia. The object of the meeting was to discuss a plan to organize public accountants into a society with the following objectives:

to elevate the standing and advance the interest of public accountants; and to direct attention to the advantages offered by, and the safeguard attending, the auditing and adjusting of books and accounts by persons thoroughly skilled and experienced as public accountants, and to establish personal reputation.[23]

The society was to be called the "Chartered Accountants' Institute," but Guthrie strongly counseled Heins and Francis to use some other name than "Chartered Accountants." He pointed out that it would conflict with the use of that title in this country by English and Scottish accountants here on professional business. This seemed to be a serious objection, because the most important and responsible business entrusted to public accountants in these days was given to visiting British accountants due to the large amounts of foreign (primarily English) investments in this country. Also, Guthrie felt that a national organization, such as the Institute of Chartered Accountants (1882) would serve these purposes better than a state society.·
Anyon immediately invited all of those present at the first meeting as well as all interested accountants to meet with him and Edwin Guthrie at the firm's office, 45 William Street, to discuss "the matter of making the profession better known, understood, and recog-

[22]James T. Anyon, *Recollections of the Early Days of Accounting, 1883-1893* (New York: published by the author, 1925), p. 16.

[23]George Wilkinson, "Organization of the Profession in Pennsylvania," *The Journal of Accountancy*, XL (September, 1927), 163.

nized by the public, and what might be done to attain this object."[24]

On December 22, 1886, six or seven persons attended such a meeting. Guthrie was asked to take the chair, and Anyon to act as secretary of the meeting. Guthrie is quoted as remarking in his address

> that it was a great privilege to him thus to have this opportunity of meeting the accountants practicing in this and other cities; that he was sorry, however, to find the profession had not materially progressed in public recognition, or in other ways, since he was last here; that in England, on the contrary, the profession was on a very high plane; that it was recognized as one of the leading professions—firms, corporations, banks, railroads, and other financial and commercial entities seeking the service of accountants in all phases of activity; that the efforts of practicing accountants in this country should be directed toward bringing about a similar institution or body to that now existing on the other side, viz., the Institute of Chartered Accountants in England and Wales, under the regulations of which competent accountants could practice and be recognized by the public as fully qualified so to do.[25]

A resolution was proposed by John Heins, who had come from Philadelphia to attend this meeting, that the accountants present should form themselves into an association for the advancement and protection of the interests of the profession, and that the qualifications for membership should be ability and fitness to practice in a public capacity. It was further proposed (Anyon states that he had the pleasure of making this motion) that the name of this organization be the American Association of Public Accountants. The motion was carried unanimously; thus came into existence, on December 23, 1886, the first organized body of professional accountants in the United States.[26] The ten members continued to advance the interests of public accounting and to further the legal recognition of the Association. Their efforts were finally successful when, on August 20, 1887, the Association was incorporated under the laws of the state of New York with the name and title

---

[24]James T. Anyon, "Early Days of American Accountancy," *The Journal of Accountancy,* XXXIX (January, 1925), 7.

[25]*Ibid.,* p. 7.

[26]*Ibid.,* p. 8.

of American Association of Public Accountants.[27] The following
is a copy of the certificate of incorporation:

The American Association of Public Accountants
Certificate of Incorporation

State of New York
City and County of New York   ss:

Be it Known, that we:
> Robert L. Fabian, of New York City
> James Yalden, of New York City
> Wm. Calhoun, of New York City
> Walter H. P. Veysey, of New York City
> Mark C. Mirick, of New York City
> Charles H. W. Sibley, of New York City
> Rodney McLaughlin, of Boston, Mass.
> John Heins, of Philadelphia, Penn.,

being persons of full age and citizens of the United States, and the majority
being also citizens of the State of New York, desiring to associate ourselves for
social and benefit purposes do hereby certify in writing, as follows, to wit:

First: That the name or title by which such society shall be known in law is
"The American Association of Public Accountants."

Second: The particular business and object of such is to associate into a
society or guild for their mutual benefit and advantage the best and most capable public accountants practicing in the United States; and through such
association to elevate the profession of public accountants as a whole, and to
promote the efficiency and usefulness of members of such society, by compelling
the observance of strict rules of conduct as a condition of membership, and
by establishing a high standard of professional attainments through general
education and knowledge and otherwise; and to transact such business as may
be necessary and incident to the establishment and conduct of an association for
the foregoing purposes.

Third: The number of trustees, directors or managers, to manage the same
shall be eight, and the names of the trustees, directors or managers for the first
year of its existence are as follows, viz.:

Robert L. Fabian, James Yalden, Wm. Calhoun, Walter H. P. Veysey, Mark
C. Mirick, Charles H. W. Sibley, Rodney McLaughlin, and John Heins.

Fourth: The district in which the principal office of such company or association shall be located is in the City, County and State of New York.

---

[27] T. Edward Ross, "Random Recollections of an Eventful Half Century," *The Journal of Accountancy*, LXIV (October, 1937), 268.

In Testimony Whereof we have made and signed the foregoing certificate, this twentieth day of August in the year one thousand eight hundred and eighty-seven.

                              (Signed) J. Yalden,
                                       John Heins,
                                       Walter H. P. Veysey,
                                       M. C. Mirick,
                                       C. H. W. Sibley,
                                       Robt. L. Fabian,
                                       Wm. Calhoun,
                                       Rodney McLaughlin.[28]

All of the American citizens present signed the certificate of incorporation. Anyon and Veysey, being British, could not join in the petition. Of the eight original signers, only two remained members after some twelve years—John Heins and James Yalden.[29]

The bylaws of the association were prepared and adopted on February 8, 1888, at a general meeting of the members of the association. A council meeting immediately followed, at which time the following officers were elected:

President .... James Yalden, New York
Vice-President .... John Heins, Philadelphia
Treasurer .... William H. Veysey, New York[30]

The first council of the association, the members of which were selected to regulate the conduct of its affairs, consisted of the following men:

James T. Anyon .... New York
Louis M. Bertheil .... New York
George H. Church .... New York

---

[28]*Fiftieth Anniversary Celebration* (New York: The American Institute of Accountants, 1937), p. 506.

[29]Sanders W. Davies, "Genesis, Growth and Aims of the Institute," *The Journal of Accountancy,* XLII (August, 1926), 105.

[30]Robert H. Montgomery, *Fifty Years of Accountancy* (New York: Ronald Press Company, 1939), p. 63.

John Heins .... Philadelphia
Mark C. Mirick .... New York
Rodney McLaughlin .... Boston, Mass.
C. H. W. Sibley .... New York
William H. Veysey .... New York
Walter H. P. Veysey .... New York
James Yalden .... New York[81]

The bylaws of the association provided that the members should be divided into two classes, Fellows and Associates, with the right to use after their names the initials F.A.A. or A.A.A., respectively. It was provided that

Fellows shall be (1) the original incorporators of the association and those who subscribe to the constitution and by-laws; and (2) all persons who have practiced as public accountants continuously for three years previous to membership in the Association.
Associates shall be all persons who obtain a certificate of their having passed the final examination hereinafter provided for.[82]

At the time of incorporation the association had thirty-one members, of whom twenty-four were fellows and seven associates.[83]

ACCOUNTING LITERATURE AND EDUCATION

Early Bookkeeping and Accounting Books

James Bennett, one of the earliest American writers on bookkeeping, published his first work, *The American System of Practical Bookkeeping*, in 1814. It met with popular response and was highly recommended by merchants, bank presidents, the Comptroller of the State of New York, the Mayor of Albany, and the Lieutenant Governor of New York.

In 1818 Bennett published a revised edition for use in schools. The title page of this edition shows him as:

---

[81]James T. Anyon, "Early Days of American Accountancy," *The Journal of Accountancy,*" XXXIX (February, 1925), 84.

[82]James T. Anyon, *Recollections of the Early Days of American Accountancy, 1883-1893*, p. 33.

[83]James T. Anyon, "Early Days of American Accountancy," *The Journal of Accountancy,* XXXIX (February, 1925), 85.

James Bennett, A. & M., Professor to the Accountants' Society of New York, late a professor to the Accountants' Society of Pennsylvania, late President of the Accountants' Society of New York, and member of Medico-Chirurgical Society of the State of New York.[84]

He probably stated this to promote his book. No other reference to the organizations in which he claimed membership could be found. The following quotations are from his book:

Natural and mathematical instruments are supplied and students will have access to a choice library. An excellent, mounted telescope for observing Satellites of Jupiter and for other astronomical purposes.[85]

The annual commencement of Bennetts' Public Lectures on Bookkeeping is on the first Monday in October, and a new class commences on the first Monday of each of the succeeding months, including April; as the lectures close annually on the 1st of May.[36]

Terms for an unlimited attendance, with the practice, $15 to be paid in advance. For private instruction, which is given at all times, $25 including books for practice. The private instruction is given in the daytime throughout the year.[37]

Mr. Bennett makes the following statement as to his ability and accomplishments:

The author has instructed in the Science and Art of Bookkeeping a far greater number of grown persons than any other person in any other country or age of the world; he has instructed persons from thirteen different nations of the earth.[38]

Another teacher-author-accountant was Benjamin F. Foster, of Boston, whom the 1834 city directory listed as an instructor. From 1835 to 1837 he was listed as an accountant. He was also a writer.

---

[34]H. C. Bentley, *A Brief Treatise on the History and Development of Accounting*, p. 27.
[35]*Ibid.*, p. 27.
[36]*Ibid.*, p. 27.
[37]*Ibid.*, p. 28.
[38]*Ibid.*, p. 28.

In 1837 Christopher C. Marsh, of New York City, published a
Lecture on the Study of Bookkeeping with the Balance Sheet, the
title page of which contained the following statement:

To Merchants and Others
Complicated Accounts Adjusted:
Opinions given on disputed points relating to accounts;
Books opened and commenced.[39]

George N. Comer, of Boston, published *A Work on Bookkeeping*
in 1842. His card as accountant stated:

Offers his services for the adjustment of disputed and complicated accounts,
Insolvent and Other Estates . . . and all business pertaining to that of an accountant, executed with fidelity and dispatch.[40]

It is clear, therefore, that these early American authors and
teachers sought engagements as public accountants. It is probable
that persons from other activities, especially from banking and
insurance, were from time to time called in for public accounting
service. After 1840, one begins to find mention of men whose
principal occupation was that of the public practice of accountancy.[41]

In 1852 Christopher C. Marsh published *Bookkeeping in Spanish*
in California. A. G. Beck was secured as a professional translator
because of his friendship for Marsh and his familiarity with the
subject matter. According to a letter dated May 20, 1888, from Beck's
son, Francis E. Beck, who was one of the earliest members of the
American Association of Public Accountants, A. G. Beck was in
public practice as an accountant in Los Angeles from 1852 to 1878.[42]

Following the Civil War, information as to accountants in public
practice, although much fuller, is far from complete.

[39]Norman E. Webster, "Public Accounting in the United States," in *Fiftieth Anniversary Celebration*, p. 106.
[40]*Ibid.,* p. 106.
[41]*Ibid.,* p. 106.
[42]*Ibid.,* p. 107.

Nineteenth Century Bookkeeping and Accounting Education

Bennett, mentioned previously as one of the early authors, also had a school which offered instruction in bookkeeping and related subjects. It has been observed by a historian:

> The school established by Bennett for the teaching of bookkeeping and mathematical science, in New York City in 1818, is doubtless the first accounting school in the United States.[43]

Attempts were made as early as 1851 to found a school of commerce at the university level. This attempt was made at the University of Louisiana but was apparently abandoned in 1857. In 1868 the University of Illinois established a school which became the School of Commerce two years later; its purpose was to prepare men for the tasks of business. Bookkeeping was one of the subjects taught. In 1880 the Board of Trustees discontinued the school since

> the attempt to construct a University School of Commerce along the lines of a business college have proven unsuccessful. The school had done little more than to prepare clerks and bookkeepers. It had not been realized that the function of a university school of commerce was to prepare for future leadership in economic enterprise, not for clerkship.[44]

The first business college of record offering instruction in accounts and related subjects was the Bryant and Stratton School, established in 1853.[45] Schools of a similar nature began to be established rather rapidly in the major cities on the east coast.[46]

The United States was the first country to recognize accounting as a proper subject or discipline to be given a place in the university

[43]H. C. Bentley, *A Brief Treatise on the History and Development of Accounting*, p. 28.

[44]Jeremiah Lockwood, "Early University Education in Accounting," *The Accounting Review*, XIII (June, 1938), 132.

[45]Norman E. Webster, "Early Movements for Accountancy Education," *The Journal of Accountancy*, LXXI (May, 1941), 441.

[46]James B. Lovette, "History of Accounting in the United States," unpublished typescript, American Institute of Accountants Library, New York, p. 14.

curriculum. The earliest known definite plan for the establishment of a collegiate school of business in the United States is described in a report made by President Robert E. Lee in 1869 to the trustees of the institution that later became Washington and Lee University. President Lee died the next year and his proposal was not carried out.[47]

The honor of establishing the first American collegiate school of business belongs to the University of Pennsylvania. Mr. Joseph Wharton gave $100,000 in 1881 to establish the Wharton School of Finance and Economy in Philadelphia.[48] The name was later changed to the Wharton School of Commerce and Finance.

The American Association's Educational Effort

On February 10, 1892, while James Yalden was President of the Association and Henry R. M. Cook Vice-President, a special meeting was called to consider a charter for an educational institution. The Vice-President, who it appears was also chairman of a committee on the charter, was authorized to go to Albany "to find out the particulars." At Albany the committee was advised by Melvil Dewey, Secretary to the Board of Regents, to present to the regents a petition for a charter for the proposed institution, embodying an outline of its form of organization, a statement of the provisions to be made for its financial stability, the curriculum which it would offer to its students, and probably the names of the persons who would constitute its faculty. On February 20, 1892, Harry A. Briggs, Richard F. Stevens, and the Committee on Charter were constituted as a Committee on Curriculum which reported on March 5, 1892, that it had agreed upon the course of study. On that date a fund of $5,000 was provided; on April 6, 1892, John L. N. Hunt was asked to take the chair of commercial law.[49]

A copy of this petition or of the curriculum is not known to exist. However, subsequent records indicate that the petition asked for a charter for a college of accountants, with the power to confer de-

---

[47]H. C. Bentley, *A Brief Treatise on the History and Development of Accounting*, p. 28.

[48]Emanuel Saxe, "The Role of the Society in Accounting Education," in *The New York State Society of Certified Public Accountants, Fiftieth Anniversary* (New York: New York State Society of Certified Public Accountants, 1947), p. 21.

[49]Norman E. Webster, "Early Movements for Accountancy Education," *The Journal of Accountancy*, LXXI (May, 1941), 443.

grees, to have a guaranty of $5,000 against deficits, to offer the courses provided for in the curriculum, and to be under the direction of the American Association of Public Accountants. The petition was endorsed by several hundred bankers, corporations, firms, and individuals of note and sent to the regents prior to May 21, 1892, because on that date the Committee informed the members that action would be taken on the petition in Albany on June 8, 1892.[50]

The minutes of the regents' meeting contain this statement:

. . . and after discussion, on motion of Regent Doane, it was voted that the Secretary be instructed to inform the petitioners in the matter of the American Association of Public Accountants of New York that the regents are not prepared to endorse the whole proposal in their petition, but are ready to open examinations for such persons as desire to become public accountants.[51]

The members of the Association's Charter Committee went to work immediately on a revision of the petition. The task was completed and the revised petition was presented to the members of the Association on December 8, 1892, when Cook submitted copies of the petition and the proposed curriculum. A brief summary of the ten sections of the petition follows:

1. It would be to the public interest to establish a professional school for accountants, under the jurisdiction of the regents, the auspices of the Association, and the guidance of members of the profession;
2. Guaranty by the Association against deficits to the extent of $2,500 a year;
3. Nominations as first trustees of the New York School of Accounts:
>   Thomas Bagot
>   Rufus G. Blandslee
>   Richard M. Chapman
>   George M. Church
>   Henry R. M. Cook
>   John L. N. Hunt
>   Lucius M. Stanton

---

[50]"A College of Accountants—Petition for It Sent to the University Regents," *The Accountant*, XVIII (June, 1892), 520.

[51]Norman E. Webster, "Early Movements for Accountancy Education," *The Journal of Accountancy*, LXXI (May, 1941), 444.

Richard F. Stevens
Frank B. Thurber
John B. Woodward
James Yalden

for terms of two years, their successors to be elected by the Association;

4. Suitable accommodations leased at 122 West 23rd Street, now available;
5. Provision of all necessary furniture, appurtenances, books and supplies;
6. Full course of instruction to extend over two years, each of forty weeks, 1000 hours;
7. Provisional Charter for two years asked;
8. After two years absolute charters to be asked on endowment of $20,000;
9. School to be self-supporting with instruction fee of $100 per annum;
10. Expenses of school estimated at $8,000 or $9,000 per annum, $5,000 subscribed to be used for furnishing the school and establishment of a library, and students estimated at not less than 100, providing an income of $10,000.[52]

The following is an outline of the proposed curriculum. It shows that the courses were for the purpose of preparing the students for the practice of public accountancy. The outlines included eight sections describing the scope of the courses that were to be studied and one section showing the time allotted to each during each of the two years.

Proposed Curriculum

Section 1. Science of double entry: elucidating the principles of original entry and posting and the primary groundwork on which bookkeeping rests.

Section 2. Keeping accounts for sole proprietors, co-partnerships, and corporations including the opening, conducting, and closing of books with the preparation of balance sheets, merchandise, and profit and loss accounts and schedules for merchandising, manufacturing, commission and brokerage, construction and shipping and commission businesses.

Section 3. Corporation accounts, state returns, reorganizations, etc.

Section 4. Judicial accounts (now commonly called fiduciary).

Section 5. Public accounts (now commonly called municipal).

Section 6. Auditing—Examination of accounts for arresting or detecting fraud; reconstruction of systems for insuring greater safety; preparing reports and statements on investigations.

Section 7. Auditing—Analyzing accounts and deducting facts therefrom for

---

[52]*Ibid.*, p. 446.

making calculations re future course of action; investigation for ascertaining actual earnings of a business; settlement of partnership interest, etc.

Section 8. Law upon mercantile, corporation, banking, judicial accounting, etc., upon matter of accounts as laid down by authorities or New York Statutes.

Section 9. First Year:

> Theory of Accounts 5 hours per week
> for 1st 20 weeks
> Profession of Public Accountancy 5 hours
> per week for last 20 weeks
> Six general classes of Accounts, each
> 2½ hours per week for full 40 weeks
> Law 2½ hours per week for full
> 40 weeks

Second Year:

> Substitute Auditing and practical
> reviews for theory and two general
> classes of accounts—others as in
> first year.

Both:

> Instruction by lectures, dictation,
> illustration, and texts.[53]

Record of action on this petition is found in the minutes of the Board of Regents for December 14, 1892:

The committee reported that the American Association of Public Accountants had withdrawn the objectionable features in their original proposal and had submitted a petition for a provisional charter for two years for the New York School of Accounts. After discussion it was voted that a provisional charter for two years be granted to the New York School of Accounts.[54]

The records of the regents also show the charter, which was as follows:

Whereas, a petition for incorporation as an institution of the University has been duly received, and Whereas official inspection shows that partial provision

---

[53]*Ibid.*, p. 447.
[54]*Ibid.*, p. 447.

has been made for buildings, furniture, equipment, and for proper maintenance, and that all other prescribed requirements will be fully met

Therefore, being satisfied that public interests will be promoted by such incorporation, the regents by virtue of the authority conferred on them by law hereby incorporate James Yalden, F. B. Thurber, Thomas Bagot, Rufus D. Chapman, Henry R. M. Cook, George H. Church, Richard F. Stevens, John B. Woodward and their successors in office under the corporate name of New York School of Accounts, with all powers, privileges and duties, and subject to all limitations and restrictions prescribed for such corporations by law or by the ordinances of the University of the State of New York. The first trustees of said corporation shall be provisionally the above named twelve original incorporators.

If all requirements prescribed by law or by the University ordinances be fully met within two years, then this charter shall be made permanent, but otherwise on December 14, 1894, it shall terminate and become void and shall be surrendered to the regents.

It is also provided that no diploma, certificate of graduation, or other credentials shall be granted except on such conditions as are from time to time certified under seal of the University as being duly approved by the regents.

In Witness Whereof the regents grant this Charter Number 680, under seal of the University at the Capitol in Albany, December 14, 1892.

Anson Judd Upon, Chancellor

Melvil Dewey, Secretary[55]

(Seal)

Even with the energetic sponsorship of the Association, the school was not a success. The movement promoted by it succeeded, however. Soon after the temporary charter expired on December 14, 1894, the regents' willingness to open examinations as early as 1892 paved the way for two bills which finally blossomed into the first state laws which set up the professional designation of Certified Public Accountant.

PROPOSED LEGAL RECOGNITION

In 1895 the accountants in California and New York were seeking legislation to obtain legal recognition and the licensing of public accountants. Early in 1895 in New York, both of the then existing accounting societies, the American Association of Public Accountants and the Institute of Accountants and Bookkeepers, had bills

[55]*Ibid.*, p. 447.

introduced in the legislature. The Association appointed a committee to promote the passage of suitable legislation, which was prepared by Francis Gottsberger and introduced on February 20. The Institute's bill was prepared by Henry Harvey early in March.[56]

The Institute's bill provided for the examination of candidates for certificates as Certified Public Accountants.

Section I of the bill stated:

Any citizen of the United States and a resident or doing business in the State of New York, over the age of twenty-one years, and of good moral character who shall have received from the University a certificate of his qualifications to practice as a public expert accountant, shall be so styled and it shall be a misdemeanor for any person not holding such certificate to assume the title of certified public accountant, or to use in connection with his name the letters C.P.A.[57]

The bills of both the Association and the Institute contained restrictive provisions which, however, differed materially in their application. The Association's bill provided

that no person shall practice as a public accountant after the passage of this act unless he be licensed by the Regents of the University of the State of New York.

The Institute's bill provided

that after July 1, 1896, only certified public accountants should be appointed or employed to act as examiners of accounts, expert accountants or paid auditors by courts, administrators, receivers, state, county or municipal officers.

Before the end of the legislative session, the Association's bill, with its restrictions of practice to those licensed by the Regents, was with-

---

[56]Norman E. Webster, "Background of the New York State C.P.A. Law of April 17, 1896, and Its Subsequent Amendments," in *The New York State Society of Certified Public Accountants Fiftieth Anniversary*, p. 32.

[57]"History of the American Institute," in *Fiftieth Anniversary Celebration*, p. 7.

drawn. The Institute's bill was defeated in the Senate because of the provision limiting practice to Certified Public Accountants.[58]

SUMMARY

It seems evident that more than seventy-five years ago some men in large cities called themselves public accountants. They audited or "checked up" books with the object mainly of discovering or preventing irregularities rather than for constructive work, although systems work was undertaken. Somewhat later the foreign shareholders and bondholders of a number of large enterprises, mainly but not exclusively railroads, desired that the accounts should be audited and sent out auditors from England to perform such services.[59] This practice led to the opening of offices in the United States by English and Scotch auditors; some of the early firms were established in this way. American accountants gave increasing competition.

The earliest accounting organization, the American Association, was formed with the purpose of raising the professional standards and "for social and benefit purposes." Early attempts to elevate the profession by means of collegiate instruction in accounting for those wishing to enter the profession were unsuccessful. Wharton's School of Finance and Economy, however, was formed in Philadelphia, and accounting was included in its curriculum.

The desire on the part of the members of the profession to receive recognition was carried to the New York State Board of Regents. With the Board's willingness to administer examinations an attempt was made to secure legal recognition from the state. The first attempt in 1895 to get legislation for the legal recognition of Certified Public Accountants failed, but during the subsequent period the public accountants continued their efforts with considerable success.

---

[58]Norman E. Webster, "Background of the New York State C.P.A. Law of April 17, 1896, and its Subsequent Amendments," in *The New York State Society of Certified Public Accountants Fiftieth Anniversary*, p. 32.

[59]Edward L. Suffern, "Twenty-five Years of Accountancy," *The Journal of Accountancy*, XXXIV (September, 1922), 174.

CHAPTER V

Public Accounting in the United States, 1896-1913

The first legal recognition of the certified public accounting profession was gained during the period 1896-1913. These were years of great expansion of accounting education, and of the founding and growth of organizations that advanced the standing of the profession. Some of the early firms discussed in this chapter are still in existence and have acquired national or international reputations.

FIRST C.P.A. LAW AND OTHER LEGISLATION

New York Legal Recognition

After the failure to get the legislature of the state of New York to pass public accounting legislation in 1895, the American Association and the Institute of Bookkeepers and Accountants united behind the Institute's bill, from which the restrictive provision which would have permitted only certified public accountants to practice accounting had been deleted.

The next year the Association appointed a committee of three to press for the Institute's bill. Its members were Frank Broaker, William Sanders Davies, and James Yalden. Davies stated that he worked for the bill only in New York City, that James Yalden was inactive, but that Frank Broaker spent nearly all his time in Albany, and that without his efforts and that of his partner, Richard M. Chapman, of the firm Broaker and Chapman, the bill would not have passed.[1] On April 17, 1896, there was enacted the first legislation in the United States to create the professional designation "Certified Public Accountant." The law reads as follows:

---

[1]Norman E. Webster, "Background of the New York State C.P.A. Law of April 17, 1896, and Its Subsequent Amendments," in *The New York State Society of Certified Public Accountants Fiftieth Anniversary* (New York: The New York State Society of Certified Public Accountants, 1947), p. 33.

Chapter 312. Laws of 1896
Passed Assembly 3 April, 1896; Passed Senate 7 April, 1896.
Signed by Governor 17 April, 1896
State of New York
An Act to Regulate the Profession of Public Accountants.

The people of the State of New York, represented in the Senate and Assembly, do enact as follows:

Section 1. Any citizen of the United States, or person who has duly declared his intention of becoming such citizen, residing or having a place for the regular transaction of business in the State of New York, being over the age of twenty-one years and of good moral character, and who shall have received from the Regents of the University a certificate of his qualifications to practice as a public expert accountant as hereinafter provided, shall be styled and known as a Certified Public Accountant; and no other person shall assume such title, or use the abbreviation C.P.A. or any other word, letters or figures, to indicate that the person using the same is such Certified Public Accountant.

Section 2. The Regents of the University shall make rules for the examination of persons applying for certificates under this act, and may appoint a board of three examiners for the purpose, which board shall, after the year eighteen hundred and ninety-seven, be composed of Certified Public Accountants. The Regents shall charge for examination and certificate such fee as may be necessary to meet the actual expenses of such examinations, and they shall report annually their receipts and expenses under the provision of this Act to the State Comptroller, and pay the balance of receipts over expenditures to the State Treasurer. The Regents may revoke any such certificate for sufficient cause after written notice to the holder thereof and a hearing thereon.

Section 3. The Regents may, in their discretion, waive the examination of any person possessing the qualifications mentioned in Section 1 who shall have been for more than one year before the passage of this Act, practicing in this State on his own account, as a public accountant, and who shall apply in writing for such certificate within one year after the passage of this Act.

Section 4. Any violation of this Act shall be a misdemeanor.

Section 5. This Act shall take effect immediately.[2]

For the first time, "Certified Public Accountant" was a term with a definite legal connotation.[3]

Acting under the authority of this act the Regents of the Univer-

---

[2]New York Laws, 1896, Ch. 312.
[3]C. W. Haskins and E. W. Sells, *The First Fifty Years, 1895-1945* (New York: Privately Printed, 1947), p. 8.

sity of the state of New York appointed Frank Broaker, C. E. Sprague, and Charles Waldo Haskins to be the first board of examiners under the new Public Accountants Act.[4] The following conditions had to be met by each candidate before a certificate could be issued under the rules of conduct. He had to be at least twenty-five years of age with three years' satisfactory experience in the practice of accounting, one of them in the office of an expert public accountant. The examinations were to cover the theory of accounts, practical accounting, auditing, and commercial law.[5] The examinations were given under the auspices of the New York State Board of Regents by a board of examiners appointed from the public accountancy profession. These examinations were under the control of the administrative board of all the educational facilities of the state of New York.

Efforts at Federal Regulation

Many of the prominent practicing public accountants in these years felt that the profession of accountancy needed federal recognition and regulation. They based their argument largely on the fact that accountancy was to a very large extent interstate. All of the large firms of public accountants, the arguments went, practiced in more than one state—in some cases in foreign countries. If the accountant could receive recognition from the national government, he would be able to practice in interstate commerce without hindrance. The profession desired a license which all states would recognize. It was pointed out by Sells that no comparable difficulty existed in the practice of the professions of law and medicine, neither of which, generally speaking, was of the same interstate character as the profession of accountancy.[6]

The reluctance of Congress to take action on legislation pertaining to one profession was one reason for not pushing for a federal law. Then, too, several states—for example California, Pennsylvania, Florida, and Maryland—had C.P.A. legislation in force, and Congress would be very reluctant to pass a law which might invade

---

[4]"Accountancy in the States," *The Accountant,* XXII (June, 1896), 504.

[5]Charles W. Haskins, "Accountancy; Its Past and Present," an address delivered before the American Association of Public Accountants, January 25, 1900 (unpublished), p. 21.

[6]C. W. Sells, "The Accountant of 1917," *The Journal of Accountancy,* III (February, 1907), 298.

THE SPREAD of ACCOUNTANCY LEGISLATION

MAP SHOWING THE THIRTY-ONE STATES IN WHICH THERE ARE LAWS PROVIDING FOR THE ISSUANCE OF CERTIFIED PUBLIC ACCOUNTANT CERTIFICATES.
Source: JOURNAL of ACCOUNTANCY, July 1913.

States' rights. Hence the idea of securing Congressional action on professional accountancy was given up or failed to gain acceptance.

Legislation in Other States

After the passage of the New York act public accountants in other states sought their own state laws. The accountants in New York were eager to offer information on their act and give assistance to other state organizations. The Pennsylvania law was enacted in 1899, the Maryland law in 1900, the California law in 1901, the Illinois and the Washington laws in 1903, the New Jersey law in 1904, and the Florida and Michigan laws in 1905.

Additional state legislation recognizing the accountancy profession was passed in Colorado in 1907, in Georgia, Connecticut, Ohio, Louisiana, and Rhode Island in 1908, in Montana, Nebraska, Minnesota, Massachusetts, and Missouri in 1909, in Virginia in 1910, West Virginia and Wyoming, 1911, and Vermont, 1912. The next year Nevada, North Carolina, North Dakota, Oregon, Tennessee, Wisconsin, Wyoming, Utah and Delaware got C.P.A. laws.

In each of these states the accountants banded together in a society which became affiliated with the American Association. By the end of the first decade of the twentieth century, there were about one thousand members of the Association. The accompanying map reflects the spread of accountancy legislation in the United States up to and including 1913. This map shows the thirty-one states which had laws governing the issuance of Certified Public Accountant certificates as of that date.

First Violation of C.P.A. Law

In 1898 the first violator of the New York C.P.A. law was brought into court. This was even before any other state had enacted such a law. The suit resulted from the publication of the following advertisement in a New York newspaper.

Accountant—a certified public accountant, highly recommended, will write up books, prepare trading accounts, make investigations etc., terms, $6 per diem, or accept permanent situation with firm or corporation—Certified Ac countant, Herald.[7]

---

[7]"Accountancy in the States," *The Accountant*, XXIV (April, 1898), 349.

In checking, authorities found that this advertisement had been inserted by one John Fenton, who pleaded ignorance of the 1896 Act and offered a full apology. Further, he stated that he was a member of the Society of Accountants and Auditors of England, but after a check had been made his name was not found among the list of members.

When Fenton appeared in court he pleaded guilty to the charge of using the professional designation "Certified Public Accountant" without having been licensed to practice by the New York State Board. He was fined $35.00 or ten days in jail for the violation. The conviction of the violator of this law was made only nine days after the violation.[8] It is clear that accountants were anxious to establish and maintain professional standards in an effort to acquire recognition. They probably wanted to make an example of the first violator of the new public accountancy act.

C.P.A. EXAMINATION, CERTIFICATION, AND PROFESSIONAL EXPANSION

Analysis of First C.P.A. Examination

The first examination was given by the New York Board of Examiners on December 15 and 16, 1896. The full text of this examination is in the Appendix. The first section of the examination, on the theory of accounts, was given on December 15, 1896 from 9:15 A.M. to 12:15 P.M. Candidates had to answer five obligatory questions and any five of the other questions. The first question pertained to the essential principles of double-entry bookkeeping as contrasted with single-entry. Other questions required the candidate to distinguish between accounts—revenue account, trading account—and to define such terms as fixed assets, cash assets, stock, capital, and loan capital.

Practical accounting was given in the afternoon from 1:15 to 4:15 P.M. There were two obligatory questions: the first required a statement of affairs, and the second had to do with a partnership problem. The third question concerned the opening of the books of a company after purchase at a receiver's sale. A balance sheet was to be made from the ledger accounts. The fourth question dealt

---

Ibid., p. 349.

with a partnership liquidation problem, the fifth with foreign exchange, and the sixth with a problem of a joint venture.

The auditing examination was the following day from 9:15 A.M.
to 12:15 P.M. Ten questions had to be answered by the candidate,
five of them required, with a choice of five from seven remaining
questions. The subject matter pertained to the duties of an auditor,
and the principal points to which he should direct his attention
while auditing a corporation. The examination then went into
specific questions in regard to auditing cash payments and receipts
as well as other specific audit procedures. The candidate had to make
a grade of 75 out of 100 on each section of the examination to pass.
The examination apparently covered the functions which the public
accountant performed during the 1890's.

The present-day C.P.A. examination covers the areas mentioned
in this first examination, but requires a longer period of time (two
and a half days) with longer sessions. The technical portion of the
test has been set at the level of a senior accountant. Thus the emphasis now is on accounting matters with much less time devoted
to bookkeeping, or even none at all.

As a result of the first examination held under the auspices of the
Regents of the State of New York under the authority granted in the
first C.P.A. law, fifty-six certificates were issued. The records of the
American Institute of Certified Public Accountants show that all of
these certificates were issued by waiver. (See Appendix B.) In fact, it
was two years before a certificate was issued upon examination, evidently because the examination papers were unsatisfactory. Some
accountants at this time began to refer to the C.P.A. title as a "degree." Webster says the term was used because the certificates issued
were from the State Board of Education of New York, and because
the initials were written after the name as are the letters of academic
degrees.[9] It was not a degree as the term is generally understood, but
a certificate of professional proficiency. Frank Broaker (Broaker &
Chapman) was issued Certificate No. 1; his partner, Certificate No.
2; Sanders Davies, Certificate No. 4; and certificates were also
granted to James T. Anyon and G. Sever, both with Barrow, Wade,
Guthrie and Company of New York.[10]

---

[9]Letter from Norman Webster, Chairman of the History Committee of the American Institute of
Accountants, to James D. Edwards, dated October 16, 1951.

[10]"Accountancy in the States," *The Accountant*, XXIII (January, 1897), 99.

Examinations—Thirty Boards

Twentieth century accountants were not satisfied with the method of examining candidates for the certificate. There was little uniformity in the requirements of the various state boards, of which there were thirty in 1913, and it was felt by some members of the profession that the C.P.A. examinations did not deserve to rank along with examinations in law and medicine.[11]

The following extract from an editorial in the July issue of *The Journal of Accountancy* reflects the opinion of the profession:

It has long been a reproach to the Accountancy profession in the United States that the examinations proposed for admission into the profession are exceedingly elementary and in no way comparable with the examinations for admission into the other learned professions. The examinations everywhere consist of questions in four subjects: theory of accounts, practical accounting, auditing, and commercial law. The questions in commercial law can readily be answered after a few days "cramming" from some elementary text books, such as White or Gano. The auditing questions require a mastery of Dicksee's auditing and little more. The theory of accounts examination usually asks of the candidate a number of elementary definitions, for example, "What is a consignment account," "Define and differentiate real and nominal accounts or controlling and specific accounts"; or such a question as this is asked, "State briefly the proper manner of conducting the following kinds of accounts: Bills receivable, Bills payable, Shipment accounts."

These are questions in bookkeeping, and their answer demands no very high order of intellectual attainment. The questions in practical accounting are of a different nature. They are almost without exception, problems of simple arithmetic which the student is required to express in "technical form." The problems themselves ordinarily present not the slightest difficulty, provided the meaning of the examiners can be clearly determined. Their expression is generally a matter of taste. A variety of methods are available if the examinee selects one which may or may not suit the examiner.

As a result of this condition, a singular situation is presented. With few exceptions, candidates for the C.P.A. degree passed the examinations in commercial law, auditing, and theory of accounts generally with high marks. Very few, however, pass the examination in practical accounting. The reason for this condition is not far to seek. It is because the first three subjects

---

[11]Edward S. Meade, "Established Preliminary Examinations in Law and Economics," *The Journal of Accountancy*, III (January, 1907), 193.

are generally too elementary to be set as a condition of examination into a profession, and because the examination in practical accounting demands of the candidate the working out of puzzles rather than the solution of problems. Even interpreted in the most kindly spirit, the practical accounting examination is an examination for accountants' assistants and not for accountants. We do not wish to be misunderstood as universally condemning all the examination questions set by the state boards of accounting examiners. As a general proposition, however, we believe that our characterization is correct.[12]

Examination Results

During the years covered in the period from 1896 to 1913, we find that a majority of the certificates issued to those in the public practice of accountancy were waiver certificates, granted to men already in practice on the date of the enactment of the C. P. A. law. Actually

ORIGINAL C.P.A. CERTIFICATES ISSUED

Year	Examination	Waiver	Reciprocity	Total	Cumulative Total
1896		56		56	56
1897		70		70	126
1898	6	1		7	133
1899	9	35		44	177
1900	16	25		41	218
1901	15	70		85	303
1902	37	24		61	364
1903	58	41		99	463
1904	67	31		98	561
1905	36	20		56	617
1906	58	20		78	695
1907	62	28	11	101	796
1908	56	229	4	289	1,085
1909	115	108	8	231	1,316
1910	201	117	8	326	1,642
1911	122	47	11	180	1,822
1912	108	9	2	119	2,021
1913	89	139	16	244	2,265

SOURCE: American Institute of Certified Public Accountants.

[12]*Ibid.*, p. 194.

the first C. P. A. certificates issued by examination according to the American Institute's records were in 1898. The preceding table reflects the number of certificates issued by states by years, whether on examination, by waiver or by reciprocity. The next column gives the cumulative total. A complete list of the certificates issued by states can be found in the Appendix.

Newly Established Firms and Branch Offices

With accounting practice moving more and more to the area of business operations, Price, Waterhouse and Company opened the following offices during the period 1896-1913: St. Louis, in November, 1901; Pittsburgh, in May, 1902; and San Francisco, in November, 1904.[13]

Some significant auditing engagements which this firm handled are presented here. In December, 1897, the firm Jones, Caesar and Company (later Price, Waterhouse and Company) accepted an engagement from J. P. Morgan & Company to make examinations of the accounts of all constituent units which were to form the American Steel and Wire Company of New Jersey. This audit was one of the first examples of the employment of public accountants during the preliminary stage leading to the negotiation of merger agreements. The consolidation was finally completed by John W. Gates in 1899 after the recovery from the recession of 1897.[14]

On February 17, 1902, the stockholders of the United States Steel Corporation elected Price, Waterhouse and Company as auditors. United States Steel was the first important industrial company to fix a policy of having the auditors elected by stockholders rather than selected by the officers or directors. The first audit certificate issued by the corporation for the year 1902 was accompanied by a certificate of chartered accountants signed by the firm.[15]

In 1906, Stuart and Young was dissolved because of disagreements between the partners, and the firm was reestablished under the name Arthur Young and Company, opening its office in 1911. It became a

---

[13]Letter from C. W. DeMond, Partner in Price, Waterhouse and Company, to James D. Edwards, dated May 6, 1952.

[14]C. W. DeMond, *Price, Waterhouse and Company in America* (New York: The Comet Press, Inc., 1951), p. 34.

[15]*Ibid.*, p. 60.

firm practicing on a national level two decades later.[16] The firm attributes its growth into a national organization to the many special jobs which were directed to it when the United States entered World War I. Many of these special jobs related to investigation of companies owned by alien enemies of the United States.[17]

Haskins and Sells opened offices in Chicago on December 1, 1900, in Cleveland and St. Louis in 1902, in Pittsburgh in 1903, in Baltimore in 1910, and in San Francisco in 1912.[18]

Lybrand, Ross Brothers and Montgomery was founded on January 1, 1898, in Philadelphia. In 1902 Montgomery was given permission by the partners to open a New York office. A Pittsburgh office was set up in 1908, and a Chicago office in 1909.[19]

In the last year of the period covered by this chapter, Arthur Andersen, head of the accounting department at Northwestern University in Chicago, became a partner in Andersen, DeLong and Company.[20] It seems that he was the first university professor to move from the teaching profession to that of public accountancy.

With over twenty-two hundred certified public accountants in the United States by 1913, it would seem safe to assume that there were several hundred public accounting firms. Most of them were probably operating in a single city. Some of the more active ones carried on regional businesses. It would be reasonable to say also that there were competent public accountants practicing in states which did not have public accounting laws.

EDUCATIONAL ACTIVITIES OF THE PROFESSION

Education and Accountancy

After the formation of the Pennsylvania Institute of Public Accountants it was realized that the upbuilding of the accountancy profession must come through education far more than through the enactment of C.P.A. laws alone. With this idea in mind, the Coun-

[16]Arthur Young and Company, *Arthur Young and the Business He Founded* (New York: privately printed, 1948), p. 15.

[17]*Ibid.*, p. 30.

[18]Charles W. Haskins and E. W. Sells, *The First Fifty Years*, 1895-1945, p. 5.

[19]William M. Lybrand, Adam A. Ross, T. Edward Ross, and Robert H. Montgomery, *Fiftieth Anniversary* (privately printed, 1948), p. 3.

[20]Charles W. Jones, "A Chronological Outline of the Development of the Firm," *The Arthur Andersen Chronicle*, IV (December, 1943), 8.

cil of the Pennsylvania Institute authorized, in the summer of 1902, the formation of classes for the study of the four subject areas in the field of Public Accounting.[21]

These classes were organized primarily for the purpose of affording technical instruction to assistants engaged in the offices of members of the Pennsylvania Institute. The restriction was not strictly enforced, because each member of the Institute had the privilege of nominating a student (not an employee) who wanted to become an accountant. The subjects taken up and the instructors lecturing thereon were:

Theory of Accounts, Robert H. Montgomery
Practical Accounts, W. M. Lybrand
Auditing, J. W. Fernley
Commercial Law, H. G. Stockwell

These classes actually did not begin until the evening school was started on October 20, 1902.[22]

By the spring of 1904 negotiations had been successfully carried out with the faculty of the Wharton School of Accounts and Finance and with the trustees of the University of Pennsylvania to turn the educational classes established by the Institute over to the University. Some members of the Institute guaranteed the expenses of conducting the classes for the first winter season, but the guarantors were never called on for any money.[23]

In 1900, the Council of New York University established in that institution a School of Commerce, Accounts and Finance, which established the world's first department of accountancy, as such.[24] Because of the impetus to business, there was greater demand for the services of accountants, and a scarcity of well-trained accountants became evident. Members of the profession felt that some steps should be taken to secure the cooperation of some educational insti-

---

[21]George Wilkinson, "Organization of the Profession in Pennsylvania," *The Journal of Accountancy,* XL (September, 1927), 162.

[22]*Ibid.,* p. 170.

[23]*Ibid.,* p. 171.

[24]Arthur H. Woolf, *A Short History of Accountants and Accountancy* (London: Gee and Company, 1912), p. 188.

tution which would establish a course in accountancy to train students to fill future needs for trained assistants.[25]

The institutions were skeptical as to the feasibility or advisability of such a step, but at length, heeding the urgings of the committee, New York University instituted the course in 1901. The Board of Regents appointed C. W. Haskins as the dean of the new school.[26]

The tentative course of study, as worked out by the New York State Society's committee included (A) Accounting (Theory of Accounts, Practice in Accounting and Auditing); (B) Finance (Money and Banking, Exchange, and Stocks and Bonds); (C) Commercial Economics (Statistics, Taxation, Public Debt, and Economic History); and (D) Commercial Law. These had been recommended at the meeting of the society in New York on December 10, 1900.

Dean Haskin's aim was "to bring together in the school such a corps of trained educators and practicing accountants as would meet the requirements of the State Board of Examiners under the Law of 1896."[27]

There was a pressing need for technical literature in those early years. Very little had been written in the United States, and schools were dependent upon English works, which, while valuable, were not wholly adapted to use in this country. Almost immediately the most essential books were published.[28]

In the year 1900 thirteen universities and colleges gave accredited courses in accounting. They were Dartmouth College, Drake University, Harvard University, Louisiana State University, the University of Pennsylvania, Temple College, the Agricultural College of Utah, the University of Vermont, West Virginia University, and the University of Wisconsin. These names were assembled after search of some twenty-two hundred college catalogues by C. E. Allen in 1927.[29] Of the thirteen schools offering courses in accounting, only four (the Agricultural College of Utah, Dartmouth, New York

---

[25]Edward L. Suffern, "Twenty-five Years of Accountancy," *The Journal of Accountancy*, XXXIV (September, 1922), 177.

[26]"Accountancy in New York State," *The Accountant*, XXVII (September, 1901), 983.

[27]Emanuel Saxe, "The Role of the Society in Accounting Education," in *The New York Society of Certified Public Accountants Fiftieth Anniversary*, p. 23.

[28]Edward L. Suffern, "Twenty-five Years of Accountancy," *The Journal of Accountancy*, XXXIV (September, 1922), 178.

[29]C. E. Allen, "The Growth of Accounting Instruction since 1900," *The Accounting Review*, II (June, 1927), 150.

University, and Temple College) had a course listed under the title of auditing.

The first course in C.P.A. problems and questions as such appeared in New York University's catalog during the period 1905-1910. It can be stated that the introduction of a course called C.P.A. Problems closely followed the passage of the state C.P.A. laws in almost every case.[80] The Graduate School of Business Administration of Harvard University, the pioneer in its field as a strictly graduate school, was founded in 1908.[81] Leland Stanford University established a graduate school of business in 1925. The University of Texas authorized a graduate degree in business in 1917.[32]

After 1905, it was decided to publish a journal which would make the accounting papers given at the conventions available to the public and the profession for educational purposes. The Accountancy Publishing Company was formed for this purpose.[33] The common stock went to the old Federation and to the Illinois Society. The preferred stock was sold to prominent public accountants in New York and Philadelphia by Robert H. Montgomery, Secretary of the Federation of Societies of Public Accountants.[34]

In November, 1905, the first issue of *The Journal of Accountancy* was published as the official organ of the profession. The co-editors were Professors Joseph French Johnson, of New York University, and Edward S. Meade, of the University of Pennsylvania. For a time these gentlemen accepted preferred stock in payment of their salaries.

The first *Journal* reviewed the status of the profession:

> Within the last decade accounting has made rapid strides. Several states have formally recognized it as a profession by providing for examinations leading to the degree of Certified Public Accountant. Five of the largest American Universities have organized instruction in Accountancy. A large number of the most important railroads and industrial corporations subject their books to periodical

---

[80]*Ibid.*, p. 155.

[81]H. C. Bentley, *A Brief Treatise on the History and Development of Accounting* (Boston: Bentley School of Accounting and Finance, 1929), p. 29.

[32]Minutes of the Board of Regents, The University of Texas, May, 1917.

[33]Sanders W. Davies, "Genesis, Growth and Aims of the Institute," *The Journal of Accountancy*, XLII (August, 1926), 107.

[34]Robert H. Montgomery, *Fifty Years of Accountancy* (New York: Ronald Press Company, 1939), p. 69.

audits by Public Accountants. Banks, trust companies and insurance companies
have more recently adopted the same plan as a guarantee of security to depositors and policy holders, and the best method of protection against fraud. Manu-
facturers are calling upon public accountants to install cost systems, banks are
requiring borrowers to secure accountants' certificates to the statement submitted as a basis for credit, and states, municipalities and public institutions
in constantly increasing numbers are engaging the services of the profession to
introduce systems and order into their affairs. These indications of the growing
appreciation of Accountancy are the source of gratification and encouragement
to its members; and there is no doubt that they will receive even more substantial recognition in the future.[35]

Once the amalgamation of the Federation and the Association
became official, many if not all of the accountant-stockholders
donated their preferred stock to the American Association of Public
Accountants. At the annual meetings of this organization in 1908
and 1909, additional capital was obtained because the editor reported that the *Journal* would not be on a self-supporting basis for
three years.

In 1911 the Council of the American Association of Public Accountants voted to assume direct control of the *Journal*. The following letter was sent to the members of the Association:

November 20, 1911

Dear Sir:

At the recent meeting of the American Association of Public Accountants at
San Francisco, the Trustees unanimously decided that the association should
itself take over the supervision of The Journal of Accountancy. This in the
opinion of the Trustees was necessary to enable The Journal to reach the position and circulation that its character justifies and that its greatest usefulness
demands.

The Association assumes direct editorial charge of The Journal, while arrangements have been made with the Ronald Press Company of New York
City for its publication and general business management. The transfer of
The Journal to the Association in the manner above described is practically
effective with the December number and will be formally effective January 1,
1912.

This means that the Association has an increased interest in The Journal's
character and success. We now ask you, as a member, to accord it your most

---

[35]Editorial, "Present Status of the Profession," *The Journal of Accountancy*, I (November, 1905),
p. 1.

active support in suggestions, in subscriptions, and in contributions of material. It is obvious that the heartier the support accorded by the members of the Association, the better, the more influential, and the more effective can The Journal be made.

We ask your support for The Journal of Accountancy because it is the official organ of your association. Beyond this, we ask it because The Journal is eminently deserving of your support—because it is the only organ of the accounting profession in this country, and because you, as an accountant, cannot be fully in touch with the best in your profession unless you are in touch with its current literature,—which for this country finds its authoritative expression in The Journal of Accountancy.

Under the new regime, there will be no lowering of The Journal's high standard. It will, however, be brought more closely in line with current accounting needs; articles on practical accounting will be given even greater prominence than heretofore; and practical discussions of these articles and of other matters of direct importance to accountants will give added interest to the magazines.

The Journal for 1912 will number the most prominent, the most progressive, and the most successful accountants of the Country among its subscribers and contributors. Will you not give it your support? If not already a subscriber, a subscription check or money order for $3, made payable to The Journal of Accountancy—198 Broadway, New York—will be immediate and gratifying evidence of your interest.

> Yours very truly,
> Edward L. Suffern,
> President American Association
> of Public Accountants[36]

Then in January, 1912, A. P. Richardson became editor and in the same year the Association assumed direct control of the *Journal* with the cooperation of the Ronald Press Publishing Company.[37]

PROFESSIONAL ORGANIZATIONS

American Association of Public Accountants

On April 18, 1896, some ten years after the Association was formed and at the time the first public accounting law was enacted and approved by Governor Levi P. Morton, the Association, according to the American Institute of Certified Public Accountants, had

---

[36]Editorial, "The Journal and The American Association of Public Accountants," *The Journal of Accountancy*, XXXII (November, 1921), 539.

[37]W. Sanders Davies, "Genesis, Growth and Aims of the Institute," *The Journal of Accountancy*, XLII (August, 1926), 107.

only forty-five active members, distributed geographically as follows: New York, thirty-seven; Massachusetts, three; California, two; and Georgia, Illinois, and New Jersey, one each.[38]

National Society of Certified Public Accountants

The legal recognition of the accounting profession in New York led to the incorporation of a National Society of Certified Public Accountants in the United States in 1897. Anyone holding a certificate from the University of the State of New York was eligible for membership. The objects of this society were to elevate the profession, to unify into one body all Certified Public Accountants practicing in the United States, to exchange professional knowledge by means of lectures, to establish a professional library, and to secure legal mutual recognition of the letters C.P.A., by and between all of the United States of America. Mr. C. W. Smith was the first president of the National Society of Certified Public Accountants. Sixty-seven accountants were admitted to membership.[39]

The organization was short-lived, for in 1899 the National Society and the American Association merged into one organization. The merger was a great advantage to the membership of both groups as well as the profession as a whole.[40] Many accountants had joined both of the original societies.

Founding of the Federation

Under the stimulus of state recognition, the profession developed rapidly. Public accountants in other states sought state laws similar to that of New York. In July, 1902, at a meeting of the Illinois Association of Public Accountants, George Wilkinson read a paper in which he set forth the great need for establishing a definite relationship among the local state societies, which at that time showed little unity of purpose in affairs of a national character. He suggested a plan for the coordination of all existing organizations by the formation of societies of public accountants.[41] In a similar search for a

---

[38]*Fiftieth Anniversary Celebration* (New York: The American Institute of Accountants, 1937), p. 7.

[39]"Accountancy in the States," *The Accountant*, XXIII (September, 1897), 858.

[40]"Accountancy in the States," *The Accountant* XXV (August, 1899), 889.

[41]James B. Lovette, "History of Accounting in the United States" (unpublished typescript, American Institute of Accountants Library), p. 14.

means of maintaining the standards set by the new laws, the practitioners in several states formed societies; practicing accountants also formed societies even in some of the states where laws had not yet been passed. It was also pointed out by Wilkinson that accountants practicing in the West did not feel that the old established American Association of Public Accountants, domiciled as it was in New York and governed by a New York board, was fulfilling its avowed purpose as a national institute.

The first convention of the Federation of Societies of Public Accountants in the United States was held at the New Willard Hotel in Washington, D.C., on October 28, 1902. At this meeting a constitution and bylaws were accepted and permanent officers elected. The officers were Charles Waldo Haskins, President; George Wilkinson, Secretary; and Robert H. Montgomery, Treasurer.[42]

The objects of the Federation, as defined in its constitution, were as follows:

(a) To bring into communication with one another the several Associations and Societies of Public Accountants, organized or to be organized under the laws of the several States of the United States of America; (b) to encourage the formation of State Associations of Public Accountants in States where they do not exist; (c) to encourage State Certified Public Accountant legislation on uniform lines; (d) to secure Federal recognition of the profession of the Public Accountant; (e) to facilitate and assist the training of young members of the profession, and to establish a uniform standard of efficiency in federal societies; (f) to disseminate throughout the United States a general knowledge of the objects of the Federation and of the utility of the Public Accountants in the industrial and financial development of the country; and (g) to further the interests of the profession of the Public Accountant generally.[43]

Though the Federation existed only from 1902 to 1905, the principle was firmly established that the interests of the profession demanded, and that the members of the profession would support, a national organization of accountants.[44]

---

[42]Edward L. Suffern, "Twenty-five Years of Accountancy," *The Journal of Accountancy*, XXXIV (September, 1922), 179.

[43]Richard Brown, *A History of Accounting and Accountants* (Edinburgh and London: T. C. & E. C. Jack, 1905), p. 277.

[44]George Wilkinson, "Organization of the Profession in Pennsylvania," *The Journal of Accountancy*, XLIV (September, 1927) 173.

First International Congress

The Federation arranged the first International Congress of Professional Accountants in connection with the Louisiana Purchase Exposition, or World's Fair, held at St. Louis in September, 1904.[45] The President of the Illinois Society of Public Accountants and one of the organizers of the Federation, George Wilkinson, was elected secretary of the Congress. He was the organizer and director of all its affairs. Joseph E. Sterrett, a prominent public accountant of Philadelphia, was permanent chairman of this first Congress. In his introductory address, Sterrett referred to the negotiations which were then under way to effect a union of the two existing "national" accounting organizations, including the state societies as well.

During the three-day Congress, several important papers were read and discussed. The first was "A Brief History of the Movement toward Uniform Municipal Reports and Accounts in the United States," by H. W. Wilmot, A.C.A., C.P.A., of the firm of Jones, Caesar, Dickinson, Wilmot and Company, and Price, Waterhouse and Company. Other papers were "Revenues and Expense as Distinguished from Receipts and Disbursements in Municipal Accounting," by Frederick A. Cleveland, Ph.D., of Haskins and Sells, Certified Public Accountants of New York, and "Appropriations," by Ernest Reckitt, C.P.A., of Chicago.

One of the primary objects of the Congress was to bring the members together for the purpose of discussing matters of common interest relating to their profession. To bring some of these matters before them, George Wilkinson, C.P.A., and Secretary of the Federation of Societies of Public Accountants in the United States, prepared and delivered a paper on "The C.P.A. Movement and the Future of the Profession of the Public Accountants in the United States of America."

Robert H. Montgomery, C.P.A. of Philadelphia, moved that the discussion of this paper be along three lines: (1) The C.P.A. Movement, (2) Audit Companies, and (3) National Organization. James Martin of London discussed the C.P.A. movement, James Miller of Cincinnati the audit companies, and A. L. Dickinson of New York national organization.

---

[45]James B. Lovette, *History of Accounting in the United States*, p. 14.

At the afternoon session of September 27, Francis W. Pixley, F.C.A., Barrister-at-Law, delivered a paper, "The Duties of Professional Accountants in Connection with Invested Capital Both Prior to and Subsequent to the Investment." This was followed by "The Importance of Uniform Practice in Determining the Profits of Public Service Corporations Where Municipalities Have the Power to Regulate Rates."

On the last day of the Congress the two following papers were read and discussed: "The Profits of a Corporation," by A. L. Dickinson, M.A., F.C.A., C.P.A., of the firm of Jones, Caesar, Dickinson, Wilmot and Company and Price, Waterhouse and Company; and "The Mode of Conducting an Audit," by Walter A. Staub, a staff member of Lybrand, Ross Brothers and Montgomery of Philadelphia.[46]

Ninety-one members attended this first International Congress in 1904.[47]

Communication on Merger

In the course of time it became apparent that if the profession desired to achieve its proper place in the business community it could not rely on state legislation alone: there were only seven C.P.A. laws by 1904, almost nine years after the New York law. Accountancy was not a local profession, even then, but was practiced nationwide, and as time went on the need for professional standards became more and more apparent. Both the American Association of Public Accountants and the New York State Society of Certified Public Accountants addressed letters to the Federation at the St. Louis Congress.[48]

At a meeting of the executive board of the Federation held during the Congress the secretary presented a communication from the secretary of the American Association of Public Accountants and one from the secretary of the New York State society expressing the opinion that there should be one national organization in which

---

[46]*Official Record of the Proceedings of the Congress of Accountants Held at the World's Fair, St. Louis, 1904*, p. 206.

[47]Norman E. Webster, "Congress of Accountants," *The Journal of Accountancy*, LXXVII (December, 1944), 514.

[48]Carl H. Nau, "The American Institute of Accountants," *The Journal of Accountancy*, XXXI (February, 1921), 104.

all public accountants should be represented by delegates. Both secretaries recommended the formation of a joint committee to consider ways and means of bringing this about.

A joint committee of nine was consequently appointed, composed of the following: W. Sanders Davies, Chairman; Duncan MacInnes, Franklin Allen, representing the American Association of Public Accountants; A. Lowes Dickinson, George Wilkinson, and Robert H. Montgomery, representing the Federation of Public Accountants. This joint committee agreed upon a plan of consolidation under which the American Association of Public Accountants would be the continuing organization after certain necessary amendments of its constitution and bylaws.

One National Organization

In 1905, as a result of efforts of a joint committee, the two organizations merged. The new constitution of the American Association of Public Accountants provided for membership by virtue of previous membership in a state society of public accountants and also for individual membership, the latter being provided for those public accountants practicing in states without societies. The new society, even with the old association's name, was not organized to supplant the various state societies of certified public accountants, nor was it formed to supplant the C.P.A. laws of the various states. It had its genesis rather in the effort to supplement both state legislation and state societies, and was at least a partial remedy for the recognized defects which had developed in former programs designed to establish professional standards and professional solidarity by enacting statutes and the issuance of certificates.[49] The amalgamation of the societies was an attempt to nationalize the profession, with a centralized control from within itself, in place of a control which lacked uniformity in both aims and ideals and was influenced by outside conditions as well as by professional considerations.[50]

The constitution of the first national organization stated the purposes of the new society as follows:

---

[49]Carl H. Nau, "The American Institute of Accountants," *The Journal of Accountancy*, XXXI (February, 1921), 105.

[50]*Ibid.*, p. 105.

1. The bringing together in friendly contact of the different state societies and members of the profession.
2. The encouragement and unification of C.P.A. legislation.

In citing these provisions, J. Edward Masters comments:

In this organization the principle was adopted that the national organization should not interfere with the local interests of the different states, but at the same time should co-operate with the constituent societies in all practicable ways.[51]

The purpose of the merger was further set forth in the words of President John R. Loomis of the American Association of Public Accountants:

This occasion celebrates the culmination of what is perhaps the most important movement ever inaugurated in the interest of the profession of public accountancy in this country—the fusion of the several societies constituting the Federation of Societies of Public Accountants with the American Association of Public Accountants. The American Association of Public Accountants stands at this time as the grand national body, representing practically all public accountants throughout the United States. Its objects are the elevation of the profession and the spreading of a knowledge and recognition of the utility and necessity for the public accountant in the industrial and financial development of our country. It is an organization that every society can stand by and that every member can work for. The hopes and plans of the past are now measurably realized, and upon a basis of absolute cause for rejoicing—the promise of the future is most encouraging.[52]

During the following years the program of the Association reflected a great interest in education for accounting. The educational committee made an effort to impress upon the members of the As-

---

[51] J. Edward Masters, "The Accounting Profession in the United States," *The Journal of Accountancy*, XX (November, 1915), 351.

[52] "History of the American Institute," in *Fiftieth Anniversary Celebration* (New York: The American Institute of Accountants, 1937), p. 9.

sociation the importance of cooperation with the universities and colleges. It also suggested that the members of the Association contribute their services, whenever the opportunity arose, as instructors and lecturers.

In these years the American Association of Public Accountants continued to foster rapid development of the profession by acting as its spokesman when the need arose, and it continued its efforts to obtain legal recognition in all the states which had not yet enacted C.P.A. laws.

FUNCTIONS OF THE PROFESSION

Audit Standards

Typical of the certificates issued during the period from 1902 to 1916 are the following three prepared by Price, Waterhouse and Company. The significance of these reports lies in what they include rather than in what they do not include. Their emphasis is clearly on valuation. In the Allis-Chalmers Company and Eastman Kodak Company reports, the auditors have specifically mentioned that the expenditures were examined to distinguish between capital and revenue expenditures. These reports state that there has been an adequate provision made for depreciation for the period. Both relate to the correct valuation of fixed assets.

In each of the reports a specific statement is made concerning the valuation of the inventories, carried at cost or market, whichever is lower, except in one instance where the finished goods inventory was carried at market. The physical inventories evidently were not taken under the supervision of the auditors, but were certified to them by the responsible officials. Then the receivables were reflected at an estimated realizable value. The auditors checked the receivables to determine the collectibility of the accounts and the adequacy of the reserves for uncollectible accounts.

The emphasis throughout the reports is on the valuation of assets. The audit reports also included a statement that all of the ascertainable liabilities had been recorded.

The statement in the 1908 Eastman Kodak Company report that "the Balance Sheet is properly drawn up so as to show the true financial position of the company," would be considered to be very strong in a present-day audit report. In the other certificates the auditor certified that the statements were "correct" or "correctly prepared therefrom." "Therefrom" signified that the Balance Sheet and Profit and Loss statements had been taken from the books and accounts of the company.

May 27, 1902

To the Directors
of the Allis-Chalmers Company:

We have audited the books, accounts and vouchers of the Allis-Chalmers Company at the general offices in Chicago, and at the offices of the several works in Milwaukee, Chicago, Scranton, Wilkes Barre and Buffalo, for the period from the commencement of the Company's operations to April 30, 1902, and we certify the accompanying Balance Sheet and Statement of Profits to be correct.

We have examined the construction accounts for the period in detail, and are satisfied that only capital additions properly so chargeable have been charged thereto, all expenditures for maintenance, repairs and renewals having been charged against revenue. Full provision has been made for depreciation of buildings, plant and machinery.

We have examined the Bills and Accounts Receivable and find the amount outstanding to be correct as stated, provision having been made for possible bad debts.

We have counted the cash on hand at the several offices and have been furnished satisfactory certificates as to the cash in banks.

We have verified the inventories by means of the cost system inaugurated by us at your request during the period. Merchandise and work in progress have been valued at factory cost, and all raw materials and supplies at cost prices or market values where the latter were less than cost.

We find that all ascertained liabilities were duly brought into the books at the close of the year, and ample reserves made for estimated outstanding accounts not yet rendered, including the estimated expense of the erection and completion of engines in course of installation.

The Company has issued no bills payable, has no bills payable outstanding, nor has it incurred any contingent liability as endorser to customers' bills receivable or otherwise.

Eastman Kodak Company:

We have examined the Books and Accounts of the B Company and its Subsidiary Companies including a subsidiary in England for the year ending

December 31, 1908, and have been furnished with certified returns from the American and Foreign Selling Agencies, for the same period, and we certify that the above Balance Sheet at that date and the relative Profit and Loss account are correctly prepared therefrom.

We have satisfied ourselves that during the year only actual Additions and Extensions have been charged to the Cost of Properties and that ample provision has been made for Depreciation on Buildings, Plant and Machinery.

We are satisfied that the Valuations of the Inventories of Stocks on Hand as certified by the responsible officials have been correctly and accurately made at cost, and that full provision has been made for Bad and Doubtful Accounts Receivable and for all ascertainable liabilities.

We have verified the Cash and Securities by actual inspection, and by Certificates from the Depositories.

And we certify that in our opinion the Balance Sheet is properly drawn up so as to show the true financial position of the Company and its subsidiary Companies, and the profits thereof for the year ending at that date.

[The American Hide and Leather Company]
Year ending June 30, 1902

We have examined the above Balance Sheet and relative Profit and Loss account with the Head Office books of the American Hide and Leather Company and its Subsidiary Companies and with the certified returns from the tanneries and we find the same to be correct. The stocks of merchandise on hand are certified by the officials as correctly taken. Hides, supplies and work in progress are valued at cost and finished leather at conservative market values, less a reserve for discounts and selling expenses.

Full provision has been made for Bad and Doubtful Debts and in our opinion the charge of Sinking Fund Appropriation to Profit and Loss is more than sufficient to provide for Depreciation.

All three of these certificates were made available for this study by C. W. DeMond, of Price, Waterhouse and Company.[53]

During this time Arthur Young, of Arthur Young and Company, made the statement regarding a merger engagement: "What you have asked from us is not an accountant's report, but our business

---

[53]Letter from C. W. DeMond, Partner of Price, Waterhouse and Company, to James D. Edwards, dated May 6, 1952.

judgment on the entire business situation."[54] Such a statement indicates that the work of the public accountant was beginning to blossom during the latter part of the period covered in this chapter.

The 1909 Tax on Corporation Income

The national tax legislation of 1909 added to the functions of the public accountant. The United States Government decided to raise some extra money in that year. An easy way appeared to be a tax on corporations, but it was not lawful for the federal government to tax income, so George W. Wickersham, United States Attorney General, suggested a franchise tax on corporation income, measured by cash receipts. This expedient may have sounded easy to those versed in law, but was an almost insurmountable task for the accountant because terms were not defined and prescribed procedures for determining income were not consistent with good accounting principles.

Therefore the following letter was sent to each member of Congress and the Attorney General:[55]

New York City, July 8th, 1909

Dear Sir:

On reading the text of the proposed corporation tax law, as reported in the Commercial and Financial Chronicle of July 3d, 1909, we have formed the opinion that some of its provisions are absolutely impossible of application, and others violate all the accepted principles of sound accounting.

Under the third clause it is provided "that there shall be deducted from the amount of the net income of each of such corporations . . . ascertained as provided in the foregoing paragraphs of this section the sum of $5,000,000, and said tax shall be computed upon the remainder of said net income of such corporation . . . for the the year ending December 31st, 1909, and for each year thereafter, and on or before the 1st day of March, 1910, and the 1st day of March of each year thereafter, a true and accurate return under oath or affirmation of its president, etc., etc."

In connection with this clause we would call attention to the fact that as you are no doubt aware, the fiscal year of a number of corporations is not and for business reasons cannot be the calendar year, and consequently, having in

[54]Arthur Young, *Arthur Young and the Business He Founded*, p. 30.

[55]Editorial, "Accounting Errors in Corporation Tax Bill," *The Journal of Accountancy*, VIII (July, 1909), 213.

mind that in such cases an inventory was not taken at the beginning of the calendar year 1909, it is and will be quite impossible for any business, corporation or institution, whose fiscal year does not terminate with the calendar year, to make a true return of its profits as required by the proposed law.

Under Clause 1 the tax is to be charged upon the "entire net income," and the net income is to be ascertained by deducting from the gross amount of the income . . . from all sources,

    (1) "Expenses actually paid"
    (2) "Losses actually sustained"
    (3) "Interest actually paid"

in each case "within the year." The words "actually paid" convey, and it is presumed are intended to convey actual disbursements out of the treasury.

The proper deductions should be:

    (1) Expenses actually incurred because the payment is not necessarily made in the year in which the expense is incurred;

    (2) Losses actually ascertained because losses may be incurred and the amount not be ascertained until a subsequent period;

    (3) Interest actually accrued because interest is never paid until the end of the period during which it accrues, and the interest accrued is the proper charge against income.

In Clause 1 the bill refers to "net income received"; in Clause 2 it refers to "gross income" without the addition of the word "received"; in Clause 3, paragraph 3, it refers to "gross income received." There is here a complete confusion between income and income received, which can only lead to endless complication.

Two methods may be adopted for taxation purposes, either

    (1) to tax the difference between actual cash receipts on revenue account and actual cash payments on revenue account, which difference will seldom if ever represent the profits of a manufacturing concern; or

    (2) to tax profits made up in the ordinary commercial way, namely, to ascertain the gross income earned whether received or not, and to deduct therefrom

        1. Expenses actually incurred during the year whether paid or not;
        2. Losses actually ascertained and written off during the year whenever incurred;
        3. Interest accrued during the year whether paid or not;
        4. A reasonable allowance for depreciation of property; and
        5. Taxes

As accountants actively engaged in the audit and examination of a number of varied businesses and enterprises, we unhesitatingly say that the law as framed is absolutely impossible of application, and would suggest that in the said Clauses 1, 2, and 3 of paragraph 2, the words "actually paid" and "actually ascertained," and the third clause be changed to read so that the return will be based on the last completed fiscal year prior to December 31st in cases where the fiscal year of a corporation is not the calendar year.

Yours very truly,

Deloitte, Plender, Griffiths & Co.
49 Wall Street

Price, Waterhouse & Co.
54 William Street

Haskins & Sells
30 Broad Street

Lybrand, Ross Bros. & Montgomery
165 Broadway

Wilkinson, Reckitt, Williams & Co.
52 Broadway

Niles & Niles
111 Broadway

Gunn, Richards & Co.
43 Wall Street

Edward P. Moxey & Co.
165 Broadway

Geo. H. Church
55 Wall Street

Barrow, Wade, Guthrie & Co.
25 Broad Street

Loomis, Conant & Co.
30 Broad Street

Marwick, Mitchell & Co.
79 Wall Street

One of the accountants received a somewhat uncordial reply, which concluded:

Your further statement "that as Accountants actively engaged in the audit and examination of a number of varied businesses and enterprises, we unhesitatingly say that the law as framed is absolutely impossible of application" causes me very great surprise. My personal acquaintance with you and a number of the other signers of the letters leads me to the belief that you have underestimated your capacity. Certainly the statement of objections made in your letter is entirely insufficient to support the conclusion which you express.[56]

After further exchange of letters, the tax discussion was closed by the following letter from Attorney General Wickersham:

In your last letter you set forth in somewhat more detail the following proposition: "But no system of accounting can give even approximately the ordinary and necessary expenses actually paid within the year out of income in the maintenance and operations of its business and properties."

I think the bare statement of that proposition would be received with very great incredulity by most minds. Certainly, I am quite unable to assent to it. However, it is now too late to attempt to recast the Corporation Tax amendment bill on the basis of such proposition.[57]

In Washington the accountants lost and the tax on corporation income became law, but the law as written was never enforced, for enforcement officials permitted determination of income on the accrual basis. In one major respect the law would have helped the accounting profession. Tens of thousands of corporations had failed to keep books and records which reflected their actual net income, and the law levied a tax on the corporation's income based on cash receipts and cash disbursements; consequently these companies were forced to set up accounting systems to determine their income. The Treasury issued regulations under which the corporation paid a tax on income measured by the accrual method, ignoring the wording of the law.[58]

---

[56]Editorial, "The Corporation Tax Correspondence," *The Journal of Accountancy*, VIII (August, 1909), 300.

[57]*Ibid.*, p. 301.

[58]Robert H. Montgomery, *Fifty Years of Accountancy*, pp. 531-534.

No strong opposition on the part of the corporations was encountered, for the rate was only 1 percent of net income, and the Treasury Department followed the liberal policies set forth in its regulations. This factor encouraged income tax proponents to sponsor an amendment to the United States Constitution which would authorize Congress to levy a tax on income without resorting to the subterfuge of continuing an excise tax measured by net income.

Public Attitude Toward the Profession

The work and attitude of the professional accountants and the way they were looked upon by the general public appears to be a unique feature of public accountancy, setting it apart from the other professions.

In the public mind, the work of the accountant must be faultless both in execution and in principle. Men in other professions may be guilty of error and their standing will not be seriously impaired, but the accountant is different in the minds of many: he must not err, he is a man of correctness, and an error cannot be overlooked or forgiven. This seemed to be the opinion of those who were engaged in the public practice of accountancy during this period. Thus in his work, service, and findings the accountant must act as much for the other man as for the client who remunerates him. The professional accountant has a responsibility to the client who employs him, but his responsibility goes much farther. Businessmen and the public will at some time rely on the accountant's opinion, either in granting credit or purchasing equities. It is evident that the public accountant has a dual responsibility in the performance of his work.

Accountancy Service for Lawyers

Lawyers were the last to recognize that accounting was a separate and distinct profession or that it played any role in the affairs of the business world. They persisted in looking upon the accountant as no more than a well-informed bookkeeper and held in contempt his claims that he was something more.

The lawyer's profession and that of the public accountant touch at many points. The statement of what a certified public accountant is should be sufficient to show to the lawyer how he may use the services of a certified public accountant in cases involving accounts that are complicated. Regardless of a lawyer's versatility, it would be difficult for him to have a thorough knowledge of the accounting problems of business unless he is a trained accountant. When he undertakes to draw up contracts dealing with accounts, he is likely to do an injustice to his own client, through lack of clear thought on the nature of income in the case of an estate. Receipts of interest are not always all income, but may be part principal and have led to controversy, because of the negligence of the attorney in failing to clarify the wish of a testator when a will is drawn. Much aid has been rendered by the accountant to the lawyer in preventing misapprehension in accounting matters and litigation.

In the case of a merger of several companies the employment of an accountant is now almost universal. No one else can render as efficient service in determining the basis on which the division of the relative interests must be made. There are so many elements affecting this basis that only a well trained accountant can adjust them in a satisfactory manner.

When a new company is organized it is not unusual for the attorney to supervise the opening entries showing the payment of stock subscriptions, and often there are errors in fundamental accounting principles which cause serious trouble. In drawing up the bylaws of the corporation there are often points to be covered that require a knowledge of business that the attorney does not always possess. Again, the lawyer may insert the provision that the accounts shall be audited once a year, but he does not specify the kind of auditor nor who shall appoint him. From the accountant's point of view it is advisable that the auditor be a professional accountant and that he be elected by the stockholders.

Another way in which the accountant has come to be of service to the attorney is by acting as receiver. The accountant's varied experience in studying all the conditions of large business enterprises fits him for dealing with the complicated problems that arise in receivership matters. His knowledge of commercial law is sufficient to enable him to know when he needs to refer a matter to the attorney. A proper knowledge of these facts by the legal profession in the United States has led to a better understanding between the two professions. The attorney has come to appreciate the fact that the accountant recognizes and fulfills his duty to point out those things which are unfavorable as well as those which make for the interests of the client.

The Supreme Court of the State of New York, in 1903, recognized the usefulness of the accountant when they made their first appointment of receivers. The appointment was in connection with a partnership action. It was not clear to what extent the accountants were allowed to control the business while it was in receivership.[59]

The late 1880's represented a period of undoubted development and advancement in accountancy both in better knowledge of the profession and its requirements, and in the fact that financial men generally began to understand the nature of its work and service. In 1891 the firm of Jones, Caesar and Company was appointed as auditor and accountant to the United States Steel Corporation, an event that contributed much to creating a realization of the real meaning of accounting and auditing on the part of the business world.

Another trend that tended to further the development of the profession was the incorporation of industrial concerns under the laws of the various states. The securities of these corporations were issued and offered to the investing public. In most of these corporations, public accounting firms were employed to make examinations and reports on the financial condition and earnings of these corporations before their securities were offered for public subscription. The first industrial firm so incorporated whose securities were offered to the public with an accountant's certificate attached to the prospectus was the firm of John B. Stetson and Company of Philadelphia.[60]

SUMMARY

From 1896, accounting became a real profession. The quality, extent and diversity of the practitioners' knowledge increasingly gave a status to the profession, and an atmosphere of learning, precision, and trustworthiness. When it was perceived that these influences formed the foundation and real essence of the profession,

---

[59]"Accountancy in the States," *The Accountant*, XXIX (November, 1903), 1,392.
[60]"Accountants as Directors," *The Journal of Accountancy*, LXIX (March, 1940), 165.

the public, the businessman, the banker, and even the lawyer generally recognized that accountancy was a good and beneficial thing.

The profession had gained such prestige among businessmen by 1909 that corporations of the better class were voluntarily adopting the practice, obligatory in England under the Companies Act of 1900, of retaining public accountants to make periodic audits.

Thus, in the auditing of accounts of corporations, in the organization of accounting systems, in the investigation of properties for prospective purchasers, and in the revision of business methods, the accountant found himself by 1913 in a favorable position in the eyes of the business community. He now found a constantly enlarging sphere of usefulness to the businesses of the United States and to the public as well as to certain other longer established professions.

CHAPTER VI

Public Accounting in the United States, 1913-1928

By 1913 the profession of public accounting was established. Much of the original impetus had been given by accountants who came to this country from England and Scotland. These accountants from abroad continued to have their influence, but the major portion of the members of the profession were now native Americans educated in the United States.

The period break of 1913 was chosen because of the tremendous effect of the income tax law on public accounting, ushering in as it did a new era for the profession. The date 1928 marks the last full year of an unprecedented prosperity that had built up in the American economy since the beginning of World War I.

Not all the developments of this period advanced the profession. The internal difficulties are evident in the fact that several national organizations purporting to represent the profession were functioning at the same time. It may have helped the profession that the internal differences were brought out very early in its development; but, on the other hand, it presented a divided front to the businessmen of this period. The separate sections of the profession were not to be entirely united by the end of this period. The period was marked by additional state adoptions of C.P.A. laws, and by the further expansion of public accounting firms.

FISCAL EVENTS AFFECTING ACCOUNTING

The Sixteenth Amendment and Accounting (1913)

One of the fiscal developments of this period which gave the profession an additional function was the enactment of a constitutional income tax law. The enactment of a 1909 franchise tax of 1 percent as measured by corporate profits encountered no strong opposition. This factor among others encouraged proponents of an income tax to redouble their efforts. But the 1894 act had been declared unconstitutional by the United States Supreme Court in the *Pollock* v. *Farmer's Loan and Trust Co.* case. It was necessary therefore that a constitutional amendment be secured before an income tax could be enacted.

By the latter part of February, 1913, the necessary number of states had ratified the sixteenth amendment to the Constitution, thus paving the way for the enactment of an income tax law on October 3, 1913, effective as of March 1, 1913.

Accountants were concerned about the enactment of an income tax law in 1913 because of their experience with the corporation tax law of 1909. Members of Congress had been unwilling to take advice from accountants before the enactment of the 1909 law, with the result that when it was enacted it was found unworkable.

The public accountant who was to be called upon to prepare the tax reports for large numbers of taxpayers under an income tax law felt a vital interest in the terms of the law and the provisions for collection. Fortunately Congress asked and received the advice of public accountants before the final income tax bill was submitted to either house.[1]

The income tax measure, which constituted a part of the Underwood-Simmons Tariff Bill, passed both houses of Congress as anticipated.[2] The tariff law of 1913, being "an act to reduce tariff duties and to provide revenue for the government and for other purposes," was approved by the President on October 3, 1913.[3]

The first income tax was a graded one, starting with a normal tax of 1 percent on all income in excess of $3,000 and increasing by degrees through the operation of an additional tax to 7 percent upon that part of a person's net income which exceeded $500,000.[4]

The enactment of the individual and corporation income tax law might have had an adverse effect on the profession had it occurred before sufficient numbers of qualified accountants were available. By 1913, however, there was already a group of well-trained members of the accounting profession ready to assist both business people and the government in this new project. The nucleus had

---

[1]Editorial, "A Federal Income Tax," *The Journal of Accountancy*, XV (January, 1913), 60.
[2]Editorial, "The Income Tax," *The Journal of Accountancy*, XVI (October, 1913), 307.
[3]Editorial, "United States Income Tax," *The Accountant*, XLIX (August, 1913), 152.
[4]John B. Niven, "Income Tax Department," *The Journal of Accountancy*, XVI (November, 1913), 384.

the immediate problem of helping hundreds of businessmen who had not previously found it necessary to prepare a statement of income and expenses. With the recognition which had previously been given the profession it was natural for taxpayers to turn to accountants for assistance in preparing their income tax returns.[5]

A feature of the law gratifying to the public accounting profession was its provision that corporations, associations, and insurance companies were at liberty to adopt the fiscal year in preference to the calendar year upon notice of such intention duly filed. This provision was not present in the 1909 tax law and caused the companies a great deal of trouble in inventory taking and getting their returns filed on time. The certified public accountants were interested in this provision because it would enable them to spread their work over the entire year. Clients would thus benefit from more thorough auditing procedures.[6]

One consequence of the income tax legislation was the inauguration of a new department, "The Tax Clinic," in *The Journal of Accountancy* (beginning with the November, 1913, issue) dealing specifically with income tax and its administration. John B. Niven was the department editor.

In establishing this feature, the editors recognized that the income tax law was to have a greater impact on the public accounting profession than upon any other. The official journal of the accounting profession was prepared to publish the latest information on new or additional income tax laws and regulations. It was felt that the practitioner should have the official releases available from the government as quickly as possible. The enactment of the 1909 corporation tax law and its administration had vastly increased the work of public accountants, but that work load was far less than the one which resulted from the new income tax law.[7]

Even so, the law brought the public accountant into a company only on a narrowly specialized engagement—income tax returns. The accountant undoubtedly brought to the client's attention the many other services that he was prepared to render. Tax engagements, for example, often led to the revision of accounting systems, in an effort to give the management more financial information;

[5]"Income Tax in the United States," *The Accountant*, XLIX (December, 1913), 861.
[6]Editorial, "The Income Tax," *The Journal of Accountancy*, XVI (October, 1913), 307.
[7]Editorial, "A New Department," *The Journal of Accountancy*, XVI (November, 1913), 373.

they led also to other accounting services which the client had no idea could be handled for him.[8] In many cases the accountant found that the records maintained by businesses were inadequate: it was necessary to reconstruct the transactions in an effort to determine the taxable net income, to design a chart of accounts to facilitate the determination of net income, and to keep the records up to date in order to reflect the earnings as time went on.

Public accountants were empowered to render further service to their clients in 1924 when the Board of Tax Appeals recognized attorneys and certified public accountants as the only representatives qualified to appear for taxpayers before the United States Board of Tax Appeals.[9]

War and Accounting (1916)

The enactment of a general income ta:. law in 1913 and the rapid increase in rates of tax that went into effect in 1917 were fiscal developments that widened the scope of accounting practice and led to a greatly enhanced standing for accountants.[10] Soon after the enactment of this bill an amendment was passed providing that income in general should be determined in accordance with the method of accounting regularly employed by the taxpayer. The broad scope of this amendment was later modified by rulings of the Bureau of Internal Revenue and the Board of Tax Appeals. Rules and regulations issued by the Internal Revenue Department set forth specific methods of determining taxable income, not necessarily in accordance with the accounting methods previously employed.

The problems of the profession and of the taxpayers were further complicated when the records of the business had to be revised to reflect statutory net income. The specific definitions set forth in the rules of the Internal Revenue Department brought about the need for adjusting the net income of a business computed according to

---

[8]Editorial, "Brighter Prospects of Accountancy," *The Journal of Accountancy*, XVI (December, 1913), 459.

[9]Editorial, "Practice before the Tax Board," *The Journal of Accountancy*, XXXVIII (November, 1924), 205.

[10]George O. May, "The Economic and Political Influences in the Development of the Accounting Profession," in *Fifty Years of Service, 1898-1948* (Newark, N. J.: New Jersey Society of Certified Public Accountants, 1948), p. 11.

good accounting principles to reflect income as defined in the law and clarified by rules of the department.

Title 2 of the Federal Revenue Act of October 3, 1917, "an act to provide revenue to defray war expenses and for other purposes," was termed the "war excess profits tax." The purpose of the law under this title was to impose a tax on those profits in excess of normal profits (as indicated by earnings made in a prewar period) made directly or indirectly through increased business arising out of the abnormal conditions of war.[11]

By this time the income tax law and the rules and regulations of the Bureau of Internal Revenue were so complex that an expert was needed to meet the requirements of the law. The public accountant was recognized as an expert who could represent business as well as government. Undoubtedly, excess profits tax legislation was one of the forces which elevated the public accountant from the status of master bookkeeper to that of a member of an honored profession.

The new and highly complex provisions of the war revenue bills, coupled with very high rates of taxation, provided the stimulus which the profession needed to get general recognition by the public.[12] The leaders among the practitioners of the day were quick to grasp the significance of the opportunity for service and were able, by word and performance, to convince the business world that the public accounting profession had the intelligence and initiative to cope with the new problem.[13]

The auditor was called with more and more frequency into conference for advice on financial transactions: not only the proper treatment of completed business, but also the best method of handling contemplated future business dealings. As a consequence, the certified public accountant was soon accepted as the most competent advisor in tax matters and was shortly to be regarded as the professional man best qualified to serve in many other important business advisory capacities. It seems reasonable to assume that the counsel of a few outstanding members of the profession had been sought by many clients prior to 1917, but before World War I the

---

[11]Editorial, "Defects of Title 2 of the Federal Revenue Act of October 3, 1917," *The Journal of Accountancy*, XXV (February, 1918), 81.

[12]Norman L. McLaren, "The Influence of Federal Taxation upon Accountancy," in *Fiftieth Anniversary Celebration* (New York: The American Institute of Accountants, 1937), p. 128.

[13]Editorial, "Preparation of Tax Returns," *The Journal of Accountancy*, XXV (June, 1918), 447.

certified public accountant was primarily an auditor of past transactions.[14] It was certainly complimentary to the public accounting profession that the leading businesses consulted their auditors. The old "holler and check" function of the auditor blossomed into more valuable undertakings and responsibilities.[15]

War Contracts and the Public Accountant

Another important development during the second decade of the new century had to do with engagements resulting from World War I. The public accountants were called upon to act as correspondents for English Chartered Accountant firms on war contracts. The entrance of the United States into the war increased the demand for accountants.

One of the more responsible engagements resulting from the war was undertaken by a national firm, Arthur Young and Company, which was retained by J. P. Morgan and Company. The latter organization had acted as purchasing agent of munitions for the British and French governments.[16]

The J. P. Morgan and Company assignment developed into a detailed study of all the transactions relating to purchases under these contracts. The detailed audit which followed contained not merely a check of the payment of vouchers, but went further and traced the receipts of goods from the time they left the contractors' plants to the time they were put on board ship. This was probably the first and largest audit conducted with such detail under modern business conditions.

Another engagement involved a company that had been making machines for the British government and had fallen down on deliveries. This failure was due largely to the frequent change in specifications for these machines—a result of abnormal developments in the industry. Arrangements were made whereby the company would be reimbursed by the British government for the cost incurred. The accountants were engaged, as representatives of the

---

[14]Norman L. McLaren, "The Influence of Federal Taxation upon Accountancy," *The Journal of Accountancy*, LXIV (December, 1937), 435.

[15]Norman L. McLaren, "Evolution of American Accountancy" (unpublished typescript), p. 5.

[16]Arthur Young, *Arthur Young and the Business He Founded* (New York: privately printed, 1948), p. 31.

British government, to determine the cost of goods manufactured.

Arthur Young and Company was also given an assignment related to the manufacturing of Enfield rifles for the British government. Three firms were involved: the Remington Arms Company of Delaware, the Remington Union Metallic Cartridge Company, and the Winchester Repeating Arms Company. Before the time of the engagement of the public accountants, the companies had not made many deliveries, although they had made large expenditures for building, machinery, and equipment. Arrangements were made between the government and the companies whereby the companies would be reimbursed for their costs up to some date in October, 1916; from then on they would continue to complete the contracts at cost. Arthur Young and Company was engaged to determine those costs.

Shortly thereafter the British representatives felt that the determination of such costs by this firm was too one-sided a matter, and another firm of accountants was called in. Arthur Young was to act for the companies and the other firm for the British government.[17]

Then, when the United States entered World War I, numerous special investigations came to the office of Arthur Young and Company, many of which involved companies owned by enemy aliens.

After the war, when additional business resulted from the merger of several small companies, the accountant was frequently called upon for advice and assistance. As an example, this firm of accountants was requested in 1919 to draw up a plan for the merger of the four largest chemical companies in the country. The plan was drawn up with the assistance of the junior executives of the companies involved, and presented for the approval of the companies. This job was completed by the firm of Arthur Young and Company before the end of 1920.[18]

These experiences are mentioned as representative of the profession; it seems safe to assume that engagements of this type were also undertaken by other firms during this period. Thus the period of the first World War helped bring the profession of accountancy to the forefront. Fortunately, the early leaders of the profession had trained enough assistants to meet this expanding demand for their services.

---

[17]*Ibid.*, p. 34.
[18]*Ibid.*, p. 37.

Advisory Committee to the Council of National Defense

Evidence of the wider scope of the profession's functions can be seen in the appointment by the president of the Institute of an advisory committee to the Council of National Defense, composed of six cabinet officers, for closer liaison between the profession and the government.

The following letter from the president of the Institute to the members of the American Institute of Accountants gives in detail the steps accountants in America had taken in the war organization, and it also demonstrates the patriotism of the profession.[19]

20 Vesey Street, New York
April 3, 1917

To the Members of the American
Institute of Accountants

Dear Sirs,

For some months past correspondence and interviews have been taking place between first the Naval Consulting Board and later the Director of the Council of National Defense, as to what Accountants could do in the event of our country's being engaged in war.

These preliminaries culminated in the appointment of the following committee to represent the Institute:

> Edward L. Suffern, Chairman
> Robert H. Montgomery
> H. A. Niles
> Elijah W. Sells
> Arthur W. Teele
> The President, ex officio
> A. P. Richardson, Secretary,

and this committee has been accepted as a sub-committee of the advisory committee to the Council of National Defense, the council, as you no doubt are aware, consisting of six cabinet officers.

The committee has taken up its work, and had its first meeting with the director of the Council of National Defense, the chairman of the Munitions Committee, and its counsel at Washington on Thursday last.

What will ultimately be required of the Committee cannot be forecast, but

---

[19] "American Institute of Accountants," *The Accountant*, LVI (April, 1917), 410.

it will act in the advisory capacity without remuneration, matters having progressed so far I feel that you should be informed of the action taken.

It is desirable that the membership should act as a body rather than as individuals. The best results can be obtained only by united efforts, and the Council of National Defense regards the Institute as the mouthpiece of the Accounting profession.

As we are now in a state of war with Germany, and Congress will declare itself on the question in the near future, will you please advise me whether you, or any members of your staff, are desirous of offering your services to the Government, either for accounting work in the department or for such work as the Government may later wish undertaken by the profession either gratuitously or on terms to be determined.

I ask this so that the Committee may be in a position to act promptly, if occasion arises.

I would suggest that members distant from New York wire me their replies.

Very truly yours
W. Sanders Davies
President

The functions of the committee to the Council of National Defense were advisory in character, and it held itself ready to consult with any governmental agency concerning any matters involving questions of accounting whether they related to principles, practice, or service.[20] The members of the committee acted as individual advisors to different agencies of the government rather than as a group. For example, Teele was a civilian member of the committee appointed to consider the determination of property accountability. Another of the committee members, Robert H. Montgomery, was called into service.[21] The entire committee acted as accountancy advisors to the War Industries Board.[22]

PROFESSIONAL ORGANIZATION

State C.P.A. Legislation

During the period 1913-1928 the enactment of C.P.A. legislation spread. Maine passed its law in 1914. The following states

---

[20]*American Institute of Accountants Year Book, 1917* (Brooklyn, New York: William G. Hewitt Press, 1917), p. 272.

[21]*Ibid., 1918,* p. 113.

[22]*Ibid.,* p. 115.

passed laws during 1915: Arkansas, Iowa, Kansas, South Carolina, and Texas. The next year Kentucky passed a public accounting law. Oklahoma and South Dakota followed in 1917. Alabama, Arizona, and Idaho passed laws in 1919, and Mississippi the next year. In 1921 the last three states to enact legislation—Indiana, New Mexico, and New Hampshire—passed such laws. After the Institute had secured a national charter and the American Society was functioning, the District of Columbia had a law passed by Congress in 1923. The accompanying map illustrates those developments.

Question of Constitutionality

In the original C.P.A. law of the state of Oklahoma there was a provision restricting the practice of public accounting to certified public accountants. This appears to have been the first such clause in public accountancy legislation. The act specifically prohibited a person from practicing as a public accountant unless he had been certified under the provisions of this act. In the legislation of other states it had been provided that nothing in the law should be interpreted as prohibiting anyone from practicing as a public account-ant. These laws had merely restricted the use of the "C.P.A." title. The American Institute and state boards of accountancy waited to see the result of such a clause in the public accounting law.[23]

The year 1924 brought the answer for which the American Institute of Accountants and the boards of other states and state organizations had been waiting, when the State Board of Accountancy in Oklahoma attempted to enjoin a group of persons from practicing as uncertified public accountants. The Board described this function as:

the holding themselves out to the public, and practicing, as professional and expert accountants and auditors for compensation, without having first appeared before the State Board of Accountancy and stood examination and received a certificate from that board authorizing them to engage in that business as professional accountants.[24]

---

[23]Editorial, "Oklahoma C.P.A. Law," *The Journal of Accountancy*, XXIII (May, 1917), 368.
[24]*State* v. *Riedell*

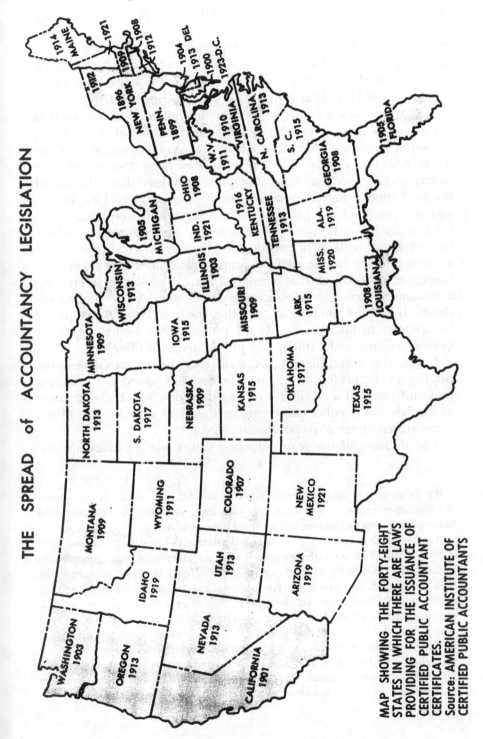

THE SPREAD of ACCOUNTANCY LEGISLATION

MAP SHOWING THE FORTY-EIGHT
STATES IN WHICH THERE ARE LAWS
PROVIDING FOR THE ISSUANCE OF
CERTIFIED PUBLIC ACCOUNTANT
CERTIFICATES.
Source: AMERICAN INSTITUTE OF
CERTIFIED PUBLIC ACCOUNTANTS

MAINE 1914
1921
1908
1912
1909
1904
DEL 1913
1900
1923-D.C.
NEW YORK 1896
1902
PENN. 1899
VIRGINIA 1910
N. CAROLINA 1913
S. C. 1915
FLORIDA 1905
GEORGIA 1908
W.V. 1911
OHIO 1908
KENTUCKY 1916
TENNESSEE 1913
ALA. 1919
MICHIGAN 1905
IND. 1921
ILLINOIS 1903
MISS. 1920
LOUISIANA 1908
WISCONSIN 1913
MISSOURI 1909
ARK. 1915
MINNESOTA 1909
IOWA 1915
NORTH DAKOTA 1913
S. DAKOTA 1917
NEBRASKA 1909
KANSAS 1915
OKLAHOMA 1917
TEXAS 1915
COLORADO 1907
NEW MEXICO 1921
MONTANA 1909
WYOMING 1911
UTAH 1913
ARIZONA 1919
IDAHO 1919
NEVADA 1913
WASHINGTON 1903
OREGON 1913
CALIFORNIA 1901

In October, 1924, the Oklahoma Supreme Court rendered a decision in the case of *State* v. *Riedell,* et al., which held that those provisions in the Accountancy Act limiting the practice of accountancy to certified public accounting were unconstitutional.

In that case it was contended by the defendants that inasmuch as the act seeks to prohibit the practice of professional accountancy without a certificate issued by the State Board of Accountancy, *it was unconstitutional on the basis that it deprived the defendants of their liberty and property without due process of law;* that it deprived them of their inherent right to liberty, the pursuit of happiness, and enjoyment of the gains of their chosen profession; that it denied, impaired, and disparaged the inherent rights of the defendants to contract in matters of private concern and in which the public at large and the public welfare, peace, health, and safety were not concerned or involved; that it violated the Bill of Rights in creating a monopoly; that it created an association to which is granted exclusive rights and immunities, and that the exercise of police power by the state in no way affected the public peace, health, safety, or general welfare, and without any public necessity therefor.

It was the contention of the state that the act prohibited the practice of the profession by one who had not passed the examination and received a certificate of qualifications, and the enactment of the law was a police power of the state and not violative of the Constitution or any of its provisions.

The decision of the State Supreme Court was stated as follows:

We think after a careful consideration of the Act as a whole, it was clearly the legislative interest to prohibit any one from practicing accountancy who has not stood the examination and received the certificate.

It is agreed that every state has a law regulating the practice of accountancy similar to this law, with the exception that no other state has attempted to prohibit the practice by those not certified. . . . Under the laws of other states, held to be valid, and under our law with sections 11 and 14 omitted, the only advantage conferred upon certified public accountants is that of having their qualifications ascertained, a degree conferred, and a certificate issued by a board created by law for that purpose. . . . The effect upon the uncertified public accountant is definite and certain. Whether it is because he stands on his belief that the Act is void and elects to stand on what he believes to be his constitutionally guaranteed rights, or because he is unable to stand the examination, or is not a citizen of the United States or does not enjoy the reputation of a good moral character, or has had his certificate revoked because of being convicted of a felony, or found guilty of conduct involving moral turpitude, or having certified to false or fraudulent statements in relation to an audit, or fraud or misrepresentation in application for the certificate, the result is the same; that after he has devoted time, effort, and expense to equip himself as an expert accountant, he is prohibited from following that calling and those dependent upon him are deprived of the fruits of that training and investment, and he is caused to seek other employment where that investment and training are of no avail for their support . . . our conclusion, therefore, is that the act, in so far as it prohibits uncertified public accountants from holding themselves out as professional or expert accountants or auditors for compensation or engaging in the practice of that profession, is in conflict with the spirit and express provision of the constitution and void, in this, that it abridges the right of private property and infringes upon the right of contract in matters purely of private concern, bearing no perceptible relation to the general or public welfare, and thereby tends to create a monopoly in the profession of accountancy for the benefit of certified accountants, and denies to uncertified accountants the equal protection of the laws, and the enjoyment of the gains of their own industry. The defendants are not engaged in the exercise of a franchise, but a constitutionally guaranteed right.[25]

After the State Supreme Court ruling that sections 11 and 14 of the accountancy law were unconstitutional, the law was then made to conform to those of other states possessing accountancy legislation. At the next session of the Oklahoma legislature the law was rewritten leaving out the sections which had previously been declared unconstitutional. For a short time then the State Board of Accountancy was operating without a law giving it a basis for operation.

A case which added greatly to the professional standing of accountancy was *J. Harold Lehman* v. *State Board of Public Accountancy*, et al., in Alabama. The Supreme Court of the United States held that the Alabama C.P.A. law was constitutional. That decision by the Supreme Court of the United States for all practical purposes placed the Alabama board in the same category as state boards governing the practice of medicine, law, and other professions. The case is No. 170, October Ten, 1923, *J. Harold Lehman* v. *State Board of Public Accountancy*, et al.

The Alabama case presented the first opportunity that the

[25]*Ibid.*

Supreme Court of the United States had had to pass on accountancy legislation. In this case the plaintiff had been a practicing accountant prior to the passage of the C.P.A. law, and the board had later cited him to show cause why his certificate should not be revoked for cause. The plaintiff sought to prevent action by the board on the ground that the law was unconstitutional. It was claimed that the determination by the board as to whether his certificate should be revoked rested wholly within the arbitrary, uncontrolled, and unappealable judgment of the board. The Supreme Court of Alabama had declared against the plaintiff on all points, but a writ of error to the Supreme Court of the United States had been granted by the Chief Justice. The Supreme Court affirmed the decision of the Alabama Court, holding that there was no equity involved, as it could not be determined in advance of the hearing that the board would sustain the charge, and added:

official bodies would be of no use as instruments of government if they could be prevented from action by the supposition of wrongful action.[26]

National Associations

Some of the members of the American Association of Public Accountants, considering it to be dominated by the New York members, felt that a reorganization was necessary to make it a truly national group. The first official intimation of the need for a change in the form of organization was the report presented by J. Porter Joplin, president of the American Association of Public Accountants, at Seattle in 1915. In his report the president drew attention to the existing conditions and asked for authority to appoint a committee to investigate matters and recommend such changes as might seem desirable. This committee was appointed, and it reported to the board of trustees of the association at its meeting in April, 1916. The board of trustees ratified the proposed change and recommended to the American Association that it adopt the plan.

In his address to the Association in Seattle in September, 1915,

---

[26]Editorial, "Court Decisions Affecting Accountancy," *The Journal of Accountancy*, XXXVII (March, 1924), 214.

President Joplin called attention to the lack of uniformity in the standards of both educational and professional attainments of the several states having C.P.A. laws. He emphasized the necessity for the establishment of a greater measure of uniformity and control. In line with this idea he suggested that a committee be appointed to study recommendations. The Association approved the president's suggestion, and the committee was appointed September 21, 1915.

The committee report was submitted to the trustees early in 1916. The following is a summary of that report: It was felt by the committee that the founders of the Association in 1887 had hoped for a national organization that would govern the profession from within. But after the passage of several state C.P.A. laws the emphasis was shifted to state regulation, although some hopes were entertained that national regulation of public accountancy might be secured by Congressional action substantially similar to that of the states.

From the outset it was found to be impossible to have strict uniformity in the state laws because of the problem involved in dealing with forty-eight different legislatures. This difficulty could be seen in the wide variation in the administration of the first two laws— New York and Pennsylvania. In the former, the administration was vested in the Board of Regents of the State University of the State of New York; in the latter, in a Board of Examiners appointed by the governor.[27]

It had been pointed out at the St. Louis Congress of 1904 that some of the state laws had serious defects. In almost every state in which there was legislation, it effectively prevented certain accountants, some of whom were members of the American Association, from securing certificates. Thus a large part of the practice of public accountancy was carried on by those who did not practice as certified public accountants. This problem was aggravated because there was no provision for reciprocity between states in the early C.P.A. laws.

Unfortunately, there was a very wide range in standards for taking the C.P.A. examination, as to both preliminary education and professional training. Some states required no preliminary education or training, while others had very high standards demanding an extensive course in accounting plus several years of experience.

In view of the foregoing, the unavoidable conclusion of the com-

---

[27]"Accountancy in the States," *The Accountant*, LV (September, 1916), 398.

116   *History of Public Accounting*

mittee was that in some states the title C.P.A. was in low repute.
Consequently the holding of a certificate from one of several states
was not sufficient qualification for membership in the American
Association of Public Accountants.

It was felt by the Association that what was needed was some form
of yardstick which could be applied fairly to accountants in every
part of the country, and which would indicate to the business public in every state that the accountants who had been measured by
it had at least attained a reasonable minimum level in preliminary
education and professional training. It was argued that the business
public demands rightfully that, upon entering the profession, an
accountant should have a sound education and should be adequately
trained to discharge the usual and ordinary duties of the profession;
and that his continued membership in a national body of accountants must be accepted as evidence that he has conducted himself
with reasonable regard to the obligations of his calling.

To foster the growth of the profession and its influence, and to
promote and conserve the interests of the business public, it was
suggested that the profession, as represented by a national organization, should assume more directly the responsibility for the establishment of uniform standards of admission to, and the maintenance
of conditions for, membership in the organized body of the profession.

To discharge its duties properly, the American Association of
Public Accountants should be truly national in its scope, and
preferably it should have a national charter. This could only be
secured through Congress, and the committee doubted that a charter could be obtained that would allow the profession to govern
itself. Hence they suggested that the organization should be incorporated under the laws of the District of Columbia, which had provision for the incorporation of educational and scientific bodies.[28]

The new name of the organization was the Institute of Accountants in the United States of America. The term *Institute* was used to
stress the educational aspects of the professional association, and the
phrase *in the United States of America* was added to show that the
organization was to be a national one.[29]

---

[28]"The Institute of Accountants in the United States of America," *The Accountant*, LV (November, 1916), 440.
[29]*Ibid.*, p. 440.

Some accountants hoped that federal regulation of the profession would follow, establishing accountancy on a national basis in the United States. But this hope was doomed from the outset because of the States' rights principle of regulating the profession within each state. However, it would have been extremely difficult to get such legislation.[30] A majority of the states had already passed some form of C.P.A. law. If an attempt had been made to supersede these laws with a federal law, a strong feeling against such a move would have arisen because of the tradition of States' rights.

Provisions of the proposal were as follows:[31]

(1) an organization embracing within its membership all of the reputable practicing public accountants in the United States;

(2) that membership therein shall be individual rather than through other societies;

(3) that the Institute, through its board of examiners, shall examine every applicant for membership, that such examinations shall be adapted to the needs of the profession, and be held at such places throughout the country as will reasonably meet the convenience of applicants;

(4) that by virtue of the maintenance of uniform and reasonably high standards a helpful influence will be exerted by the Institute upon accountancy education;

(5) that the profession of the entire country will be represented by a national organization which will be not only responsive to the best thought of the profession, but will also be capable of maintaining its dignity and honor;

(6) that through the maintenance of proper standards of admission to and continuance of admission a substantial recognition of the profession can be secured from governmental trade bodies.

The drafts of the bylaws and constitution were submitted to the Association on September 19, 1916, and approved. All members of the American Association of Public Accountants in good standing on that date became members of the American Institute of Accountants in the United States of America. There were 1,150 initial members of the Institute.

---

[30]"Accountancy in the States," *The Accountant*, LV (November, 1916), 398.

[31]"The Institute of Accountants in the United States of America," *The Accountant*, LV (November, 1916), 442.

The first officers of the Institute were:[32]

President	W. Sanders Davies
Vice-Presidents	Carl H. Nau and Harvey S. Chase
Treasurer	Adam A. Ross

The American Institute of Accountants was not formed to supplant either the various state societies of certified public accountants, or the C.P.A. laws of the various states. It had its genesis rather in the effort to supplement both state legislation and state societies and was at least a partial remedy for the defects which had developed in the program that attempted to establish professional standards and professional solidarity by enacting statutes and issuing certificates.[33]

A group of state societies must inevitably be characterized by differences of opinion, and in many cases, jealousies were to be expected. With all its merits, the American Association of Public Accountants was, in the last analysis, considered by some to be only a group of state societies.

The American Institute of Accountants, however, with membership entirely irrespective of residence or of membership in a state organization, was to represent the combined opinion and abilities of all its members. If differences of opinion arose, they would be between members—not between organizations.[34]

The name of the Institute was shortened in January, 1917, to The American Institute of Accountants, dropping the words "in the United States of America" for the sake of brevity. The new name went into effect after a two-thirds vote of the members on January 22, 1917.[35]

The National Association of Certified Public Accountants

National representation and peace in the public accountancy profession was short-lived: in 1921 came the formation of an association, privately incorporated, which threatened to destroy the American

---

[32]*Ibid.*, p. 444.

[33]Carl H. Nau, "The American Institute of Accountants," *The Journal of Accountancy*, XXXI (February, 1921), 105.

[34]"The Record of the American Institute of Accountants," *The Accountant*, LVII (December, 1917), 453.

[35]*American Institute of Accountants Year Book, 1917*, p. 144.

Institute by issuing C.P.A. certificates to those who supposedly took examinations and paid a fee. From the information available, the emphasis was placed on the payment of a fee and the dues to the organization and maintenance of a bond. The bond was maintained to protect the members of this organization from suits brought against them for negligence in the fulfillment of their duties.

The purpose of the National Association, according to its articles of incorporation, was as follows:

The purpose for which said corporation is to be formed: To bring together in one common union certified public accountants who are now, or heretofore have been, engaged in the practice of professional accounting; also those who, by virtue of education, personal endowments, technical training and experience are qualified to perform the duties pertaining to professional accounting; to provide for the admission of members; and when said members shall have presented satisfactory evidence of knowledge in the theory and practice of accounting, and shall have satisfactorily passed the prescribed qualifying examinations of the Association, to admit said members to the degree of certified public accountant, and to issue to such members the association's formal certificate to that degree pertaining; to safeguard the rightful professional interests and promote the friendly, and social, and public relations of the members of this corporation; and to do all else incident, appurtenant, and germane to the purpose and objects of this corporation.[36]

This organization purported to give examinations to applicants before issuing C.P.A. certificates, but actually it was simply a certificate mill from which anyone, without regard to training or experience, could secure a C.P.A. certificate for a price. In fact, during its short life, 1920 to 1923, it issued something like three thousand certificates to those taking "examinations."

The National Association of Certified Public Accountants gave the following explanation for the bond required of members:

The National Association, representing the majority of its members' views, always has held firmly to the belief that all human nature is weak at best, and that that weakness extends even to Public Accountants, certified or otherwise.

---

[36]Editorial, "Certificate of Incorporation of the National Association of Certified Public Accountants," *The Certified Public Accountant Bulletin*, II (December, 1923), 4.

With this belief, the National Association devised and supplied to its members a fidelity bond for their protection and for the protection of the public.[37]

This organization lasted only a short time. The government brought suit against the National Association of Certified Public Accountants to prevent, by injunction, the issuance of certificates which purported to entitle holders to describe themselves as certified public accountants. The injunction was upheld by the Court of Appeals in the District of Columbia, which based its decision on the states' rights under the Constitution of the United States to regulate the activities of a profession. If the association, a private corporation, had been held to have the right to issue certificates, serious disagreements and confusion would certainly have resulted. The editors of the *Journal* asserted that injury would have been done to all holders of certified public accountant certificates properly issued by state boards.[38] Moreover, other corporations would have been formed which would have completely destroyed the C.P.A. designation.

The federal courts were chosen to bring the injunction against the association. This organization was operating on a nationwide basis, and so, instead of fighting it in each of the states, suit was brought in federal courts to settle the dispute with finality. Actually court action against the National Association continued in several states until 1928, one of the most prominent cases being tried in Illinois.

The initiative taken by the federal government in the District of Columbia against the National Association, as mentioned previously, marks the point when the state's right to license public practitioners was established. No further attempts have been made by private organizations to issue certificates nor has the federal license been sought for certified public accountants.

American Institute and Federal Charter

Before the injunction was issued against the National Association of Certified Public Accountants in 1923, the organization's opera-

---

[37]W. R. Anderson, "The Surety Bond," *The Certified Public Accountant Bulletin*, IV (October, 1925), 4.

[38]Editorial, "Injunction against National Association of Certified Public Accountants," *The Journal of Accountancy*, XXXVI (July, 1923), 30.

tions had had a profound influence on the public accounting profession. The effect was of such proportions that the American Institute met in 1921 to clarify the use of the professional title C.P.A.

During the five years of its existence the Institute had grown in membership and influence so rapidly that it appeared to members of its council that the time had come for a charter of more general scope and greater effect than was possible under the laws of the District of Columbia. Accordingly, a committee was appointed in April, 1921, to prepare a bill for the incorporation of the Institute by act of Congress.[39]

At the next regular meeting of the council of the American Institute of Accountants in Washington, September 19, 1921, the special committee on a national charter reported that it had given consideration to obtaining this from Congress. The committee expressed the opinion that the charter could be obtained and proposed that the following act of incorporation be introduced in Congress:

An Act to Incorporate The American Institute of Chartered Accountants

Be it enacted by the Senate and House of Representatives of the United States of America in Congress assembled; that the persons following, namely:

Carl H. Nau	James D. M. Crockett
William P. Hilton	W. Sanders Davies
T. Edward Ross	Page Lawrence
Joseph E. Sterrett	Ernest Reckitt
John F. Forbes	William A. Smith
J. Porter Joplin	Edward L. Suffern
Waldron H. Rand	J. S. Morris Goodloe
Frederick A. Ross	Elmer L. Hatter
Elijah W. Sells	Clifford E. Isyard
Frederic A. Tilton	J. Edward Masters
William Jeffers Wilson	James S. Matteson
Hamilton S. Corwin	Robert H. Montgomery
Ernest Crowther	W. Ernest Seatree
Edward E. Gore	Joseph E. Hutchinson
Charles S. Ludlow	Fedmond W. Lafrentz
Overton S. Meldrum	William R. Mackenzie

---

[39]Editorial, "For Federal Incorporation," *The Journal of Accountancy*, XXXIII (January, 1922), 37.

Adam A. Ross   Walter Mucklow
Cassius M. William   John B. Niven
Harvey S. Chase   John R. Ruckstell
                        and Francis F. White

their associates and successors duly chosen are hereby incorporated and declared
to be a body corporate by the name, title and style of the American Institute
of Chartered Accountants, and by that name shall be known and have perpetual
succession with the powers, limitations and restrictions herein contained.

Section 2. That the objects for which said corporation is incorporated shall
be (a) To promote education in the science of accounts and in the practical
application of that science throughout the United States of America and its
territories and possessions.

(b) To maintain a library of works treating upon the subject of accountancy
and upon related subjects, and to encourage the production of such works.

(c) To publish books, pamphlets and periodicals for the increase of information and education in the science of accounts.

(d) To establish and maintain standards of qualifications of persons who
desire to enter into practice as professional public accountants and who desire
to be known and designated as American Chartered Accountants.

(e) To receive and hold by gift, bequest, device, grant or purchase, any real
or personal property, and to use and dispose of the same for the purpose of the
Corporation.

Section 3. That the government of said corporation shall be vested in a council composed of not less than thirty-five members, not more than five of whom
shall be residents of the same state or territory.

Section 4. That no part of any net income or profit earned or realized by said
corporation shall inure to the personal gain of any individual or be devoted
to any purpose foreign to the objects herein set forth.

Section 5. That said corporation may make all by-laws, rules and regulations
not inconsistent with law that may be necessary or expedient to accomplish the
purposes of its creation; and it may hold real estate and personal property in
the United States and any foreign country for its proper use and purposes to an
amount not exceeding two million dollars.

The principal office of said corporation shall be in the City of New York,
in the State of New York, but it may establish and maintain offices, and hold
regular or special meetings in such places as its by-laws may provide.[40]

The bill as proposed by the original committee was not introduced
in Congress. It was moved before the report was passed that as an
amendment the words "Certified Public Accountants" be substi-

---

[40]"Council Meeting Proceedings," in *American Institute of Accountants Year Book, 1921*, p. 82.

tuted for "Chartered Accountants" in the committee's report, but the suggested amendment was lost.[41] The occasion for the amendment to the original draft of the proposed federal charter was the formation of a competing organization, the American Society of Certified Public Accountants. Before the end of 1921 the American Society was formally organized as a federation of the state societies with the avowed purpose that it

shall be to protect and foster the certificate of certified public accountants, as granted by the States and political subdivisions of the U.S. of America.[42]

The American Institute then revised the bill requesting federal incorporation and excluded the "chartered accountant" provisions.

The attempt to eliminate the designation only added to the controversy among the members of the national organization. The first purpose of the Institute, "to unite the accountancy profession of the United States," was in serious jeopardy. Actually the difference of opinion brought about a split and the formation of another national accounting organization—The American Society of Certified Public Accountants.[43] This organization will be discussed in more detail later in this chapter.

Federal Incorporation of the American Institute of Accountants

The council of the Institute continued in its efforts to obtain a federal charter. This had been one of the original objectives when the American Institute of Accountants was formed in 1916.

Another draft of a bill was drawn, changing certain sections, and this later draft was finally introduced by Representative Rodenberg of Illinois, December 9, 1921, and referred to the Committee on the District of Columbia. This reference, however, was erroneous, and the bill was transferred to the Committee on the Judiciary.[44] The text of the bill, introduced on December 9, 1921, follows:

[41]*Ibid.*
[43]Alexander S. Banks, "Problems Now Confronting the Public Accounting Profession," *The Certified Public Accountant,* III (January, 1924), 17.
[43]Carl H. Nau, "The Aims of the Institute," *The Journal of Accountancy,* XXXI (May, 1921), 322.
[44]Editorial, "Federal Incorporation of the Institute," *The Journal of Accountancy,* XXXIII (April, 1922), 287.

67th Congress
 2 D Session
  H.R. 9446
In the House of Representatives
  December 9, 1921
Mr. Rodenberg introduced the following bill; which was referred to the Com-
mittee on the District of Columbia and ordered to be printed.

A Bill

To Incorporate the American Institute of Accountants

Be it enacted by the Senate and House of Representatives of the United
States of America in Congress assembled, That the persons following, namely:
Carl H. Nau, John B. Niven, Arthur W. Teele, Joseph E. Sterrett, John F.
Forbes, J. Porter Joplin, Waldron H. Rand, Frederick A. Ross, Elijah W. Sells,
Frederic A. Tilton, William Jeffers Wilson, William R. Tolleth, Ernest Crow-
ther, Edward E. Gore, Charles S. Ludlow, Overton S. Meldrum, Adam A. Ross,
T. Edward Ross, William Hilton, Frederick Hurdman, James D. M. Crockett,
W. Sanders Davies, Page Lawrence, Ernest Reckitt, William A. Smith, Edward
L. Suffern, J. S. Morris Goodloe, Elmer L. Hatter, Clifford E. Isyard, J. Edward
Masters, James S. Matteson, Robert H. Montgomery, Albert T. Bacon, Joseph
E. Hutchinson, senior, Charles E. Mather, William R. Mackenzie, Walter Mucklow, John R. Ruckstell, and Lewis G. Fisher, their associates and successors duly
chosen, are hereby incorporated and declared to be a body corporate by the
name, title, and style of the American Institute of Accountants, and by that
name shall be known and have perpetual succession, with the powers, limitations, and restrictions herein contained.

Section 2. That the objects for which said corporation is incorporated shall
be—

(a) To promote education in the science of accounts, and in the practical
application of that science, throughout the United States of America and its
territories and possessions.

(b) To maintain a library of works treating upon the subject of accountancy
and upon related subjects and to encourage the production of such works.

(c) To publish books, pamphlets, and periodicals for the increase of information and education in the science of accounts.

(d) To establish and maintain standards of education for, and to pass upon
and determine the qualifications applying to it for membership.

(e) To issue its diplomas attesting the degree of proficiency in the science
of accounts of such persons as may submit themselves to it for examination
and to confer upon such persons as it may deem entitled thereto such degree,
title, or designation as is not inconsistent with existing laws or with established
educational ethics.

(f) To receive and hold by gift, bequest, device, grant, or purchase any real or personal property and to use and dispose of the same for the purposes of the corporation.

Section 3. That the government of said corporation shall be vested in a council composed of not less than thirty-nine members, not more than six of whom shall be residents of the same state or territory.

Section 4. That no part of any net income or profit earned or realized by said corporation shall inure to the personal gain of any individual or be devoted to any purpose foreign to the objects herein set forth.

Section 5. That said corporation may make all by-laws, rules, and regulations not inconsistent with law that may be necessary or expedient to accomplish the purpose of its creation, and it may hold real estate and personal property in the United States and any foreign country for its proper use and purposes to an amount not exceeding $2,000,000.

The principal office of said corporation shall be in the City of New York, in the State of New York, but it may establish and maintain offices and hold regular or special meetings in such places as its by-laws may provide.[45]

Changes from First Bill Drafted

The first major difference or change from the original draft was the inclusion of a subsection authorizing the issuance of

diplomas attesting the degrees of proficiency in the science of accounts of such persons as may submit themselves to it for examination and to confer upon such persons as it may deem entitled thereto such degree, title, . . . with existing law. . . .

Here is found the acceptance of the C.P.A. designation as prescribed by the state laws of the several states.

In the first proposal one of the objects of the American Institute of Accountants under this charter was:

To establish and maintain standards of qualifications of persons who desire to enter practice as professional public accountants and who desire to be known and designated as American Chartered Accountants.

---

[45]Editorial, "For Federal Incorporation," *The Journal of Accountancy*, XXXIII (January, 1922), 39.

It is significant that the following section was substituted for the one above:

To establish and maintain standards of education for, and to pass upon and determine the qualifications of persons applying to it for membership.

It would appear from the wording of the original draft that the American Institute of Accountants would have the power to determine who was eligible to practice public accounting. In the final draft the emphasis was shifted to the determination of those eligible for membership in the organization. This change may have been made to avoid the claim that the organization would have had a monopoly and that the Institute would have violated States' rights in determining who could practice accounting.

Another change in the proposed charter was the increase in the number of members on the Council from thirty-five to thirty-nine with no more than six from one state instead of five. This alteration was made to impress upon the members as well as the public the fact that the Institute was a national organization.

It was suggested prior to the federal incorporation that the only way to regulate the public accounting profession was to set up federal certification procedure. Had this been brought forth in a positive way, the ever-present States' rights principle would have in all probability defeated any such proposal.

If the bill had been passed by Congress, the American Institute of Accountants would have had for the first time a certificate of incorporation of a national character. It is significant that, in the final bill submitted by the Council of the Institute, the title "Chartered Accountant" was excluded. It seems logical to assume that the reason for the exclusion of this title was an effort to smooth the already ruffled feathers of many members of the profession, some of whom had organized the American Society of Certified Public Accountants by this time. Another possible reason is that all of the states' public accounting laws had included in them the distinguishing title of "C.P.A." It would then seem unreasonable for the Institute to reject the title which had come to be identified with public accountancy by those in business and the general public.

Some members of the American Institute of Accountants felt

that membership in that organization had become the real measure of professional ability and standing, rather than the possession of a C.P.A. certificate. Hence there was an attempt to change the name of the Institute to the Institute of Chartered Accountants and to dispense with the C.P.A. designation as far as their organization was concerned. But this idea was dropped after the Society was formed with the avowed purpose of maintaining and protecting the C.P.A. certificate as granted by the several states.[46]

American Society of Certified Public Accountants

Dissatisfaction with the policies of the American Institute was a factor which led to the organization of the Society in 1921. The Institute was still admitting noncertified public accountants to membership and was not promoting the passage of additional C.P.A. laws with the aggressiveness that some members felt it should. On the other hand some state examinations were not recognized by the Institute, and C.P.A.'s in those state were excluded from membership in the Institute unless they submitted to another examination given by the Board of Examiners of the Institute. Then, too, it was thought by some that the American Institute of Accountants had not taken any positive action against the National Association. Hence a number of members of the Institute felt that there was room for an organization composed exclusively of certified public accountants, which could continually emphasize the value of the certificate and devote a major portion of its energies to development of state societies. These members met in Chicago under a charter obtained from the District of Columbia and formed the American Society of Certified Public Accountants.[47]

The American Society of Certified Public Accountants represented the "liberal" element of the public accounting profession and the American Institute of Accountants represented the "conservative" element.[48] The Society was almost exclusively concerned with the C.P.A. movement; in fact, it wanted to push for laws in every

---

[46]D. W. Springer, "Institute-Society-Institute," *The Certified Public Accountant*, XVI (December, 1936), 744.

[47]Robert H. Montgomery, *Fifty Years of Accountancy* (New York: Ronald Press Company, 1939), p. 69.

[48]Henry J. Miller, "The American Society and the American Institute," *The Certified Public Accountant*, V (December, 1925), 157.

state. Once a person received a C.P.A. certificate granted by a state, he was eligible for membership in the Society.

The American Society of Certified Public Accountants was organized in Chicago on December 12, 1921, as a result of a series of events in the field of public accountancy at that time. The three immediate and compelling causes were:

(1) The organization of the "National Association of Certified Public Accountants" in Washington on June 4, 1921, which organization was designed to destroy the title "C.P.A."

(2) The failure of the American Institute of Accountants, at its annual meeting in September, 1921, to take any official action against or notice whatever of the "National Association" but instead made a move to abandon support of the C.P.A. certificate and adopt the title "Chartered Accountant," and

(3) The lack of a national organization for expressing the will in a national way of ALL Certified Public Accountants of ALL the states.[49]

Then there was a feeling among many members of the profession outside the eastern area of the United States that the American Institute was being run by just a few members.[50] It seems significant that the Institute, in its federal incorporation act, had a governing body composed of thirty-nine representatives with no more than six from any one state. The Council was composed of representatives from almost all the states that had C.P.A. laws at that time.

Article II of the constitution of the American Society of Certified Accountants states:

The object of the society shall be to protect and foster the certificate of Certified Public Accountants, as granted by the States and political subdivisions of the United States of America.

Article III states:

The membership of this society shall consist of certified public accountants.

[49]"The American Society and the American Institute," *The Certified Public Accountant*, III (October, 1924), 244.
[50]*Ibid.*, p. 247.

Every member shall be the legal holder of a certified public accountant's certificate issued by a state or political subdivision of the United States of America.[51]

The constitution of the American Society of Certified Public Accountants goes on to say that the United States would be divided into districts. Each state would have the right to elect one representative for each fifty members or major fraction thereof, and any state with less than fifty members would elect one representative. The district representatives would then elect directors annually to serve on the board of directors, which was the governing body of the organization.

It was felt by the members of the American Society of Certified Public Accountants that the problem of winning complete public recognition and respect was greater than any other problem facing the public accountancy profession. The aims of the Society, in an effort to achieve this status, were:[52]

    (1) to co-operate effectively with the state societies;
    (2) to promote the prestige of the state societies;
    (3) to protect and foster the state-granted certificates;
    (4) to educate the public generally, and businessmen specifically, to understand the importance and advantages of C.P.A. service;
    (5) to co-operate financially and other ways with the state societies fighting adverse legislation;
    (6) to stimulate education of all accountants now certified, and those who are working to earn their certificates.

Soon after the formation of the Society, as early as 1924, there were attempts to consolidate the two national organizations. This merger did not come about for several years thereafter and will be discussed in detail in a later chapter. Both of the national public accounting organizations continued to operate and in many cases performed duplicate functions. In fact, many of the leading professional public accountants in practice during the tenure of the

---

[51]"Constitution and By-Laws of the American Society of Certfieid Public Accountants," *The Certified Public Accountant*, II (August, 1923), 213.

[52]Alexander Banks, "Problems Now Confronting the Public Accounting Profession," *The Certified Public Accountant*, III (January, 1924), 20.

two organizations held membership in both. Individuals who held these memberships did so in good faith although leaders such as Robert H. Montgomery did not approve of the two different organizations and worked very diligently for their merger.

Institute Rejects an Amendment

During the annual meeting of the American Institute of Accountants in 1925, there was introduced an amendment to that organization's constitution to restrict membership to Certified Public Accountants. An earlier attempt to bring about this change had been defeated by a very small majority. Some of the leading practitioners felt that membership in the national organization should be restricted to those who had C.P.A. certificates, yet when the amendment was presented for a vote it was overwhelmingly defeated. The amendment's importance was enhanced rather than diminished by the practically unanimous nature of the opposition to it; however, when the amendment to restrict admission was put to a vote, there were only two who desired to be recorded in favor.[53]

The overwhelming action by the members of the Institute can be partially explained. Some of them were not C.P.A.'s, since one of the purposes of the organization was to admit those qualified public accountants who could not meet the requirements of state legislation. Moreover, the American Society had restricted its membership to Certified Public Accountants. If the Institute had done the same thing, the two organizations would have been practically identical.

American Institute of Accountants Board of Examiners

The American Institute of Accountants was seeking to avoid the charge of being a closed corporation, a trust or any of the other reprehensible things which are apt to frighten the American mind. It was the Institute's desire to have on its roll every accountant, honestly engaged in public practice, who had a sufficient knowledge of accounting to justify him in offering his services to the public without jeopardy to the public interest.[54]

---

[53]Editorial, "The Institute Rejects an Amendment," *The Journal of Accountancy*, XL (November, 1925), 355.

[54]"Growth of Accountancy," *The Accountant*, LVII (August, 1917), 135.

Up to this time each of the states that had C.P.A. laws in force prepared its own examination. This led to varying requirements and standards of admittance to the profession. Some of the states' examinations were considered to be exclusive in nature.

A board of examiners of the Institute was appointed September 21, 1916, and organized by the election of Arthur W. Teele as chairman. They met again on November 10, 1916, to formulate rules and regulations for the conduct of examinations.[55]

There was a provision in the rules and regulations that an applicant possessing such qualifications as the board might from time to time prescribe might, at the discretion of the board and upon the request of the applicant, be subjected to oral instead of written examinations in one or more subjects. The oral examinations were given to satisfy those members of the profession who felt that some examination should be given to all members regardless of how long they had been practicing accountancy. This practice was adopted because of the difficulty of arriving at a satisfactory definition of what constituted the practice of public accountancy.[56]

It was decided to offer the first examination on June 14, 1917, under the auspices of the American Institute of Accountants. The following states used this first examination given by the Institute: California, Colorado, Florida, Michigan, Missouri, Nebraska, New Hampshire, New Jersey, and Tennessee. A copy of this examination can be found in the July, 1917, *Journal of Accountancy*.[57]

In all probability, the number of applicants eligible for oral examination was greater at this first examination than at any subsequent time. Some members of the American Institute of Accountants felt that a considerable number of men in different parts of the country, whose qualifications for membership were satisfactory, had, for one reason or another, been prevented from becoming C.P.A.'s. Lacking this qualification, these men were not eligible for membership in the American Association after the change in the bylaws which became effective in 1913.

It was felt by the members of the American Institute of Account-

[55]"The Institute of Accountants in the United States of America," *The Accountant*, LV (November, 1916), 445.

[56]"Accountancy in the States," *The Accountant*, LVI (January, 1917), 81.

[57]Letter from Robert L. Kane, Educational Director of the American Institute of Accountants, to James D. Edwards, dated June 2, 1952.

ants that many of the questions on the state examinations had been ultra-technical and that a man who had been in practice for a number of years could not answer them, while one fresh from an accounting school could. Also, many of the state examinations were designed to exclude rather than to admit, and questions had been formulated which, in many cases, were susceptible to more than one answer. The applicant who gave the answer selected by the examiners would pass, whereas the applicant giving another answer equally accurate would receive no credit whatever.[58]

In 1917 the newly-formed American Institute of Accountants, through its Board of Examiners, made every attempt to overcome these obstacles. It seemed sufficient that the board was set up so that it would not include among its members any representative from an accountancy school. The first examination was given in the fields of accounting theory and practice, auditing, and commercial law.[59]

American Institute of Accountants Library

George O. May, one of the partners of Price, Waterhouse and Company, discussed with members of the American Institute of Accountants, in 1917, the question of founding a library and bureau of information, to which members might submit questions confronting them without disclosure of names on either side; they could thus receive opinions from other members who were qualified to answer them, and other general information on accountancy. May offered a subscription in the name of his firm for the purpose of establishing such a library. This recommendation, backed by the subscription, resulted in an endowment of over $200,000 for the establishment of a library and research staff by the Institute.[60]

American Institute of Accountants Bureau of Research

The American Institute of Accountants proceeded to carry out the previously mentioned provisions as set forth in its federal char-

---

[58]Editorial, "Institute Examinations," *The Journal of Accountancy*, XXIII (February, 1917), 133.

[59]Editorial, "American Institute of Accountants Board of Examiners," *The Journal of Accountancy*, XXIV (July, 1917), 20.

[60]Sanders W. Davies, "Genesis, Growth and Aims of the Institute," *The Journal of Accountancy*, XLII (August, 1926), 108.

ter. At the annual meeting of the Council of the American Institute held in April, 1926, the Committee on Endowment recommended the establishment of a bureau of research, to investigate various areas in accounting and make this information available to the profession. It was to function along with the library and department of information which had previously been established. The report of the committee was unanimously approved by the Council, and the bureau was established shortly thereafter.[61]

The bureau served a very useful purpose for the profession of accountancy for some twenty-five years. It no longer exists, however. The issuance of an important Federal Reserve pamphlet a short time thereafter was the first accomplishment. This booklet was the first of many publications to come from the Institute's Bureau of Research.

Practice before the Board of Tax Appeals

The Board of Tax Appeals was established by the 1924 Revenue Act of the Congress of the United States. The most immediate problem facing the board after it was organized in the latter part of 1924 was to establish who was qualified to practice before the board. There had been some representatives appearing before it who were not qualified to represent the taxpayers.

The Board of Tax Appeals in its first ruling included a provision that practice before the board would be restricted to attorneys and certified public accountants. The rule provided for admission to practice of the following:

1. Attorneys-at-law who have been admitted to practice before the courts of the States, territories, or District of Columbia, in which they maintain offices, and who are lawfully engaged in the active practice of their profession.

2. Certified Public Accountants who have duly qualified to practice as certified public accountants in their own names, under the laws and regulations of the states, territories, or District of Columbia, in which they maintain offices, and who are lawfully engaged in active practice as certified public accountants.[62]

[61]Editorial, "A Bureau of Research," *The Journal of Accountancy*, XLI (May, 1926), 354.
[62]Editorial, "Board of Tax Appeals," *The Journal of Accountancy*, XXXVIII (November, 1924), 206.

The purpose of the Board of Tax Appeals rule was to bar undesirable and poorly qualified representatives of taxpayers (such as the self-styled "tax experts") from appearing before the board on behalf of their clients.

Federal Reserve Board Requests a Pamphlet

The promulgation by the Federal Reserve Board of a ruling calling for public accountants' certification of statements presented in support of application for discount of commercial paper, brought into prominence a question which had been frequently discussed at conventions of the American Association of Public Accountants. This ruling added even more impetus to the growth of the profession and engaged the attention of its leaders in the national scope of the work of the public accountant.[63]

The American Institute of Accountants' committee on federal legislation was instructed to cooperate with the Federal Trade Commission. The committee consisted of the president, W. Sanders Davies, Harvey S. Chase, George O. May, and Robert H. Montgomery. This committee was successful in persuading the Commission to dispense with the idea of a uniform accounting system and be satisfied with a more specific statement, "Approved Methods for the Preparation of Balance Sheet Statements."

Other members of the American Institute of Accountants were consulted during the preparation of the committee's report, and the council of the Institute unanimously approved the audit program which was recommended. The Federal Reserve Board then had the report published in the Federal Reserve Bulletin in 1917.[64]

This publication, *Approved Methods for the Preparation of Balance Sheet Statements*, was a statement of what the Board believed a balance sheet audit should entail. Subsequently, after the Federal Reserve Board had adopted it as semi-official, the document became the standard authority on minimum requirements in balance sheet audits.[65] The demand for the pamphlet was so great that it went through several printings.

---

[63]Editorial, "National Aspects of Public Accountancy," *The Journal of Accountancy*, XIX (January, 1914), 46.

[64]Editorial, "How the Text Was Published," *The Journal of Accountancy*, XLVII (May, 1929), 358.

[65]Editorial, "Significance of an Accountants' Certificate," *The Journal of Accountancy*, XLI (January, 1926), 33.

Education for Accountancy

The importance of education in the minds of accountants is confirmed by the stated objectives of the American Institute of Accountants, as found in its charter:

(a) To promote education in the science of accounts, and in practical application of that science, throughout the United States of America and its territories and possessions

(b) To maintain a library of works treating upon the subject of accountancy and upon related subjects and to encourage the production of such works

(c) To publish books, pamphlets, and periodicals for the increase of information and education in the science of accounts.[66]

The American Society of Certified Public Accountants also wrote into its constitution, as one of its objectives, the following: " (6) to stimulate education of all accountants now certified, and those who are working to earn their certificates."[67]

The American Society of Certified Public Accountants then acknowledged the need for instruction of candidates preparing for the examination and also for a continuing educational program for the certified man.

Universities and technical schools, recognizing this need for training, and possibly foreseeing the part which the accountant would be called upon to play in the modern industrial world, readjusted and expanded their curricula to provide intensive training for the student of accountancy. By 1920 most of the major universities and colleges not only had accounting courses in their curricula but were offering degrees in business administration with a major in accounting.[68] The increase from fifty-two such colleges in 1910 to one hundred and sixteen in 1916 is an indication of the expansion of educational opportunities for accounting students. It is noteworthy, moreover, that forty-eight of these institutions were offering courses which pointed specifically toward securing the C.P.A. certificate.[69]

---

[66]Editorial, "For Federal Incorporation," *The Journal of Accountancy*, XXXIII (January, 1922), 39.

[67]Alexander Banks, "Problems Now Confronting the Public Accounting Profession," *The Certified Public Accountant*, III (January, 1924), 2.

[68]Editorial, "Growth of Accountancy," *The Accountant*, LVII (August, 1917), 134.

[69]C. E. Allen, "The Growth of Accounting Instruction Since 1900," *The Accounting Review*, II (June, 1927), 160.

Further indication of the significance of university training in accounting is the formation of a national organization of instructors. In Washington, D.C., during December, 1915, a group of accounting instructors decided on this move, but it was not until the next year, on December 28, 1916, at Columbus, Ohio, that the organization came into existence as the American Association of University Instructors in Accounting. The purpose of the Association as stated in its constitution was: "To advance the cause of Instruction in Accounting."[70]

Technical education was also being carried on by correspondence with some success. As an example, the LaSalle Extension University of Chicago had over ten thousand accounting students in 1917. Another of the early accounting correspondence schools was the Walton School of Commerce. Students included not only clerks, bookkeepers, and junior accountants, but also senior accountants, auditors, and comptrollers of large corporations as well as public accountants who understood the value of continuous training in their profession.[71]

Expansion of C.P.A. Firms

Along with the increasing emphasis on educational standards of public accountants, more and more public accounting firms were being established. Most of these practiced on a local basis; however, many developed regional practices and most of them attained reputations for such professional competence as to rate their work equal with that of the national firms. In many areas of the United States audit reports of certain local and regional firms have always been and continue to be just as acceptable to bankers, investors and creditors as those of the national firms. While most of the distinguished local firms are located in the larger cities such as New York, Chicago, San Francisco, Houston, St. Louis, Denver, and Omaha, occasionally an individual or a firm in a community of less than 100,000 population makes such an outstanding contribution to the profession as to be recognized nationally or even internationally.

---

[70]Editorial, "American Association of University Instructors in Accounting," *The Journal of Accountancy*, XXV (February, 1918), 155.

[71]Arthur W. Chase, "University Education of Accounting Students in the United States," *The Accountant*, LVII (September, 1917), 179.

In 1959 there were about sixty-five hundred local certified public accounting firms in the United States. The number of public accounting firms is in distinct contrast to the approximately one hundred firms in 1900 and the one thousand in 1915.

In the aggregate these local public accounting firms handle a larger volume of work than do the dozen or so national ones. These local practitioners are the business advisors to the small businessmen on matters of taxation and other government regulations. These local and regional firms render real assistance to their clients in systems work and budgeting. Their clients generally are the small and medium-sized businesses, but some obtain audit engagements with larger corporations.

The tendency today, however, is for national public accounting firms to grow larger by absorbing the practices of local firms. In the process the national firms have acquired a major portion of the audits of large corporations. Despite this trend toward national public accounting firms, many local firms have grown stronger and have resisted offers of national firms to purchase their practices. The local certified public accountants remain the mainstay of the accounting profession in the United States.

While the number of local and regional C.P.A. firms multiplied rapidly, national public accounting firms continued to increase the number of branch offices. The firm of Lybrand, Ross Brothers, and Montgomery, which had been formed in 1898, opened offices in widely scattered sections of the country. In 1919 Lybrand opened its Washington, D.C., office in order to have closer contact with the federal government. The two offices opened the next year were in widely separated sections of the country: Detroit and Seattle. In 1923, offices were opened in Cleveland and Cincinnati and, in 1924, in San Francisco, Los Angeles, and Baltimore.[72]

Price, Waterhouse and Company, organized in 1890, opened offices from one end of the country to the other during the period 1913 to 1928. That in Milwaukee was opened in 1914 and the Detroit one the next year. After four years, the Cleveland office was opened in 1919; then came Providence in 1920. In 1921 the Washington, D. C., office was opened and also the Portland, Oregon,

---

[72]William N. Lybrand, T. Edward Ross, Adam A. Ross, and Robert H. Montgomery, *Fiftieth Anniversary* (privately printed, 1948), p. 24.

office. An eastern office, in Buffalo, and a southern one, in Atlanta, were opened in 1928.[73]

The Milwaukee office of Arthur Andersen and Company was opened in 1915 in order that the firm might better serve its clients in that area. Then came the opening of the New York office and the Washington, D. C., office in 1921. After the lapse of two years the Kansas City branch was started in 1923. The firm spread to the west coast by opening offices in Los Angeles in 1926, and in San Francisco in 1928.[74]

The firm of Ernst and Ernst started in 1903. Offices for this firm were opened in St. Louis in 1913. In 1915 Dallas and Pittsburgh offices were opened, and in 1916 one in Detroit. The next year offices were opened in Boston and Houston. Two middle western ones were opened in 1918 in Minneapolis and Toledo, as well as an eastern one in Philadelphia. Then, in 1919, offices were opened in Buffalo, Washington, Kansas City, Indianapolis, Fort Worth, and Atlanta. The greatest expansion occurred in 1920, with branches set up in such cities as Providence, Canton, St. Paul, Richmond, Grand Rapids, Denver, New Orleans, Columbus, and Kalamazoo. Then came offices in Youngstown, Baltimore, Erie, and Dayton in 1921; Akron, San Antonio, and Rochester in 1922; Milwaukee, San Francisco, and Los Angeles in 1923; Memphis in 1924; Miami in 1925; Winston-Salem in 1926; and Seattle in 1928.[75]

Reasons for Growth of National Firms' Branch Offices

The public accounting practice of many an individual calls for travel from one state to another during the year. Thus the certified public accountant is brought under the jurisdiction of state governments other than that which granted him his certificate. Many firms are engaged in practice in several states, and they are, as indicated in the previous section and in the last chapter, compelled to select one state as their principal headquarters and to conform to the requirements of that state.[76]

---

[73]Letter from C. W. DeMond, partner in Price, Waterhouse and Company, to James D. Edwards, dated May 6, 1952.

[74]Charles W. Jones, "A Chronological Outline of the Development of the Firm," *The Arthur Andersen Chronicle*, IV (December, 1943), 14.

[75]Letter from J. A. Lindquist, partner in Ernst and Ernst, to James D. Edwards, dated May 21, 1952.

[76]Editorial, "National Aspects of Public Accountancy," *The Journal of Accountancy*, XIX (January, 1914), 49.

Many objections are raised to the establishment of branch offices of accounting firms, the most important of which has been the criticism of the local practitioner who feels that the national firms are invading his territory by establishing branch offices.

In all professions the work was originally almost wholly an individual matter. The lawyer, for instance, had his offices in which he met his clients and personally served their needs. In the beginning the accountant, too, worked in a somewhat similar fashion.

The corresponding relationships thus established were ideal in many respects, and might have continued undiminished but for the growth of the volume of business and the variety and extent of engagements. Accountancy has been and is more closely connected with this development of business than perhaps any other profession. As a business service accountancy must conform in its development to the necessities imposed upon it by the changing structure of business.[77]

Neither the financial nor the physical operations of business are completely local any longer, and it is this change in conditions which makes the branch office system in public accounting necessary. As incorporated business organizations became larger and began to open branch offices, so did the accounting firms. The major reason for the opening of branch offices by accounting firms was to serve their clients more efficiently. If a C.P.A. firm did the auditing for the home office, it usually was the policy to have the same firm audit the branch offices. Many auditors originally depended on a correspondent firm to handle the audit of far-flung offices and plants, but it was much more satisfactory to have an office of one's own firm in that area to ensure better control over the audits.

Branch offices of accounting firms are usually staffed to furnish the same services as the home office, yet they maintain a national reputation because the home office has the responsibility of reviewing the work performed.[78]

The capital that big business needs has always been obtained in large measure from commercial banks and investment bankers in the financial centers of the country rather than locally. Almost universally the audit certificate of a certified public accountant is re-

[77]Editorial, "Branch Office Ethics," *The Journal of Accountancy,* XXVIII (September, 1919), 212.
[78]T. A. Ross, "Growth and Effect of Branch Offices," *The Journal of Accountancy,* XXX (October, 1920), 256.

quired in connection with the transaction. It is generally agreed that the bankers' requirement of the certificate of an accountant is in the interest of sound business in having a review of the records made by an independent third party.

The acceptance of certificates issued by branch offices of a public accounting firm is a result of the confidence in standards and methods which has been inspired by work well done locally. At bottom, the firm with a branch office organization and the firm whose practice is confined to a restricted territory are in the same position, in that the acceptability of their certificates depends on the reputation enjoyed in the locality where the certificate is to be used. Generally, the national firm's certificate will have a much wider range of acceptance than the certificate issued by a local C.P.A. because of the national firms being known in industrial and financial circles.

Reporting Standards for Certified Statements

The pamphlet *Approved Methods for the Preparation of Balance Sheet Statements,* issued in 1918, detailed what the Federal Reserve Board considered to be the minimum auditing procedures. The Federal Reserve Board was the first governmental agency to approve what they considered minimum standards.

As early as 1919, *The Journal of Accountancy* frequently urged the placing upon the shoulders of the accountant of full responsibility for his work. The lack of court decisions in the United States dealing with the accountant's responsibility resulted in a wide difference of opinion as to the liability involved.

For years the general opinion seemed to favor the theory advanced in several English cases (London and General Bank, Ltd., The Leeds Estate, Building and Investment Company, and the Kingston Cotton Mill Company, presented in a previous chapter) to the effect that the accountant must exercise reasonable care in the preparation and certification of reports. It is the duty of the auditor to inquire into the substantial accuracy of the accounting reports. But the point is established in America only when some accountant is charged with neglect of his professional obligations and damages are assessed.[79] Auditing standards are established by the profession, but

---

[79]Editorial, "Holding the Accountant Responsible," *The Journal of Accountancy,* XXVIII (July, 1919), 39.

court decisions affect what the profession considers minimum auditing standards. This will be shown here and also in other cases in a later chapter.

Auditor's Responsibility and the Law

The responsibility of the auditor for the maintenance of minimum auditing standards and procedures has been defined in several American court decisions. The most prominent of these was handed down by Judge Cardozo in *Ultramares Corporation* v. *Touche* et al. (255 N.Y. 170, 174 N.E. 441 [1931].) This case is discussed in some detail here to convey its background as well as the final decision.

In January, 1924, the firm of Touche, Niven and Company, public accountants, was engaged by Fred Stern and Company, Incorporated, to prepare and certify a balance sheet for the Company as of December 31, 1923. This same firm of accountants had prepared the statements of this company during the previous three years.

When the audit was completed in February, 1924, the balance sheet was made up. The balance sheet stated that the assets were $2,550,671.88 and that the liabilities were $1,479,956.62, thus showing a net worth of $1,070,715.26. Attached to the balance sheet was the following auditor's certificate:

Touche, Niven & Co.
Public Accountants
Eighty Maiden Lane
New York

February 26, 1924

Certificate of Auditors

We have examined the accounts of Fred Stern and Company, Inc., for the year ending December 31, 1923, and hereby certify that the annexed balance sheet is in accordance therewith and with the information and explanations given us. We further certify that, subject to provision for federal taxes on income, the said statement, in our opinion, presents a true and correct view of the financial condition of Fred Stern and Company, Inc., as of December 31, 1923.

Touche, Niven and Company
Public Accountants[80]

---

[80]*Ultramares Corp.* v. *Touche*, 255 N.Y. 170, 174 N.E. 441, 442 (1931).

It was known to the accountants that the company used the statements to finance their operations, which involved extensive borrowing of large sums from banks. The auditors also knew that the statements given Fred Stern and Company would be exhibited by them to bankers, creditors, and stockholders, according to the needs of the occasion, as the basis of financial dealings. When the balance sheet was made up, the accountants supplied the Stern Company with thirty-two copies certified with serial numbers as counterpart originals.

The president of the Stern Company later requested loans from the Ultramares Company, which had not previously advanced money to Stern. He submitted with his request one of the statements certified by Touche, Niven and Company. All the loans that were subsequently made by the Ultramares Corporation were, by agreement, to be secured by assignment of accounts receivable. The conditions of the agreement were fulfilled with respect to the earliest loans, but later the lending corporation did not insist upon the prompt assignment of the accounts and in particular failed to require the assignment of accounts in support of the loans which were not paid.

Then Fred Stern and Company was declared bankrupt on January 2, 1925. In November, 1926, the Ultramares Corporation brought suit against the auditors, Touche, Niven and Company, to recover the amounts which had not been repaid. The plaintiff stated that had the audit been made carefully it would have been shown that Fred Stern and Company was insolvent in 1923 instead of having a surplus, but the plaintiff relied on the statements of the auditor and granted loans. The action was first brought against the auditors for negligence, and later a second cause of action alleging fraud was added.

In the first trial the judge, at the close of the testimony, directed a verdict for the defendant on the fraud charge, but left it to the jury to decide whether the defendants had been negligent. The jury rendered a verdict against the accountants and made an award of $187,576.32, which Judge Walsh set aside on the ground that negligence is not actionable unless there is a breach of duty by the defendant (in this case Touche, Niven and Company) to the plaintiff (Ultramares Corporation).

The case was then appealed to the Appellate Division of the

Supreme Court of New York, which affirmed the lower court's dismissal of the complaint of fraud, but reserved the decision of dismissing the complaint of negligence. The verdict of the jury in favor of the plantiff granted a judgment for the sum of $203,058.97. Again the case was appealed, this time by both sides, the accountants on the second count and the company on the fraud case. The case then went to the Court of Appeals of the State of New York.[81]

The plaintiff maintained that the certificate of the auditor, previously given in this chapter, was erroneous in two respects. The first was the asserted correspondence between the accounts and the balance sheet, purporting to be made as a matter of knowledge of the auditors. The second was the auditors' certification that the conditions reflected in the balance sheet presented a true and correct picture of the resources of the business, stated as a matter of opinion. If correspondence, however, be assumed, a closer examination of supporting invoices and records, or a fuller inquiry directed to the persons appearing on the books as creditors or debtors, would have exhibited the truth. In fact, accounts receivable had been placed on the books and substantiated by invoices which actually did not exist. It was maintained that proper scrutiny would have revealed this fact to the auditors.

The following are excerpts from the decision of Judge Cardozo of the Court of Appeals:

The defendants owed to their employer a duty imposed by law to make their certificates without fraud, and a duty growing out of contract to make it with the care and caution proper to their calling. Fraud included the pretense of knowledge when knowledge there is none. To creditors and investors to whom the employer exhibited the certificate, the defendants owed a like duty to make it without fraud, since there was notice in the circumstances of its making that the employer did not intend to keep it to himself. A different question develops when we ask whether they owed a duty to these to make it without negligence. If liability for negligence exists, a thoughtless slip or blunder, the failure to detect a theft or forgery beneath the cover of deceptive entries, may expose accountants to a liability in an indeterminate amount for an indeterminate time or to an indeterminate class. The hazards of a business conducted on these terms are so extreme as to enkindle doubt whether a flaw may not exist in the implication of a duty that exposes to these consequences. We put aside for the moment any statement in the certificate which involves the representation of a

[81] *Ibid.*, p. 441.

fact as true to the knowledge of the auditors. If such a statement was made, whether believed to be true or not, the defendants are liable for deceit in the event that it was false. The plaintiff does not need the invention of novel doctrine to help it out in such conditions. . . .

Our holding does not emancipate accountants from the consequence of fraud. It does not relieve them if their audit has been so negligent as to justify a finding that they had no genuine belief in its adequacy, for this again is fraud. It does no more than say that if less than this is proved, if there has been neither reckless misstatement nor insincere profession of an opinion, but only honest blunder, the ensuing liability for negligence is one that is bounded by the contract, and is to be enforced between the parties by whom the contract has been made. We doubt whether the average business man receiving a certificate without paying for it and receiving it merely as one among a multitude of possible investors, would look for anything more. . . .

The correspondence to be of any moment may not unreasonably be held to signify a correspondence between the statement and the books of original entry, the books taken as a whole. If that is what the certificate means, a jury could find that the correspondence did not exist and that the defendants signed the certificates without knowing it to exist and even without reasonable grounds for belief in its existence. . . .

The defendant's attempt to excuse the omission of an inspection of the invoices proved to be fictitious by invoking a practice known as that of testing and sampling. A random choice of accounts is made from the total number on the books, and these, if found to be regular when inspected and investigated, are taken as a fair indication of the quality of the mass. The defendants say that about 200 invoices were examined in accordance with this practice, but they do not assert that any of the seventeen invoices supporting the fictitious sales were among the number so selected. Verification by test and sample was very likely a sufficient audit as to accounts regularly entered upon the books in the usual course of business. It was plainly insufficient, however, as to accounts not entered upon the books where inspection of the invoices was necessary, not as a check upon accounts fair upon their face, but in order to ascertain whether there were any accounts at all. If the only invoices inspected were invoices unrelated to the interpolated entry, the result was to certify a correspondence between the books and the balance sheet without any effort by the auditor, as to $706,000 of accounts, to ascertain whether the certified agreement was in accordance with the truth. How far books of account fair upon their face are to be probed by Accountants in an effort to ascertain whether the transactions back of them are in accordance with the entries, involves to some extent the exercise of judgment and direction. . . .

We conclude, to sum up the situation, that in certifying to the correspondence between balance sheet and accounts the defendants made a statement as true to their own knowledge, when they had, as a jury might find, no knowledge on the subject. If that is so, they may also be found to have acted without information leading to a sincere or genuine belief when they certified to an opinion that the balance sheet faithfully reflected the condition of the business.

Whatever wrong was committed by the defendants was not their personal act or omission, but that of their subordinates. This does not relieve them however, of liability to answer in damages for the consequences of the wrong, if wrong there shall be found to be. . . .[82]

After this judge had written such a descriptive decision on the responsibility of the public accountant, he ordered a new trial in the case. The case was not taken to court again, but there was a settlement out of court sometime later.

Judge Cardozo's decision was the most prominent of all American court cases on the responsibilities of the auditor and his responsibility to third parties. It would appear that such a decision would have its inevitable influence on the practitioners in this country. The profession would then be put on guard in the performance of the duties of auditors.

Judge Cardozo actually confirmed the common law concept, current in the United States and England, that an auditor should not be held liable to third parties for negligence. The injured party could not hold the accountant responsible for errors in judgment except when fraud was present. In this case the suit brought on the grounds of fraud was settled out of court; no public record was made of the settlement.

State Street Trust Co. v. *Ernst* was substantially analogous to the Ultramares case.[83] Prior to these decisions it had been generally believed that the auditor owed no duty whatsoever to persons who were not his clients. Since there was no contract with third parties, it was queried as to how there could possibly be any responsibility to them. In other words, accountants at that time claimed that even if they were negligent the only person who had a right to complain was the client.

However, these two decisions held that:

a. The client may recover from an accountant where the accountant had been negligent;

---

[82]*Ibid.*, pp. 444-450.
[83]*State Street Trust Co.* v. *Alwin C. Ernst*, 278 N.Y. 104 (1938).

b. Third parties (investors and creditors) cannot recover from an accountant where he has been merely negligent;

c. Third parties (investors and creditors) may recover from an accountant where fraud can be proved;

d. Gross negligence on the part of accountants is sufficient evidence from which a jury may infer fraud.[84]

The auditor's responsibility to his client has been ruled on in several cases, the most notable being *Craig* v. *Anyon*, 212 App. Div. N.Y. 55 (1925) affirmed 242 N.Y. 569, [85] and *National Surety* v. *Lybrand*, 9 N.Y. 52d 554 App. Div. 226, 233.[86]

In *Craig* v. *Anyon* the auditors failed to discover, over a period of five years, defalcations exceeding a million dollars. The trial court held the auditors liable and assessed damages for the amount of the plaintiff's loss. The amount of damages was reduced on appeal to $2,000, the fee paid to the defendant auditors for their services. The nominal amount of damages was due to the defense plea that plaintiff clients had been contributorily negligent in the supervision—or lack thereof—over their own malfeasant employee. Thus it was felt that if an auditor could show that his client had himself been negligent, he had a defense against any suit for negligence.[87]

But this idea that contributory negligence would be an adequate defense was shattered by the *National Surety* v. *Lybrand* decision in 1939. This case was another of those that established the liability of an auditor for his negligence in performing an audit. As in the Craig case, a trusted employee was involved. The employee's theft covered a period of nine years without detection. The cashier had managed to hide his embezzlements from the three accounting firms by knowing when the audits were to be performed. All three accounting firms were sued by the plaintiff's surety company. After the first decision was appealed it was held that a *prima facie* case for liability had been made out. The decision included the definite and import-

---

[84]Boris Kostelanetz, "Auditors' Responsibilities and the Law," *The New York Certified Public Accountant*, XIX (February, 1949), 94.

[85]*William R. Craig* v. *James T. Anyon*, 242 N.Y. 569 (1926).

[86]*National Surety Corp.* v. *Lybrand*, 256 App. Div. 226, 9 N.Y. 52d 554 (1939).

[87]Boris Kostelanetz, "Auditors' Responsibilities and the Law," *The New York Certified Public Accountant*, XIX (February, 1949), 93.

ant statement that "it is undisputed that cash in bank can be verified absolutely"; therefore, the "lapping" and "kiting" system used by the cashier should have been detected by the auditors.[88] Further, the decision implied that the only kind of contributory negligence which would be a defense is that which amounts to an interference with the auditor's conduct.

Later when the Securities Acts were passed, statutes were enacted to establish the accountant's liability to third parties. These statutes will be discussed in the following chapter.

SUMMARY

By the end of this period, 1913-1928, the public accounting profession had attained national prominence. The American Institute of Accountants was now well established; in 1917 it began to offer two examinations yearly for candidates who desired admission to the Institute. There was also another national organization representing the liberal element of the C.P.A. movement, the American Society of Certified Public Accountants. Many practitioners held membership in both groups.

The public accounting profession grew rapidly under the influence of the income tax law of 1913 and the excess profits tax of 1917. These laws had established a new phase of operations for the public accountant. In the preparation of the income tax returns the accountant was able to furnish his client other beneficial services. Then, too, many companies engaged auditors on a regular basis for the first time. These developments were reflected in the expansion of national and local public accounting firms.

By 1924 all of the states and territories had enacted C.P.A. legislation. There was no strict uniformity in the laws of the several states nor in the examinations given to candidates. The examination given by the American Institute of Accountants was to be used in future years to establish uniform examination standards for all C.P.A.'s.

The Cardozo decision in the Touche, Niven and Company case was to have an effect on the profession. The status of the profession and the fixing of their responsibilities in auditing engagements was to be reflected in the Securities Act of the federal government.

---

[88]*Ibid.*, p. 93.

CHAPTER VII

Public Accounting in the United States, 1928-1949

In this period, 1928 to 1951, the public accounting profession attained many of the goals it had been seeking for several decades. Now that businesses recognized the value of the accountant and conferred with him regularly, his services were sought not only for auditing and tax services but also for his wide experience and knowledge as a business consultant.

These years mark the advent of a major governmental agency having some influence on the establishment of accepted accounting principles, in some cases as a result of the enactment of laws which have continued to have an effect upon the profession. The significant movements in legislative influences will be discussed in this chapter. Also, the court decisions of the 1930's are here studied for their influence upon the development of the profession.

All of the events discussed in this chapter have not yet had their full impact on the profession, but influences that are apparent are discussed as completely as possible. The most recent of these is the conflict between the accounting and the legal professions during the period from 1945 to 1949.

Influence of the Depression

Despite availability of the Federal Reserve Board's and the American Institute of Accountants' previously mentioned bulletins, businessmen, bankers, and accountants may not have given the proper emphasis to the auditing standards set forth therein. One of the effects of the depression was greater reliance upon accountancy on the part of businessmen. Legal restrictions placed on business in the 1930's had the same result. The defalcations which unfortunately resulted emphasized the importance of auditing in the case of those companies which were not of sufficient magnitude to justify the maintenance of an adequate system of internal check. There were also incidents that demonstrated the importance of external audits in the case of companies with more elaborate accounting systems. Companies whose size and importance had seemed to place them beyond the need of auditing by outside accountants now began to consult them. Due to the magnitude of the depression and the complications of business, accounting firms of all sizes experienced a permanent growth in their work.[1]

REPORTING STANDARDS FOR CERTIFIED STATEMENTS

Revised Auditing Pamphlet

From a very early date, the organized profession aggressively championed sound accounting principles and full disclosure of material facts. This attitude was reflected in the cooperation given the Federal Trade Commission in an earlier issue of the pamphlet entitled "Approved Methods for the Preparation of Balance Sheet Statements." This pamphlet was revised under the auspices of the Federal Reserve Board in 1929. It was issued under the title "Verification of Financial Statements," with the hope that something could be done to encourage the adoption of proper precautions by preparing and distributing a set of instructions which would serve as a guide to accountants, bankers, credit men, and the business public. Such a prescription was not intended to be complete or restrictive, but it purported to show the level below which the accountants could not go and still certify the validity of the accounts.[2]

Effect of the New York Securities Exchange Requirements

The Committee on Business Conduct of the New York Stock Exchange evolved, in 1921 and 1922, a plan for obtaining periodic direct statements of the financial condition of each stockbroker or stockbrokerage house. The requirement sought to get a statement of financial condition direct from each member. The request for a statement was in the form of a questionnaire; it could be made at

---

[1]George O. May, "Influence of the Depression on the Practice of Accountancy," *The Journal of Accountancy,* LIV (November, 1932), 336.

[2]Victor H. Stempf, "The Securities and Exchange Commission and the Accountant," *The New York Certified Public Accountant,* VIII (April, 1938), 12.

any time by the committee, and usually was planned to come as a surprise. The questionnaire called for an audit of the books coincident with the completion of the questionnaire; the audit was to be made in conformity with the regulations prescribed by the Committee on Business Conduct. It was also stipulated that the firm's name must not appear on the questionnaire; instead, by using a system of key numbers, the confidential nature of the answer was maintained. The answer to the questionnaire was to be accompanied by a certificate signed by each member of the firm and by those who conducted the audit—whether the internal auditors of the company or a certified public accountant. The certificate stated that the questionnaire was prepared after an audit had been prescribed by the Committee on Business Conduct and that the answers were correct in every detail.[3]

The questionnaire that was requested of these firms in the early twenties was the forerunner of the request for similar statements from listed companies. Perhaps the Committee felt that only after the brokerage houses had put their own records in order could the companies which had their stocks listed on the Exchange be expected to cooperate.

New York Stock Exchange Statement

For several years before formally audited statements were required of the companies with stocks listed on the New York Exchange, the regular statements of these companies had to be filed with the Exchange. This practice began in the early 1920's. At first these statements could be prepared by company accountants, but when the process of filing them became known to the public accounting profession, the leaders of the Exchange were cautioned against such a policy of filing uncertified statements. The only result of these protests was that the Exchange then asked for quarterly financial statements to be sent to them.[4]

Tremendous losses were suffered from the fall in stock prices in 1929. With the realization that proper accounting methods and independent audits might have prevented some of the financial

[3]Harlan Johnson, "New York Stock Exchange Questionnaire," *The Journal of Accountancy*, XLVIII (July, 1929), 19.

[4]"Financial Statements for Stock Exchange," *The Journal of Accountancy*, XLII (July, 1926), 37.

losses that took place, conferences began between the New York Stock Exchange and the American Institute of Accountants. These talks continued in 1932 and 1933 and led to two important results. First came the announcement of the Exchange on January 6, 1933, that it would require all those requesting permission to list their stock on the Exchange to have an audit certificate of an independent certified public accountant. The second step was the adoption by the Exchange (announced on October 24, 1933), of proposals regarding accounting methods which had been made by an Institute committee.[5]

Accountants were gratified by the announcement made by Richard Whitney, president of the New York Stock Exchange, explaining the requirement adopted by the Exchange that listed companies should have their annual accounts audited by independent public accountants. This statement was dated January 6, 1933, and read as follows:[6]

Since April, 1932, all corporations applying for the listing of their securities upon the New York Stock Exchange have been asked to enter in an agreement to the effect that future annual financial statements published more than three months after the date of the agreement shall be audited by independent public accountants, qualified under the laws of some state or country, and shall be accompanied by a certificate of such accountants showing the scope of the qualifications, if any, made by them in respect thereto. The committee on stock list has considered reasons advanced why this procedure should not apply in particular cases, but has made exceptions only in the case of certain railroad companies.

During this period, the New York Stock Exchange has not required that audited statements be filed with applications for listing, because it was felt that applicants who had relied upon the former practice of the exchange would have been subjected to undue delay if the committee had pursued any other course.

The New York Stock Exchange now announces that its present policy in this respect will be continued until July 1, 1933, after which date all listing applications from corporations must contain the certificate of independent public

[5]George O. May, "The Economic and Political Influences in the Development of the Accounting Profession," in *Fifty Years of Service, 1898-1948* (Trenton: New Jersey Society of Certified Public Accountants, 1948), p. 11.

[6]Editorial, "Stock Exchange Demands Audits of Listed Companies," *The Journal of Accountancy*, LV (February, 1933), 82.

accountants, qualified under the laws of some state or country, certifying to the correctness of the balance-sheet, income statement and surplus statement for the most recent fiscal year. In general, the audit or audits must cover all subsidiaries, and the scope of the audit must be not less than that indicated in a pamphlet entitled "Verification of Financial Statements" issued by the Federal Reserve Board in May, 1929, and obtainable from that board at Washington, D.C. All applications must include an agreement to the effect that future annual reports published or sent to stockholders will be similarly audited and accompanied by a similar certificate.

The Committee on Stock List may make exceptions to these requirements in unusual or extraordinary cases where the enforcement of the requirements would, in its opinion, be manifestly unwise or impracticable. The committee has concluded that for the present it will not require audited statements from railroad companies, except in the case of those railroads whose accounts have heretofore been currently audited by independent accounts.

Representative houses and banks of issue have been advised of the foregoing program and have expressed themselves as in accord with the plan outlined above, which they believe is sound and consistent with the importance of affording to the public the most complete and accurate information in regard to the financial condition of corporations whose securities are publicly dealt in.

The second phase of this program was included in the following letter from Richard Whitney, president of the New York Stock Exchange. Highly important conversations between the Committee on Stock List of that exchange and accountants had preceded its writing. The letter was addressed to every corporation whose securities were listed:[7]

The New York Stock Exchange has recently announced its intention of requiring audited statements in connection with the listing applications made after July 1, 1933. The public response to this announcement indicates clearly that independent audits are regarded by investors as a useful safeguard.

If, however, such a safeguard is to be really valuable and not illusory, it is essential that audits should be adequate in scope and that the responsibility assumed by the auditor should be defined. The exchange is desirous of securing from companies whose securities are listed, and which now employ independent auditors, information which will enable it to judge to what extent these

[7]Editorial, "Accountants and the New York Stock Exchange," *The Journal of Accountancy*, LV (April, 1933), 242.

essentials are assured by such audits. In furtherance of this end, we should be greatly obliged if you will secure from your auditors, upon the completion of the audit for the year 1932, and furnish to the committee on stock list, for its use and not for publication, a letter which will contain information on the following points:

1. Whether the scope of the audit conducted by them is as extensive as that contemplated in the Federal Reserve Bulletin, *Verification of Financial Statements*.

2. Whether all subsidiary companies controlled by your company have been audited by them. If not, it is desired that the letter should indicate the relative importance of subsidiaries not audited, as measured by the amount of assets and earnings of such companies in comparison with the total consolidated assets and earnings, and should also indicate on what evidence the auditors have relied in respect of such subsidiaries.

3. Whether all the information essential to an efficient audit has been furnished to them.

4. Whether in their opinion the form of the balance-sheet and of the income, or profit and loss, account is such as fairly to present the financial position and the results of operations.

5. Whether the accounts are in their opinion fairly determined on the basis of consistent application of the system of accounting regularly employed by the company.

6. Whether such system in this opinion conforms to accepted accounting practices, and particularly whether it is in any respect inconsistent with any of the principles set forth in the statement attached hereto.

I shall personally appreciate very much your prompt consideration of this matter and any cooperation which you may extend to the exchange in regard thereto. . . .

Probably these New York Stock Exchange rulings were among the most important forward steps in the field of auditing within recent years. No one who has been interested in the public accounting profession can fail to recognize their significance, or the added burden of responsibilities which they placed on the entire profession, especially on those practitioners engaged by companies listed on the Exchange. Upon their success in living up to the new responsibilities that were placed upon them depended in great measure the future standing of the profession.[8]

These accomplishments in the field of auditing have had a stimulating effect not only on those firms that have been the auditors for the companies listed on the Exchange but also throughout the whole public accounting profession. This was the first time that the stockholders' annual reports of the companies with stock listed on the New York Stock Exchange had to be certified by public accountants. Recognition was given the certified public accountant by the New York Stock Exchange for the first time on a national level by this requirement. The stipulation laid upon management of listed companies to obtain this certification was one of the moves most stimulating to the development of public accounting as a profession.

Requirement of Independent Audits by Chicago Stock Exchange

Following the action taken by the New York Stock Exchange in 1933, requiring that all applications for listing of corporation securities be supported by financial statements certified by independent certified public accountants, the second largest exchange took similar action. On March 21 the Chicago Stock Exchange adopted regulations from which the following excerpts are taken:

> Clear and informative financial statements, including a balance-sheet, profit and loss statement and an analysis of surplus, shall be submitted as part of each application. Such financial statements shall truly disclose the past operations and present conditions of the company and shall be certified to the Chicago Stock Exchange by duly qualified independent public accountants, whose certificate shall be set forth in full as a part of the application.[9]

Securities Act of 1933

While the United States was vacillating between neutrality and participation in World War I, a new arm of the government was created, the Federal Trade Commission. One of its functions of interest to accountants was to investigate all corporations in interstate commerce except banks and common carriers and require financial reports from them.

Legislation for the protection of investors was pushed during the

---

[8]Editorial, "Great Responsibility and Great Opportunity," *The Journal of Accountancy*, LV (February, 1933), 83.

[9]Editorial, "Chicago Stock Exchange Requires Certified Statement," *The Journal of Accountancy*, LV (May, 1933), 321.

depression of the 1930's. When the Securities Act went into effect after its passage on May 27, 1933, public confidence had been dealt a staggering blow by the disclosures of defalcations in financial circles. During the "New Economic Era" a large number of issuers of securities were found to have grossly misrepresented values and concealed essential facts and information.

Another factor which might be considered instrumental in the passage of the Securities Act of 1933 was the growth of the corporation from a firm in which the ownership was vested in a few individuals to one collecting funds from all types and classes of investors. This situation is evidenced by the fact that the number of shares listed on the New York Stock Exchange was .9 billion in 1929 as compared with 1.3 billions in 1933 and 2.1 billions in 1950.[10] Thus, the corporate form of business operation and the bigness of the corporation were having an effect on the public. The demand for the control over the security issues could be considered a reflection of the feeling on the part of the public toward bigness.

The first major legislation dealing with such matters was the Securities Act of 1933. This was defined in its preamble as:

> An act to provide full and fair disclosure of the character of securities sold in interstate and foreign commerce and through the markets, and to prevent frauds in the sale thereof, and for other purposes.[11]

Further, the statute provided for the registration of securities with the Federal Trade Commission by the filing of registration statements in regard to such securities sold in interstate markets. These statements were to reveal all pertinent financial information as required in Section 7 of the act.[12] Also, the form of the statement had to follow the form that was set forth in Schedule A of the act.[13] These statements then had to be accompanied by a certificate of an independent public accountant regarding the financial condition of the issuing company.

---

[10]*New York Stock Exchange Yearbook, 1951* (New York: Department of New York Stock Exchange), p. 30.

[11]Securities Act of 1933, An Act of May 27, 1933, 48 Stat. 74.

[12]*Ibid.*, Section 7, p. 78.

[13]*Ibid.*, Schedule A, Subsection 1, p. 88.

The passage of the Securities Act somewhat disturbed the profession both because of what the public accountants considered an unreasonable degree of liability imposed upon them, and because it was feared that the enormous power conferred originally on the Federal Trade Commission, which included the power to prescribe forms of financial statements, might not be wisely administered.[14]

Liability of Accountant under Act

Section 11a of the Securities Act of 1933 has the following statement pertaining to the liability of the accountant:

> In case any part of the registration statement, when such part became effective, contained an untrue statement of a material fact, or omitted to state a material fact required to be stated therein not misleading, any person acquiring such security . . . may sue . . . every accountant . . . who has by his consent been named as having . . . certified any part of the registration statement . . . with respect to the statement . . . which purports to have been . . . certified by him.[15]

It was clear that the accountant might be held liable under the act without being guilty of either moral culpability or recklessness, if a court held that (a) facts within his knowledge were presented in such a way as to mislead; or (b) the tests which he gave were not sufficiently extensive to justify him in forming a belief; or (c) he was not justified in forming a belief on the evidence which he examined without probing deeper. The act stresses the obligation to state every material fact necessary to make the registration statement not misleading in any way.[16]

The officers and directors of the issuing corporation who sign the registration statement, and the directors upon whom liability was imposed by the act, might be sued with respect to any part of the registration statement. The accountant, however, could be sued

---

[14]*Ibid.*, Section 11a, p. 82.

[15]Andrew Stewart, "Accountancy and Regulatory Bodies in the United States," *The Journal of Accountancy*, LXV (January, 1938), 36.

[16]George O. May, "The Position of Accountants under the Securities Act," *The Journal of Accountancy*, LVII (January, 1934), 34.

only with respect to the statement, report or valuation which purports to have been prepared or certified by him. The accountant was not responsible for any other part of the registration statement.[17]

The certified public accountant was pleased at the legal recognition, but he was worried by the burden of responsibility that was thrust upon him. The risk assumed by an accountant who signed the registration statement submitted to the Securities Commission of the Federal Trade Commission under the 1933 act seemed quite out of proportion to the possible material benefits that could be derived from the services rendered. It was not surprising that some accounting firms accepted the offers to certify registration statements only after having found protection against their liability in indemnity letters. Actually, only a minor portion of the fees collected by these firms were from the services rendered to corporations making new security issues.[18]

Administration of the Act

Accountants had another reservation, about the administration of the act. The Federal Trade Commission called for advice and assistance from the American Institute of Accountants in an earnest desire to make the new law not only protective, but also workable. A committee was appointed by the president of the Institute to cooperate with the Federal Trade Commission, and the Commission, for its part, appointed a subcommittee of advisors on its regular staff to draft rules and regulations which were to be the subject of joint consideration by the two committees before promulgation.[19]

With its direct provision that the financial statements accompanying a registration statement "shall be certified by an independent public accountant," this 1933 act had more direct effect on the public accountant than any previous piece of federal legislation in that it required certified financial data from companies in interstate commerce making original stock issues.[20]

---

[17]Spencer Gordon, "Accountants and the Securities Act," *The Journal of Accountancy*, LVI (December, 1933), 439.

[18]Robert Weidenhammer, "The Accountant and the Securities Act," *The Accounting Review*, VIII (December, 1933), 272.

[19]"Administration of Federal Securities Act," *The Journal of Accountancy*, LVI (July, 1933), 7.

[20]"American Institute of Accountants," *The Accountant*, XC (February, 1934), 197.

Securities Exchange Act of 1934

The purpose of the Securities Act of 1934 was stated in the preamble as follows:

An act to provide for the regulation of security exchanges and of over-the-counter markets operating in interstate and foreign commerce and through the mails, to prevent inequitable and unfair practices on such exchanges and markets, and for other purposes.[21]

In 1934 several amendments to the Securities Act of 1933 were passed by Congress. One of these amendments took the administration of the acts away from the Federal Trade Commission and gave it to a new Securities and Exchange Commission. Among the extensive regulatory powers conferred upon the commission were those relating to standards of accounting and financial disclosure of all corporations making public offerings of securities in interstate commerce through the mails, and of all corporations registered with national security exchanges.[22]

The 1934 amendments brought all security exchanges under the Securities and Exchange Commission. Financial statements filed with all of the Security Exchanges as well as the Securities and Exchange Commission had to be certified by a public accountant, whereas in the 1933 act the certified statements applied to the issuance of new certificates. The 1934 act then further broadened the area of auditing functions of the certified public accountant.

The new commission approached the problems at the outset by calling a group of prominent accountants into consultation and asking them to appoint a committee to cooperate in setting up reporting forms. After many months of study by this committee and the representatives of the Commission, basic forms for reporting accounting information were agreed upon. This action taken by the Securities and Exchange Commission was a source of gratification to many accountants, who considered that the Securities and Exchange Commission could render effective some standards of

---

[21]Securities Exchange Act of 1934, An Act of June 6, 1934, 48 Stat. 881.
[22]Chester T. Lane, "Cooperation with the Securities and Exchange Commission," *The New York Certified Public Accountant*, VIII (April, 1938), 6.

reporting which had long been advocated by the accounting profession itself.[23,24]

Liability of Accountants under the Securities and Exchange Act

The cause for alarm over the Securities Act of 1933 was removed, in large measure, by the 1934 amendments affording a sounder basis for recovery and reducing from ten to three years the period within which action could be taken. Under the 1934 act, the party suing had to rely on the statements issued. Only damage caused by such reliance on the statements could be recovered.[25]

Perhaps too much emphasis has been laid on the unlimited liability imposed by the acts, although unquestionably the hazards of continuing in professional practice have been greatly increased. However, if it was possible for the accountant signing a registration statement to satisfy himself that he had been dealing with a client who was both ethical and responsible, if his examination was complete and extensive so that it could be favorably compared with other standards of the profession (for example, the auditing procedures set forth in the American Institute and Federal Reserve Board's pamphlet "Verification of Financial Statements"), if he had satisfied himself by using the procedures covered in this outline, the auditor could give an unqualified opinion without fear of assuming any undue liability.[26]

Commission's Dependence on Public Accountants

The Securities and Exchange Commission has depended a great deal upon the independent public accountants and has not attempted to lay down hard and fast rules regarding the type of audit or the specific form of the financial statements required. Certain minimum requirements are specified in each form, but much is

[23]Andrew Stewart, "Accountancy and Regulatory Bodies in the United States," *The Journal of Accountancy*, LXV (January, 1938), 37.

[24]T. H. Sanders, "Recent Accounting Developments in the United States," *The Accountant*, C (April 1939), 542.

[25]Spencer Gordon, "Liability of Accountants under Securities Act of 1934," *The Journal of Accountancy*, LVIII (October, 1934), 257.

[26]Rodney F. Starky, "Practice under the Securities Act of 1933 and the Securities Exchange Act of 1934," *The Journal of Accountancy*, LVIII (December, 1934), 447.

left to the judgment of the accountant.[27] Thus the public accountant has a direct professional interest in one part of the Securities
and Exchange Commission's operations, the registration division.
The registration requirements of the Securities and Exchange Commission which cover new issues under the Securities Act as well as
securities listed on national exchanges under the Securities Exchange Act demand financial statements certified by indpendent
public accountants.[28]

These Securities Acts of 1933 and 1934 were indirectly very
beneficial for auditing standards in engagements not covered by the
laws. The auditor could point for the first time to rulings of a
government agency which set the minimum auditing and reporting
standards for markets covered by the acts. The client could no
longer dictate what the auditor should include in his certificate on
the audits performed under the Securities Acts. Nor could he go
to another auditor to get a certificate more to his liking, inasmuch
as that accountant would have to observe the same minimum
standards.

The importance of the Securities Acts in this respect cannot be
overemphasized. The laws affected not only the standards of those
firms practicing before the Securities and Exchange Commission,
but also those of the entire profession. Accountants with the forti-
tude to stand firm on their convictions were now backed by federal
law.

With so much emphasis being placed on auditing and auditing
standards and later on auditing procedures, this might be called
the period of the independent audit.

Opinions of the Commission

On April 1, 1937 the Securities and Exchange Commission made
an important announcement: the Commission intended to publish from time to time its opinions on certain accounting principles
as they might arise in specific cases.[29] These releases and the financial

---

[27]Carman G. Blough, "The Relationship of the Securities and Exchange Commission to the Accountant," *The Journal of Accountancy*, LXIII (January, 1937), 25.

[28]C. Aubrey Smith, "Accounting Practice under the Securities and Exchange Commission," *The Accounting Review*, X (December, 1935), 325.

[29]Editorial, "Accounting and the Securities and Exchange Commission," *The Journal of Accountancy*,
LXIII (May, 1937), 323.

statement forms required by the Commission have profoundly influenced the financial reporting of corporations. As cited in *The Journal of Accountancy,* one of their special reports states:

> At all times the commission had drawn heavily on the experience and counsel of . . . professional associations of accountants.
>
> . . . It has often been said that the objectives of the accounting profession and the Securities and Exchange Commission are much the same. Both believe in providing investors with an independent and objective view of the affairs of corporations in which the public invests its savings.[30]

Both the profession and the Commission have contributed to the development of generally accepted accounting procedures. The reports contain references both to the Accounting Series Releases expressing the opinions of its chief accountant, and to the Accounting Research Bulletins published by the American Institute of Accountants.

Independence of Accountants in Reporting to the Securities and Exchange Commission

A real independence for the auditor is as necessary in the fulfillment of his functions as an unofficial representative of the investing public as the recognition of privileged communications is to the fulfillment of the lawyer's function. It is the public accountant's well-developed sense of professional independence as quasi-public representative of the interest of inarticulate and scattered investors that places so much responsibility on the profession. They are, as A. C. Littleton says, professional men who already are well suited to "protect those whom they serve against spoliation."[31]

The Commission, in Accounting Series Release No. 2, indicated that the independence of an auditor might be questioned if in his capacity as accountant he had had too much to do with management decisions reflected in the accounts. This is the area in which

[30]Editorial, "Ten Years of Securities and Exchange Commission," *The Journal of Accountancy,* LXXIX (June, 1945), 427.

[31]A. C. Littleton, "Auditor Independence," *The Journal of Accountancy,* LIX (April, 1935), 290.

there appear to have been the greatest differences of opinion between the Commission and the profession.

There are two approaches to the problem of independence. One is the application of what has been called objective standards—that is, rules describing certain relations—which the accountant must avoid or be found lacking in independence. An example is the generally accepted rule prohibiting the holding by an accountant of a substantial financial interest in the company which he audits. The other approach originates in the recognition that independence is an attitude of mind and a manifestation of integrity and character. This latter attitude seems to belong to those professional accountants who have the interest of the profession as well as their own in mind.

The concern of the Securities and Exchange Commission, in giving attention to the subject of independence, is presumably about the reliability of the information made available to investors. The Commission desires reasonable assurance that auditors who certify financial statements will express honest and impartial opinions. If auditors maintain relationships which are obviously inconsistent with this purpose, the Commission has the right to consider them not independent under its rules. If no such obviously inconsistent relationship appears to exist, the Commission should have before it evidence that the opinion of the auditor is in fact not honest or impartial before it holds him not independent.[32]

The practice of accounting under the requirements of the Securities and Exchange Commission, Securities Act of 1933, and the Securities Exchange Act of 1934, has been beneficially affected not only by the recognition of the advantage to stockholders of requiring examinations by public accountants, but also by the enunciation by a government agency of certain accounting principles without attempting uniformity.[33] Thus the Securities Act of 1933 and the Securities and Exchange Act of 1934, insofar as they relate to accounting matters, are designed to obtain and present to the investor information regarding a registrant's financial condition and operations adequate for making sound judgments as to the value of its securities.

---

[32]Editorial, "Securities and Exchange Commission Release on Independence of Public Accountants," *The Journal of Accountancy*, LXXVII (March, 1944), 181.

[33]Albert J. Watson, "Practice under the Securities Act," *The Journal of Accountancy*, LIX (June, 1935), 445.

Auditing standards are often changed as a result of court decisions. Securities and Exchange Commission investigations have had an even more direct and certain effect on the responsibility of the independent auditor. Perhaps the most noted investigation was the McKesson & Robbins case.

McKesson & Robbins Case—Background

The McKesson & Robbins case brought out the necessity for additional auditing standards. It occurred at a time when the American Institute of Accountants had issued the 1936 statement on auditing procedures to be followed prior to certifying the financial condition of an enterprise. The pamphlet published by the Institute was supposed to have been the latest thing in auditing standards and procedures. Yet less than two years later the McKesson & Robbins case proved the inadequacy of the procedures prescribed in this statement.

In February, 1938, Julian Thompson, one of the lenders to McKesson & Robbins, began to notice that, although the crude drug operations showed the best profits of all the McKesson divisions, these profits were always plowed back into new purchases, no cash ever accruing to the company. The directors, who had previously voted to reduce inventories by $4 million in four months, again requested Mr. Coster, president, to make the reduction. However, by the end of the year, crude drug inventories of McKesson & Robbins had risen another $1 million. Questions addressed to Coster drew evasive answers, so Julian Thompson refused to sign $3 million worth of debentures until proof of the physical existence of the assets of the crude division was furnished. Soon thereafter the Securities and Exchange Commission investigated McKesson & Robbins.

The Securities and Exchange Commission examiners discovered that during the previous twelve years Coster and his confidants had stolen about $2.9 million of McKesson & Robbins money. They also found that the crude drug division was separated into two parts, one domestic and legitimate, and the other foreign and wholly fictitious. Costers' fraud consisted of pretending to purchase crude drugs from drug sources, paying for them with company funds, pretending to sell them to bona fide foreign dealers, and paying the company back part of its own money through dummy corporations.[34]

The auditors were furnished inventory sheets signed or initialed by company employees prior to 1935; they test-checked the items to the perpetual inventory records and checked the inventory sheets for clerical accuracy. After 1934, the auditors obtained confirmations of the quantities presumably in the hands of suppliers who were supposed to have held the goods until they were sold. In addition the auditors checked the prices shown in the inventory sheets by reference to purchase invoices covering a substantial portion of the quantities of each item. The auditor also obtained certificates signed by two or more McKesson officials covering quantity and condition of inventories stated in the balance sheet.

The auditors were furnished detailed lists of customers' accounts, verifying the total of open balances with the general ledger controls. Accounts covering the sale of crude drugs were test-checked as to charges with perpetual inventory records, copies of customers' invoices and shipping advices supporting these debits. These documents were all forgeries. Credits to customers' accounts were checked to cash records and to statements or credit advices from Manning and Company (forgeries). Coster asked that these accounts not be confirmed directly.[35]

Public Hearings before Securities and Exchange Commission

On January 5, 1939, the Securities and Exchange Commission began public hearings in New York City before Adrian C. Humphreys, Examiner, for the purpose of determining the scope, character, and detail of the audit in the preparation of the financial statements of McKesson & Robbins, Incorporated; also the extent to which generally accepted auditing procedures had been adhered to in the performance of the audit by Price, Waterhouse and Company.

By February 20, 1939, the witnesses for McKesson & Robbins and the accounting firm had been heard, and the first stage of the investigation was complete. At that time the Commission began the examination of expert witnesses for the purpose of defining gener-

[34]C. W. DeMond, *Price, Waterhouse and Company in America* (New York: The Comet Press, Inc., 1951), p. 262.
[35]*Ibid.*, p. 264.

ally accepted auditing procedures by means of a sampling of the opinions of a cross section of the public accounting profession.

The following twelve representatives of the public accounting profession were examined by William W. Werntz, chief accountant of the Commission:

Samuel J. Broad, New York
C. Oliver Wellington, New York
Victor H. Stempf, New York
William H. Bell, New York
Norman J. Lenhart, New York
John K. Matheison, Philadelphia
Henry A. Horne, New York
Charles B. Couchman, New York
Hiram T. Scovill, Urbana, Illinois
Joseph J. Klein, New York
George D. Bailey, Detroit
Charles W. Jones, Chicago

Most of the questions asked these men related to "Examination of Financial Statements by Independent Public Accountants," a bulletin reissued by the American Institute of Accountants in 1936. It was the general agreement of the witnesses that the purpose of the statement was to formulate generally accepted practice for the benefit of the profession and the public, rather than to introduce new procedures or to make improvements upon old ones.

In the opinion of these witnesses, the procedures followed by the accounting firm were such as were generally accepted at that time. It was not customary for the auditors to confirm receivables directly, nor was it necessary for them to check the physical existence of inventories. The Kingston Cotton Mills case was the only court decision at the time in which inventories had been considered, and this did not require physical test of inventories by public accountants.

In answer to one of the questions regarding the discovery of fraud, Mr. Bell answered:

An examination made in accordance with the bulletin ought, in my opinion, to disclose any fraud of relatively large amount except perhaps where there has been widespread collusion or forgery of records.[36]

[36]"Testimony of Expert Witness at Securities and Exchange Commission Hearings," *The New York Certified Public Accountant*, IX (April, 1939), 318.

Commission's Conclusion

The commission concluded that the audits performed by Price, Waterhouse and Company substantially conformed, in scope and procedure employed, to what was generally considered mandatory during the period of Girard-McKesson engagements. The accountants' failure to discover the gross overstatement of assets and of earnings was attributable to the manner in which audit work was done. In carrying out the work, the auditor failed, in the opinion of the S.E.C., to employ that degree of vigilance, inquisitiveness, and analysis of the evidence available that is necessary in a professional undertaking and that is recommended in all well-known and authoritative works on auditing. In addition, the overstatement would have been disclosed if the auditors had corroborated the company's records by actual observation and independent confirmation through procedures involving regular inspection of inventories and confirmation of accounts receivable. Though these audit procedures were considered better practice and were used by many accountants, they were not considered mandatory by the profession prior to the hearing.[37]

Letter from Price, Waterhouse and Company

On November 15, 1940, the firm of Price, Waterhouse and Company sent the following letter to William Wardell, Trustee of the estate of McKesson & Robbins, Inc.:

> You have informed us of certain losses sustained by McKesson & Robbins, Inc., Debtor, and its predecessor and subsidiary companies, in connection with the fraud and dishonesty of the former President of the Debtor, his three brothers, and certain other persons, who were engaged in a conspiracy to defraud the companies concerned. You have also publicly asserted that certain of the officers and directors of McKesson & Robbins, Inc., may have been negligent in the performance of their duties in failing to discover the existence of the fraud and hence legally responsible for losses thereby occasioned.
>
> You have discussed with us your claim that we, as independent public accountants, may also be responsible for such losses, by reason of the fact that our examinations of the books and records of the McKesson & Robbins Companies did not disclose such fraud, dishonesty and negligence.

---

[37]C. W. DeMond, *Price, Waterhouse and Company in America,* p. 274.

As we have already advised you, it is our firm conviction, formed after a review of all the facts, even in the light of hindsight, both by the Securities and Exchange Commission and by members of our firm acting independently, that our work during the entire period of our relationship with the McKesson & Robbins companies was conducted carefully and in accordance wtih generally accepted accounting practice and procedure.

Although subsequent disclosures suggest possibility that certain additional procedures might have resulted in discovery of the fraud, such procedures were neither required nor customary under generally accepted accounting practice and could not have been undertaken except upon the express instructions of those officers of the McKesson & Robbins companies who engaged our services. Those officers did not so instruct us, although they were advised by us in writing that our examinations were not sufficiently extensive to reveal either possible misappropriations of funds or manipulations of the accounts.

It is our position that in the conduct of the limited character of examination for which we were employed, and which was described by our certificates and by our reports, we were not guilty of any negligent act or omission or otherwise at fault, but that we were victims of the same fraud of which the McKesson & Robbins companies were victims. Furthermore, we believe that this position would be sustained in any litigation by which you might seek to impose liability upon us in connection with the losses in question.

As a result of the fraud practiced upon us by the former President of McKesson & Robbins, Inc., and others, we have from time to time expressed opinions to the effect that various financial statements of the McKesson & Robbins companies fairly presented their position and the result of their operations. These opinions have, with the discovery of the fraud, proved to be mistaken. Nothwithstanding the fact that the opinions were given in good faith, after the performance of the work for which we were employed with due care and in accordance with the highest professional standards, we are willing, and hereby offer, to refund to you the sum of $522,402.29, the total amount received by us from McKesson & Robbins companies in respect of all such opinions subsequent to January 1, 1933.[38]

The trustee recommended that the offer made by Price, Waterhouse and Company was fair and that it was in the best interest of McKesson & Robbins to accept the offer. Thereupon the court instructed the trustee to accept the firm's proposal.

The following words of caution were given the profession in the United States in *The Accountant,* the official public accounting publication in England:

---

[38]*Ibid.*, p. 273.

A case so extremely exceptional as McKesson & Robbins, though rightly the occasion of heartsearching, cannot properly be used as the basis of general action. Hard cases make bad law, and in the sphere of accounting and auditing it would, in our judgment, be the very extremity of folly to prescribe panic measures because a single corporation, conceived, conducted and supported in the vilest form of collusive fraud, has succeeded for a time in eluding the ordinary vigilance of an auditor. McKesson & Robbins was not one case in a hundred, or even one case in a million; it was the grand exception unlikely ever to be repeated and unworthy of being the occasion for the laying of burdens and expense on a community in which, after all, honesty is the prevailing rule.[39]

The significant development of the McKesson & Robbins case was not in this case itself nor in the fact that the American Institute of Accountants took action in revising the minimum auditing procedures. Even before the case was ruled on by the Commission, the public accounting profession, through its national organization, had taken steps to re-examine the then generally accepted auditing standards and procedures. It was through these revised standards and extension of procedures that the case affected the profession and contributed to national recognition for it and for the Institute. Then, too, members of the profession were increasingly looking toward their organization as the medium through which the profession could operate cooperatively to raise its standards and to enhance the prestige of accountancy.

The refund of accounting fees to the clients of the public accountant in this case indicated to the profession that their liability could be tremendous if found guilty by the Securities and Exchange Commission. In such a case the public accountant would show less persistence in the future in carrying out examinations of wide scope, and businessmen would be more reluctant to place limitations on the audit than in the past.

Extension of Audit Procedures

The importance of the McKesson & Robbins case, however, was such as to require a thorough re-examination of the auditing procedures previously accepted as standard.

---

[39]"Independent Audits in America," *The Accountant*, CII (April, 1940), 370.

The American Institute of Accountants announced publicly that it intended to review carefully customary auditing procedures because of the events brought to light by the Securities and Exchange Commission's investigations of this case and then to recommend what, if any, changes in procedures should be adopted by the profession. The American Institute and the New York State Society of Certified Public Accountants arranged for informal conferences with representatives of the Securities and Exchange Commission to discuss the character and scope of generally accepted auditing procedures and the possibility of improvement.[40]

The starting point for the discussion of the Committee on the Extension of Auditing Procedure was the pamphlet published in January, 1936, by the American Institute of Accountants entitled "Examination of Financial Statements," which was rather more than a restatement of the 1929 pamphlet. Neither pamphlet required circularization of receivables or observation or testing physical quantities of inventories.[41] A committee was appointed by the president of the Institute to study this document and make recommendations for changes.

The report of the committee on auditing procedures on May 9, 1939, made recommendations on the following matters:

Examination of inventories
Examination of receivables
Appointment of independent certified public accountants
Form of independent certified public accountant's report.[42]

The major point made by the committee on inventories was that the corroboration of inventory quantities either by observing the taking of inventories or by physical test should be accepted as a normal audit procedure. With regard to receivables, the committee recommended that all receivables should be verified by direct communication with the debtor, by either negative or positive methods. The committee further recommended that the auditor

[40]"The American Institute and Audit Procedure," *The Accountant*, C (February, 1939), 263.

[41]Victor H. Stempf, "The Securities and Exchange Commission and the Accountant," *The New York Certified Public Accountant*, VIII (April, 1938), 12.

[42]"Extension of Auditing Procedure," *The Accountant*, C (June, 1939), 850.

should be selected by the directors and voted on by the stockholders, and, lastly, that the scope and opinion sections should be distinct on the auditor's report.[43]

This pamphlet, which was the first of several, was entitled "Extension of Auditing Procedure." The report, in effect, became a part of the generally accepted standards of auditing procedure after issuance because it was approved by the American Institute of Accountants.[44] For example, the inclusion of verification of inventory quantities on a physical basis and the direct confirmation of receivables with the debtor have become a part of the auditor's standard procedure since 1939. This statement, and others later, have been made in an effort to raise the standards of auditing practice.

Prior to the McKesson & Robbins case, some segments of the profession had been desirous of extending the minimum auditing procedures. This case brought action by the profession on a national level.

Reporting Problems As a Result of the War

The effect of World War II on the profession can best be shown by reference to the Accounting Research Bulletins. The first of seven bulletins published as a result of the onset of the war was No. 13, issued in January, 1942. It pertained to accounting for special reserves arising out of the war, and the methods of handling possible costs or losses resulting from the war.[45]

A major problem for the accounting profession arose as a result of the War Profits Control Act.[46] Under this act, contractors and subcontractors had to maintain adequate records so that profits could be determined with reasonable certainty prior to the completion of the contract. The government had the right to renegotiate the contract and recover that portion of the price found to be excess profits.

In December, 1942, a bulletin was issued entitled "Post-War Refund of Excess Profits Tax." The Treasury Department had to

[43]*Ibid.*, p. 850.

[44]Norman J. Lenhart, "Development in Auditing Procedures Since the Extension of Such Procedures in 1939," *The New York Certified Public Accountant*, XVII (September, 1947), 565.

[45]*Accounting Research Bulletin No. 13*, January, 1942, pp. 111-118.

[46]*Accounting Research Bulletin No. 15*, September, 1942, pp. 123-134.

make a credit in each taxpayer's account for 10 percent of the excess profits paid, thus providing a fund that would be available for the conversion to peace-time production.[47]

Bulletin No. 19, "Accounting under Cost-Plus-Fixed-Fee Contracts," was issued in 1942. The procurement of war materials had greatly extended the use of this type of contract, under which the contractor was periodically reimbursed for his expenditures plus a fixed fee. This procedure resulted in many accounting problems. one of which was when to recognize profits. In such cases the committee recognized the special nature of such contracts and approved the recognition of profits upon partial fulfillment of the contract.[48]

A supplement to Bulletin 15 was issued in 1943. It was entitled "Renegotiation of War Contracts" and dealt further with the problems of financial reporting when long periods of time elapse between cancellation of a contract or completion and final settlement.[49]

In April, 1945, the sixth bulletin dealing directly with war problems was issued under the title "Accounting For Terminated War Contracts." This bulletin was concerned with the problems of fixed-price contracts that were terminated. The recognition of profits accruing as a result of cancellation of these contracts for the convenience of the government and the claims of the company against the government should be given full disclosure.[50]

The October, 1946, bulletin, No. 26, was entitled "Accounting for the Use of Special War Reserves." This concerned the handling of losses or costs resulting from the facilities acquired by the companies for war purposes.[51]

The American Institute of Accountants Committee on Auditing Procedures issued several bulletins on war problems of the auditor. The first bulletin, that of June, 1942, was a joint report of the Committee and the New York State Society. It was stated therein that the auditor's work should be spread throughout the year. Also, more emphasis should be placed on the system of internal control and the adequacy of the system.

[47]*Accounting Research Bulletin No. 17*, December, 1942, pp. 147-150.
[48]*Accounting Research Bulletin No. 19*, December, 1942, pp. 155-162.
[49]*Accounting Research Bulletin No. 21*, December, 1943, pp. 171-177.
[50]*Accounting Research Bulletin No. 25*, April, 1945, pp. 203-214.
[51]*Accounting Research Bulletin No. 26*, October, 1946, pp. 215-222.

The major accounting problem arising from World War II was the confirmation of physical inventories. Under the conditions of war, it was considered increasingly acceptable for the accountant to use sampling techniques in verifying the physical existence of inventories.

These problems, along with the reduction in the number of accountants available to practice, put a terrific strain on the profession. Many qualified accountants were called into service. Even under these adverse conditions the profession made an important contribution to the war effort by maintaining high professional standards with small numbers of qualified experienced assistants.

Drayer-Hanson Case

The war had an effect on the profession lasting for several years after the war ended. One of the cases tried was Drayer-Hanson, which arose as a result of an audit performed by Barrow, Wade, Guthrie and Company.

On April 29, 1946, the corporation filed a registration statement with the Securities and Exchange Commission, as specified under the Securities Act of 1933, covering the issuance of Class A stock to the public. The registration statement was accompanied by the financial statements of the company as a partnership and pro forma statements as a corporation. The statements were certified by Barrow, Wade, Guthrie and Company. These financial statements represented the net income to be approximately $260,000 for the partnership for a period of ten months ending April 30, 1946, and $91,000 when computed as though the partnership had been incorporated.

The following is an excerpt from the auditor's statement of opinion:

We were present only during the taking of a physical inventory, which did not include work in process, as at March 31, 1946, and satisfied ourselves as to the procedure followed in the determination of inventory quantities as to that date.

Sometime in June, 1947, the Commission was advised by Barrow, Wade, Guthrie and Company and Drayer-Hanson, Incorporated, that the April 30, 1946, balance sheet and income statement were in error. The error consisted of an overstatement of the work-in-process inventory amounting to $87,000, resulting in an overstatement of the net income and net worth as of April, 1946. The public accounting firm contributed $87,500 (the approximate amount of the inventory error) to Drayer-Hanson so the financial condition of the company would not be damaged as a result of the error.

After the evidence was presented to the Commission, they took into account the fact that the public accountants had at once revised their procedure to prevent a recurrence. Moreover, the firm's prompt reporting of the incident and the payment of an amount sufficient to cover the shortage reflected a cooperative attitude. The recommendation was not to bar Barrow, Wade, Guthrie from practice before the Commission, either temporarily or permanently because of their role in this case.[52]

The proceedings in this case emphasized the need for more intensive training on detailed audit procedures. Consequently the more progressive public accounting firms began setting up training programs for newly-hired junior accountants. The programs have not been restricted to this group, but have been extended to each classification that a firm might have in its auditing department. The purpose of these training programs is to keep the practicing auditors up to date as well as to review the basic auditing programs and standards of the firm.

PROFESSIONAL ORGANIZATION AND JURISDICTION

Public Accounting Legislation

For the protection of investors and businessmen, legislation to regulate the profession had been advocated for several years. In several states regulatory laws had been passed with the purpose of limiting the practice of public accounting to certified public accountants and registered noncertified public accountants.

In the United States recognition and regulation of the public accounting profession is a function of state government. The first C.P.A. law (New York, 1896) provided for the issuance of the

[52]"After Hearings, the S. E. C. Dismisses 11(e) Proceedings against Barrow, Wade, Guthrie and Company Growing out of Drayer-Hanson Case," *The Journal of Accountancy*, LXXXVII (June, 1949), 514.

174   *History of Public Accounting*

C.P.A. certificate by a political authority, not a professional society. There was no attempt in the early C.P.A. laws to recognize or regulate noncertified public accountants.[53]

Prior to the enactment of regulatory legislation, noncertified public accountants performed the same functions as the certified public accountant. Many C.P.A.'s believed that the public interest required regulatory legislation.

There have been four major legal decisions dealing with regulatory legislation. The first two are *The State* ex rel. *Short, Attorney General* et al. v. *Riedell* et al. in Oklahoma in October, 1924, and *Frazer* v. *Shelton* in Illinois in 1926. These two decisions held that when practice is restricted to those having a certificate from the State Board of Accountancy it "is an unwarranted regulation of private business and the right of the citizen to pursue the ordinary occupations of life."[54] In 1932 the Tennessee Supreme Court held that it was unconstitutional to prohibit all work involved in the practice of public accountancy by those not licensed as certified accountants or public accountants and cited the above mentioned Oklahoma and Illinois cases.

The fourth case on constitutionality was decided in December, 1936, by the Wisconsin Supreme Court in the case of *Wangerin* et al. v. *Wisconsin State Board of Accountancy*, et al. This decision held that the Wisconsin accountancy law was constitutional and that it did not limit the right to perform accounting work to persons certified under the act, but expressly permitted such work by others so long as their work was not held out as that of a public accountant.[55]

The court further held that all qualified persons seeking a license as certified public accountants were entitled to receive it upon compliance with the law; that the law made provision for those already engaged in the practice of accountancy who do not seek license as certified public accountants by permitting them to practice as public accountants; that by the terms of the act all those who were engaged in the profession of public accounting when the act took effect were entitled to certificates of authority; and

[53]Jay A. Phillips, "A Summary of State Legislation during the 1946-1947 Season Affecting Accountants," *The Journal of Accountancy*, LXXXIV (August, 1946), 131.

[54]Charles F. Coates, "State Legislation Relative to the Practice of Accountancy," *The Journal of Accountancy*, LXXXII (September, 1946), 224.

[55]*Ibid.*, p. 225.

finally that in making provisions for those already engaged in the practice of accountancy, the legislature followed the established precedent of the medical and other professions.

The work of a public accountant was distinguished from that of a public bookkeeper:

> A person may under contract act as bookkeeper for as many persons or firms as he chooses. It is when he holds himself out to the public as one skilled in the profession of accounting that he comes within the statute.
> . . . A bookkeeper can do anything now that he could do before the chapter was enacted, except that he cannot represent himself to be a public accountant. He can render the same service to his employers as any other accountant may render, but it cannot be put before the public as work of a public accountant or a certified public accountant.[56]

The Wisconsin act limited the practice of accountancy to holders of state-granted certified public accountant certificates and to a closed class consisting of those who were in practice at the date of enactment and presented evidence of four years' experience. They received certificates of authority to continue in practice as "public accountants." This instance was the first in which an accountancy act of the two-class restrictive type was clearly held by a state supreme court to be constitutional.[57]

By 1960, thirty-two states and Puerto Rico had regulatory type accounting laws under which no one may practice as a public accountant who is not in possession of a license or certificate issued by the respective state authorities.

The form of the restrictive legislation may vary, but it has a fundamental substance. The following is the core of a model bill:

A. Model bills
  (1) Give a legal status to accountants.
  (2) Require that certified public accountants register with a board of registered accountants.
  (3) Establish the two-class system—certified public accountants and public.

---

[56]*Ibid.*, p. 226.
[57]Editorial, "Restrictive Act Upheld," *The Journal of Accountancy*, LXIII (January, 1937), 10.

(4) Permit the registration of public accountants without examination: tax consultants, accountants, bookkeepers, or those holding themselves out as public accountants.

B. A waiver of certain requirements now existing to attain the status of C.P.A. (educational) (experience).

(1) Dying Class.

(2) Grandfather clause.[58]

Modern regulatory accountancy legislation has two principal purposes. The first is to restrict to certified and registered public accountants the right to use the title Public Accountant and express opinions regarding financial statements of clients. The second is to control the ethics of the profession by authorizing the State Board of Accountancy to promulgate rules of professional conduct.[59] In other words, the idea is, first, to close the profession to all except certified public accountants and registered non-certified public accountants, and then to control the activities of the members of the profession by the enforcement of a strict code of professional ethics.[60]

Because of assumed constitutional restrictions, such limiting legislation usually establishes a temporary class of public accountants which, during its continuance, has all the privileges of practice accorded to certified public accountants. This group, however, usually carries a special designation other than certified public accountant and, in theory, is limited to those entering at or about the date on which restrictive legislation becomes effective.[61]

The usefulness and the prestige of the profession depend on uniformly high standards of performance. Hence, it is in the public interest as well as that of the profession that such work be controlled and, so far as possible, limited to persons of established fitness. As stated by Wilcox, opinion reports should be issued only

[58]James Langan, "Problem Encountered in Sponsoring or Opposing State Regulatory Legislation," *How to Improve Accounting and Tax Service to American Business* (New York: American Institute of Accountants, 1950), p. 188.

[59]William R. Winn, "The Case against Regulatory Accountancy Legislation," *The South Carolina C.P.A.*, V (October, 1947), 4.

[60]Robert L. Miller, "Why Regulatory Accounting Legislation Is Unsuccessful," *Public Relations and Legislative Control of the Accounting Profession* (New York: American Institute of Accountants, 1951), p. 30.

[61]William D. Cranstoun, "Restrictive Legislation," *The New Jersey C.P.A. Journal*, XXII (November, 1951), 1.

by certified public accountants; this restriction of practice can be made only by legislation. However, the immediate effect of such legislation would be to deprive some persons of an existing right to make a living, thus interfering with constitutional rights.[62] An interim period is necessary during which noncertified public accountants already in practice are permitted to continue. The officially adopted policy of the American Institute of Certified Public Accountants has the long-range objective, after the transitional class of registered accountants has disappeared, of limiting practice as professional public accountants to C.P.A.'s.

The American Institute of Certified Public Accountants estimates that there are three or four noncertified public accountants for each certified one in the United States. At the inception of any regulatory law, there are many noncertified accountants who have not demonstrated their qualifications or competency. Some members of the profession argue that recognition of persons outnumbering the certified public accountants in the particular state without any test of the competency of these individuals cannot improve professional work or conduct, but serves rather to dilute the quality of professional work and conduct to the extent of the incompetency of the persons so licensed.[63]

The question then arises whether the standards of the profession should be lowered in order to help raise the noncertified public accountants to a level which some are unwilling or unable to attain through their own efforts. Some C.P.A.'s argue that the registration of noncertified accountants might well lead to a situation which would place the entire future of the profession in jeopardy. The standing of the accountancy profession depends upon the confidence of the public. The public expects the profession to set forth the facts in an unbiased manner and relies on the facts which it presents. If the profession supports permissive legislation for those accountants who are known to be less than fully qualified, public confidence in the profession will probably be shaken.[64]

The most logical method of maintaining confidence in public

---

[62]E. B. Wilcox, "The Pros and Cons of Regulatory Legislation," *The Indiana Certified Public Accountant* (May, 1948), 3.

[63]Robert L. Miller, "Why Regulatory Accounting Legislation Is Unsuccessful," *Public Relations and Legislative Control of the Accounting Profession*, p. 31.

[64]William R. Winn, "The Case against Regulatory Accountancy Legislation," *The South Carolina C.P.A.*, V (October, 1947), 7.

accountants is to have a "closed" clause in the restrictive legislation. In this way the nonregistered accountants that are licensed will become a "dying class." However in some states which have enacted regulatory laws the time for initial registering has been extended. In other states public accountants have been members of the state board, and the practice of public accountancy by other than certified public accountants and licensed public accountants has been authorized. Worst of all, some have granted C.P.A. certificates by waiver.[65] This practice, however, has not been common in the last twenty years.

The profession has not attempted to create a monopoly, or reserve the practice of public accountancy for the benefit of a special group.[66] It would be difficult to enumerate any phases of accounting practice which call for neither education, skill, nor experience.

The laws, then, do not prohibit a noncertified or nonregistered accountant from performing the many other functions of public accountants—tax returns, systems, etc.—so long as he does not hold himself out as a public accountant.[67]

In the following twenty-nine states and the District of Columbia, accounting laws of a permissive type have been passed, and anyone may practice public accounting, but only those persons who hold a C.P.A. certificate of the state concerned may use the title C.P.A.:

Alabama	Massachusetts	Oklahoma
Arkansas	Minnesota	Pennsylvania
*Connecticut	Montana	Rhode Island
Delaware	Nebraska	South Carolina
District of Columbia	Nevada	South Dakota
Hawaii	New Hampshire	*Tennessee
Idaho	New Jersey	*Utah
Indiana	*New York	Vermont
Kansas	North Dakota	*West Virginia
Maine	*Ohio	Wyoming

Source: Topical Law Reports
*These states now have regulatory laws (J.D.E.)

---

[65]Robert L. Miller, "Why Regulatory Accounting Legislation Is Unsuccessful," *Public Relations and Legislative Control of the Accounting Profession*, p. 31.

[66]William D. Cranstoun, "Restrictive Legislation," *The New Jersey C.P.A. Journal*, XXII (November, 1951), 2.

[67]E. B. Wilcox, "The Pros and Cons of Regulatory Legislation," *The Indiana Certified Public Accountant* (May, 1948), 3.

In the state of Pennsylvania the Institute of Certified Public Accountants actually sponsored a permissive accounting law which would permit public accountants to practice without any regulation.[68] In fact, all permissive accountancy laws allow this.

College Degree as Prerequisite to Taking the C.P.A. Examination

Dissatisfaction with the poor showing of many candidates on the C.P.A. examination led to the inevitable stiffening of the educational prerequisite for admission to the examination. The New York practitioners were persuaded of this formal educational need, and in 1929 a new law, paragraph 1498-a, provided that on and after January 1, 1938, every candidate for examination for the C.P.A. certificate must be a graduate of an approved course of study at the college level, following completion of an approved four-year high school course. The content of the college course was divided—half to liberal arts subjects and half to professional studies, with a minimum of 24 hours in accountancy, eight hours in commercial law, eight in finance, and six in economics.[69]

This law, the first one requiring graduation from college as a prerequisite for the C.P.A. certificate, went into effect January 1, 1938. The popularity of the idea among professional accountants indicates that it may be a precedent which will be written into laws in other states, but actually only two other states have enacted such laws. In the United States all professions depend heavily upon the universities. The apprenticeship system does not seem adequate.[70] But a slow evolutionary period will have to follow before a reasonable balance is reached between educational and apprenticeship training. Most state C.P.A. laws, however, reduce or eliminate the experience requirement if the candidate has a college degree. Thus some recognition is given even now to the value of study in colleges and universities.

The American Institute of Accountants Committee on Education, even as late as 1945, recommended that all candidates should have

[68]Jay A. Philips, "A Summary of State Legislation during the 1946-1947 Season Affecting Accountants," *The Journal of Accountancy*, LXXXIV (August, 1947), 135.

[69]Emanuel Saxe, "Rule of the Society in Accounting Education," *The New York State Society of Certified Public Accountants, Fiftieth Anniversary.*

[70]Editorial, "College Degree as C.P.A. Prerequisite," *The Journal of Accountancy*, LXIII (May, 1937), 321.

at least a high school education.[71] It seems evident, then, that the Institute's Committee is pessimistic about raising the educational requirements for candidates in the near future. The American Institute has recently appointed a committee to study this problem thoroughly. It will probably be several years, if not decades, before all of the states require college training. At the present time there are only three states which require college degrees as a prerequisite to taking the C.P.A. examination.

One National Organization

As early as 1924, soon after the injunction against the National Association of Certified Public Accountants, attempts were made to consolidate the American Society of Certified Public Accountants and the American Institute of Accountants. These attempts failed because the members did not feel that there was any necessity to form a solid front.

During 1934 and 1935 a movement was inaugurated by the New York State Society of Certified Public Accountants looking toward the substitution of a single national organization for the then existing national organizations, the American Institute and the American Society. The two organizations appointed committees to meet in an effort to reach a common basis for the merger.

After the joint committee had reached an agreement to the effect that the profession had progressed to the point of needing a single national organization, and had listed its ideas on the major needs for immediate changes in organization, a conference of state society presidents or delegates was held in Atlantic City in 1936. Following the Atlantic City meeting, the American Institute of Accountants and the American Society of Certified Public Accountants committees prepared a joint report which, it was hoped, would receive the approval of both organizations. The entire Institute committee approved it, but two members of the Society committee declined to sign the report. One of them objected because of the increase in the dues and the other one on the grounds that while "a single national organization representing the recognized profession of accountancy in the United States is highly desirable," the

---

[71]Editorial, "Educational Program of the American Institute," *The Journal of Accountancy*, LXXIX (March, 1945), 228.

joint merger report trusted too much to future possibilities rather than being based on any definite knowledge of what the profession really desired.[72]

The following are significant passages from the merger recommendation:

MERGER PLAN

It is proposed to merge the membership of the American Institute of Accountants, hereinafter called the "Institute," and the membership of the American Society of Certified Public Accountants, hereinafter called the "Society," on the following basis:

1. The Institute shall continue as the active national organization.

2. The Institute shall be furnished with a list of the members of the Society as of August 31, 1935, certified by the President and Secretary of the Society. Each of the members of the Society whose name appears on such certified list shall upon subscribing to the by-laws and rules of professional conduct of the Institute, become a member or associate of the Institute, as he elects, without examination or initiation fee.

3. Amendments to the by-laws of the Institute shall be adopted as follows:
. . .

    b. To require that after January 1, 1936, an applicant for membership or associateship in the Institute must hold a valid and unrevoked certified public accountant certificate issued by the legally constituted authorities of a State or territory of the United States of America, provided, however, that this by-law shall not in any way affect the membership rights of any present members of the Institute who do not hold such certificates.

Two matters have been considered which the undersigned believe should be left for the consideration and action of the united membership after the merger, viz.:

    a. Whether or not the name of the Institute should be changed to include in it the words "certified public" so as to read, say, American Institute of Certified Public Accountants;

---

[72]Editorial, "A Single National Organization," *The Certified Public Accountant*, XV (October, 1935), 604.

    b. Whether or not the election of members of the council of the Institute
should be on a regional basis instead of at large as at present.[73]

    The two matters last mentioned were to be submitted to the entire membership of the new organization after the merger.

    Under the arrangement made, the bylaws of the American Institute of Accountants were amended to provide for the admission of members of the Society in good standing on August 31, 1936.[74]

    These proposals were all agreed upon by the two organizations. The vote for one national organization was 1,571 in favor and 70 against out of 2,835 who were entitled to vote. All members were given an opportunity to express their opinion on the merger.[75] The will of the majority had been expressed—The American Society of Certified Public Accountants and the American Institute of Accountants became one national organization, retaining the name American Institute of Accountants.[76] The last annual meeting of the Society was held at Fort Worth, Texas, October 17 and 18, 1936, at which time the final arrangements were made to transfer the members to the Institute.[77] At the meeting of the Institute in Dallas, Texas, October 19-22, 1936, the merger of the two organizations was completed and the list of members of the Society eligible for membership was agreed upon.[78]

    The two points left to decide were the inclusion of "Certified Public" in the name of the organization and the method of nomination and election of the members of the governing body.

    None of the proposed amendments of the bylaws of the American Institute of Accountants, submitted to all members in a referendum ballot dated December 3, 1936, received an affirmative vote of a majority of the members prior to expiration of the 60-day limit for voting on February 1, 1937. The following is the result of the balloting:[79]

---

[73]*Ibid.*, p. 606.

[74]"Amalgamation in America," *The Accountant*, XCVI (March, 1937), 372.

[75]"One National Organization," *Bulletin of the American Institute of Accountants*, No. 152, December, 1936, p. 3.

[76]Harry M. Jay, "Consolidation—Now What," *The Certified Public Accountant*, XVI (October, 1936), 569.

[77]Editorial, "The Consolidation," *The Certified Public Accountant*, XVI (September, 1936), 517.

[78]Editorial, "Institute's Annual Meeting," *The Journal of Accountancy*, LXII (September, 1936), 164.

[79]Editorial, "Proposed Amendments to By-Laws," *The Certified Public Accountant*, XVII (February, 1937), 10.

Entitled to vote	3,807
Majority necessary to approve an amendment	1,904

Proposed change in name of the Institute:

In favor	1,662
Against	624

Proposed change of method of electing members of council:

First Plan—elect half of council at large and half by regions:

In favor	1,100
Against	133

Second Plan—seven members of the council elected each year
from twelve districts:

In favor	151
Against	526

Against both plans	854
In favor of both plans	130

The proposed change in the method of electing the council goes back to the early formation of the American Association in 1887. Soon after organization it became known as a "State of New York" organization. That was one of the sore spots with practitioners west of New York and the New England states. The members in the South, Middle West, and West wanted equal representation on the governing body of the new organization.

The problem of council representation arose again when the American Society of Certified Public Accountants and the American Institute of Accountants merged. The first proposal for a changed method of electing members of the council was submitted by the Institute's executive committee. This proposal provided for the election of half the members of the council by regional districts and half by the membership as a whole after consideration of the suggestions of the nominating committee. The second recommendation was for the election of seven council members each year for five years, from not less than twelve districts composed of the United States and its territories.[80] Neither of the plans received the necessary number of votes for approval.

The power of electing the council of the Institute remained

---

[80]"One National Organization," *Bulletin of American Institute of Accountants*, CLI (November, 1936), 7.

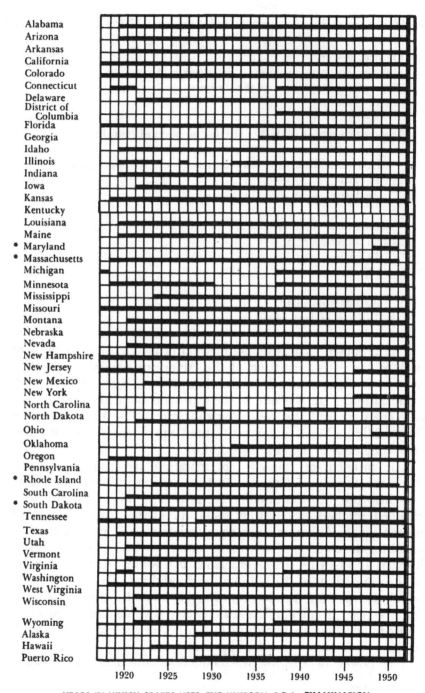

Alabama
Arizona
Arkansas
California
Colorado
Connecticut
Delaware
District of
    Columbia
Florida
Georgia
Idaho
Illinois
Indiana
Iowa
Kansas
Kentucky
Louisiana
Maine
* Maryland
* Massachusetts
Michigan
Minnesota
Mississippi
Missouri
Montana
Nebraska
Nevada
New Hampshire
New Jersey
New Mexico
New York
North Carolina
North Dakota
Ohio
Oklahoma
Oregon
Pennsylvania
* Rhode Island
South Carolina
* South Dakota
Tennessee
Texas
Utah
Vermont
Virginia
Washington
West Virginia
Wisconsin
Wyoming
Alaska
Hawaii
Puerto Rico

1920   1925   1930   1935   1940   1945   1950

YEARS IN WHICH STATES USED THE UNIFORM C.P.A. EXAMINATION

* One examination a year and that in November   Source: A.I.C.P.A.

with the entire membership of the organization. There were thirty-five men in the council, seven of them to be elected each year. No more than six members could be from one state, and by custom no more than two could be members of the same firm.

Publishing Company

In 1931 there was formed the American Institute Publishing Company, Inc., all of whose capital stock was owned by the Institute, and subsequently liquidated. Though the enterprise was undertaken in a period of economic adversity, the members of the Institute wanted to keep control of publications of their organization and to further the communications going on within the profession during a period when it was important to keep in close contact with the developments in business, as well as in the accountancy profession.

This company assumed direct publication of *The Journal of Accountancy* and the *Certified Public Accountant Bulletins.* It also published several books, among them *Evolution of Accounting to 1900,* by A. C. Littleton, *Twenty-five Years of Accounting Responsibility,* by George O. May, and *Origin and Evolution of Double-Entry Bookkeeping,* by Edward Peragallo. Of the monographs put out by the Institute's publishing company the most notable is *A Statement of Accounting Principles,* by Sanders, Hatfield and Moore (originally published by the Haskins and Sells Foundation).

Planned Examinations

In 1941 the Association of C.P.A. Examiners and the board of examiners of the American Institute of Accountants met in Detroit. They considered the topic of planned examinations for future C.P.A. candidates. The following recommendations were drawn up and approved by both committees and were included in the section entitled "Scope."

7. There should be four separate subjects in the general examination; namely, auditing, law, accounting theory, and accounting practice. Each should be the subject of at least a half-day examination.

8. The general subject examination should be extended to 2½ days consisting of three mornings of 3½ hours each and two afternoons of 4½ hours each.

9. The various topics under each subject should be included in the scope of the examinations with major topics appearing frequently, and minor topics being rotated in such a manner as to cover the entire subject in a five-year cycle.

10. Topics properly a part of one subject should not be transferred to another subject since in most states candidates are given final credit by subjects.

11. The C.P.A. examination should be set at a level to test the ability of the candidate to qualify as a senior accountant.[81]

The accompanying chart shows the years each state has used the uniform C.P.A. examination. There were ten states which stopped using the examination at one time or another. In 1937 four states, Connecticut, Michigan, Minnesota, and Wyoming, began using the examination again after the merger of the American Society and the Institute.

Practice before Treasury Department

Before May 15, 1939, applicants for enrollment to practice before the Treasury Department of the United States were required to show

that they are of good character and in good repute, possessed of the necessary qualifications to enable them to render such claimants valuable service, and otherwise competent to advise and assist such claimants in the presentation of their cases.

It was further provided by the Committee on Enrollment and Disbarment that applicants must demonstrate, by passing a prescribed examination, that they possessed

---

[81]Norman E. Webster, "Planned Examination," *The Journal of Accountancy*, LXXV (April, 1943), 348.

the educational background, technical knowledge and ability essential to the proper understanding of federal tax matters and the presentation of the same before the Treasury Department.

Attorneys at law and certified public accountants who had received their certificate by examination were exempt from this special test.

On the same date the Committee amended the regulations so as to restrict further admissions to practice to attorneys and certified public accountants. (There were further changes in 1958-59.) The amended regulation read as follows:

Qualifications for enrollment. (a) Persons of the following classes who are found, upon consideration of their applications, to possess the qualifications required by these regulations may be admitted to practice before the Treasury Department as attorneys or agents respectively:

1. Attorneys at law who have been admitted to practice before the courts of the States, territories, or District of Columbia, in which they maintain offices, and who are lawfully engaged in the active practice of their profession.

2. Certified public accountants who have duly qualified to practice as certified public accountants in their own names, under the laws and regulations of the states, territories, or District of Columbia, in which they maintain offices, and who are lawfully engaged in active practice as certified public accountants.[82]

There was another amendment to the rules providing for special enrollment for the presentation of matters before a particular bureau or division of the Treasury. This amendment would permit an applicant not an attorney nor a certified public accountant to become enrolled by satisfying the Committee on Enrollment and Disbarment, by examination and otherwise, of his qualifications to render valuable services to claimants.[83]

---

[82]Editorial, "Practice before Treasury Department," *The Journal of Accountancy*, LXVIII (July, 1939), 1.

[83]Editorial, "Practice before Treasury Department," *The Journal of Accountancy*, LXVIII (August, 1939), 79.

Lawyers and Accountants Conflict

For thirty-eight years public accountants have been engaged in federal income tax practice, as reflected in the Treasury Department's rules and regulations mentioned earlier in this chapter.

One of the primary functions of a certified public accountant in auditing corporate books is to determine the corporation's income from its books of accounts and to express an opinion on the financial statement. But when the federal tax on income was accepted as a constitutional amendment in 1913, it was necessary that this information contained in the income statement compiled by the corporation's auditor be adapted to a tax return. Before the federal income tax law became so complex, it was a simple matter for the C.P.A. to do this. As he was on the ground, and knew the situation, it was natural for a corporation to call upon its auditor to prepare its tax returns. This practice became generally accepted.

Many lawyers considered that the preparation of such returns by an accountant and the activities involved in preparing returns amounted to the practice of law. This issue was to be raised in litigation on several occasions, the most prominent of which was the Bercu case, which will be discussed later in this chapter.

In 1935, the American Bar Association first considered the question of tax practice by accountants and discussed the matter with the American Institute of Accountants' Committee on Cooperation with the Bar Association. In 1938 the Bar Association's Committee on the Unauthorized Practice of Law, under the chairmanship of Stanley H. Houck, issued a formal statement in the section devoted to accountants. The statement is as follows:

It is the view of the Committee that it is the practice of law to engage in any of the following activities:

(1) To give advice regarding the validity of tax statutes or regulations or the effect thereof in respect of matters outside of accounting procedure.

(2) To determine legal questions preliminary or prerequisite to the making of a lawful return in a lawful manner.

(3) To prepare protests against tax adjustments, deficiencies, or assessments.

(4) To represent a taxpayer at a conference with administratives in relation to matters outside of accounting procedure.

(5) To prepare claims for refunds of taxes.

(6) To prepare petitions, stipulations, or orders incident to the review of assessments by the United States Board of Tax Appeals or any like administrative tribunal.

(7) To conduct the trial of issues before the United States Board of Tax Appeals or any like administrative tribunal.[84]

Shortly after the issuance of this statement, the Unauthorized Practice of Law Committee met with representatives of the American Institute of Accountants to discuss the matter. The discussion extended over several months, but the two groups were unable, or unwilling, to reconcile their points of view.

Finally the negotiations ceased altogether, and both lawyers and certified public accountants continued to engage in tax practice. The feeling of antagonism between the two professions may have been intensified.

It had long been the conviction of eminent members of the legal profession and of the accounting profession that the two had many common interests. The close relationship between lawyers and accountants in practice, especially in dealing with problems of corporations, led to a belief that there should be a closer relationship between the organizations representing the two professions. In 1944, a step toward achievement of this objective was taken with the adoption of resolutions by the House of Delegates of the American Bar Association and the Executive Committee of the American Institute of Accountants, authorizing the establishment of a national conference of lawyers and accountants composed of five representatives from each organization. The representatives from each profession were to be appointed by the respective presidents.

The objectives of the new organization, the National Conference of Lawyers and Accountants, as expressed after this first meeting on May 6, 1944, in Philadelphia were as follows:

1. To further the development of professional standards in both professions.

2. To encourage cooperation between the two professions for the benefit of each and the public.

---

[84]David F. Maxwell and William Charles, "National Conference of Lawyers and C.P.A.'s," *The Journal of Accountancy*, LXXXI (February, 1946), 121.

3. To consider misunderstandings, involving fundamental issues, between the two professions and recommend means for disposing of them.

4. To devise ways and methods of expanding the usefulnesss to the public of both.

5. To seek means of protecting the public against practice in these respective fields by persons not qualified to serve the public.[85]

Then the committee set about the difficult task of drawing up a declaration of principles which would serve as a guide for the conduct of the two professions in their relations with the public. Certain fundamental principles were recognized immediately. The lawyers who were members of the conference conceded that where an income tax return simply required the setting down of factual data from the income statement of a corporation, a C.P.A. was qualified to prepare it. On the other hand, the accountant members of the group conceded that they were not qualified to prepare legal documents such as articles of incorporation, contracts, deeds, wills.

Then, on September 10, 1944, the following agreement was placed in writing:

Whereas, Lawyers and Certified Public Accountants are trained professional men, licensed by the several states, and required to bring to their public service qualifications both as to competency and character; and

Whereas, The American Bar Association and the American Institute of Accountants have adopted codes of ethics to assume high standards of practice in both professions;

Be it Resolved, In the opinion of the National Conference of Lawyers and Certified Public Accountants

1.That the public will be best served if tax returns are prepared either by certified public accountants or lawyers.

2. That it is in the public interest for lawyers to recommend the employment of certified public accountants and for certified accountants to recommend the employment of lawyers in any matter where the services of either would be helpful to the client; and that neither profession should assume to perform the functions of the other.

3. That certified public accountants should not prepare legal documents, such as articles of incorporation, corporate by-laws, contracts, deeds, trust agree-

ments, wills, and similar documents. Where, in connection with such documents, questions of accountancy are involved or may result, it is advisable that certified public accountants be consulted.[86]

Although the National Conference of Lawyers and Certified Public Accountants and the local organizations seemed to be making progress toward reconciling the problem, the following series of rather significant events occurred that have thrown the conflict once more into an area of combat:

1. The Bercu case
2. The Administrative Practitioners Bill
3. The introduction of HR 3214—which would make the Tax Court a court of record.

These events are discussed in detail below.

The Bercu Case

Bernard Bercu was a certified public accountant in New York City and a member of the New York State Society. In 1943 he prepared a memorandum regarding the deductibility, in the federal income tax return of the Craft Streets Products Company, Inc., for that year, of additional sales taxes for the years 1935, 1936, and 1937, the liability for which was in dispute. Settlement with the City of New York was reached in 1943, and payment of these taxes in the sum of $12,000 dollars was made in that year. Bernard Bercu expressed the opinion that under a Treasury ruling they were properly deductible in 1943, in which year the Craft Company had a substantial profit and was in the excess-profits-tax bracket. The company's accountant, who was also a lawyer, had previously advised that they could only be deducted in the earlier years to which they applied, in which years there had been losses and no benefit would be obtained. Mr. Bercu did not prepare the income tax return

---

[86]David F. Maxwell and William Charles, "The National Conference of Lawyers and Certified Public Accountants," *The Journal of Accountancy*, LXXXI (February, 1946), 124.

for the Craft Company and was not the company's regular accountant.[87]

On December 31, 1943, Mr. Bercu submitted a bill for services
rendered in the amount of $500, which was not paid, and he sued
for collection. The Municipal Court dismissed the case on motion of
the defense counsel to the effect that Bercu had been engaged in the
unlawful practice of the law. Bercu started an appeal but discontinued it because of the expense involved. The New York County
Lawyers' Association thereupon petitioned the Supreme Court of
New York to punish Bercu for contempt and to enjoin him from the
further unlawful practice of the law. At this point the New York
State Society of Certified Public Accountants joined in the defense
of Bercu and was assisted by the American Institute of Accountants.
Hearings were held on March 18, 1947. Excerpts from the decision
follow:

. . . the advice which the respondent Bercu gave in this case was based upon
a ruling of the Income Tax Unit of the Treasury Department. This is an administrative ruling which does not even bind the Department, much less the
courts. The Department promulgating these rulings is staffed principally by
accountants. Bercu undoubtedly knew this and treated the ruling as amounting
to what was considered by accountants to be sound accounting practice. . . . .

Perhaps the entire subject of unlawful practice of law in this state should
be studied by a legislative commission or by the existing Law Revision Commission. The problem, as has been indicated, is essentially one for the legislature and not for the courts.

The motion is accordingly disposed of as follows: In so far as it seeks injunc-
tive relief, it is dismissed for noncompliance with the provision of article 75-a
of the Civil Practice Act; in so far as it seeks to punish for contempt, it is denied
and the proceeding dismissed on the merits. Settle order.[88]

The case was then appealed to the New York Appellate Court of
the State of New York. In February, 1948, this court reversed the
decision handed down by the state Supreme Court. They ruled
as follows:

---

[87]Percival F. Brundage, "The Bercu Case," *The New York Certified Accountant*, XVII (May
1947), 278.

[88]"Official Decisions and Releases—Text of the Bercu Case," *The Journal of Accountancy*, LXXXIII
(April, 1947), 348.

. . . When, however, a taxpayer is confronted with a tax question so involved and difficult that it must go beyond its regular accountant and seek outside tax law advice, the consideration of convenience and economy in favor of letting its accountant handle the matter no longer apply, and consideration of public protection requires that such advice be sought from a qualified lawyer. At that point, at least, the lines must be drawn. The line does not impinge upon any of the business or public interests which respondent cites or oust the account- ant from the tax field or prejudice him in any way in the pursuit of his pro- fession or create any monopoly in the tax field in favor of the legal profession. It allows the accountant maximum freedom of action within the field which might be called "tax accounting" and is the minimum of control necessary to give the public protection when it seeks advice as to tax law.

The order appealed from should be reversed, respondent adjudged in con- tempt and fined $50 and an injunction as prayed for issued.[89]

This case was not yet settled even with this decision. It was ap- pealed to the Court of Appeals of the State of New York. That court, the highest in the state, on July 19, 1949, affirmed unanimously, without opinion, the appelllate division's decision against Mr. Bercu.[90]

This first major case on the practice of law by accountants is high- ly significant for several reasons. First, it had been generally assumed that questions such as the deductibility of proposed expenditures for tax purposes were matters of tax accounting, on which certified public accountants were fully qualified to advise. Second, the case will ultimately have an effect on the development of public ac- counting practice in the United States.

The Administrative Practitioners Bill

HR 2657, the Administrative Practitioners Bill, was sponsored by the American Bar Association and introduced in the United States House of Representatives on March 20, 1947. The bill provided (1) for a single national register of all practitioners admitted to practice before administrative agencies and (2) for the creation of a Credentials Committee to pass on all persons desiring to practice

[89]"Official Decision and Releases—Lawyers' View of Accountants' Practice before Tax Court," *The Journal of Accountancy*, LXXXV (May, 1948), 434.

[90]Editorial, "Bercu Case on Tax Practice Upheld in New York Court of Appeals," *The Journal of Accountancy*, LXXXVIII (August, 1949), 93.

before such agencies. The Committee was authorized to issue credentials to nonlawyers certified by the appropriate agency as qualified technically and legally, and found by the committee to meet ethical and moral requirements.[91]

The Administrative Procedure Act of 1946, which was endorsed by the American Bar Association, the American Institute of Accountants, and the National Conference of Accountants and Certified Public Accountants, provided that persons other than lawyers may appear before the administrative agencies. The Institute opposed HR 2657 on the grounds that the creation of the Credentials Committee would involve additional expense and might create a lawyers' monopoly of practice before administrative agencies of the federal government. Accordingly, the Institute filed with the Judiciary Committee of the House a statement opposing the provisions of the bill, and urging an amendment instead. The Institute recommended that a simple bill be devised which would admit all lawyers to practice before administrative agencies and let each individual agency set up its own rules about who else should be admitted to practice. The Institute felt that the original bill as it stood would involve considerable expense and duplication. Moreover, nonlawyers would be put into a precarious position since they could practice before administrative agencies only with the approval of the Credentials Committee, which would be composed of five members, four of them lawyers. The Institute in its statement to Congress urging amendments to the bill stated that an enormous amount of informal practice is now conducted before the agencies at which the presence of lawyers is often unnecessary and undesirable.[92]

The bill was opposed by the Treasury Department and almost all other important government agencies on the ground that it would prevent nonlawyers from appearing in proceedings in which a record is made which might be the subject of judicial review.[93]

The American Bar Association stated that the bill was designed "to protect the public with respect to practitioners before admin-

---

[91]"Practice before Government Agencies," Official Decisions and Releases, *The Journal of Accountancy,* LXXXVIII (June, 1947), 535.

[92]Louis Goldberg, "A Plague on Both Their Houses: The Accountant-Lawyer Difference over Tax Practice," *The Journal of Accountancy,* LXXXIV (September, 1947), 188.

[93]Editorial, "Lawyers Testify on Administrative Practitioners Bill," *The Journal of Accountancy,* LXXXIV (September, 1947), 178.

istrative agencies." The Bar Association reacted violently to the proposed amendment by the Institute and referred to the accountants' brief as a "masterpiece of innuendoes, specious pleas, irrelevancies, and evasions of the esssential issue."[94] Mr. John D. Randall, chairman of the Unauthorized Practice of Law Committee of the Bar Association, in his testimony before the Judiciary Committee on the bill, explained that lawyers have certain disabilities according to their code of ethics which nonlawyers who practice before agencies would not have. He also pointed out that lawyers are required to submit to intensive training, and it would not be logical to allow nonlawyers to practice on the same basis. He stated further that nonlawyers would be permitted in minor cases which did not call for judicial review and that the Credentials Committee was created only to pass on character and repute and not on other qualifications.[95]

Mathis F. Correa, counsel of the New York State Society of Certified Public Accountants, presented the Society's objections to the bill. He described it as monopolistic and discriminatory and stated further that there had been no showing of public necessity for regulation of nonlawyers before federal agencies.[96] This bill has not yet passed the House.

HR 3214—Tax Court of Appeals a Court of Record

HR 3214, which would make the Tax Court of Appeals a court of record, was passed by the House on July 7, 1947, with an amendment providing that no qualified person be denied the right to practice before the court.[97]

The Tax Court of Appeals does not consider certified public accountants as engaged in the practice of law even though they are permitted to practice before the court. The court recognizes certified public accountants as especially qualified to appear before

---

[94]Louis Goldberg, "A Plague on Both Their Houses: The Accountant-Lawyer Difference over Tax Practice," *The Journal of Accountancy*, LXXXIV (September, 1947), 195.

[95]"Testimony on Administrative Practitioners Bill," Official Decisions and Releases, *The Journal of Accountancy*, LXXXIV (September, 1947), 261.

[96]"Accounting Organizations Oppose Administrative Practitioners Bill," *The Journal of Accountancy*, LXXV (March, 1948), 187.

[97]Editorial, "House Passes Bill Making Tax Court a Court of Record," *The Journal of Accountancy*, LXXXIV (September, 1947), 180.

the court. Since they are not familiar with the rules of procedure of the court, the accountants are required to pass an examination.[98]

The main objection to the bill, as presented by nonlawyers, was that cases could not be handled as informally and expeditiously as they had been in the past. Several cases recognized the Tax Court as an administrative agency and not as a court. Members of the legal profession contended that in 1942, when the name of the United States Board of Tax Appeals was changed to the United States Tax Court, it was intended that the Court should function as a judicial body and not as an administrative agency.[99]

In spite of these and other developments that have heightened the conflict between the accountant and the lawyer, the outlook for the future is brightened considerably by the growing realization on the part of members of the bar that it is desirable and necessary to cooperate with accountants. This is evident in the 1951 statement of principles, mentioned earlier in this section, of the National Conference of Lawyers and Certified Public Accountants.

More and more, both professions are realizing that the best criterion in every case is to ascertain which profession can best serve the interests of the client, and that for most cases the best results can be reached by a proper combination of legal and accounting services. With more and more of the law schools of the country offering courses in accounting and taxation and business schools offering courses in law, there should develop a better understanding on the part of both groups.

National Firms and Their Continued Spread

The firm of Lybrand, Ross Brothers and Montgomery continued to expand throughout the United States. They opened offices in Rockford (Illinois) in 1929, in St. Louis, Atlanta, and Dallas in 1930, and in Houston and Louisville in 1931.[100]

The decade beginning with 1930 was one of remarkable growth and expansion in the practice of Arthur Andersen and Company.

---

[98]William P. Jordan, "Accountancy and Law," *The Journal of Accountancy,* LXXXIII (February, 1947), 161.

[99]"Debate on HR 3214 Making Tax Court a Court of Record," Official Decisions and Releases, *The Journal of Accountancy,* LXXXIV (September, 1947), 249.

[100]William M. Lybrand, Adam A. Ross, T. Edward Ross, and Robert H. Montgomery, *Fiftieth Anniversary* (New York: privately printed, 1948), p. 12.

The Detroit office was opened in 1930, and the Houston office in 1937. Others were opened as follows: Minneapolis in 1940; St. Louis and Seattle in 1943; Cleveland and Philadelphia in 1946; and Dallas and Omaha in 1951.

The very rapid opening of offices continued for Ernst and Ernst. During 1929, offices were opened in Portland (Maine), Birmingham (Alabama), and Reading (Pennsylvania). Then, in 1948, offices were opened in Salt Lake City; in 1949, in Portland (Oregon), Des Moines, and Colorado Springs; in 1950, in Lancaster (Pennsylvania), Decatur (Alabama), Oakland (California), and Columbus (Georgia); Lansing and Spokane in 1951, and finally in Worcester (Massachusetts) in 1952.[101]

Price, Waterhouse and Company opened offices in Houston in 1938 and in New Orleans in 1943.

This information is given again to illustrate the expansion of the public accounting profession. The growth of selected firms can give the reader an idea of the continued growth of the profession throughout the United States.

SUMMARY

The responsibility of the public accounting profession has been extended by the re-emphasis on auditing occasioned by the enactment of the securities acts and the regulations of the Securities and Exchange Commission.

The public accounting professsion, with the merger of the American Society of Certified Public Accountants and the American Institute of Accountants, seems finally to have achieved unity. Aside from the influence of the federal government in the field of auditing, the national professional organization itself has defined and elaborated the generally accepted auditing procedures. The Institute's Committee on Audit Procedures and its Committee on Accounting Procedures have become established as the authority on matters of public accounting theory and practice.

The continued acceptance of certified public accountants as qualified to practice before the Treasury reflects the recognition given the profession by the government. The friction between the

---

[101]Letter from J. A. Lindquist, Partner in Ernst and Ernst, to James D. Edwards, dated May 21, 1952.

legal profession and certified public accountants has not been allev-
iated, although the National Conference of Lawyers and Certified
Public Accountants has established rules under which accountants
continue to do tax practice.

World War II resulted in new demands on the accounting profession which it met with notable success. Cost-plus contracts, renegotiation, and contract termination all called for skilled accounting work. The profession undertook this work and also played an
important part in the formation of the policy of the government
in regard to these matters.

Many of the new responsibilities assumed by the profession have
not yet developed to a stage where their full implications can be
determined.

CHAPTER VIII

Public Accounting in the United States During the 1950's

In the decade of the 1950's the public accounting profession had to face some of the problems of a profession coming of age. The primary cause of the problems was the rapidity with which the independent certified public accountant's role in the business community was becoming recognized. His services now extended beyond the expression of the auditor's opinion on the financial condition of a business enterprise, and touched increasingly on income, estate, and gift tax matters, and the rapidly growing management services field. The extension of the functions performed by the certified public accountant brought about additional tensions with other professional groups concerned with federal income tax practices. The tax practice conflict extended from New York State, with its Bercu case, to California, with its Agron case.

The influence of the Securities and Exchange Commission since 1933 was evident in the several suspensions of public accounting firms from practicing before it. Some of these cases will be cited in this chapter. In addition, the development of some of the American Institute committees will also be discussed. These activities are in the areas of professional development, theory, auditing, and ethics.

Not all the events discussed in this chapter have had their full impact on the public accounting profession. Still in process of growth and change are professional curricula in colleges and universities, and the continuing education activities of the American Institute of Certified Public Accountants. The long-standing question of the relationship of the C.P.A. with noncertified public accountants remains unresolved, and the Accounting Principles Board's impact is yet to be felt. Since it is too early to make final evaluation of many of these events, the chapter's structure is almost entirely chronological.

Expanding Field of Auditing

The primary responsibility of an auditor (C.P.A.) today is the expression of an informed and responsible opinion on whether financial statements fairly present the financial position and operations of a business enterprise.

Until recently, independent audits were confined chiefly to non-regulated, privately owned, profit-making businesses. Within the last decade there has been rapidly growing recognition of the value of independent auditors' opinions on financial statements in many other segments of the economy.

During 1956 and 1957 the American Institute of Certified Public Accountants established or re-established four committees to deal with the expanding areas of service of the independent auditor. These committees were concerned with relations with bankers, (originally appointed in 1923) accounting for non-profit organizations, the special problems of audits of insurance companies, and (at the suggestion of a vice president of the New York Stock Exchange) relations with the Interstate Commerce Commission. These committee appointments and their subsequent activities are just a few major examples of the growing acceptance of responsibility and accountability in all segments of American society. The new American Institute committees have the challenging task of opening up large new areas where C.P.A.'s have been only occasionally used before.[1]

AFL-CIO and Independent Audits

In 1957, the AFL-CIO Council adopted a code calling for virtually all affiliated unions to have independent audits. The stipulation reads as follows:

At least annually, an audit of the accounts of each affiliate, except directly affiliated local unions of the AFL-CIO, should be made by independent certified public accountants. A summary of such audit approved by such independ-

---

[1]Editorial, "Expanding Fields for Auditing." *The Journal of Accountancy*, CIV (July, 1957), 23.

ent certified accountants should be available to the membership of the affiliate and to the public.[2]

Committee on Relations with I.C.C.

The committee on relations with the Interstate Commerce Commission was charged with studying the difference between railroad accounting and accounting for other industries. The committee members were Arthur J. Abbott, William R. Blew, Nels C. Nelson, Russell D. Tipton and Howard D. Murphy, Chairman.[3] Phillip L. West, vice president of the New York Stock Exchange, had suggested the establishment of such a committee in a letter of May 17, 1956, to Anthony F. Arperia, Interstate Commerce Commission Chairman. The function of such a committee should be:

to bring railroad accounting into agreement with generally accepted accounting principles and to have the opinions of independent public accountants included in reports to stockholders of railroad companies conform to the practice followed in all other industries.[4]

Mr. West stated that a study of railroad accounting practices was needed to determine whether they might be brought into conformity with generally accepted accounting principles so that the opinions of independent certified public accountants, as published on railroad company annual reports, can then affirm that the accounts are in accordance with those principles. At that time, the opinions of independent accountants usually state that the reports conform with Interstate Commerce Commission accounting requirements.

In the railroad industry, the system of accounts promulgated by the I.C.C. in 1907 was in many respects superior to general practice

---

[2]Official Releases, "AFL-CIO Code of Union Financial Practice—Official Text," *The Journal of Accountancy*, CIV (July, 1957), 54.

[3]News Report, "Railroad Accounting Committee," *The Journal of Accountancy*, CII (August, 1956), 7.

[4]Editorial, "Railroad Accounting," *The Journal of Accountancy*, CIII (May, 1957), 25.

at the time. Unfortunately, because of the resistance to change that is inherent in the nature of a governmental agency, the accounting regulations of the I.C.C. have not been revised sufficiently to keep pace with the subsequent improvements in accounting adopted by most unregulated businesses. The major problem lay in the fact that income and results of financial operations have not been reported on a basis comparable with the income of most other public corporations.

Report of the Committee

In its report to the Interstate Commerce Commission, the Committee listed six main variations between present railroad accounting practice and generally accepted accounting principles. In brief, the committee covered the following areas:

1. Charging of items to retained income account instead of to income.

2. Charging current income with such items as sinking funds which are not customarily charged to income.

3. Treating all income tax accruals and adjustments as railway operating expenses instead of allocating them where appropriate to other accounts or other years.

4. Failure to identify and segregate items in the acquisition adjustment account, and provide for their disposal when that should be done.

5. Failure to list long-term debt maturing within one year as a current liability.

6. Showing outstanding voucher drafts as liabilities rather than reductions in cash.[5]

Railroad Accounting Incident

On February 13, 1957, an article in *The Wall Street Journal* reported a speech given the previous day to the Milwaukee Control

---

[5]Editorial, "Railroad Accounting," *The Journal of Accountancy*, CIII (May, 1957), 26.

of the Controllers' Institute of America, entitled "Professional Accountants and Their Public Responsibility." The speech was given by Leonard Spacek, partner, Arthur Andersen & Co., Certified Public Accountants; it took sharp issue with accounting procedures for railroads prescribed by the I.C.C. Mr. Spacek alleged that divergencies between I.C.C. railroad accounting procedures and generally accepted accounting principles result in overstatement of current income and inaccurate property accounting. He further stated that these divergencies are of such magnitude that the investing public, which deserved protection from the I.C.C., was being led to a "shearing."[6]

The Journal of Accountancy reported as follows:

In his speech, Mr. Spacek criticized the use of replacement accounting for railroad-track structures. Replacement accounting requires that most of the costs of new rails and ties be charged as expense items rather than being set up as capital assets with regular depreciation charges as would be required if generally accepted accounting principles were followed. Spacek attacked the reliability of railroad current income statements which he said reflect tax refunds and tax credits from other years (adherence to generally accepted accounting principles would require that tax adjustments for prior years be made through the surplus account rather than be shown as current income). He also said that railroads do not charge current income with tax deferrals resulting from rapid amortization of emergency facilities purchased under the provisions of Section 168 of the Internal Revenue Code of 1954 (or Section 124A of the 1939 Internal Revenue Code). As a result, he alleged, current income is further overstated because of the payment of unusually low taxes due to rapid tax amortization. He also stated future income will be deflated when the taxes deferred as a result of the tax amortization are paid, because no reserve for deferred taxes is prescribed under I.C.C. accounting procedures.[7]

Furthermore, in regard to the report of the Committee on Relations with the Interstate Commerce Commission, the *Journal* stated:

Mr. Spacek charged interference with the inquiry by some railroad officials and some members of the A.I.A. Committee. He said that the railroads had told the

---

[6]Official Releases, "Railroad Accounting Procedures," *The Journal of Accountancy*, CIV (November, 1957), 69.

[7]*Ibid.*, p. 69.

A.I.A. Committee to make sure that "no recommendations are made which would affect the railroad companies adversely from the standpoint of regulation or income taxes."[8]

There was an American Institute Committee appointed to investigate the charge by Mr. Spacek, which was "not sustained."

Shortly after the speech, and after staff study of the issues, a subcommittee held informal conferences with Spacek and with representatives of the I.C.C. On March 5, 1957, the subcommittee met with Mr. Spacek. On March 7, after a transcript of his views was made available to the I.C.C., the subcommittee of the American Institute met with the chairman and staff representatives of the Commission. Public hearings on railroad accounting procedures prescribed by the I.C.C., with particular emphasis on the divergencies from generally accepted accounting principles, began on April 3, 1957, and ended on May 3, 1957.

On March 28, 1957, the report of the American Institute's Committee on Relations with the I.C.C. was forwarded to the chairman of the I.C.C.

Attached to the report, in addition to one member's dissent (principally with respect to "betterment of accounting"), was a memorandum setting forth details of each of the six variations between present railroad accounting and generally accepted principles.

The Official Release of the *Journal* stated further:

Some measure of the intensity of differences among accountants on railroad accounting procedures is evidenced by the resignation from the A.I.A. by the dissenting committee member, and in the investigating of Mr. Spacek's charges by the American Institute of Accountants, as a result of his public criticism of the A.I.A. committee on relations with the Interstate Commerce Commission.[9]

Arthur Andersen & Co. and Rule 5(e)

In reporting on the financial statements of railroads, most public accounting firms generally have certified to the effect that the state-

[8]*Ibid.*, p. 69.
[9]*Ibid.*, p. 72.

ments present fairly the financial position and results of operations in conformity with accounting principles and practices prescribed or authorized by the Interstate Commerce Commission, without making any reference in their certificates to conformity with generally accepted accounting principles.

The firm of Arthur Andersen & Co. questioned whether this form of auditor's certificate is acceptable under Rule 5 (e) of the Rules of Professional Conduct of the American Institute of Certified Public Accountants, since it does not say whether the financial statements are in conformity with generally accepted accounting principles. Rule 5 (e) reads, in part, as follows:

(5) In expressing an opinion on representations in financial statements which he has examined, a member may be guilty of an act discreditable to the profession if . . . (e) he fails to direct attention to any material departure from generally accepted accounting principles. . . .[10]

On July 1, 1959, the firm stated that in two important areas the accounting prescribed by I.C.C. and followed by the railroads fails to conform to generally accepted accounting principles:

(1) The railroads are not permitted to defer the current income-tax reductions resulting from the use of accelerated depreciation for tax purposes in excess of the depreciation recorded in the accounts. Under generally accepted accounting principles (ARB No. 44, Revised), such tax reduction should be deferred as reserves for the increased income taxes that will be payable in the future when the depreciation deductible for tax purposes falls below that recorded in the accounts.

(2) That railroads are required to use replacement accounting for track property. This requires that the replacement expenditures be charged to operating expense. This practice is not in accordance with generally accepted accounting principles, which require the capitalization of such expenditures, the concurrent retirement of property removed from service, and the depreciation of the cost of new property over its useful life.[11]

---

[10]Russell Morrison, George R. Catlett, "Inquiry Regarding Compliance of Auditors' Certificate on Financial Statements of Railroad with Rule 5(e) of the Rules of Professional Conduct of the American Institute of Certified Public Accountants," Arthur Andersen & Co., 1959, p. 1.

[11]*Ibid.*, p. 2.

Leonard Spacek wrote a letter of inquiry, dated July 29, 1958, to the members of the American Institute Committee on Professional Ethics, pointing out several auditors' certificates of railroad companies which were not qualified, while the Arthur Andersen & Co. certificate was qualified. Mr. Spacek asked whether, in the opinion of the committee, the certificates were in conflict with Rule 5 (e).

On March 23, 1959, the Chairman of the American Institute Committee on Professional Ethics, Thomas G. Higgins, wrote in his reply that the committee's opinion was that an auditors' certificate stating the financial statements of a railroad are in conformity with accounting principles and practices prescribed or authorized by the Interstate Commerce Commission is permissible under Rule 5 (e).

The Ethics Committee's two main reasons for this conclusion were briefly as follows:

(1) [There is] strong presumption that the accounting prescribed by the I.C.C. constitutes generally accepted accounting principles in that industry.

(2) The Institute's Auditing Procedure Committee has not spoken specifically on the reports on railroads or other regulated companies. In the absence of some authoritative statement by the committee prescribing the standards for what has been concluded is a special reporting problem, the validity of any reporting practice must rest on general use and general acceptance. The practice of reporting on railroad financial statements in terms of accounting principles prescribed or authorized by the Interstate Commerce Commission appears to be widespread.[12]

The inquiry of Mr. Spacek to the Ethics Committee was handled as a complaint, rather than a question regarding compliance of several railroad certificates with Rule 5 (e).

Management Services by C.P.A.'s

A significant development in the practice of the public accounting profession, which reached full bloom in the decade of the 1950's, was the growth in the management services field. This expansion

---

[12]*Ibid.*, p. 4.

of the audit function had started during World War I, when Arthur Young & Co. was asked to work for the British government on a contract with the Remington Company. Many other public accounting firms have performed some services of this type regularly for many years. Though this does not represent a new field for C.P.A.'s, the American Institute Committee on Management Services has come to feel that the activity now warrants separate recognition and treatment by the profession; accordingly, in 1957 it issued a pamphlet dealing with possible services that C.P.A.'s could perform, rather than areas that they should or should not serve.

The members of the Committee on Management Services by C.P.A.'s at the time the pamphlet was issued were:

Roger Wellington, Chairman
Carroll W. Cheek
Warren B. Cutting
Henry J. Harder
Joseph J. Hartnett
Ralph F. Lewis
Arthur F. Morton

Lawrence P. Quill
Louis A. Ryan
Willard E. Slater
Mark C. Walker
Carman G. Blough, Director of
    Research

The committee set forth the meaning of the term *management services* as follows:

1. It refers to services that are being rendered by an appreciable number of CPAs to business management in addition to the conventional or traditional services rendered by a public accountant.

2. The traditional services offered by CPAs include auditing, tax service, preparation of financial statements of various types and advice on matters of accounting principle or treatment. These are, in the broad sense, services to management but they are excluded from the extensions of service to which the term management services refers. Some services, such as accounting systems work, may be a "traditional service" for some practitioners and a "management service" for others. The line of distinction between the traditional services and management services cannot be sharply drawn, and it is not important to do so as long as there is an understanding of the general nature of the term.

3. The term "management services" includes, but is not restricted to, assisting the client in problems of managerial accounting, e.g., reporting, budget-

ing, cost accounting and cost analysis, and operating cost control. It also includes the problems of office operation and office equipment.

4. It includes services which CPAs are asked to perform primarily because
of existing confidence in individuals and firms, and because of the reputation
which the profession in general has for integrity and independence. Examples
are: acting as arbitrator, and accumulating statistics for a trade association.

5. It includes various kinds of services performed for clients in conjunction
with other expert advisers, such as attorneys, investment bankers, insurance
counselors and industrial engineers.

6. Management services by CPAs tend to originate in connection with
accounting records and problems, but often lead into areas which are related
to the problem under consideration but not directly related to accounting.
The internal use of accounting is only one part of overall business management, and well-rounded advice to management must consider all aspects of
the management task. The services, then, may often appear to be unrelated to
accounting, especially where the CPA and his staff members have had experience and training in other fields of business and management.[13]

The qualifications of the C.P.A. for management services are
based in part upon his training for professional accounting and his
analytical approach to his clients' problems, but to a larger degree
upon his experience in observing and working with the problems of
his clients. The intimate knowledge thus gained enables him to
offer useful counsel and guidance on various phases of business
problems.

In the area of qualifications and standards of performance the
Committee on Management Services emphasized that a C.P.A.
should make sure that he is clearly qualified to render a particular
service before he offers it to his clients. Further, in extending the
scope of the C.P.A.'s services to his audit clients, the accountant
will not jeopardize his position as an independent auditor. The
management services are performed on behalf of management without responsibility to third parties and therefore the concept of
independence is somewhat different than that applicable to auditing.

The areas of management services by C.P.A.'s were classified
according to major functions of business management. The examples
were intended to be illustrative, to suggest possibilities and to stim-

---

[13]Committee on Management Services by CPAs, "Management Services by CPAs," (New York:
American Institute of Certified Public Accountants, 1957), p. 6.

ulate interest, but not to constitute a check list of the areas within which any C.P.A. should be qualified to render service. The committee's list is as follows:

I General Management
   General Management: objectives and policies
   Organization
   Management controls: system of internal reporting; cost and
      expense controls; budgetary control
   Special investigations: purchase or sale of business

II Finance
   Financial structure: types and sources of capital or financing
   Financial requirements: short and long term needs
   Financial policies: retention or distribution of earnings; credit
      and collection
   Financial planning: forecasting; operating budgets; cash bud-
      gets; capital budgets
   Insurance: coverage; records
   Cost accounting: systems; standards; principles and procedures
   Pensions and profit sharing
   Government contracts: cost, renegotiation or redetermination

III Production
   Plant and equipment: economic justification; depreciation
      and obsolescence
   Production standards
   Production control: records and statistics; inventory control
   Material control

IV Sales
   Distribution and merchandizing: distribution costs and
      statistics
   Sales management: pricing; sales results

V Office Management
   Systems and records: accounting systems; forms and records;
      data processing
   Office equipment
   Office layout and space utilization
   Office organization
   Office personnel: workloads and standards; evaluation

VI   Purchasing
     Purchasing procedures
     Inventory control

VII Traffic and Transportation
     Transportation equipment: operating costs

VIII Personnel
     Recruitment or interview: office personnel
     Training: accounting personnel
     Job classification and evaluation
     Compensation: types of work; wage incentives; profit sharing
         distributions
     Employee benefit programs[14]

Bulletins on Management Services

Several studies followed the policy statement of the Committee on Management Services by C.P.A.'s. The bulletins were published by the American Institute to help professional accountants expand their management services to small business clients. The first series of studies reviewed principles and techniques in the areas of finance and control and included descriptions of actual services performed. The materials should prove extremely useful to every practitioner as well as to the business executive who may have responsibility in the areas covered. Series I of the Management Services by C.P.A.'s contained the following studies:

1. The Concept of Management Services
2. Budgeting For Profit in Small Business
3. Financing the Small Business
4. Cost Reduction and Cost Control
5. Office Management

The function already filled by certified public accountants in the area of management services will continue to grow in importance.

New National and International Offices

The national public accounting firms continued to open offices in the various business centers throughout the United States. The

---

[14]*Ibid.*, p. 10.

certified public accountant's general acceptability in the business world and his desire to render service to his clients gave great impetus to the national and international growth. The fact that American business operations spread into many international markets with large investments of capital contributed to the international recognition of the certified public accountant.

The editor of *The Journal of Accountancy* felt that the continued changes in the constitution of some well-known firms merited reporting. One of the major developments in mergers of firms came on November 21, 1950 when Peat, Marwick, Mitchell & Co. merged with Barrow, Wade, Guthrie & Co. under the former's name. In another such step, McLaren, Goode & Co. with headquarters in San Francisco, merged with the New York firm of West, Flint & Co. under the name of McLaren, Goode, West & Co.

In 1950, Arthur Young & Co. merged with two firms: Wideman, Madden, Dolan & Co., of Toledo, and Lunsford, Barnes and Company, of Kansas City.[15]

During the last decade, the firm of Arthur Andersen & Co. opened ten additional offices in the United States and sixteen outside the United States.[16] The United States offices were as follows:

Dallas, Texas	1951	Pittsburgh, Pennsylvania	1957
Omaha, Nebraska	1951	Charlotte, North Carolina	1958
Denver, Colorado	1956	New Orleans, Louisiana	1958
Cincinnati, Ohio	1957	Phoenix, Arizona	1958
Oklahoma City, Oklahoma	1957	Tulsa, Oklahoma	1958

The same firm's offices outside the United States which were opened during the 1950's were:

San Juan, Puerto Rico	1956	Brussels, Belgium	1957
London, England	1957		

---

[15]Editorial, "Many Accounting Practices Have Been Merged in Recent Months," *The Journal of Accountancy*, XCI (January, 1951), 68.

[16]Letter from Paul D. Williams, Arthur Andersen & Co., to James D. Edwards, dated January 13, 1960.

Milan, Italy	1957	Maracaibo	1958
Oslo, Norway	1957	Bogotá, Colombia	1958
Brazil:		Buenos Aires, Argentina	1959
Rio De Janeiro	1957	Montevideo, Uruguay	1959
Santos	1957	Australia:	
Sao Paulo	1957	Melbourne	1959
Venezuela:		Sydney	1959
Caracas	1958	Perth	1959

The new offices of Ernst & Ernst during the same period were as follows:[17]

Charlotte, North Carolina	May 1, 1958
Hartford, Connecticut	January 1, 1959
New Haven, Connecticut	May 1, 1958
Stamford, Connecticut	January 1, 1959
Winsted, Connecticut	May 1, 1958
Lancaster, Pennsylvania	January 1, 1950
Newark, New Jersey	May 1, 1955
Worcester, Massachusetts	May 1, 1952
Columbus, Georgia	June, 1951
Charleston, West Virginia	October 1, 1952
Athens, Alabama	July 1, 1959
Decatur, Alabama	February 1, 1950
Huntsville, Alabama	October, 1959
Mobile, Alabama	September 24, 1955
Knoxville, Tennessee	October 1, 1952
Nashville, Tennessee	August 1, 1956
Clarksville, Tennessee	August 1, 1956
Lebanon, Tennessee	August 1, 1956
McMinnville, Tennessee	August 1, 1956
Murfreesboro, Tennessee	August 1, 1956
Shelbyville, Tennessee	August 1, 1956
Sparta, Tennessee	August 1, 1956
Hopkinsville, Kentucky	August 1, 1956
Syracuse, New York	November 1, 1958
Lima, Ohio	August 1, 1958
Lansing, Michigan	September 5, 1951

---

[17]Letter from F. H. Hass, Partner in Ernst & Ernst & Ernst, to James Don Edwards, dated January 26, 1960.

Saginaw, Michigan	October 1, 1956
Port Huron, Michigan	July 1, 1958
Albuquerque, New Mexico	December 1, 1954
Terre Haute, Indiana	December 1, 1959
Evansville, Indiana	November 1, 1956
Oklahoma City, Oklahoma	December 1, 1957
Wichita, Kansas	May 1, 1956
Shreveport, Louisiana	October 1, 1958
Anchorage, Alaska	May 1, 1959
Boise, Idaho	September 28, 1954
Phoenix, Arizona	July 1, 1959
San Diego, California	July 1, 1957
San Jose, California	October 1, 1957
Sacramento, California	September 1, 1954
Oakland, California	December 1, 1950
Spokane, Washington	September 1, 1951
San Juan, Puerto Rico	May 1, 1952

At the time of the merger of Touche, Niven & Co., Allen R. Smart & Co., and George Bailey & Company on September 1, 1947, they had ten offices located in New York City, Cleveland, Pittsburgh, Detroit, Dayton, Chicago, St. Louis, Minneapolis, Los Angeles, and Seattle. The new firm name was Touche, Niven, Bailey & Smart. Their other offices were opened in the following years:[18]

Boston, Massachusetts	1948	Modesto, California	1954
Houston, Texas	1948	Rochester, New York	1954
Milwaukee, Wisconsin	1948	Honolulu, Hawaii	1954
San Francisco, California	1950	Dallas, Texas	1956
San Jose, California	1950	Washington, D. C.	1957
Kansas City, Kansas	1951	Atlanta, Georgia	1958
Grand Rapids, Michigan	1952	Philadelphia, Pennsylvania	1958
Portland, Oregon	1954	Denver, Colorado	1959

The firm of Lybrand, Ross Bros. & Montgomery opened offices in five cities during the 1950's. They were as follows:[19]

---

[18]Letter from Donald H. Cramer, Partner in Touche, Ross, Bailey & Smart, to James D. Edwards, dated January 14, 1960.

[19]Letter from Frank P. Smith, Lybrand, Ross Bros. & Montgomery, to James D. Edwards, dated January 22, 1960.

Tulsa, Oklahoma	1952	Hartford, Connecticut	1958
Birmingham, Alabama	1953	Portland, Oregon	1959
Atlanta, Georgia	1953		

The firms Touche, Niven, Bailey & Smart of the United States of America, Ross, Touche & Co. of Canada, and George A. Touche & Co. of the United Kingdom announced their affiliation in international public accounting practice and the change of their firm names to Touche, Ross, Bailey & Smart effective January 1, 1960.

Offices of the new firm Touche, Ross, Bailey & Smart outside the United States are as follows:

Canada:
  Calgary
  Edmonton
  London
  Montreal
  Ottawa
  Regina
  St. John
  Saskatoon
  Toronto
  Vancouver
  Victoria
  Winnipeg
United Kingdom:
  Birmingham
  Edinburgh
  London
Belgium:
  Brussels
France:
  Paris
West Germany:
  Berlin
  Bielefeld
  Bremen
  Cologne
  Düsseldorf
  Frankfurt

  Hamburg
  Hanover
  Lübeck
  Munich
  Nurnberg
  Stuttgart
Mexico:
  Mexico City
Barbados:
  Bridgetown
Jamaica:
  Kingston
Panama:
  Panama City
Holland:
  Almelo
  Amsterdam
  Breda
  Rotterdam
  The Hague
Switzerland:
  Geneva
Puerto Rico:
  San Juan
Australia:
  Adelaide
  Brisbane
  Canberra

Melbourne	New Zealand:
Perth	Auckland
Sydney	Christchurch
	Wellington

The flow of investment funds among the nations of the free world has been at a high level since World War II. This movement of capital has inevitably stimulated the requirement for world-wide professional accounting and auditing services, performed on the basis of reasonably uniform standards. In answer to this need the firm of Lybrand, Ross Bros. & Montgomery announced the formation of the international firm of Coopers & Lybrand on January 2, 1957. The partners in the firm of Coopers & Lybrand were to continue to practice public accounting under their own names in the United States, the United Kingdom, Canada, Mexico, and West Germany.[20]

The old American and English public accounting firm, Price, Waterhouse & Co., opened new offices during the decade of the 1950's as follows:[21]

Baltimore, Maryland	Newark, New Jersey
Battle Creek, Michigan	Peoria, Illinois
Beverly Hills, California	Phoenix, Arizona
Columbus, Ohio	Saginaw, Michigan
Denver, Colorado	Santa Ana, California
Hartford, Connecticut	Syracuse, New York
Kansas City, Missouri	Toledo, Ohio
Knoxville, Tennessee	Wheeling, West Virginia
Nashville, Tennessee	

The new offices outside the United States during the 1950's were as follows:

---

[20]Coopers & Lybrand, *L. R. B. & M. Journal*, published by Lybrand, Ross Bros. & Montgomery, XXXIX (January - March, 1958), 1.

[21]Letter from E. V. Thompson, Partner, Price, Waterhouse & Co., to James D. Edwards, dated February 8, 1960.

Canada:
  Edmonton
  Halifax
  Hamilton
Continental Europe:
  Duesseldorf, Germany
  Hamburg, Germany
  Frankfurt am Main, Germany
  Genoa, Italy
  Barcelona, Spain
  Geneva, Switzerland
Caribbean Area:
  Ciudad Trujillo, R. D.
  San Juan, P. R.
South America:
  Cordoba, Argentina
  Cochabamba, Bolivia
  Belo Horizonte, Brazil
  Porto Alegre, Brazil
  Asuncion, Paraguay
Australia, New Zealand and Fiji:
  Canberra
  Geelong, Victoria

Hobart, Tasmania
Townsville, North Queensland
Fiji, Suva
Africa and Middle East:
  South Africa
    Durban
  Central African Federation
    Salisbury, Southern Rhodesia
  North Africa
    Algiers, Algeria
  Cyprus
    Nicosia
  Ethiopia
    Addis Ababa
  Libya
    Tripoli
    Aden
Asia:
  Pakistan
    Chittagong, East Pakistan
  Thailand
    Bangkok

During the ten-year period Arthur Young & Company opened offices in the following United States cities:[22]

Detroit, Michigan	1950	Seattle, Washington	1956
Toledo, Ohio	1950	Washington, D. C.	1956
Wichita, Kansas	1950	Buffalo, New York	1957
Cleveland, Ohio	1951	St. Louis, Missouri	1957
Atlanta, Georgia	1952	Bluefield, West Virginia	1959
Denver, Colorado	1955	Newark, New Jersey	1959
Cincinnati, Ohio	1956		

The firm of Arthur Young & Co. operates under its own name, or through affiliations and associations with other firms, in foreign countries as follows:

---

[22]Letter from L. S. Dunham, Arthur Young & Company, to James D. Edwards, dated January 21, 1960.

Australia:
  Adelaide
  Brisbane
  Fremantle
  Hosham
  Melbourne
  Perth
  Sydney
Canada:
  Calgary
  Edmonton
  Hamilton
  London
  Montreal
  Regina
  Toronto
  Vancouver
  Windsor
  Winnipeg
Italy:
  Genoa
Mexico:
  Mexico City
Philippine Islands:
  Cebu
  Davao
  Manila

Union of South Africa:
  Cape Town
  Johannesburg
  Paarl
Southwest Africa:
  Windhoek
Argentina:
  Buenos Aires
  Mendoza
Brazil:
  Sao Paulo
France:
  Paris
Germany:
  Berlin
  Düsseldorf
  Frankfurt
  Hamburg
Great Britain:
  London
Chile:
  Santiago
Colombia:
  Bogotá
  Medellin
Uruguay:
  Montevideo
Venezuela:
  Caracas

Peat, Marwick, Mitchell & Co. opened United States and international offices as follows:[28]

United States:

Cincinnati, Ohio	1950	Waterbury, Connecticut	1950
Oklahoma City, Oklahoma	1950	Billings, Montana	1951
Omaha, Nebraska	1950	Buffalo, New York	1951
San Jose, California	1950	Lincoln, Nebraska	1951

[28]Letter from Carl A. Newlin, Jr., Peat, Marwick, Mitchell & Co., to James D. Edwards, dated February 18, 1960.

Shreveport, Louisiana	1951	Costa Rica:	
Columbus, Ohio	1951	San Jose	1958
Louisville, Kentucky	1954	Germany:	
Nashville, Tennessee	1954	Berlin	1958
Richmond, Virginia	1954	Düsseldorf	1958
Cedar Rapids, Iowa	1955	Frankfurt am Main	1958
Des Moines, Iowa	1955	Hamburg	1958
Albuquerque, New Mexico	1956	Munich	1958
Hilo, Hawaii	1956	Holland:	
Honolulu, Hawaii	1956	The Hague	1959
Lihue, Hawaii	1956	Italy:	
Sante Fe, New Mexico	1956	Milan	1958
Kingman, Arizona	1957	Rome	1959
Phoenix, Arizona	1957	Jamaica:	
Birmingham, Alabama	1958	Kingston	1958
Greenville, South Carolina	1958	Montego Bay	1958
Hartford, Connecticut	1958	Japan:	
St. Paul, Minnesota	1958	Tokyo	1955
San Antonio, Texas	1958	Puerto Rico:	
Fort Worth, Texas	1959	San Juan	1958
Kingston, New York	1959	Republic of Panama:	
Troy, New York	1959	Panama City	1958
International:		Switzerland:	
Bahamas:		Basle	1959
Nassau	1958	Lausanne	1959
Canada:		Zurich	1958
London, Ontario	1955	Venezuela:	
Halifax, Nova Scotia	1959	Caracas	1958
Colombia:			
Bogotá	1955		
Cali	1959		

Regulatory Legislation and the American Institute

The official policy of the American Institute in regard to "regulatory" C.P.A. legislation was adopted by the Institute's Council in April, 1956. This replaced the "neutral" position on regulatory and permissive legislation which it had held for eight years.

Under the new policy the Institute will support state laws providing for the registration of all accountants in public practice, either as C.P.A.'s or P.A.'s. After a cutoff date for registration of all individuals already in practice, the right to practice as a public accountant will be limited to those who pass the C.P.A. examination.[24]

States With Regulatory Legislation

The states with regulatory public accounting laws are the following:

STATES WITH REGULATORY PUBLIC ACCOUNTING LAWS

State	Year of Enactment of Initial Accounting Law	Year Law Became Regulatory
1. *Alaska	1923	1949
2. *Arizona	1919	1933, 1955
3. California	1901	1945
4. Colorado	1907	1937
5. Connecticut	1907	1955
6. Florida	1905	1927
7. *Georgia	1908	1943
8. Hawaii	1923	1955
9. Illinois	1903	1927, 1943
10. Iowa	1915	1929
11. Kentucky	1916	1946
12. Louisiana	1908	1924
13. Maryland	1900	1924
14. Michigan	1905	1925
15. Mississippi	1920	1930
16. Missouri	1909	1943
17. Nebraska	1909	1957
18. *New Mexico	1921	1947
19. New York	1896	1959
20. North Carolina	1913	1925
21. *Ohio	1908	1959
22. *Oregon	1913	1951
23. *Tennessee	1913	1955
24. Texas	1915	1945
25. Utah	1907	1959

---

[24]News Report, "The Top News Stories of 1956," *The Journal of Accountancy*, CI (January, 1956), 6.

State		Year of Enactment of Initial Accounting Law	Year Law Became Regulatory
26.	*Vermont	1912	1928
27.	Virginia	1910	1949
28.	Washington	1903	1959
29.	West Virginia	1911	1935
30.	Wisconsin	1913	1945
31.	Puerto Rico	1927	1957
32.	Virgin Islands	1942	1953

*Law provides for continuing registration of public accountants.
Note: All other jurisdictions have accountancy laws of the "permissive" type.[25]

Public Accountants and the Institute's Legislative Policy

In the winter of 1959 there were forty-six state legislatures in session and they were asked to consider many bills affecting public accounting statutes. Some of the legislative proposals sponsored by non-C.P.A.'s provided for the continuing and reopening of registration in states where it has already been closed under regulatory legislation.

The American Institute's position is that no one benefits if such proposals are enacted into law. The general public, business executives, and government are then confronted forever with a confusing array of accountants who, despite their different standards, are authorized to use similar titles and perform identical services. Such a neglect of the public interest cannot in the long run advance the interests of either Certified Public Accountants or noncertified public accountants.

The proposed legislation in many states deserves serious attention because it reflects a genuine fear on the part of public accountants (noncertified) that C.P.A.'s want "to put them out of business." Even if the C.P.A.'s wished to do this, constitutional guarantees would protect the noncertified public accountants' right to continue practice.

The American Institute of Certified Public Accountants has indicated its readiness to work with public accountants toward gradual

---

[25]Letter from Katherine Michaelsen, Librarian, American Institute of Certified Public Accountants, to James D. Edwards, dated February 18, 1960.

unification of the accounting profession. The institute has offered technical and educational assistance to the noncertified public accountants.

Essentially, the policy of the American Institute on achieving professional harmony would require legislation to accomplish the following:

1.   Public accountants would be entitled to register when the legislation is enacted and would be permitted to perform all the accounting activities they now perform. Their constitutional right to earn a livelihood in their chosen field would not be infringed in any way.

2.   Only public accountants and certified public accountants registered under the law would be authorized to use professional titles and to sign financial statements in a way that enhances their credibility in the eyes of "third parties."

3.   Unregistered persons would still be permitted to render general accounting and tax services under other titles.[26]

The objective of this policy is to follow the pattern established by other professions; it is reasonable to hope that *ultimately* there will be only one class of professional accountants, all members of which will have met the same standard of qualifications and will be subject to the same ethical disciplines.

As the public accounting profession expands into new areas of services, as business grows larger and more complex, demands on the profession will require higher standards. A college or university degree with a major in accounting will be expected of all who enter the field of public accounting. The public interest will demand that every practitioner demonstrate his competence by passing a searching examination, and all professional public accountants will be obliged to increase their technical knowledge and skills throughout their working life by participating in continuing education programs. In the future everyone entering the profession will want to be a C.P.A.[27]

Walter Gellhorn, Professor of Law at Columbia University, presented a salutary analysis of the whole regulatory-licensing situation

[26]Editorial, "Public Accountants and the Institute's Legislative Policy," *The Journal of Accountancy*, CVII (January, 1959), 25.

[27]*Ibid.*, p. 26.

at the American Institute's 1959 annual meeting held in San Francisco. Recognizing the genuine need for protecting the public in the regulation of the professions, he said:

> Members of your profession as well as my own came under public superintendence in one degree or another because, like physicians, they performed highly responsible services of great moment to clients themselves unable, in most instances, to judge the practitioners' qualifications; a test of those qualifications was needed in advance, lest the client be destroyed in the process of appraising his servitor.[28]

At the same time, Professor Gellhorn is inclined to think that the public is given sufficient protection if the use of titles indicating recognized competence is restricted. He deplores the tendency to "stake out a professional empire" and rather disarms criticism by saying, "my own profession, clamoring as it does about the 'unauthorized practice of law,' set a bad example."

In most of the states which have regulatory accounting legislation, the principal restriction is on the use of the titles "Certified Public Accountant," "Public Accountant," or any designation which might be confused with them. This is also the principle restriction in the form of regulatory legislation recommended by the American Institute.

The one area of professional accounting work which, in the public interest, it seems necessary to restrict to licensed practitioners is the expression of an opinion. The American Institute's regulatory bill, and legislation now in force in a number of states, allow only C.P.A.'s and registered P.A.'s to sign financial statements as accountants or auditors, or in such a way as to indicate "expert knowledge in accounting or auditing." It seems reasonable to provide that only competent and responsible practitioners may sign reports on which creditors and investors might risk their money.[29]

Professional Education for the C.P.A.

A Commission on Standards of Education and Experience was formally created in April 1952. The chairman of the Commission

---

[28]Editorial, "Legislation Regulating Professions," *The Journal of Accountancy*, CIX (January, 1960), 27.

[29]*Ibid.*, p. 28.

was Donald P. Perry and the secretary was Robert L. Kane, Jr.
The members of the commission were:

Elmer G. Beamer	Thomas W. Leland
Herman W. Bevis	J. Cyril McGarrige
Ralph L. Boyd	Hermann C. Miller
Thomas H. Carroll	Carroll V. Newson
Richard S. Claire	Donald P. Perry
Clem W. Collins	R. G. Rankin
Robert L. Dixon	Emanuel Saxe
Ira N. Frisbee	J. S. Seidman
S. Paul Garner	Frank P. Smith
Raymond E. Glos	A. Frank Stewart
Clifford V. Heimbucher	William W. Werntz
Richard L. Kozelka	Robert E. Witschey

The establishment of the commission represented the result of
at least twenty years of effort by successive committees of the American Institute, and the Association of C.P.A. Examiners, to bring
about more uniform and more realistic standards for the qualification of C.P.A.'s.

There were two events that occurred in 1959 which resulted in the
formation of the Commission: in that year the American Institute Committee on State Legislation undertook the preparation
of a revised accountancy statute, and at about the same time the
Association of C.P.A. Examiners appointed a committee to study
education and experience as a prerequisite for the C.P.A. examination. The widely differing points of view on education and experience expressed in the replies to a questionnaire completed by
a large number of practitioners resulted in the following proposal,
put forward in 1951 by Donald P. Perry at the 64th Annual Meeting of the American Institute of Accountants:

I should like to see the executive committee and the council of the Institute
take the following steps in the near future:

1. Pass and publish a resolution, subsequently to be ratified by the membership, to put the Institute on record as favoring state legislation and state
board regulation which would foster adoption of uniform examination, educa-

tional, and experience requirements for the issuance of C.P.A. certificates throughout the nation.

2. Nominate and elect a Commission or Board on Standardization of Requirements for the Certificate, to cooperate or merge with the committee of the Association of Public Accountant Examiners, for the purpose of developing and publishing what it considers currently the minimum standards of examination, education, and experience. Such a commission should include representatives from state boards, from educators in the accounting field, from the committee on education, selection of personnel and state legislation, and generally be composed of respected members who would bring to the commission the authority of broad experience and acknowledged interest in the welfare of the profession. Their responsibility should not be confined to the initial task of formulating standards for the present, but should be a continuing endeavor to see that standards are changed with changing conditions and raised as rapidly as will meet with general acceptance.[30]

On April 18, 1952, J. William Hope, the Institute President, with the approval of the Executive Committee, created a small committee to undertake study of the proposal set forth in this statement. The President of the Institute and its Executive and Educational Directors met with S. Paul Garner, Raymond E. Glos, J. Cyril McGarrige, and Donald P. Perry, to consider the desirability and feasibility of creating an independent commission to formulate standards of education and experience for C.P.A.'s. This group unanimously approved the creation of a commission.

The commission was primarily concerned with the *preparation* of individuals for public accounting practice as C.P.A.'s and with the *process* by which the individual is designated as a C.P.A. The commission recognized that there was little collegiate training in accounting in 1900 when there were approximately 250 C.P.A.'s, whereas programs in accounting are now available throughout the United States and there are about 65,000 C.P.A.'s. The American Institute's uniform C.P.A. examination, which was introduced in 1917, is now used by all states in the United States. Thus, ideally, all C.P.A.'s should have free entry into all political jurisdictions. The first important step toward uniformity—the C.P.A. examination—has been taken. The next step, agreement upon educa-

[30]Donald P. Perry, "Public Relations and Legislative Control of the Accounting Profession," *Proceedings of the 64th Annual Meeting of the American Institute of Accountants*, p. 40.

tion and experience requirements, is necessary before the C.P.A. can have common national significance.

Professional training for public accounting, then, is primarily dependent upon the formal educational process which facilitates a logical division of preparation for professional practice into two distinct parts, one to be accomplished through the formal educational process prior to admission, and the other through practical experience acquired subsequent to admission.[31]

Regarding the location of the academic facilities for training, it was stated that:

. . . the Commission does not believe that the existing undergraduate programs in schools of business administration generally provide the depth and comprehensiveness of training for a definite professional objective which are needed by the C. P. A.'s of today and tomorrow.[32]

The Commission reported that adequate preparation for the profession of public accountancy requires additional academic training beyond present four-year undergraduate programs. The additional educational program should be within the framework of collegiate schools of business administration. Moreover, the Commission recommended that the C.P.A. examination be given at the conclusion of the training acquired through the recommended formal educational process: practical experience should follow rather than precede admission to the examination of the accountant who has completed the recommended educational program. Accreditation of the programs, once established by the colleges and universities, would facilitate the maintenance of a desirable level of quality in the training provided by educational institutions.[33]

The Commission clearly stated that the accountant who has been designated as a C.P.A. on the basis of prescribed educational preparation and satisfactory completion of the examination is not an experienced practitioner. Regarding experience for C.P.A.'s the Commission stated:

---

[31] *Standards of Education and Experience for Certified Public Accountants,* Published for the Commission by the Bureau of Business Research, University of Michigan, (Ann Arbor: Bureau of Business Research, 1956), p. 119.

[32] *Ibid.,* p. 120.

[33] *Ibid.,* p. 123.

. . . practical experience advances the competence of a public accountant throughout his career, that some experience in practice has generally been relied upon in the past, and is being presently relied upon as a prerequisite for issuance of the C.P.A. certificate.[34]

The recommendations of the Commission may be summarized under five heads:

1. College graduation from a fifth-year professional accounting program, with classroom material drawn from public practice, with faculties experienced in public accounting.

2. A qualifying examination that would test the college graduate's intellectual capacity, his academic achievements, and his aptitude for public accounting.

3. A professional academic program which would require a fifth year, which would require the undergraduate curricula to adjust to the principal areas in accounting and the specialized subject matter would be at the postgraduate level in preparation for public accounting.

4. An internship program of approximately three months should be included in the professional program, to be completed generally during the period of December - April.

5. The Uniform C.P.A. Examination—as a long-range goal to become effective as professional academic programs are developed, that individuals be admitted to the C.P.A. examination upon completion of the recommended educational preparation and, if successful, that they be awarded the certificate.[35]

There were several Commission members who dissented as regards the meaning of the C.P.A. or the experience requirements. The dissenters were J. Cyril McGarrige, Emanuel Saxe, J. S. Seidman, and Richard S. Claire.

Council of American Institute Position on Standards

On April 22, 1959, the Council of the American Institute of Certified Public Accountants adopted the recommendations of the Special Committee that was appointed to study the Report of the Commission on Standards of Education and Experience for C.P.A.'s.

[34]*Ibid.*, p. 124.
[35]*Ibid.*, p. 136.

The committee members were George D. Bailey, Chairman, William H. Holm, C. A. Moyer, John C. Potter, and T. Dwight Williams.

The Council of the American Institute then took the educational lead by adopting the following resolutions:

1. That the long-established meaning of the C.P.A. certificate as evidence of demonstrated competence for the practice of public accounting be continued.

2. That a baccalaureate degree be made a requirement for the C.P.A. certificate; that proportions among accounting, business, and nonbusiness subjects in the curriculum recommended by the American Accounting Association Standards Rating Committee are desirable; that those earning baccalaureate degrees with considerable variations from these proportions be considered deficient and be required to present evidence of equivalent study.

3. That studies be made by the Institute's committee on personnel testing to ascertain whether the tests in the Institute's testing program can be adopted or new tests developed to serve the purpose of screening applicants for postgraduate accounting educational programs.

4. That postgraduate education for careers in public accounting is desirable and that as soon as it is feasible postgraduate study devoted principally to accounting and business administration become a requirement for the C.P.A. certificate.

5. That an advisory committee of the Institute preferably acting with representatives from the American Accounting Association, and the American Association of Collegiate Schools of Business, be formed to assist interested schools in planning and revising courses and programs for educating accountants and to assist existing accrediting agencies and associations in evaluating accounting courses and curriculums.

6. That student internship as a part of the student's educational program be optional; that plans be developed by a committee of the Institute so that internships may be well organized and carefully supervised by schools and practitioners when used; and that serious effort be made toward answering the problem of whether internships should be provided to all who qualify.

7. That an experience requirement be retained; that with the baccalaureate degree with or supplemented by evidence of study of accounting to the extent set forth in Resolution 2 the experience be not less than two years; that as education is extended beyond the baccalaureate degree the length of experience should be reduced but should not be less than one year; that the experience should be under the guidance of a C.P.A. and some of the experience should be in the area of third-party reliance; and that a committee of the Institute should prepare a statement as to what, in general, should be an acceptable type of experience for the C.P.A. certificate.

8. That the existing purposes and level of the C.P.A. examination be continued.

9. That a candidate be permitted to take the examination when he feels adequately prepared but not before he has successfully completed the recommended educational requirements.

10. That the C.P.A. certificate be awarded after the candidate has successfully completed the examination and experience requirements.

11. That individual practitioners and the American Institute of Certified Public Accountants co-operate in rendering assistance to colleges by such means as providing instructional materials drawn from business; providing student scholarships and internships; providing funds for advanced study by faculty members; endowing professorial chairs; providing faculty residencies; and by serving as or providing special lecturers.

12. That state society committees on state legislation should consider local conditions in timing any recommendation for necessary legislation.

13. That the American Institute of Certified Public Accountants take the leadership in causing periodic reviews of education and experience for C.P.A.'s.[36]

Graduate School in Accounting

The first graduate school of public accounting specifically designed for liberal arts graduates wishing to obtain C.P.A. certificates was established in 1955 by Rutgers University as a division of its School of Business Administration. The school awards the Master's degree in business administration. As a part of the academic program, between the fall and spring semesters, degree candidates are required to work for a firm of C.P.A.'s.

Serving as the advisory committee which assisted in the founding of the Graduate School in Public Accounting were:

Samuel J. Broad	Maurice E. Peloubet
Albert J. Eckhardt	Abraham H. Puden
Arthur B. Foye	Ira A. Schur
Thomas G. Higgins	Charles H. Towns
Charles A. Hoyler	George Wagner
John B. Inglis	Roger Wellington
Alvin R. Jennings	William W. Werntz[37]

[36]Official Releases, "Education and Experience for C.P.A.'s," *The Journal of Accountancy*, CVIII (June, 1959), 71.

[37]News Report, "Education—Graduate School in Accounting," *The Journal of Accountancy*, CI (May, 1956), 14.

The first graduate was John D. Campbell of Belleville, Pennsylvania. The director and originator of the program was Professor William J. vonMinden.

Continuing Education and the Institute

At the Spring 1958 meeting the American Institute's Council approved an appropriation of $50,000 to engage a competent administrator and inaugurate an expanded program to provide both staff training for junior accountants in smaller firms, and more professional courses for practicing Certified Public Accountants. The plan was not only to develop additional materials for continuing education, but also to recruit and train teachers for the program, and to assist state C.P.A. societies and chapters which sponsor the course.

About the continuing education program the editor of *The Journal* stated:

> It is perhaps not too much to hope that availability of post-collegiate courses for staff and partners of accounting firms will have a beneficial effect on accounting education generally, by encouraging emphasis on cultural subjects and significant theory in the college curriculum. This should be a desirable trend even if the Collegiate accounting course is expanded to five years or more.[38]

Shortly after the American Institute's Council approved the continuing education program, Lewis W. Matusiak was appointed director.

The American Institute of C.P.A.'s initiated its formal continuing program in 1956. It was a modest beginning, which required only a part-time director. Under his auspices three continuing education courses were set up: Report Writing, Tax Practice Administration, and Accountants' Legal Responsibility.

In December, 1958, the continuing education function was transferred from the Education Division of the Institute and made the sole activity of the newly created Division of Professional Development. At present, in addition to a director, the division employs

[38]Editorial, "More Professional Education," *The Journal of Accountancy*, CVI (June, 1958), 26.

three technical assistants and an administrative assistant. Two new seminars have been developed, Accountants' Fees and Budgeting.

The cumulative enrollments in continuing education courses through 1959 are:

1,823 in Report Writing
  631 in Tax Practice Administration
  476 in Accountants' Legal Responsibility
1,608 in the seminar on Accountants' Fees
   34 in the seminar on Budgeting for Profit in Small Business.

The total enrollment in continuing education courses is 4,572. It is apparent that the Institute's Professional Development Program has made tremendous strides in a few short years.

Public Accountants' Cooperation With Bankers

One of the developments of the 1950's was the steady growth in cooperation between the public accounting profession and the banking fraternity.

Evidence of this cordial spirit was shown in a report issued by Arthur L. Nash of the Robert Morris Associates' committee on cooperation with public accountants. Mr. Nash discussed two important projects in his report resulting from the joint efforts of R.M.A. and the American Institute, first the survey of audit reports submitted to banks by Certified Public Accountants, and second the memorandum for the auditor's file. The results of these surveys disclosed that there is still considerable room for improvement in audit reports.

Mr. Nash candidly told the R.M.A. annual meeting that the survey also revealed another fact:

The difficulties of analyzing the individual reports from banks and the variations in the replies to a standard set of questions give rise to the thought we bankers need to expand our knowledge of auditing standards, methods and procedures if we are to properly evaluate and criticize an audit report.[39]

---

[39]Editorial, "Cooperation Between Accountants and Bankers," *The Journal of Accountancy*, XCVIII (November, 1954), 597.

State Society of C.P.A.'s Anniversary

The two oldest state societies of C.P.A.'s both celebrated their sixtieth anniversary in 1957. The New York Society, founded in January, 1897, has grown from 16 charter members to more than 8,500. The Pennsylvania Institute, only two months younger, started with 15 members, and now has approximately 2,800.[40]

Women C.P.A.'s

According to the American Women's Society of C.P.A.'s there have been 900 C.P.A. certificates issued to women since the first received her certificate in 1899.[41]

The Journal's Birthday

The first 50 years were eventful to *The Journal.* One of the pioneer C.P.A.'s, Colonel Robert H. Montgomery, once said that fifty years ago the public accountant was "little known, little recognized, little wanted. . . ." By contrast, the editors of *The Journal* state:

Today far from being little known, recognized, or wanted, the C.P.A. is summoned to high posts of duty in the government; he is welcomed in the board rooms of multi-billion dollar corporations; he is selected for top executive positions in industry; he is consulted by Congress on matters of grave import to the nation; and he is a subject of growing interest to the press.[42]

The editors go on to say that the profession had to produce technical and ethical standards to justify continued acceptance of its work. It has had to establish organizations for the orderly determination of professional policies.

The circulation of *The Journal,* which had begun in November, 1905, reached approximately 90,000 per month by the end of 1959.

---

[40]News Report, "State Society Anniversaries," *The Journal of Accountancy,* CIII (March, 1957), 14.

[41]News Report, "Survey of Women C.P.A.s," *The Journal of Accountancy,* CIII (February, 1957), 16.

[42]Editorial, "*The Journal of Accountancy* Has A Birthday," *The Journal of Accountancy,* XCIX (November, 1955), 29.

American Institute's Committee on Research Program

The Special Committee on Research was appointed in December, 1957 to consider a new approach and the means whereby accounting research should be undertaken, accounting principles should be promulgated, and adherence to them should be secured. This action followed an address by Alvin R. Jennings, a past president of the Institute, at the annual meeting in New Orleans in October, 1957, in which he cited some of the difficulties of the present approach to the problem (that is, the issuance of accounting and auditing research bulletins on specific subjects) and suggested possible alternatives.

Members of the Special Committee were Weldon Powell, Chairman, Andrew Barr, Carman G. Blough, Dudley E. Browne, Arthur M. Cannon, Paul Grady, R. K. Mautz, Leonard Spacek, and William W. Werntz.

The report of the committee was made in September, 1958. The report of the special committee on research programs of the American Institute is of vital importance not only to the public accounting profession, but to all others who are concerned with accounting: business management, government agencies, investors, banks and other financial organizations, industry associations, security analysts, economists, teachers, controllers and internal auditors—everyone who has to do with financial reporting in a free society. The report suggests procedures which would assure even more extensive discussion and interchange of opinion before statements are given final approval. The American Institute accounting procedures committee had always attempted to consult interested groups before the issuance of its bulletins.

The well-received Accounting Research Bulletins issued by the American Institute's committee have gone a long way toward achieving their major objective: "to narrow the areas of difference in corporate financial statements."[43]

Of primary importance in the report on research programs is the stipulation that the new Accounting Principles Board and accounting research staff be under specific instructions to study the problems of financial accounting at four levels: postulates, princi-

---

[43]Editorial, "Accounting Research and Accounting Principles," *The Journal of Accountancy*, CVI (December, 1958), 28.

ples, rules or guides for the application of principles, and research.

Of almost equal significance is the plan for greater participation by individuals and groups both inside and outside the public accounting profession. Instead of sending out accounting research bulletins for comment in semi-final form after extensive discussion by the accounting procedures committee, there would ordinarily be published an initial research study, issued on the authority of the Director of Accounting Research and those associated with him in the specific project. While in preparation, these studies would be publicly announced, and comments requested. After publication, there would be further opportunity for suggestions and criticisms before the Accounting Research Board decided whether or not to embody the conclusion of the research study in a Statement of Generally Accepted Accounting Principles.[44]

The Special Committee on Research in its report specifically proposed that the organization carry out the accounting research program and related activities of the Institute; it would consist of an Accounting Principles Board and an accounting research staff.

The Board, consisting of eighteen members of the Institute, would be designated a senior technical committee, the sole group in the Institute having authority to make pronouncements on accounting principles. The accounting research staff would comprise, on a permanent basis, a director of accounting research, three to five senior members, two to three junior members, and necessary secretarial assistance. The Director of Accounting Research would be the administrative head of the accounting research staff, and would have active charge and direction of the carrying out of the accounting research program. The following statement sets forth the purpose of the research:

The principal products of the proposed accounting research program and related activities would be a series of accounting research studies and a series of statements on generally accepted accounting principles.[45]

The research studies and statements on generally accepted accounting principles, issued under the name of the Director of Re-

[44]*Ibid.*, p. 28.
[45]Official Releases, "Report to Council of the Special Committee on Research Program," *The Journal of Accountancy*, CVI (December, 1958), 64.

search, would be tentative and not authoritative. They would furnish a vehicle for the exposition of matters for consideration and experimentation.

The statements of generally accepted accounting principles would be issued by the Board of Accounting Principles and *would be expected to be regarded as an authoritative written expression of what constitutes generally accepted accounting principles.* They ordinarily would be based on accounting research studies previously prepared by the accounting research staff. As in the case of the accounting research studies, the statements on generally accepted accounting would be framed in relation to basic postulates and broad principles.

The various statements on generally accepted accounting principles would not be presented to the Council or to the membership of the American Institute of Certified Public Accountants for approval, except in rare cases. The Accounting Principles Board would replace the committees on accounting procedures and on terminology.

The Council of the American Institute of Certified Public Accountants, in 1959, unanimously approved the proposal of the Special Committee on Research programs. At the same meeting of the Council a new Institute staff division was created under a director of accounting research.

An Accounting Research Board was elected by the Institute Council, and it superseded the Accounting Procedures Committee at the end of the 1959 fiscal year. The following members of the Institute were elected to serve on the Accounting Principles Board:

Weldon Powell, Chairman	Joel Hunter, Jr.
Arthur M. Cannon	Ira A. Schur
Ira N. Frisbee	John H. Zebley
Thomas G. Higgins	Carman G. Blough
Alvin R. Jennings	Gordon S. Battelle
C. A. Moyer	John B. Inglis
Henry T. Chamberlain	John W. McEachren
James L. Dohr	Herbert D. Miller
James E. Hammond	Hassel Tippit[46]

---

[46]News Report, "Professional-New Institute Research Program," *The Journal of Accountancy*, CVIII (June, 1959), 7.

One of the first objectives of the program will be a study of the basic postulates underlying accounting principles. It is also expected that the Accounting Principles Board will concern itself with the preparation of a statement of broad principles of accounting to serve as the foundation for future pronouncements on accounting matters.

Prior to the publishing of any pronouncement a public announcement will be made and interested parties will be invited to submit their views. After the study has been issued it will be reviewed by the Accounting Principles Board and may be accepted as a basis for the issuance of a statement of generally accepted principles, rejected with a public explanation, or laid aside for future action.

Prior to the formation of the accounting research program there were criticisms of the accounting profession and the accounting function. Most of the criticisms were concerned with alleged inconsistencies or inadequacies in financial statements prepared for investors and the public. There are also disturbing signs that business executives find accounting in some respects unsatisfactory for their own decision-making purposes. Some examples of these criticisms will illustrate their general tenor. The financial vice president of the Chesapeake and Ohio Railroad asserts:

> The role of accounting in management affairs has been grossly misrepresented, grossly overstated. . . . Offhand, I cannot think of a single major decision that we make by going back to these books to find out what the dividend rate of the Chesapeake and Ohio Railroad should be. We did not rush to these books to decide whether or not we should spend $125 million this year on capital improvements . . . as a practical matter, there is no single set of statements, there is no single accounting system that anybody can devise, whether it be the Institute of Accountants or the Interstate Commerce Commission, which would serve all of the purposes of investors, all of the purposes of management, and all of the purposes of government agencies, regardless of whether they be for taxing purposes or for purposes of regulation. Vast additional data of all sorts is necessary to keep these folks properly informed.[47]

This view was echoed in a statement filed with the Interstate Commerce Commission December 30, 1957, on behalf of the Association of American Railroads:

---

[47]Editorial, "New Solution for New Problems," *The Journal of Accountancy*, CV (March, 1958), 29.

Once again the theoretical pedantic approach . . . illustrates why business management is so little influenced by bookkeeping practices.[48]

As for labor's attitude, a criticism from AFL-CIO president George Meaney, on December 29, 1958, stated:

Currently published profit pictures are understated by as much as $3 billion to $4 billion, because the methods of computing depreciation allowances have been changed.[49]

Accounting Research, Terminology, and Auditing Bulletins

Some significant contributions to the field of accounting literature and accounting theory in the series of *Accounting Research Bulletins, Accounting Terminology Bulletins,* and *Statements on Auditing procedures* issued by the American Institute during the 1950's are listed herewith.

ACCOUNTING RESEARCH BULLETINS
ISSUED FROM 1950 to 1959

No.	Date Issued	Title
40	September, 1950	Business Combinations

This statement differentiates between two types of corporate combinations. Where there is a continuance of the former ownership it is known as a "pooling of interests." Where there is a new ownership it is known as a "purchase." The accounting treatment applicable to each type of combination is considered.

| 41 | July, 1951 | Presentation of Income and Earned Surplus (Supplement to Bulletin No. 35) |

This bulletin confirms bulletin No. 35 which states that those extraordinary items which are

---

[48]*Ibid.,* p. 29.
[49]*Ibid.,* p. 30.

omitted from the determination of net income should be shown in the surplus statement and not as deductions from or additions to net income in the income statement. The committee holds to this opinion even though Rule 5-03, Regulation S-X of the Securities and Exchange Commission makes provision for the addition or deduction of such extraordinary items at the bottom of the income statements filed with the commission. The committee is of the final opinion that either the form recommended in Bulletin No. 35 or the form required by Regulation S-X is acceptable.

13   July, 1951   Limitation of Scope of Special War Reserves
(Addendum)

This addendum merely voided the use of Bulletins No. 13 and 26, dealing with the establishment and use of special war reserves.

26   July, 1951   Limitation of Scope of Special War Reserves
(Addendum)

This addendum was the same as the addendum on Bulletin Number 13. It merely stated that Bulletins No. 13 and 26, dealing with the establishment and use of special war reserves were no longer applicable.

42   November, 1952   Emergency Facilities—Depreciation, Amortization, and Income Taxes

11   November, 1952   Accounting for Stock Dividends and Stock Split-
(Revised)   Ups

37   January, 1953   Accounting for Compensation Involved in Stock
(Revised)   Option and Stock Purchase Plans

This bulletin considers the problems of compensation raised by stock option plans and stock purchase plans. Accordingly it considers, rights involving compensation, rights not involving compensation, time measurement of compensation, manner of measurements, and disclosure.

43   1953   Restatement and Revision of Accounting Research
                                    Bulletins

                                    This is a very important bulletin in that it can-
                                    celled and replaced the first 42 bulletins issued
                                    from 1939 to 1953, with the exception of the eight
                                    terminology bulletins. Its purposes were to elimin-
                                    ate what was no longer applicable, to condense
                                    and clarify what continued to be of value, to re-
                                    vise where changed views required revision, and
                                    to arrange the retained subject matter by subjects
                                    rather than in the order of issuance. This examin-
                                    ation of previous pronouncements and the changes
                                    brought forth by such scrutiny were a definite
                                    contribution to the entire profession of account-
                                    ing by the committee on accounting procedure.

44   October, 1954   Declining-balance Depreciation

                                    The declining-balance method is "systematic and
                                    rational." It is a very satisfactory allocation of
                                    cost where the expected productivity or revenue-
                                    earning power of an asset is relatively greater
                                    during its early life, or where maintenance charges
                                    tend to increase during the later years.

45   October, 1955   Long-term Construction-type Contracts

                                    This bulletin covers accounting problems re-
                                    lated to construction type contracts of a long-
                                    term nature. Two generally accepted methods, the
                                    percentage-of-completion method and the com-
                                    pleted-contract method, are discussed.

46   February, 1956   Discontinuance of Dating Earned Surplus

                                    The dating of earned surplus following a quasi-
                                    reorganization would rarely be of significance
                                    after a period of ten years. Under exceptional cir-
                                    cumstances, the discontinuance of the dating of
                                    earned surplus could be justified in a lesser period.

47   September, 1956   Accounting for Costs of Pension Plans

This bulletin considers the treatment of costs of pension plans in the accounts and reports of companies having such plans.

48   January, 1957   Business Combinations (Supersedes Chapter 7 (c) of Accounting Research Bulletin No. 43)

This bulletin considers the accounting problems involved in two types of business combinations namely, a purchase and a pooling of interests.

49   April, 1958   Earnings per share

This bulletin deals with several problems arising in the computation and presentation of data on earnings per share. It covers single-year computations, comparative statistics, earnings of senior securities, and dividends per share.

44   July, 1958   Declining-balance Depreciation
(Revised)   (Supersedes Bulletin No. 44)

This bulletin supplements Bulletin No. 44. It considers the problem where the declining-balance method is adopted for income-tax purposes but other appropriate methods are used for financial accounting purposes. It is recommended that recognition should be given to deferred income taxes if the amounts thereof are material, except in those cases where charges for deferred taxes are not allowed for rate-making purposes, in which case accounting recognition need not be given to deferred taxes if it can reasonably be expected that future rate determinations will cover the expected increased future income taxes, resulting from the earlier deduction of declining-balance depreciation for income tax purposes only.

50   October, 1958   Contingencies

                    This bulletin treats the disclosure of those con-
                    tingencies in which the outcome is not sufficiently
                    predictable to permit recording in the accounts,
                    but in which there is a reasonable possibility of an
                    outcome which might materially affect financial
                    position or results of operations.

51   August, 1959   Consolidated Financial Statements

                    This bulletin concerns problems dealing with
                    consolidated statements. It has sections dealing
                    with the purpose of consolidated statements, con-
                    solidation policy, general consolidation procedure,
                    elimination of intercompany investments, minor-
                    ity interests, income taxes, stock dividends of sub-
                    sidiaries, unconsolidated subsidiaries in consoli-
                    dated statements, combined statements, and par-
                    ent-company statements.

ACCOUNTING TERMINOLOGY BULLETINS
ISSUED 1950 to 1959

No.   Date Issued   Title

1   1953   Review and Resumé

                    The purpose of this bulletin was to initiate a
                    series of bulletins on terminology separate from
                    those on accounting procedure. Therefore, this
                    bulletin was primarily a review of the past ac-
                    counting Research Bulletins dealing with termin-
                    ology (Nos. 7, 9, 12, 16, 20, 22, 34, and 39). This
                    bulletin includes the terms value, assets, liabilities,
                    accounting, accountancy, accounting principles and
                    postulates, balance sheet, income, income state-
                    ment, profit, profit and loss statement, undistri-
                    buted profits, earned surplus, audit, opinion re-
                    port or certificate, depreciation, depreciation ac-
                    counting, reserve, and surplus.

2   March, 1955   Proceeds, Revenue, Income, Profit, and Earnings

The use of the terms revenue, income, profit,
and earnings (and sometimes proceeds) generally
relate to an increase (or decrease) in the owners'
equity which results from operations of the enterprise. To promote uniformity of usage these
terms were defined and recommendations for their
use were made in this bulletin.

3   August, 1956   Book Value

This bulletin discusses the meaning of "book
value" and when such term should and should not
be employed.

4   July, 1957   Cost, Expense and Loss

Definitions of and recommendations for the use
of the terms cost, expense, and loss are included
in this bulletin.

STATEMENTS ON AUDITING PROCEDURE
ISSUED 1950 to 1959

No.	Date Issued	Title
	1951	Codification of Statements on Auditing Procedure

This pamphlet was prepared by the committee
on auditing procedure to consolidate the more
valuable and useful information of Statements on
Auditing Procedure, Nos. 1 to 24 inclusive. It
eliminated obsolete material and condensed, clarified, and revised the materials currently applicable. In so doing, this statement represented a
definite contribution to the entire profession of
accounting, particularly to the auditing area.

25	October, 1954	Events Subsequent to the Date of Financial Statements

This statement considers and clarifies the extent of the auditor's responsibility in connection with the disclosure of events occurring or becoming known subsequent to the date of the statements on which he is expressing an opinion.

26	April, 1956	Reporting on Use of "Other Procedures"

This statement arrived at the conclusion that in all cases in which the extended auditing procedures are not carried out with respect to inventories or receivables and they are a material factor, the independent CPA should not only disclose, in the general scope section of his report the omission of the procedures, regardless of whether or not they are practicable and reasonable, but also should state that he has satisfied himself by means of other auditing procedures if an unqualified opinion is to be expressed.

27	July, 1957	Long-Form Reports

This statement deals with the long-form report and the application of standards of reporting.

28	October, 1957	Special Reports

This statement covers the applicability of generally accepted auditing standards to "special reports." This includes wording of the opinion. These special reports may cover reports on financial statements of companies not using the accrual basis of accounting, the reports on financial statements of some nonprofit organizations, and reports prepared for limited purposes.

29	October, 1958	Scope of the Independent Auditor's Review of Internal Control

This statement considers the scope of the independent auditor's review of internal control as it pertains to his examination leading to an expression of an opinion on the fairness of the financial statements.

Cooperation with Noncertified Public Accountants

The 1959 decision of the Institute Council to cooperate with non-certified public accountants was consistent in following its legislative policy on restrictive legislation. The council voted to:

foster closer relations between C.P.A.'s and non-C.P.A.'s licensed to practice accounting with the purpose of improving educational, technical, and ethical standards.[50]

Sixth International Congress

The Council of the Sixth International Congress on Accounting, 1952, appointed Sir Harold Gibson Howitt president of the Congress to be held in London in June, 1952. Sir Harold is a past president of the Institute of Chartered Accountants in England and Wales. Charles Percival Barrowcliff, Past President of the Society of Incorporated Accountants and Auditors, was appointed vice president of the Congress.[51] The concept of one world is not likely to become a reality for some time, but progress toward one accounting world was greatly accelerated by this meeting. There were about 80 American C.P.A.'s in attendance at the Sixth International Congress. In total, there were 2,500 representatives of 36 nations in attendance.

George O. May, C.P.A., of the United States, was the only attender who had also been an active participant in the First International Congress held at St. Louis, Missouri, in 1904.

The following general observation was made on the technical portions of the program:

[It is a] basis for the free exchange of technical information and professional opinion, and possibly for future efforts to cooperate in the development of common terminology and technical standards.[52]

---

[50]News Report, "Professional-New Institute Research Program," *The Journal of Accountancy*, CVIII (June, 1959), 7.

[51]Current Notes-Briefs, "The Council," *The Journal of Accountancy*, XCII (December, 1951), 656.

[52]Editorial, "Toward One Accounting World," *The Journal of Accountancy*, XCIV (August, 1952), 163.

The following subjects were the topics covered at the Congress:

(1) Fluctuating Price Levels in Relation to Accounts (eight papers by representatives of seven countries, including Professor Willard J. Graham and Edward
B. Wilcox of the U.S.A.); (2) Accounting Requirements for Issues of Capital
(five papers by representatives of six countries); (3) The Accountant in Industry (seven papers by representatives of six countries, including Clinton W.
Bennett of the U.S.A.); (4) The Accountant in Practice and in Public Service
(eight papers by representatives of seven countries, including T. Coleman An-
drews of the U.S.A.); (5) The Incidence of Taxation (seven papers by representatives of seven countries, including Thomas J. Green of the U.S.A.).[53]

Seventh International Congress

More than 2,800 accountants gathered in Amsterdam on September 9 to 13, 1957, for the Seventh International Congress of Accountants. Accountants from 40 nations were present, representing
104 accounting organizations; the United States representation was
about 110. Ninety members of the American Institute of Certified
Public Accountants were listed, ten representatives of the National
Association of Accountants, five of the Institute of Internal Accountants, five of the Institute of Internal Auditors, four of the
American Accounting Association, and two of the Controllers Institute of America.

American participation in the technical programs included the
papers and discussions listed herewith.

Arthur B. Foye and Carman G. Blough, on the topic "Principles for the Accountants Profession."

Donald J. Bevis, was the author of a paper "Verification of the Existence of
Assets."

Joseph Peleg, contributed a paper on "Budgeting and Corresponding Modern-
ization of Accounting."

---

[53]John L. Carey, "One Man's View of the Sixth International Congress on Accounting," *The Journal
of Accountancy*, XCIV (September, 1952), 307.

W. A. Walker, authored a paper on "The Internal Auditor." W. R. Davis was a member of a discussion panel on the same topic.

G. L. Phillippe, was the author of a paper entitled "Business Organization and the Public Accountant."

Ira N. Frisbee, was author of a paper and member of the panel on the subject "Ascertainment of Profit in Business." Weldon Powell was a member of the same panel.[54]

Committee on Long-Range Objectives of the Profession

The purpose of this committee was to clarify the objectives and goals of the American Institute, and recommend to the council resolutions which would make such goals part of the official policy of the organization.

The members of the Committee on Long-Range Objectives during the 1958-59 year were J. S. Seidman, Chairman, Herman W. Bevis, Robert M. Trueblood and Robert E. Witschey. As a result of their work, the Institute's Council adopted two basic objectives in 1958:

1. It is an objective of the Institute to serve as the national organization of certified public accountants in and out of public practice, and to develop and maintain the form of organization best adapted to the needs of all its members.

2. It is an objective of the Institute to encourage co-operation and consultation among national organizations of accountants to the end that the entire accounting function may make its greatest contribution to the public welfare.[55]

American Institute's Films

The first of the Institute's films, entitled "Accounting—The Language of Business," was produced in 1953. Primarily intended

[54]John L. Carey, "The Seventh International Accounting Congress," *The Journal of Accountancy*, CIV (December, 1957), 35.

[55]Official Releases, "Long-Range Objectives of the Accounting Profession," *The Journal of Accountancy*, CVII (May, 1959), 71.

to attract young people to the profession, it has been shown 21,845 times before audiences of students, service clubs and business groups totaling well over one million people. The movie has been telecast 501 times to an estimated audience of 39 million, has won two awards for excellence among educational films, and has received enthusiastic praise from teachers who have used it in their classes.

A second film, "Helping the Taxpayer," which dramatizes the work of the certified public accountant in tax practice, has been shown 11,384 times to live audiences in less than five years, and 1,101 times on television to audiences of over 100 million. "CPA," the third Institute release, came out late in 1959. The film presents the highlights of one day in the life of a certified public accountant.[56]

C.P.A. Examiners Meet

The first meeting of the Association of Certified Public Accountant Examiners was held in Atlantic City on October 20-22, 1908, attended by the representatives of ten state boards. The Association's golden anniversary meeting convened in New Orleans on October 26 and 27, 1957. The Uniform C.P.A. Examination is now used by all 50 states.[57]

Institute Membership

The American Institute of Certified Public Accountants passed another milestone in 1959 when the total membership reached 35,000. The upward trend is even more significant in that in 1946 the number reached 10,000. In 1950 there were 15,000, in 1952, 20,000, and in 1955, 25,000.[58]

A.I.A. Becomes A.I.C.P.A.

The first proposal to change the name of the American Institute of Accountants to the American Institute of Certified Public Accountants was rejected by the membership.

---

[56]Editorial, "Dramatizing the Accounting Profession," *The Journal of Accountancy*, CVIII (December, 1959), 29.

[57]News Report, "C.P.A. Examiners Meet," *The Journal of Accountancy*, CIV (December, 1957), 10.

[58]Editorial, "Thirty Thousand Members," *The Journal of Accountancy*, CIV (October, 1957), 30.

In order to pass, the measure had to be voted upon by one third of the membership and receive the approval of two thirds of those voting. The proposal was voted down in a count of 10,363 in favor to 6,992 against.[59]

However, on the second time of proposing, the name change was approved by the membership, to become effective June 1, 1957. The final vote was 18,885 in favor to 1,042 opposed. Membership at the time of the mailing of the ballots was 27,850. Reconsideration of the name change had been urged by the Public Relations Committee of the Institute, and approved by the Council and by members present at the annual meeting in September of 1956. Reasons given for the change stressed the desirability of keeping the title Certified Public Accountant before the public and making clear in the name that the Institute is the national professional organization of C.P.A.'s.[60]

What's in a Name?

On June 3, 1957, the American Institute of Accountants became the American Institute of Certified Public Accountants. This alteration was made in recognition of a change which had taken place years before in the qualification for new members.

When the original organization was incorporated as the American Association of Public Accountants on August 13, 1887, there were no C.P.A.'s. The title did not come into use until the New York State accountancy law was enacted in 1896.

The name was changed to the American Institute of Accountants in 1917. At that time the organization had a membership of 1,150, and there were scarcely more than 3,000 C.P.A.'s in the United States. One of the first major activities of the Institute was the development of the examination, originally for admission to membership, which, over the years, has been adopted by state boards of accountancy as the Uniform C.P.A. Examination. Successful completion of the examination is now the prerequisite to becoming a C.P.A. in every state.

Since the American Society of C.P.A.'s was merged with the

---

[59]News Report, "AIA Name Change Rejected," *The Journal of Accountancy*, CI (February, 1956), 7.

[60]News Report, "Name Change Approved," *The Journal of Accountancy*, CIII (January, 1957), 8.

American Institute in 1936, the Institute has been the only national
organization of C.P.A.'s.[61]

Institute and Accounting Opinions

In 1959 three public utility companies obtained a series of temporary injunctions against the Institute of C.P.A.'s, preventing
issuance of a letter interpreting Accounting Research Bulletin
Number 44 (Revised) which had been approved by eighteen of
the twenty-one members of the accounting procedures committee.
The utility companies which had obtained the injunction contended that removal from the equity sections of their balance
sheets of amounts which had been shown there as "earned income
taxes" would limit their short-term borrowing power and otherwise interfere with their activities. The utilities said in their complaint that because of the "prestige and authority of the Institute
and the Committee," issuance of the letter would:

cause substantial numbers of accountants, financial institutions, investment banking concerns, rating services, financial analysts and governmental agencies to
question the continued inclusion of credits for deferred taxes in the earned surplus accounts of plaintiffs. . . .[62]

The plaintiffs claimed that because of the prestige of the Institute
and its committee, dissemination of the opinion would cause them
"irreparable damage."

The plaintiffs asked specifically that the Accounting Procedures
Committee be restrained from issuing the letter until other groups
were given an opportunity to comment.

The first temporary restraining order had been issued, without
notice or hearing, on April 15, 1959, and a hearing was held on
May 7, 1959. Following the hearing, on May 20, the position of the
Institute and the Accounting Procedures Committee was upheld in
a decision by Judge Levet of the United States District Court for
the Southern District of New York. Judge Levet said:

[61]Editorial, "What's in a Name?," *The Journal of Accountancy*, CIV (June, 1957), 30.
[62]News Report, "Institute Wins Court Case," *The Journal of Accountancy*, CVIII (August, 1959), 7.

The purposes of the defendant Institute are adequate justification, if justification indeed be required, to permit the proposed communications. There is no adequate proof (even if the plaintiffs had any right to insist on the committee procedures they mention) that the Institute's rules have been or are about to be violated. In fact, the contrary appears.

There is no allegation that the method of accounting proposed by defendants is inherently false or fraudulent. On the contrary, it is supported by respectable authority. Neither is there any allegation of special damages, except in the most general and speculative terms.[63]

However, Judge Levet issued a temporary injunction enjoining the mailing of the letter pending a hearing by the Court of Appeals on a motion to be made in that court for an injunction. After hearing arguments from both sides, the Court of Appeals on June 17, 1959 unanimously affirmed the decision of the District Court, and dissolved the injunction.

On June 19, 1959, Judge Lumbard of the Court of Appeals reinstated the injunction, pending a hearing by a Justice of the United States Supreme Court on an application for a further injunction. Such an application was heard and denied by Justice Brennan of that court on July 6, 1959. In denying the application Justice Brennan said:

. . . in my judgment none of the questions proposed to be presented in the petition for certiorari have the prospect of commanding four votes for review.[64]

The right to issue such opinions has been upheld by a U. S. District Court and the Court of Appeals for the Second Circuit of New York. The decisions of the District Court and the Court of Appeals both contain language of far-reaching significance. The Institute's new Accounting Principles Board was thus given the opportunty to carry out its function of formulating basic accounting postulates and statements on accounting principles.

---

[63]*Ibid.*, p. 7.
[64]News Report, "Supreme Court Review Requested," *The Journal of Accountancy*, CVIII (November, 1959), 7.

The plaintiffs did not challenge the right of the Institute or its committee to issue opinions in the field of accounting. Instead, they protested that the committee had not submitted an "exposure draft" of its opinion to other interested organizations. The Institute has an expressed policy of expanding its consultation with other groups before statements on accounting principles are issued. However, the final responsibility for its opinions and procedures must rest with the Institute, or with the appropriate committee or board to which it delegates such responsibility. This principle has been upheld by the court decisions.

In rejecting the contention of the plaintiffs, Judge Levet of the U. S. District Court (Southern District, New York) said:

. . . the communications which defendants intend to promulgate do not mention plaintiffs. The plaintiffs, like other business enterprises which may be affected, may, if they so elect, appear before the appropriate governmental body to sustain their own contentions. There is no misrepresentation, no fraud. The acts of the defendants can hardly be termed wanton. The purposes of the defendant Institute are adequate justification, if justification indeed be required, to permit the purpose communications. There is no adequate proof, even if the plaintiffs had any right to insist on the Committee procedures they mention, that the Institute's rules have been or are about to be violated. In fact the contrary appears.[65]

The Court of Appeals, in its unanimous *per curiam* opinion upholding Judge Levet, went even further in establishing the right of the American Institute of C.P.A.'s, as a professional organization, to issue statements in the area of its professional competence.

The Court of Appeals said:

On the merits we agree with Judge Levet's reasoned opinion below, D.C.S.D. N.Y., May 20, 1959. We think the courts may not dictate or control the procedures by which a private organization expresses its honestly held views. Defendant's action involves no break of duty owed by them to the plaintiffs. On the contrary, every professional body accepts a public obligation for un-

---

[65]Editorial, "Institute's Right to Issue Accounting Opinions Upheld by Courts," *The Journal of Accountancy*, CVIII (August, 1959), 23.

fettered expression of views and loses all right to professional consideration, as well as all utility, if its views are controlled by other criteria than the intellectual conclusions of the person acting. Absent a showing of actual malice or its equivalent the courts would be making a great mistake, contrary indeed to their own ideas and professions, if they assumed to restrict and denigrate this widely recognized and assumed professional duty.[66]

The authority of the American Institute's accounting research bulletins has always been widely recognized; this legal affirmation of the Institute's rights and obligations came at an opportune time, as the new Accounting Principles Board prepared to take up its duties.

Rules of Professional Conduct

The rules of professional conduct for all members of the American Institute of Certified Public Accountants indicate the high professional standards that must be maintained. These rules are as follows:

RULES OF PROFESSIONAL CONDUCT
American Institute of Certified Public Accountants
As Revised January 20, 1958

(These rules of conduct supplement the disciplinary clauses of the by-laws.)

(1) A firm or partnership, all the individual members of which are members of the Institute, may describe itself as "Members of the American Institute of Certified Public Accountants," but a firm or partnership, not all the individual members of which are members of the Institute, or an individual practicing under a style denoting a partnership when in fact there be no partner or partners, or a corporation, or an individual or individuals practicing under a style denoting a corporate organization shall not use the designation "Members of the American Institute of Certified Public Accountants."

(2) A member shall not allow any person to practice in his name who is not in partnership with him or in his employ.

---

[66]*Ibid.*, p. 24.

(3) Commissions, brokerage, or other participation in the fees or profits of professional work shall not be allowed directly or indirectly to the laity by a member.

Commissions, brokerage, or other participation in the fees, charges, or profits of work recommended or turned over to the laity as incident to services for clients shall not be accepted directly or indirectly by a member.

(4) A member shall not engage in any business or occupation conjointly with that of a public accountant, which is incompatible or inconsistent therewith.

(5) In expressing an opinion on representations in financial statements which he has examined, a member may be held guilty of an act discreditable to the profession if

(a) he fails to disclose a material fact known to him which is not disclosed in the financial statements but disclosure of which is necessary to make the financial statements not misleading; or

(b) he fails to report any material misstatement known to him to appear in the financial statement; or

(c) he is materially negligent in the conduct of his examination or in making his report thereon;

(d) he fails to acquire sufficient information to warrant expression of an opinion, or his exceptions are sufficiently material to negative the expression of an opinion; or

(e) he fails to direct attention to any material departure from generally accepted accounting principles or to disclose any material omission of generally accepted auditing procedure applicable in the circumstances.

(6) A member shall not sign a report purporting to express his opinion as the result of examination of financial statements unless they have been examined by him, a member or an employee of his firm, a member of the Institute, a member of a similar association in a foreign country, or a certified public accountant of a state or territory of the United States or the District of Columbia.

(7) A member shall not directly or indirectly solicit clients by circulars or advertisements, nor by personal communication or interview, not warranted by existing personal relations, and he shall not encroach upon the practice of

another public accountant. A member may furnish service to those who request it.

(8) Direct or indirect offer of employment shall not be made by a member to an employee of another public accountant without first informing such accountant. This rule shall not be construed so as to inhibit negotiations with anyone who of his own initiative or in response to public advertisement shall apply to a member for employment.

(9) Professional service shall not be rendered or offered for a fee which shall be contingent upon the findings or results of such service. This rule does not apply to cases involving federal, state, or other taxes, in which the findings are those of the tax authorities and not those of the accountant. Fees to be fixed by courts or other public authorities, which are therefore of an indeterminate amount at the time when an engagement is undertaken, are not regarded as contingent fees within the meaning of this rule.

(10) A member shall not advertise his professional attainments or services:

(a) The publication of what is technically known as a card is restricted to an announcement of the name, title (member of American Institute of Certified Public Accounts, CPA, or other professional affiliation or designation), class of service, and address of the person or firm, issued in connection with the announcement of change of address or personnel of firm, and shall not exceed two columns in width and three inches in depth if appearing in a newspaper and not to exceed one-quarter of a page if appearing in a magazine or similar publication.

(b) A paid listing in a directory is restricted to the name, title, class of service, address and telephone number of the person or firm, and it shall not appear in bold type, box, or other form of display, or in a style which differentiates it from other listings in the same directory.

(11) A member shall not be an officer, director, stockholder, representative, or agent of any corporation engaged in the practice of public accounting in any state or territory of the United States or the District of Columbia.

(12) A member shall not permit his name to be used in conjunction with an estimate of earnings contingent upon future transactions in a manner which may lead to the belief that the member vouches for the accuracy of the forecast.

(13) A member shall not express his opinion on financial statement of any enterprise financed in whole or in part by public distribution of securities, if he owns or is committed to acquire a financial interest in the enterprise which is substantial either in relation to its capital or to his own personal fortune, or if a member of his immediate family owns or is committed to acquire a substantial interest in the enterprise. A member shall not express his opinion on financial statements which are used as a basis of credit if he owns or is committed to acquire a financial interest in the enterprise which is substantial either in relation to its capital or to his own personal fortune, or if a member of his immediate family owns or is committed to acquire a substantial interest in the enterprise, unless in his report he discloses such interest.

(14) A member shall not make a competitive bid for professional engagements in any state, territory, or the District of Columbia, if such a bid would constitute a violation of any rule of the recognized society of certified public accountants or the official board of accountancy in that state, territory, or District.

(15) A member engaged in an occupation in which he renders services of a type performed by public accountants, or renders other professional services, must observe the by-laws and rules of professional conduct of the Institute in the conduct of that occupation.

(16) A member shall not violate the confidential relationship between himself and his client.

(17) A member in his practice of public accounting shall not permit an employee to perform for the member's clients any services which the member himself or his firm is not permitted to perform.

(18) A member who receives an engagement for services by referral from another member shall not extend his services beyond the specific engagement without consulting with the referring member.

(19) A member shall not permit his name to be associated with statements purporting to show financial position of results of operations in such a manner as to imply that he is acting as an independent public accountant unless he shall: (1) express an unqualified opinion, or (2) express a qualified opinion, or (3) disclaim an opinion on the statements taken as a whole and indicate clearly his reasons therefor, or (4) when unaudited financial statements are presented on his stationery without his comments, disclose prominently on each page of the financial statements that they were not audited.[67]

---

[67]Rules of Professional Conduct, American Institute of Certified Public Accountants, p. 14.

The January 20, 1958 rules of professional conduct of the American Institute of Certified Public Accountants have changed over the years in accordance with the needs of the emerging profession of public accountancy. It is significant to note the change in the rules since the American Institute of Acountants was formed in 1917 under that name. The significance is not in the number of rules or their increase from eight to nineteen, but rather in their exemplification of the importance of ethics for a new profession. It should be remembered that in 1917 all of the states did not yet have C.P.A. laws.

The rules of professional conduct of the American Institute of Accountants as approved by the council of the Institute were as follows:

AMERICAN INSTITUTE OF ACCOUNTING
Rules of Professional Conduct

Prepared by the Committee on Professional Ethics and approved by the Council April 9, 1917.

(1) A firm or partnership, all the individual members of which are members of the Institute, may describe itself as "Members of the American Institute of Accountants," but a firm or partnership, all the individual members of which are not members of the Institute, or an individual practising under a style denoting a partnership when in fact there be no partner or partners, or a corporation, or an individual or individuals practising under a style denoting a corporate organization, shall not describe themselves as "Members of the American Institute of Accountants."

(2) The preparation and certification of exhibits, statements, schedules, or other forms of accountancy work, containing an essential mis-statement of fact, or omission therefrom of such a fact as would amount to an essential mis-statement shall be, *ipso facto*, cause for expulsion, or for such other discipline as the Council may determine, upon proper presentation of proof that such mis-statement was either wilful or was the result of such gross negligence as to be inexcusable.

(3) No member shall allow any person to practice in his name as a public accountant who is not a member of this Institute, or in partnership with him or in his employ on a salary.

(4) No member shall directly or indirectly allow or agree to allow a commission, brokerage, or other participation by the laity in the fees or profits of his professional work, nor shall he accept directly or indirectly from the laity any such commission, brokerage or other participation for professional or commercial business turned over to others as an incident of his services to clients.

(5) No member shall engage in any business or occupation conjointly with that of a public accountant, which in the opinion of the Executive Committee or of the Council is incompatible or inconsistent therewith.

(6) No member shall certify to any accounts, exhibits, statements, schedules or other forms of accountancy work which have not been verified entirely under the supervision of himself, a member of his firm, one of his staff, a member of this Institute or a similar association of good standing in foreign countries which has been approved by the Council.

(7) No member shall take part in any effort to secure the enactment, alteration, or amendment of any state or federal law, or any regulation of any governmental or civic body, affecting the practice of the profession without giving immediate notice thereof to the Secretary of the Institute, who in turn shall at once advise the Executive Committee or the Council.

(8) No member shall directly or indirectly solicit the clients nor encroach upon the business of another member, but it is the right of any member to give proper service and advice to those asking such service or advice.

Enforcement of Professional Ethics

There have been nine significant opinions on professional ethics since December, 1956. The American Institute's Committee on Professional Ethics is, and has been, active in the development of professional ethics and conduct for certified public accountants. The opinions of the Trial Board are on various subjects, ranging from newsletters, publications, and confidence of a client to sharing of fees and distribution of literature. The nine recent decisions of the Trial Board are briefly reported here to show the range of activities of the Committee on Professional Ethics. Without professional standards there can be no real recognition as a profession. The opinions follow:

COMMITTEE ON PROFESSIONAL ETHICS
Numbered Opinions

Opinion No. 1

Newsletters, Publications

Impropriety of member furnishing clients and others with tax
and similar booklets prepared by others and imprinted with
firm name of member.

In the opinion of the committee, imprinting the name of the accountant on newsletters, tax booklets or other similar publications which are prepared by others and distributed by a member of the Institute does not add to the usefulness of the material to the reader. Use of the imprint, in the committee's opinion, is objectionable in that it tends to suggest (and has been interpreted by many as a means of) circumventing Rule 10 of the rules of professional conduct, which says that a member shall not advertise his services.

It is the conclusion of the committee that distribution of newsletters, tax booklets or similar publications, prepared by others, when imprinted with the name of the accountant furnishing the material, is not in the interest of the public or the profession.

The committee sees no grounds for objection to furnishing material of the type indicated to clients or others provided that such material does not carry the imprint described and provided that such distribution is limited in a manner consistent with Rule 7.

(Published in The CPA, December 1956)

Opinion No. 2

Responsibility of Member for Acts of
Third Parties on His Behalf

Member may not carry out through others, acts which he is
prohibited from directly performing under Institute by-laws
and rules of professional conduct.

A member should not cause others to carry out on his behalf either with or without compensation acts which, if carried out by a member, would place him in violation of the Institute's rules of professional conduct if, with his approval:

1. A nonprofit organization in recognition of accounting services which had been rendered by a member placed without charge an advertisement of the firm in the organization's bulletin;

2. A bank announced to its depositors that a CPA would be at a desk on the main floor of the bank at certain hours and days during the tax season to assist customers in preparation of tax returns for a fee;

3. A trade association in its official publication announced that a certain certified public accountant, member of the Institute, who long had served the association as independent accountant, was especially well qualified and available to assist association members in dealing with accounting and tax problems peculiar to the industry.

(Published in The CPA, December 1956)

Opinion No. 3
Confidence of a Client

> Seller of accounting practice should not give the purchaser access to working papers, income tax returns, and correspondence pertaining to accounts being sold without first obtaining permission of client.

The seller of an accounting practice has a duty under Rule 16, pertaining to confidential relations, first to obtain permission of the client to make available to a purchaser working papers and other documents.

(Published in The CPA, January 1957)

Opinion No. 4
Authorship—Propriety of Showing
Firm Affiliation of Author

> Responsibility of author for publisher's promotion efforts.

Many certified public accountants, members of the Institute, are especially well qualified to write authoritatively on accounting, taxes, auditing, management and related subjects, and in the interests of the public and the profession are encouraged to write under their names articles and books for publication. In the opinion of the committee it is of value to the reader to know the author's background (degrees he holds, professional society affiliation, and the firm with which he is associated). It is held that publication of such information is not in violation of Rule 10.

It is the opinion of the committee that an author who is a member of the Institute has the responsibility to ascertain that the publisher or others promoting distribution of his work keep within the bounds of professional dignity and do not make claims concerning the author or his writing that are not factual or in good taste.

(Published in The CPA, February 1957)

Opinion No. 5

Prohibited Self-Designations—
Use of Title "Tax Consultant,"<br>"Tax Specialist," or Similar
Description Forbidden

The "Statement of Principles Relating to Practice in the Field of Federal Income Taxation, Promulgated in 1951 by the National Conference of Lawyers and Certified Public Accountants," was approved by the Institute's Council. Section 5 of this statement reads as follows:

"5. Prohibited Self-Designations. An accountant should not describe himself as a 'tax-consultant' or 'tax expert' or use any similar phrase. Lawyers, similarly, are prohibited by the canons of ethics of the American Bar Association and the opinions relating thereto, from advertising a special branch of law practice."

Under Article V, Section 4, of the Institute's by-laws a member renders himself liable to expulsion or suspension by the trial board if he refuses to give effect to any decision of the Institute or the Council.

It is the opinion of the committee that a reasonable period of time has elapsed since the adoption of the Statement of Principles by Council within which the members could revise their stationery, directory and other listings so as to conform with the Statement.

(Published in The CPA, March 1957)

Opinion No. 6

Concept of "Laity" in Sharing of Fees

Concept of laity as used in Rule 3, interpreted to prohibit sharing of fees, profits, or commissions with others not in public practice; propriety of joint services.

Rule 3 provides that: "Commissions, brokerage, or other participation in the fees or profits of professional work shall not be allowed directly or indirectly to the laity by a member.

"Commissions, brokerage, or other participation in the fees, charges, or profits of work recommended or turned over to the laity as incident to services for clients shall not be accepted directly or indirectly by a member."

There has been no precise definition of the word "laity" as used in Rule 3, and it is the belief of the committee that no useful purpose would be accomplished by attempting to establish a special definition for use solely within the accounting profession which would include certain non-accounting professional groups and exclude other such groups. It is the view of the committee that Rule 3 should be interpreted as intending to prohibit a member in public practice from receiving or paying a commission or sharing a fee with *any individual or firm not engaged or employed in the practice of public accounting.*

Rule 3 is not intended to apply to payments to a retired partner of a public accounting firm or to the heirs of a deceased partner or of a deceased member. Also in view of the fact that the term "laity" has not been authoritatively defined, the committee feels it would be unreasonable to apply its present interpretation to arrangements made in good faith and already existing between certified public accountants and individuals not presently in the practice of public accounting. It is the hope of the committee that within a reasonable time Rule 3 may be amended so as to clarify the word "laity" by referring instead to any individual or firm not engaged or employed in the practice of public accounting. In the meantime an understanding of, and voluntary compliance with, the committee's views should facilitate the transition.

The committee believes there is nothing contrary to the public interest or in violation of the rules of conduct in a firm of certified public accountants coordinating its work with that of an engineering, legal or other professional firm on a specific project for a single client. In such cases care should be taken by the accounting firm not to extend its services beyond its particular field and that any reports or recommendations rendered make clear the limitation of responsibilities assumed and services rendered.

Neither Rule 3 nor any of the other Institute rules of professional conduct at present prohibit a partnership by a member of the Institute in public practice with a person who is not a certified public accountant. The committee, however, looks forward to the day when such public accounting partnerships will be composed solely of certified public accountants.

(Published in The CPA, January 1958)

Opinion No. 7
Statistical Tabulating Services

The committee on professional ethics has, in recent years, responded to several inquiries in regard to the possible violation of the Institute's rules of professional conduct by members who operate statistical tabulating service bureaus.

In practically all cases the tabulating services include or contemplate the accumulation of data to be used for accounting purposes, the maintenance of accounts, and bookkeeping services. This type of service is similar to so-called "write-up work" or bookkeeping service rendered by many public accountants.

Some members have formed separate partnerships which perform statistical tabulating services. Some of these organizations were apparently formed under the erroneous impression that the Institute's rules of professional conduct would not be applicable.

The committee finds it is proper for members to conduct statistical tabulating service bureaus. The committee holds, however, that any such separate organization in which a member has an interest should not be permitted to do things which the member in public practice is prohibited from doing as a member of the Institute, such as advertising, soliciting business, or practicing in corporate form.

It is the opinion of the committee that any member of the Institute who has any interest in an organization which renders statistical tabulating services is either directly or indirectly rendering the "type of service commonly rendered by public accountants" and, therefore, must observe the by-laws and Rule 15, which requires compliance with all of the rules of professional conduct of the Institute.

(Published in The CPA, December 1958)

Opinion No. 8

Denial of Opinion Does Not Discharge Responsibility in All Cases

> Where the CPA believes financial statements contain false or misleading information, mere denial of opinion held insufficient.

Rule 5 deals with a member's responsibilities in expressing an opinion on representations in financial statements. The rule does not, however, specifically refer to situations where an opinion is denied, either by disclaimer or by reference to the statements as "prepared without audit." When an accountant denies an opinion on financial statements under Rule 19, which incorporates the provisions of Auditing Statement ·23, he is in effect stating that he has insufficient grounds for an opinion as to whether or not the statements constitute a fair presentation. Rule 19 provides that where an opinion is denied, the accountant must indicate clearly his reasons therefor.

In a circumstance where a member believes the financial statements are false or misleading as a whole or in any significant respect, it is the opinion of the committee that he should require adjustments of the accounts or adequate disclosure of the facts, as the case may be, and failing this the independent accountant should refuse to permit his name to be associated with the statements in any way.

(Published in The CPA, February 1959)

Opinion No. 9
Distribution of Literature

There has come to the attention of the committee with increasing frequency printed material bearing a member's name and address or that of his firm, which is devoted either to informing others of the services the member of his firm is prepared to render or dealing with a specialized subject in a manner that might suggest the firm's ability to serve in a specialized field or geographical area.

The committee feels that such material is entirely proper when its distribution is carefully restricted to clients, but that failure to control the circulation of such literature directly or through third parties may place the member whose name it bears in violation of Rule 10 of the Institute's rules of professional conduct prohibiting advertising.

The committee believes that a member who produces any literature, or material which may be considered promotional in nature, must assume responsibility to guard and control its distribution. It is recognized by the committee that in isolated cases a client, not knowing the profession's restrictions on the distribution of such material, may pass on to the client of another member material he found of interest. Such an isolated instance would not necessarily be viewed as unethical practice. Where there is evidence that reasonable control has not been maintained to limit distribution of such material, it is the view of the committee, that it must, in the interest of the profession, strictly enforce both the spirit and the letter of Rule 10, which provides "A member shall not advertise his professional attainments or services. . . ."

Accountant's Legal Responsibility

An Illinois appeals court has revised a trial court decision and found a C.P.A. firm negligent for failure to detect defalcations during its audit of a client's books.

In *Cereal Byproducts Company* v. *Roy Hall, J. Leonard Penny,* et al., appealed in January, 1956 to the Appelate Court of Illinois, First Division, the conduct of the C.P.A. defendants in the confirmation of accounts receivable was characterized as "inexcusable negligence for which defendants are liable."

The C.P.A.'s failed to confirm 29 accounts receivable totaling $28,964 in 1957. Plaintiff charged breach of contract and negligence and carelessness in the audit. Justice Niemeyer said:

Although the discovery of defalcations is not in most cases the objective of an ordinary examination of books, it is necessary that certain examinations or checks be made which would show defalcations before the auditor could render an opinion on the balance sheets and financial statements as showing the worth of the firm whose books are examined.[68]

Securities and Exchange Commission's Influence

The Securities and Exchange Commission announced the decision on October 31, 1952 suspending the public accounting firm of Haskins & Sells, because of the Thomascolor case, and one of its partners, Andrew Stewart, individually, from appearing or practicing before the commission for a period of ten days, effective November 29, 1952.

The basis for the decision was a finding by the Commission that the financial statements prepared and certified by the respondents and included in the registration statement filed by Thomascolor, Incorporated, were defective.

The Commision stated in the findings:

. . . respondents' accounting treatment and disclosures were materially inadequate and the financial statements certified by them were materially misleading in important respects. Those deficiencies resulted directly from respondents' failure to follow generally accepted accounting and auditing principles and practice and professional standards, and rules, regulations and prior decisions of this Commission.[69]

The deficiencies in the financial statements of the Thomascolor Case related primarily to a $2,014,941.03 item in the balance sheet,

---

[68]News Report, "Accountants Found Negligent." *The Journal of Accountancy*, CI (April, 1956), 5.

[69]Official Decisions & Releases, "SEC Accounting Series Release No. 73: The Thomascolor Case," *The Journal of Accountancy*, XCV (January, 1953), 83.

captioned "Patents and Patent Applications," which represented all but $536,642.37 of the company's assets. The Commission noted that the public was being asked by Thomascolor, Incorporated, to invest $10 million in a "highly speculative venture" against a background of a long history of attempts to develop and exploit inventions in color photography which had involved the expenditures of large sums of money without any evidence of commercial success. The Commission further stated:

> It was against this background that respondents prepared and certified balance sheets which grossly overstated intangible assets by the arbitrary use of the par and stated value of shares of stock issued to acquired the assets, including shares expected to be reacquired from promotions as a donation, and attributed to apparently potentially productive items material amounts which should have been shown as promotion services.[70]

In its Findings and Opinion the Commission accepted Haskins & Sells' assertion that they acted in good faith, and accordingly did not find any willful or deliberate disregard of its rules or accepted accounting practice. The suspension of Haskins & Sells by the Commission was the first instance in the history of the S.E.C. that disciplinary action has been based on differences of judgment as to proper accounting treatment.

It was the opinion of Haskins & Sells that it was proper to carry this item (Patents and Patent Applications), at the amount stated because, among other things, it resulted from a series of transactions involving substantial elements of arm's-length bargaining, and that there was adequate disclosure in the balance sheet and footnotes concerning this item.[71]

Dangerous Precedent Set by S.E.C.

The October, 1956 suspension of Haskins & Sells from practicing before the Commission for a period of ten days established a dangerous precedent.

---

[70]*Ibid.*, p. 83.

[71]Official Releases & Decisions, "Comment Released by Haskins & Sells," *The Journal of Accountancy*, XCV (January, 1953), 85.

The basis for the suspension under Rule II (e) of the Commission's Rules of Practice is stated to be that the respondent's accounting work was so deficient

as a result of their failure to give this professional undertaking the degree of care and inquiry it demanded under the circumstances, that disciplinary action is required.[72]

The specific provision of Rule II (e) under which the suspension was made was "improper professional conduct."

During the hearing three C.P.A.'s, two of them past presidents of the American Institute, testified as expert witnesses, without contradiction, that the accounting treatment complained of by the Commission was proper.

The record shows that the balance-sheet on which the complaint was based was amended before acceptance by the Commission, so that the original financial statements to which they took exception were never issued to the public. Furthermore, the time period for the processing of the complaint was as follows: the original statements were filed in 1947, the disciplinary proceedings against Haskins & Sells were begun in 1948, the final arguments were given in 1950, and the Commission issued the suspension order two and one half years later.

Regarding the suspension, the editors of *The Journal* stated:

This decision, we believe, constitutes a dangerous precedent for all accountants who may certify statements filed with the S.E.C. Any accountant certifying such a statement may be disciplined for improper professional conduct, regardless of his good faith and competence, if the Commission disagrees with the accounting treatment of any important item. . . . Demonstration of substantial authoritative support for the accounting procedure originally followed provides no protection—the Commission regards as final its own judgment of what is sound accounting.

. . . .

---

[72]Editorial, "Suspension of Accountants by SEC a Dangerous Precedent," *The Journal of Accountancy*, XCV (January, 1953), 33.

In these circumstances the S.E.C. occupies not only the position of prosecutor, judge, and jury, but by asserting its authority to decide, regardless of evidence, what is and what is not proper accounting, it also takes over the function of legislator of the "law of accounting."[73]

C.I.T. Case—Liability to Third Parties

The decision of the United States Court of Appeals for the Second Circuit in this case of *C.I.T. Financial Corporation U.P.W.R. Glover* et al., was a crucial decision on accountants' liability. The suit was brought against a number of individuals who were partners in the firm of Barrow, Wade, Guthrie & Co., which was a national firm of certified public accountants.

The plaintiff in the case was not a client of the accountants but a creditor of the client. The case involved an attempt to broaden the scope of accountants' liability to third parties for mere negligence.[74] A unanimous verdict on all counts in favor of the former accounting firm of Barrow, Wade, Guthrie & Co. was returned by the Federal District Court.

The plaintiff in the action was the C.I.T. Financial Corporation, which loaned $1.5 million in 1945 to another commercial finance company, the Manufacturers Trading Corporation, with headquarters in Cleveland. The borrower, M.T.C., became involved in financial difficulties in 1948 and was finally adjudicated bankrupt in 1950.

The complaint in the court action alleged that the loan had been made in 1945 in reliance upon the audit reports of the defendants, Barrow, Wade, Guthrie & Co., and that, during the life of the loan, there had been further reliance upon semi-annual audit reports, all of which were alleged to have been inaccurate and misleading in material respects.

The opinion of the certified public accountants was qualified in each report and the auditors disclaimed any responsibility for the valuation or collateral held by their client in connection with the commercial receivable appearing in the balance sheet.[75]

The plaintiff-appellant contended that their accountants knew that their reports would be relied upon by this creditor and that

---

[73]*Ibid.*, p. 34.

[74]Saul Levy, "The C.I.T. Case," *The Journal of Accountancy*, C (October, 1955), 31.

[75]News Report, "Accounting Firm Upheld," *The Journal of Accountancy*, XCVII (May, 1954), 520.

this specific identification of the third party was sufficient to support the claim asserted in the third cause of action, though it involved negligence rather than fraud.

The Court of Appeals in its opinion stated:

> The jury went on, however, to find that defendants' representations had not been negligently false or misleading, and this second finding alone bars recovery on this count. [76]

The plaintiff, C.I.T., who had loaned M.T.C. $1.5 million, claimed that defendants' auditors were totally inadequate for failure to disclose overvaluation of loans to debtors. The plaintiff argued that defendants should have pointed out the necessity for larger reserves due to the stagnancy of certain collateral, and due to its concentration in certain types of merchandise and in certain individual debtors. Further, reference was made to alleged misclassification of particular items as accounts receivable, rather than inventory loans.

The defense relied on the special nature of M.T.C.'s business and on plaintiff's knowledge of this. Defendants maintained that M.T.C., in its financial transaction, had always relied primarily on the borrower's collateral, rather than on his financial condition. The auditors claimed that they had never asserted their own special competence to make such appraisals, but that they had inserted in their audit reports appropriate disclaimers qualifying their general assertions about M.T.C.'s financial stability. Further, the accountants claimed that M.T.C.'s business was such that the accountants had to rely to a great extent on management statements about the nature and the value of the collateral, and that, since the audit reports disclosed this reliance, defendants were not liable for whatever factual errors might have occurred.

Each of the audit reports of the public accounting firm had a disclaimer in these or similar words:

> While it was not within our province to pass upon or assume responsibility for legal or equitable title to the commercial receivables purchased by the

---

[76]Saul Levy, "The C.I.T. Case," *The Journal of Accountancy*, C (October, 1955), 32.

companies or the valuation of any security thereto accepted and held by them, it was apparent from their books and records and by opinion of counsel, that their contractual and assignment forms are adequate for their legal protection in connection with the collection and liquidation of commercial receivables purchased.[77]

The final paragraph of the decision of the United States Court of Appeals was as follows:

Plaintiff argues vigorously the importance of this case in holding accountants in strict liability for their audits, and, in effect, for increasing that liability. But we do not believe we should attempt to go beyond the standards of the market place, as reflected in current judicial decisions. So when, after a fair and carefully conducted trial under the function of the courts should be considered fulfilled. Judgment affirmed.[78]

S.E.C. Criticizes Report

The Securities and Exchange Commission permanently suspended the Regulation A exemption of the Coastal Finance Company and criticized its certified public accountants, O'Connell and Company of Silver Springs, Maryland, for an "inaccurate and misleading" report.

The Commission's action, announced on April 10, 1957, was taken on the grounds that a stock offering circular issued by Coastal Finance contained false and misleading information, failed to disclose transactions with and securities held by officers and directors, and misleadingly represented that the public accountants' examination was in accordance with generally accepted auditing standards.

O'Connell and Company's certificate, dated August 3, 1955, covered Coastal's financial statements for the six months period ending June 30, 1955. The Commission charged that O'Connell had not examined the company's field officers during the period, and had not audited a new office which Coastal acquired in February, 1955. The accounting firm was said to have performed only bookkeeping at Coastal's home office.

---

[77]*Ibid.*, p. 42.
[78]*Ibid.*, p. 42.

The Commission said that when O'Connell made a routine audit of one of Coastal's offices on August 16, 1955, after the date the certificate was issued, it discovered evidence of improper renewals of delinquent loans to prevent their being charged off as a bad debt. After a special audit by O'Connell, revised figures were issued for the August 3 report which showed a $128,130 operating loss, compared to an operating profit of $107,695 shown in the financial statement in the stock offering circular.[79]

S.E.C.—Seaboard Case

On March 28, 1957, the Securities and Exchange Commission temporarily suspended Touche, Niven, Bailey & Smart, C.P.A. firm, and two of its partners from practice before the Commission for a fifteen-day period effective May 1, 1957. The decision, issued pursuant to Rule II (e) of the Commission's Rules of Practice, was based in findings of improper professional conduct in connection with the firm's certification of financial statements of Seaboard Commercial Corporation for 1947 which were included in Seaboard's annual report for 1947 filed with the Commission pursuant to the Securities Exchange Act of 1934.

Seaboard was a commercial finance company, but by the end of 1947 its financial condition had drastically changed as a result of the concentration of its funds in six companies, all of which had experienced increasingly serious financial difficulties in 1946 and 1947. The Commission found, among other things, that the $857,729 reserve for losses and contingencies in Seaboard's certified balance sheet was materially inadequate, and that the respondents in certifying to statement including this reserve failed to follow generally accepted accounting and auditing standards and failed to exercise an independent and informed judgment. It was noted that the senior in charge of the field work for Touche, Niven, Bailey & Smart, had estimated, at the conclusion of his work, that a reserve of $1,453,551 was required. Thereafter the partner in charge of the audit, following a conference with management, had arrived at an estimated reserve of $1,345,000 and a draft certificate used by the respondent after several meetings with Seaboard's management referred to a need for a reserve of $1,345,000.

---

[79]News Report, "SEC Criticizes CPA's Report," *The Journal of Accountancy,* CIII (June, 1957), 13.

The Commission found that the respondents, Touche, Niven, Bailey & Smart, improperly deferred to management's wishes in deleting from their certificate language indicating the financial condition of Seaboard's major accounts. The inadequate addition to the reserve of $750,000 was not charged to income, notwithstanding that an addition to the reserve was necessitated by developments during 1947. Had the $750,000 addition to the reserve been charged to income, Seaboard's net income of almost $250,000 would have been converted to a net loss of approximately $500,000.

The suspension of Touche, Niven, Bailey & Smart took place nine years after the audit report of the Seaboard Commercial Corporation. The partners suspended were William W. Werntz and Henry E. Mendes, who retired from active practice in 1950. The Commission did not institute ·the proceedings against Touche, Niven, Bailey & Smart until 1952, after Thomas W. Brown, the partner in charge of the audit, had died. The burden of the details of the audit fell on William W. Werntz, Brown's assistant. Werntz was not admitted to partnership in the firm until 1950.

Seaboard's own balance sheet at the year end of 1947 carried a reserve against losses of $107,000 and all of its advances to debtors were carried on the balance sheet as current assets. The audit firm's regular procedures disclosed not only the concentration of receivables in a small number of accounts but also the possibility that serious losses would be sustained. It was, therefore, determined to undertake supplementary audit procedures to develop and to obtain a more detailed knowledge of the debtor companies. The additional audit procedures convinced the auditors that substantial additional reserves for losses would be required and that a considerable portion of the receivables classified as current should be reclassified as noncurrent. The management of Seaboard vigorously denied this and insisted that the loan would be worked out without loss, or with losses not exceeding the reserve which Seaboard had itself established. The public accounting firm refused to certify the balance sheet as presented because, in their judgment, the reserves were inadequate and the current assets overstated. With the establishment of a reserve of $857,000 and the reclassification of approximately $1 million in receivables, a certificate was signed by the auditors.

The auditors stated, in regard to the case, that ". . . the case should be sent back with instructions that it should be heard again with hindsight evidence excluded. . . ." Subsequent to 1947, the Seaboard Company was liquidated with substantial losses.[80]

T. N. B. & S. Statement on the Seaboard Case

The audit of the Seaboard Company occurred during the first audit season of the new firm of Touche, Niven, Bailey & Smart. Thomas W. Brown was the only member of the firm familiar with Seaboard's affairs, and it was not until after his death in 1950 that the Commission instituted the proceedings. Thus the burden of defending Brown's decision fell on William Werntz, who had been his assistant, and had shortly before joined one of the constituent firms in the merger as an employee, after serving for nine years as chief accountant for the Securities and Exchange Commission. He did not become a partner until 1950.

Seaboard's own balance sheet at the year end of 1947 carried a reserve against losses of $107,000 and all of its advances to debtors were carried on the balance sheets as current assets. After undertaking supplementary audit procedures, Touche, Niven, Bailey & Smart concluded that a substantial addition to the reserve for losses would be required and that a considerable portion of the receivables was improperly classified as current assets and should be reclassified as noncurrent receivables. Seaboard management vigorously denied this and insisted that the loans would be worked out without loss, or with losses not exceeding the reserves which Seaboard had itself established.

At the conclusion of a series of conferences during which management insisted that the accounting firm was being harshly pessimistic, the auditors made three stipulations: a reserve of $857,000, the exclusion from current assets of approximately $1 million of receivables from debtors and a subsidiary, and the disclosure in a footnote that $3,158,000 of receivables were due from three customers, if the auditors were to give an unqualified opinion on Seaboard's financial statements. These conferences extended over a period of two weeks and were held with the president of the company, the executive vice-president, and other officers of Seaboard.

---

[80]Official Releases, "Official Summary of SEC Accounting Studies Release Number 78 and Statement of Touche, Niven, Bailey & Smart," *The Journal of Accountancy*, CIII (June, 1957), 62.

Management finally agreed and the balance sheet was changed accordingly.

Seaboard's banker creditors became very disturbed upon the receipt of the audit report with the disclosure of the increase in the reserve for losses to $857,000, the reclassification of approximately $1 million of receivables as noncurrent assets, and the concentration of loans in a few debtors. In the words of one of the banker creditors, the audit report had "certainly hung out all the red flags."[81]

Atlas Plywood Story

Fortune in January, 1958 aroused considerable comment by raising a number of questions about the Atlas Plywood Corporation. The dispute arose regarding the determination of the operating loss of $10,818,645, of Atlas Plywood, including special charges against income of $6,300,000. In January, 1957 a new management assumed control of Atlas Plywood and terminated the engagement of Peat, Marwick, Mitchell & Co. as auditors, engaging Arthur Andersen & Co. instead. In its opinion on the 1947 financial statements Arthur Andersen & Co. stated:

We are not in a position to determine what portion of the net loss including special charges for the year ended June 30, 1957, should be attributed to prior years. . . .[82]

A year later, on July 23, 1958, the treasurer of Atlas Plywood wrote to the senior partner of Peat, Marwick, Mitchell & Co., with the knowledge and written approval of his board of directors, that the procedures followed by the auditors ". . . would not in any way indicate improper auditing or reporting by Peat, Marwick, Mitchell & Co., in connection with their examinations of these companies." In the opinion accompanying the June 30, 1958 financial statements Arthur Andersen & Co. stated:

---

[81]Statement of Touche, Niven, Bailey & Smart, With Respect to the Decision of the Securities and Exchange Commission in the Seaboard Commercial Corporation Proceedings, p. 3.

[82]Editorial, "Conclusion of the Atlas Plywood Story," *The Journal of Accountancy*, CVI (November, 1958), 32.

. . . the results of its operations included special charges for the two years then ended, and were prepared in conformity with generally accepted accounting principles applied on a basis consistent with that of the preceding year.

As Peat, Marwick, Mitchell & Co. said in a statement issued in 1958, this is a "clean" certificate, and it

confirms that the losses, including special charges, reported in 1957 were attributable to that year—not to previous years. Thereby, it substantiates without equivocation Peat, Marwick, Mitchell & Co.'s certification of the balance sheet at June 30, 1956.[83]

In the opinion of the editor of *The Journal,*

The incident emphasizes once again the urgency of better public information about the nature of accounting and auditing, and the responsibilities of management, as well as auditors, for the representations in financial statements.[84]

Use of C.P.A. Title by Partnerships

A tabulation by the American Institute of state law provisions regarding the use of the C.P.A. title or term "certified public accountants" by partnerships was gathered from the Accounting Law Reporter of the Commerce Clearing House. These laws sometimes require that titles other than C.P.A. be used on audit certificates. Many C.P.A. firms cannot use "C.P.A.'s" on their letterheads and firm title in some states. Some 12 million stockholders receive reports containing opinions of "Accountants and Auditors" or "Public Accountants," not Certified Public Accountants. This is a significant public relations loss to the C.P.A.'s. The following shows the results of the survey of the Accounting Law Reporter:

---

[83]*Ibid.*, p. 34.
[84]*Ibid.*, p. 34.

STATE LAW PROVISIONS REGARDING THE USE OF THE
CPA TITLE BY PARTNERSHIPS

Require each partner of a firm to possess a CPA certificate of that state

#Arizona
Delaware
District of Columbia
#Florida
#Georgia
Indiana
#Iowa*
#Louisiana
Maine
#Maryland
Massachusetts
#Michigan
#North Carolina
North Dakota
Oklahoma
South Carolina**
South Dakota
#Tennessee
#Virginia

Require each partner personally engaged within the state; each resident manager in charge of an office in the state to be CPAs of that state, and each non-resident partner to be a CPA of some state

#Colorado
Minnesota
#Missouri
Pennsylvania
#Wisconsin

Require all members personally engaged or practicing within the state to be CPA's of that state

#Alaska††
#Illinois
New Hampshire
#New Mexico
#Utah
#West Virginia

*Not a statutory requirement. Provided for in Regulations.
**Not a statutory requirement. Provided for in Board Code of Ethics.
†Does not require each resident manager to be a New York CPA.
††Not a statutory requirement. Provided for in Regulations. Non-resident partnerships also provided for in Regulations requiring each partner to have essential qualifications that would qualify him for practice in Alaska.
#States with regulatory public accounting laws.[85]

[85]Letter from Roderic A. Parnell, to Secretaries of the State Boards of Accountancy.

Require at least one general partner; each partner personally engaged within the state; each resident manager in charge of an office in the state, to be CPA's of that state, and each non-resident partner to be a CPA of some state

#California
#Connecticut
Kansas
#Kentucky
#Nebraska
#Nevada
#New York†
#Ohio
#Oregon*
#Texas
#Washington
#Puerto Rico
#Virgin Islands

Have no provision regarding the use of the title "CPA" by firms within their borders, but do restrict its use by individuals

Alabama
Arkansas
#Hawaii
Idaho
#Mississippi
Montana
New Jersey
Rhode Island
#Vermont
Wyoming

Certified Public Accountants and Lawyers Conflict: The Conway Case

The decision of the Supreme Court of Minnesota in *The Matter of Ramsey County Bar Association* v. *Conway* was of one of the major decisions on the subject of unauthorized practice of law in the field of income taxation.

The Conway case decision held that the defendant was engaged in the practice of law when he advised a client on whether he was in partnership with his wife, whether his common-law wife entitled him to claim an exemption for her, and certain other questions. A private investigator employed by the Unauthorized Practice of Law Subcommittee of the Ramsey County Bar Association, using an assumed name, approached Conway with a hypothetical tax problem, apparently calculated to tempt Conway into the rendering of services upon which plaintiff hoped later to prosecute him. Conway, apparently believing the investigator to be a bona fide client, undertook to advise him.[86]

In this case the defendant was found to have engaged in the practice of law in that he

advised and determined for the taxpayer whether the latter had attained the status of lawful marriage with a woman with whom he had been living but to whom he had never been ceremonially married. He further gave advice as to whether such taxpayer and his consort should file separate or joint returns.[87]

This decision appears to be slightly at variance with the Bercu case, which generally has been understood to mean that an accountant can properly advise on questions of law if they are incidental to his regular work as an accountant. The Minnesota court stated that the "incident" test is of no value except in a negative sense; that legal service is the practice of law unless it is incidental to the regular calling of a nonlawyer furnishing such service, but the mere fact that it is incidental is not decisive; and that when this service involves advice or a decision on difficult or doubtful legal questions, it is the practice of law whether incidental or not.

The editors of *The Journal* stated:

As a matter of fact, the court's opinion appears at no point to be in direct opposition to the Statement of Principles. The opinion must be appraised in the light of the fact that the defendant was not a certified public accountant. His lack of professional qualifications was stressed throughout the litigation.[88]

Agran Case

The editors of *The Journal* expressed the apparently inescapable conclusion that a purposeful minority within some of the bar associations was making a conscious effort to take away from accountants

---

[86]Current Notes, "Decision in Conway Appeal Holds Tax Consultant Practiced Law," *The Journal of Accountancy*, XCII (August, 1951), 135.

[87]Editorial, "The Conway Decision," *The Journal of Accountancy*, XCII (September, 1951), 289.

[88]*Ibid.*, p. 290.

a substantial part of the tax practice in which they had traditionally engaged, and make it a monopoly for lawyers, whether taxpayers want lawyers to serve them or not.

This position was arrived at in reaction to a June, 1954, decision of an appellate court in California, which held that a C.P.A., Reuben Agran, enrolled to practice before the U. S. Treasury Department, had invaded the field of "unauthorized practice of law" in settling a regular client's federal income tax liability with the Internal Revenue Service.

The views of the California State Bar's Committee on the Unauthorized Practice of Law on the proper functions of the accountant in income tax practice were clearly stated in a report issued in the fall of 1953, which said in part:

No accountant except one who is an employee of the taxpayer (as distinguished from an independent contractor) may advise as to the Income Tax effect or consequences of a transaction or transactions already completed or contemplated by the taxpayer.

Upon the instigation of an audit, it is recommended that an accountant should advise the retention of an attorney; and upon the issuance of a 30-day letter by the Treasury Department, an accountant shall do nothing further in the matter except under the supervision of and in aid of an attorney.[89]

On various occasions, other state bar associations (e.g. Massachusetts, Illinois, New York, Minnesota, and Florida) supported substantially the same views.

The case in question arose when Reuben Agran, a C.P.A. holding a Treasury card, handled federal income tax matters for clients, as C.P.A.'s have done since the income tax was first levied. One of his clients refused to pay for such services, so Agran sued for the fee. The trial court awarded Agran the full amount of the claim. On appeal by the client and in the appellate court the Cailfornia State Bar intervened, claiming that Agran had engaged in the "unauthorized practice of law" in settling a tax difference with an

---

[89]Editorial, "CPAs' Tax Practice Seriously Threatened," *The Journal of Accountancy*, XCVIII (August, 1954), 161.

internal revenue agent involving an operating loss carryback. The Superior Court of Los Angeles County held that Agran dealt with a "difficult and doubtful" question of law in that he interpreted and applied the Internal Revenue Code and related regulations and decisions in arguing how the loss should be classified for tax purposes.

The following excerpts show where a logical extension of the appellate court's assumptions had to lead:

For the sake of clarity and for the protection of those dealing with such matters, only those functions which clearly constitute the practice of law should be prohibited to the accountant.

A return may be characterized as an "ex parte" declaration by a taxpayer as to the amount of taxes he owes. If the return is accepted by the Treasury Department no other services by the person preparing the return are required. Up to this point it would be impossible to determine the extent to which the person preparing the return has relied on his knowledge of law and his knowledge of accounting.

Difficulties do not arise until the collecting agency takes the position that additional taxes are due. . . .

An issue was framed in this matter when an agent from the Treasury Department indicated in connection with an audit of the 1949 return that he did not agree that the Pritchard transaction was a "net operating loss from the operation of a trade or business."

No dispute ever arose out of the facts of the Pritchard loss nor of accounting matters connected therewith. The only question, as stated before, was as to the type of loss, purely a question of law. The basic question is whether or not after the framing of the issues, plaintiff as a certified public accountant could continue without the assistance of an attorney in his efforts to sustain the position previously taken. . . .

A definition which is especially pertinent is found in *State* ex rel. *McKittrick* v. *C. S. Dudley & Co.*, 102 S. W. 2d 895, 898; 340 Mo. 852: "A person is engaged in the 'practice of law'; when he, for a valuable consideration, engages in the business of advising persons, firms, associations or corporations as to their rights under the law, or appears in a representative capacity as an advocate in proceedings pending or prospective, before any court, commissioner, referee, board, body, committee or commission constituted by law or authorized to settle controversies, and there, in such representative capacity, performs any act or acts for the purpose of defending the rights of their clients under the law." The prime definition of Advocate is given in Webster's *New International Dictionary*, Second Edition, Unabridged, as: "One who pleads the cause of another. Specif., one who pleads the cause of another before a tribunal or judicial court; a counselor."

It has always been assumed that the right to practice law included the exclusive right to appear as an advocate in any type of proceedings where the rights of a litigant depended on questions of law, particularly the construction and interpretation of difficult statutory provisions. No other profession but law requires the training necessary to properly resolve difficult and complex questions of statutory construction.

The expert witness for defendant testified that in discussion with an agent from the Collector's office, similar to that testified to by plaintiff, they would proceed in precisely the same manner and do the same preparatory research as though the matter were to be tried before a judge. . . .

The public interest may only be protected by a requirement that such efforts be restricted to attorneys at law.

Based on a consideration of all these matters, this court holds that all services performed by plaintiff from the time of the first conference with the agent from the Treasury Department, in which the deductibility of the Pritchard loss was first questioned (referred to as item 20 at the time of the trial), until the successful termination of the plaintiff's efforts (items 28), constituted the practice of law, for which services he must be denied recovery.[90]

The court ignored the fact that the determination of income and the classification of a loss is an accounting process in which lawyers generally profess no competence. In effect, the court held that Agran "practiced law" because he practiced before the Treasury Department, as the Treasury Department authorized him to do by issuing him a card.

The editors of *The Journal* had the following to say:

The Treasury Department can bring us back to reality. It has unchallengable authority in this area. If it will say clearly what its rules mean, the fantasy will be ended.[91]

---

[90]Editorial, "Agran in Wonderland," *The Journal of Accountancy*, C (August, 1955), 29.
[91]*Ibid.*, p. 30.

The subsequent issuance of Circular 230 by the Treasury Department was an effort to clarify the practice before the department in federal income tax matters.

American Institute Withdraws from Agran Case

Following the statement by the Secretary of the Treasury, the American Institute and the California Society of Certified Public Accountants subsequently decided to drop the Agran case. Since the case had become something of a *cause célèbre,* an explanation of the circumstances seems in order.

Agran sued a client, Shapiro, for a fee for services rendered, including settlement of tax liability with the Internal Revenue agent. He won the case in municipal court and was awarded the full amount of the fee claimed.

On appeal, the Appellate Department, Superior Court of Los Angeles County, California, held that Agran's work constituted in part the unauthorized practice of law, and remanded the case to the lower court for decision as to how much fee he was entitled to for that part of his work which was not considered the practice of law.

This case followed the heels of the Bercu case in New York, the Conway case in Minnesota, and others of less importance in other states, in which unauthorized practice committees of local bar associations had charged that various activities of accountants in the field of tax practice constituted practice of law.

The Agran case was the first in which a C.P.A. who held a Treasury card had been attacked apparently for doing only what the Treasury authorized him to do. The implications of the Agran decision seemed so ominous that the Council of the American Institute resolved to ask the Treasury Department to clarify the right of enrolled C.P.A.'s to represent their clients before the Department.

In the light of the improved relations with the organized bar, and the Treasury interpretation of its regulations, the Council of the Institute at its April, 1956 meeting decided that there was no necessity to participate further in the Agran case, which in the meantime had been retired with a decision adverse to the C.P.A. plaintiff. The final decision, upon appeal, of the Appellate Department of the Superior Court of Los Angeles County was handed down September 30, 1956. It was again adverse to the C.P.A. plaintiff.[92]

Practice Before Treasury Department

The Treasury Department statement on January 30, 1956 seems to clearly confirm the long-established practice of enrolled agents before the Department and to make it clear that regulation of this practice is within the exclusive province of the Secretary of the Treasury.

The statement of the Secretary was made for the following reason:

Recently it has been contended that some phases of practice before the Department constituted the "practice of law," that the state courts had power to regulate the practice of law, and that the state courts, therefore, could properly prevent nonlawyers from doing things, in representing taxpayers before the Treasury Department, which the court held to be within the exclusive domain of lawyers.[93]

The Treasury Department opened practice before it to some individuals not enrolled by proposed revisions of Circular 230 announced October 31, 1958.

One significant change in policy allows those who prepare tax returns for others to represent taxpayers before revenue agents without being enrolled. A second proposal provides a less difficult examination for enrollment.

Under the terms of the second change, a simplified examination has been instituted to enable qualified persons, other than C.P.A.'s, lawyers, and former Internal Revenue Service personnel, to be specially enrolled to practice before the I.R.S. "The new examinations," the I.R.S. announced, "will not be as difficult as those presently given." They are, however, designed to test adequately the competency of candidates to represent taxpayers at all levels of the I.R.S. About 2,500 candidates passed the first examination for Treasury cards.

[92]Editorial, "The Agran Case in Perspective," *The Journal of Accountancy*, CII (December, 1956), 30.

[93]Editorial, "Practice Before Treasury Department Clarified," *The Journal of Accountancy*, CI (April, 1956), 29.

Under the proposed revisions, any person who prepares a return for a taxpayer would be permitted to appear as the taxpayer's representative, with or without the taxpayer's presence, before revenue agents and examining officers in the District Director's office (but not at the important conference level) in connection with the returns prepared by him.[94]

On January 30, 1956, the Secretary of the Treasury issued a statement interpreting Treasury Department Circular 230 relating to practice before the Treasury Department. In this statement the Secretary mentioned the need for uniformity in interpretation and administration of the regulations governing practice before the Department and stated that it has properly placed on lawyers and accountants, under the Department's ethical requirements, responsibility for determining when the assistance of a member of the other profession is required.

After the Treasury statement and the end of the Agran case, voluntary machinery was re-established under the 1951 Statement of Principles to encourage self-discipline and to enable differences between lawyers and C.P.A.'s to be resolved as they may arise (whether in tax practice or elsewhere) by conference and negotiation, and not by litigation. A special Committee on Professional Relations of the American Bar Association and the American Institute's Committee on Relations with the Bar have agreed that the National Conference of Lawyers and C.P.A.'s, composed of members of the two committees, should serve as a joint committee to consider differences arising between the two professions involving questions of what constitutes the practice of law or that of accounting.

The joint committee made the following recommendations as to procedures:

1. That with respect to the field of federal income taxation, the two professions continue to adhere to the Statement of Principles, approved by the governing bodies of the American Bar Association and th American Institute of Accountants in 1951. It is recognized that the statement is a guide to co-operation and does not presume to be a definition of the practice of law or the practice of accounting.

---

[94]News Report, "Treasury Practice Rules Eased," *The Journal of Accountancy*, CVI, (December, 1958), 7.

2. That state organizations of the two professions consider the establishment in each state of a joint committee similar to the National conference for consideration of differences arising between and members of the two professions.

3. That before any state organization of either profession shall institute or participate in litigation or disputes involving differences between members of the two professions, or involving questions of what constitutes the practice of law or accounting, such differences and questions be referred to joint committees of state organizations of the two professions, where such committees exist, or to the National Conference.

4. That, in the interest of uniformity, state committees maintain close coordination with the National Conference; and if resolution of differences seems impossible at the local and state level, they be referred to the National Conference. Particularly in the early years, it would seem to be in the best interest of all concerned for the National Conference to participate actively in the consideration and settlement of disputes which might serve as guides and precedents for other cases.

5. That—again in the interest of uniformity—where joint committees at the state level are appointed to deal with any differences which may arise, they be limited, where possible, to one to a state, and their structure and procedure follow the pattern of the National Conference.

It is hoped and believed that resolution of specific cases as suggested above will in time provide a body of precedent which will come to serve as a guide to members of the two professions. Such a body of precedent will, we think, prove of more practical value than attempts to find acceptable definitions of the fields of the two professions.

The efforts of the National Conference are not, of course, intended to be punitive in nature. Their objective will be to avoid conflict and to encourage and enable continuing co-operation between lawyers and certified public accountants in accordance with the ethical standards of the two professions.

> For the American Bar Association
> William J. Jamison, Chairman
> Special Committee
>
> For the American Institute of
> Accountants
> John W. Queenan, Chairman Committee
> on Relations with the Bar[95]

---

[95]Official Release, "Joint Report of Special Committee on Professional Relations of American Bar Association and Committee on Relations with the Bar of American Institute of Accountants," *The Journal of Accountancy*, CIII (January, 1957), 54.

Bar Lists Seven Objectionable Tax Activities

The American Bar Association Committee on Unauthorized Practice of Law, in its eighth annual report to the Association, discussed the relation of accountants and lawyers in tax practice, and expressed the opinion that it was the practice of law to do any of the following:

1. To give advice regarding the validity of tax statutes or regulations of the effect thereof in respect of matters outside of accounting procedures.

2. To determine legal questions preliminary or prerequisite to making of a lawful return in a lawful manner.

3. To prepare protests against tax adjustments, deficiencies or assessments.

4. To represent a taxpayer at a conference with administrative authorities in relation to matters outside of accounting procedures.

5. To prepare claims for refund of taxes.

6. To prepare petitions, stipulations or orders incident to the review of assessments by the U. S. Board of Tax Appeals or any like administrative tribunal.

7. To conduct the trial of issues before the U. S. Board of Tax Appeals or any like administrative tribunal.[96]

Lawyers and C.P.A.'s Co-operation

After the Bercu case the National Conference of Lawyers and Certified Public Accountants had further meetings, out of which came a statement which was unanimously approved by the American Institute of Accountants and the Board of Governors and House of Delegates of the American Bar Association. This statement was made in an effort to prevent future occurrences such as the Bercu case and public conflict between the two professions.

Excerpts from the statement of principles relating to practice in the federal income taxation field follow:

1. Collaboration of Lawyers and Certified Public Accountants Desirable. . . . Lawyers should encourage their clients to seek the advice of certified public accountants whenever accounting problems arise and certified public account-

---

[96]Official Decisions & Releases, "American Bar Association Committee Lists Seven Tax Activities It Considers To Be Practice of Law," *The Journal of Accountancy*, XCI (February, 1951), 307.

ants should encourage clients to seek the advice of lawyers whenever legal questions are presented.

2. Preparation of Federal Income Tax Returns. It is a proper function of a lawyer or a certified public accountant to prepare federal income tax returns.

3. Ascertainment of Probable Tax Effects of Transactions. . . . In many cases, therefore, the public will be best served by utilizing the joint skills of both professions.

4. Preparation of Legal and Accounting Documents. Only a lawyer may prepare legal documents such as agreements, conveyances, trust instruments, wills. . . .

Only an accountant may properly advise as to the preparation of financial statements included in reports as submitted with tax returns, or as to accounting methods and procedures.

5. Prohibited Self-Designations. An accountant should not describe himself as a "tax consultant" or "tax expert" or use any similar phrase. Lawyers, similarly, are prohibited by the canons of ethics of the American Bar Association and the opinions relating thereto, from advertising a special branch of law practice.

6. Representative of Taxpayers before Treasury Department. . . . If in the course of such proceedings, questions arise involving the application of legal principles, a lawyer should be retained, and, if in the course of such proceedings accounting questions arise, a certified public accountant should be retained.

7. Practice before the Tax Court of the United States. Under the Tax Court rules nonlawyers may be admitted to practice. . . .

Here also, as in proceedings before the Treasury Department, the taxpayer, in many cases, is best served by the combined skills of both lawyers and certified public accountants, and the taxpayers, in such cases, should be advised accordingly.

8. Claims for Refund. Claims for refund may be prepared by lawyers or certified public accountants, provided, however, that where a controversial legal issue is involved or where the claim is to be made the basis of litigation, the services of a lawyer should be obtained.

9. Criminal Tax Investigation. When a certified public accountant learns that his client is being specially investigated for possible criminal violation of the income tax law, he should advise his client to seek the advice of a lawyer to determine his legal and constitutional rights.[97]

---

[97]"National Conference of Lawyers and Certified Public Accountants," *The Journal of Accountancy*, XCI (June, 1951), 871.

It was the hope of both professions that under these rules the professions could continue in income tax practice. Every effort was made by the two groups to reconcile their differences in an honorable way.

The New York State Society of Certified Public Accountants and the New York State Bar Association reached a formal agreement which was wholly consistent with the Statement of Principles in the Field of Federal Income Taxation, adopted by the National Conference of Lawyers and C.P.A.'s in 1951. The New York C.P.A. Society and the Bar Association specifically "concur in and ratify" the national statement.

The following paragraph in the agreement is of special significance:

These procedures are intended to provide voluntary means for the amicable solution of any controversies which may arise between the two professions. To this end it is agreed that, in so far as may be compatible with law and except where necesssary to protect its rights in any case, neither the Bar Association nor the Society of Certified Public Accountants will institute or participate in litigation or a dispute involving the interests of the two professions without first submitting such question to the Joint Practice Committee.[98]

The New York agreement established a Joint Practice Committee for dealing with potential sources of disagreement, especially when a member of either profession is charged with invading the province of the other.

In the state where the two professions were on opposite sides of the Bercu case only a decade ago, this is a constructive achievement in which both can take proper pride. Further, during the years immediately following the National Conference's adoption of the Statement of Principles in 1951, formal or informal agreements were reached between bar associations and C.P.A. societies in more than half the states.[99] Since the 1957 National Statement (Jamison-Greenman), no serious conflicts have arisen. The National Conference or state groups have settled questions by friendly negotiation. Relations in 1960 are the best in twenty years.

---

[98]Editorial, "Lawyer - CPA Co-operation," *The Journal of Accountancy*, CVII (March, 1959), 27.
[99]*Ibid.*, p. 28.

Ethics and Practice of Law and Public Accounting

The following may be cited as an example of one view of the ethical considerations involved in practicing law and public accounting in one office. The New York County Lawyers Association received a question from a member regarding the practice of law and public accounting from the same office. The answer given the lawyers and certified public accountants by the committee on professional ethics of the New York Lawyers Association was as follows:

Question

Is it professionally proper for AC and BC, two brothers, who are both members of the New York Bar and also certified public accountants of the State of New York, to practice accountancy at the same office, in New York City where they practice law, placing on their office door the following legends:

C & C
Attorneys and Counselors at Law
C & Company
Certified Public Accountants

Answer

Two principles are involved in the consideration of this question. The first, grounded on canon 27, is that an attorney at law, acting as such, may not by any form or medium of advertising, announce to the public at large that he has a special skill in a particular branch of the law. This prohibition extends to every type of publicity, including legends on office doors, stationery, announcements, letters, circulars, etc.

The other principle, also established by canon 27, is that a lawyer may not solicit professional employment by advertisements, circulars, or by personal communications or interviews not warranted by personal relations.

We are aware that the committee on professional ethics and grievances of the American Bar Association, in its opinion 272 (October 25, 1946), expressed the view that a lawyer could not, as a practical matter, carry on an independent accounting business from his law office without violating canon 27. With all due respect to the committee on professional ethics and grievances of the American Bar Association, we have come to the conclusion that neither of the aforesaid prohibitions of canon 27 would be violated by the procedure set forth in the question, provided that AC and BC, in the practice of their

profession as certified public accountants, adhere to the professional standards applicable to attorneys at law with respect to advertising and solicitation.
In our opinion the proposed legends on the office door would merely identify
the firms occupying the premises and the professions practiced by them therein,
and would not constitute either advertising or solicitation by AC and BC
within the meaning of canon 27.[100]

Employment of Lawyers by CPA Firms

Dean Erwin N. Griswold of the Harvard Law School, who succeeded Judge Jamison as co-chairman of the National Conference
of Lawyers and C.P.A.'s in 1958, has taken a helpful interest over
the past few years in minimizing friction and misunderstanding
between lawyers and certified public accountants in the field of
tax practice. This interest has led to occasional informal exchanges
of views on specific questions between Dean Griswold and representatives of the American Institute of Certified Public Accountants.

Recently Dean Griswold wrote the Institute on a subject which
has caused a great deal of irritation in bar association circles—the
employment of lawyers by accounting firms. The Dean wrote as
follows:

In a purely personal and wholly unofficial way, I want to pass on to you a
paragraph from a letter which has just come to me from a lawyer friend. I believe that it summarizes what is perhaps the really most difficult problem in the
lawyer-accountant area. At least it shows the way some thoughtful lawyers
are thinking. The paragraph in question reads as follows:

"With regard to the CPA item, nothing is surprising in this field. A large
accounting firm now has approximately ten lawyers in the 'Tax Department'
of its local office alone, having only one approximately three years ago. Another
firm has about twenty-five lawyers and lawyer-CPAs in its 'Tax Department'
and thirty-five in its 'Auditing Department.' "

One of the accounting firms referred to was discovered to be
Lybrand, Ross Bros. & Montgomery, of which Alvin R. Jennings,

---

[100]Official Decisions & Releases, "New York County Lawyers Association Answers a Question on
Ethics," *The Journal of Accountancy*, LXXXIX (January, 1950), 72.

nominee for the presidency of the Institute, is senior partner. The matter was brought to his attention, and Mr. Jennings wrote Dean Griswold as follows:

Before dealing with the substance of your correspondence, I would like you to know that I share the feeling which is general in our profession that your personal participation in the efforts to further the understanding between our two professions has been profoundly helpful. From your writings and otherwise I have the impression that your views generally on the proper place of the certified public accountant in the field of tax practice are very similar to those held by our partners.

As a firm, we wholeheartedly endorse the purposes and aims of the National Conference of Lawyers and Certified Public Accountants. We acknowledge a responsibility for identifying and, if possible, for eliminating causes of friction between the two professions. We have no desire to practice law and I am sure, in all material respects, there is no disagreement between your views and ours on what might constitute the practice of law.

The question of the propriety of the employment of lawyers by firms of CPAs has been raised with some frequency. It has been said that some of the national accounting firms "have law departments." it has been charged that some such firms give legal advice. I would suppose that, so long as differences of opinion exist on what constitutes maintenance of "legal departments" or of "legal advice," the problem will remain with us.

Our firm organization includes a relatively few men who have law degrees. Almost without exception, these men have never practiced law but came to us initially out of college with a law degree or attended law school nights while employed by us. Almost without exception the men with law degrees also are certified public accountants or are presently preparing themselves to become such. Because we recognized that employment by accounting firms of lawyers was a source of misunderstanding, our firm, more than a year ago, issued a statement of policy on the subject. I am enclosing a copy for your information.

I am unable to accept the idea that there is anything improper, per se, in the employment of a lawyer by a firm of CPAs or the employment of a CPA by a firm of lawyers. As you can determine from our own statement on the subject, we do believe that, if a firm of CPAs should have among its employes those who possess law degrees, the firm should do everything possible to avoid the impression that it is competent to practice law or holds itself out as doing so. In my opinion, it would be a bad thing for both our professions if the Bar were to adopt a canon which would prevent one of its members from accepting employment with a firm of certified public accountants. However, it does not seem to me unreasonable that the Bar should take the position that one of its members cannot serve in both capacities at the same time and that a member of the Bar who accepts employment in the office of a certified public accountant should, in effect, consider his right to practice law to be restricted so long as he is so employed.

There may be strong reasons why the Bar would be reluctant to prohibit its members from accepting employment as corporate officials or employment in any other field of their choosing. Do there exist reasons why the Bar could not restrict the right of one of its members to practice law so long as by his own choice he was employed in a field in which the Bar believed that the practice of law was incompatible? If such restrictions were generally regarded by members of the Bar as desirable, could not the Bar associations do a great deal to set the whole problem at rest by amending their canons of practice to achieve this result?

If you would like further details concerning our organization or our policy regarding the employment of members of the Bar, I hope that you will feel free to write me.

The statement of policy to which Mr. Jennings refers is the following:

Subject: Employment of Members of the Bar

February 8, 1956

To All Partners:

The American Institute of Accountants has devoted a great deal of time and effort to finding a workable solution to the controversy over the proper place of the accountant in the field of federal tax practice.

Several responsible spokesmen of the Bar have asserted that the large national accounting firms maintain legal departments and give legal advice to clients. The AIA has made efforts to find out what, if any, factual basis there may be for such assertions. While these efforts have not disclosed any such cases, they do suggest the possibility that the misunderstanding grows out of the employment of attorneys by accounting firms.

An example in point may be cited from an article by a prominent member of the Bar which appeared last summer in the *Arkansas Law Review* in which the author says:

"A word at this point about the employment of lawyers by accounting firms. While employment of an attorney by the major accounting firms is not per se unlawful, it is evidence that these firms are practicing law in the giving of general advice to clients. This advice not only includes pure tax practice, but in many instances, includes a consideration of property and other laws, the consideration of which is necessary to the answer to the particular tax problem. While the employment of the attorney is not itself unlawful, it is what the attorney does for the accountant that is unlawful. The giving of the opinion by the lawyer, acting for the accountant, where the lawyer is simply the employee or agent, is the giving of the opinion by the principal, and not by the agent. This would be true even though the accountant himself, as partner, happens to be also a lawyer. It is the accounting firm, over its letterhead, that purports to answer the questions and to give the advice, and the fact that its agent in giving the advice is a lawyer, does not mean that the advice by the firm is thereby legalized. The American Institute should adopt a firm rule that accountants shall not, as a matter of policy, employ attorneys. If they do not succeed in this, action should be taken by the American Bar Association."

Some of our partners and staff have legal in addition to accounting degrees. In a relatively few cases members of our tax staff who have law degrees are not yet CPAs. These circumstances do not alter the fact that our practice is that of public accounting. We do not practice law and we have no desire to do so. Possession of a CPA degree is essential for advancement to positions of responsibility in our profession. Accordingly, our personnel policies stress the importance of attaining the degree. This is so without regard to whether the staff member may be employed in the auditing, special management or tax areas of our practice. At no point should we require that the possession of a law degree be a requisite for employment or advancement. Possession of a law degree, on the other hand, should not prevent us from employing anyone who has the requisite accounting education or experience.

To avoid the unwarranted implication that we are holding ourselves out as competent to practice other than in the field of public accounting, our Executive Committee believes that we should not approve any public reference to law degrees which may be held by partners or staff. Articles written or talks given by partners or staff members who possess dual degrees may properly describe the author as a CPA but should not identify him as a member of the Bar. If a member of the staff who does not hold the degree of CPA should publish an article, or appear on a program, his identification with the firm may be stated but no reference to a legal degree, if any, should be approved.

Sincerely,

A. R. Jennings

To this communication Dean Griswold replied:

Thank you very much for your letter of June 17. I am glad to hear from you. I suspect that one of the major areas of friction between lawyers and accountants lies in the employment of lawyers by accounting firms. Where these persons are primarily and basically accountants, who have simply studied law in the evenings as an aid and background to their accounting work, I doubt if much problem arises. On the other hand, though, where the persons are basically and essentially lawyers, with their primary training as lawyers, I am inclined to think that a good many difficulties and misunderstandings can arise. This is particularly true where they are not certified public accountants. It is also true to a considerable extent where they do qualify for the CPA after having full legal training and experience.

Thank you for sending me your policy statement of February 9, 1956. This is very interesting. It seems to me to be an important step in the right direction. I am sure that if all accounting firms would adopt this policy, and would carry it out, there woud be a considerable drop in friction between lawyers and accountants. This is something which might be considered in more detail by the National Conference of Lawyers and Certified Public Accountants.

This correspondence may raise the question why accounting firms employ men with law degrees in the first place. Frequently men with law degrees apply for positions in accounting firms. There has been an urgent need for good men in the rapidly growing profession of accounting. A promising man with a trained mind is welcomed as a recruit today by almost any accounting firm, whether he is skilled in law, engineering, science, economics or any other discipline. It goes without saying that such recruits .must study accounting and obtain the CPA certificate before they can advance in the accounting profession. Again, accountants on the staffs of accounting firms have studied law in the belief that it would be a useful additional discipline.

There may be a few exceptions. Perhaps some certified public accountants, without giving the matter much thought, have assumed that it is all right to employ lawyers on a salary to deal with legal aspects of tax work for clients of the CPAs. Any such CPA, or accounting firm, would be open to charges of unauthorized practice of law, since the proprietor or partners of the firm would be accepting fees for the legal work done by their employees. Any such situation should be corrected immediately. No employee of an accounting firm should be permitted to render services which the employer is not permitted to render.

At best, the presence of law-trained assistants on a CPA's staff may be regarded as circumstantial evidence of improper intentions. For this reason, any accounting firm which employs men with law degrees, even if they do nothing but accounting work, might do well to follow the policies adopted by Mr. Jennings' firm.[101]

Use of Title "Tax Consultants"

The American Institute's Committee on Relations with the Bar agrees that it would be desirable for an accountant to discontinue the use of the designation "tax consultant" in conjunction with his name in the telephone directory. The bar association cited the decision of the New York Court of Appeals in the Bercu case which prohibited the defendant from using the designations "Tax Counsel," "Tax Consultant" or similar designations.[102]

The American Bar Association Standing Committee on Unauthorized Practice of Law adopted an opinion on the use of the title "Tax Consultant." The complete text of the views is given here because of the magnitude of the lawyer-accountant conflict of the past dozen years.

---

[101]Editorial, "Employment of Lawyers by Accounting Firms," *The Journal of Accountancy,* CIV (September, 1957), 30.

[102]Editorial, "Use of Designation 'Tax Consultant' Is Challenged," *The Journal of Accountancy,* XC (July, 1950), 5.

OPINION NO. C OF 1950
FROM THE
STANDING COMMITTEE ON UNAUTHORIZED
PRACTICE OF LAW
OF THE
AMERICAN BAR ASSOCIATION

In many cities Classified Telephone Directories are published which contain a separate listing of persons and firms describing themselves as "Tax Consultants."

An analysis of the listing in the Classified Telephone Directory in one city (Manhattan, New York City Directory) discloses the names of 125 persons and firms who designate themselves as "Tax Consultants"; of these, 36 appear to be certified public accountants, 11 appear to be lawyers, (some of whom are also certified public accountants) and as to the rest, except for 18 public accountants, a special investigation of each would be required to ascertain what claim is made to professional status.

The American College Dictionary defines the word "consultant" as "one who gives professional or expert advice." Therefore, the listing under the designation "Tax Consultant" can have only one purpose, and that is to make the public believe that the persons listed under such designation are experts in tax law problems and are qualified to give tax law advice.

The title "Tax Consultant" is self-bestowed. It does not represent any degree or designation awarded by any court, college or statute. Obviously, neither the publishers or these directories nor the telephone companies can, nor do they, attempt to ascertain or apply to these listees any standards of competency, of good character or fitness which might entitle them to be represented to the public as "Tax Consultants."

In all of the professions admission is not easy and a license to practice is granted only after rigid examinations as to competence and character. In the field of legal advice and the practice of law, statutes require that persons rendering such services shall be competent and qualified, shall conform to high ethical principles and maintain professional standards of practice. Thus every effort is being made so that the public should have competent and qualified legal advice from persons who must undergo a course of study and pass examinations, whose good character is passed upon as well, and who, after they are licensed as lawyers, will give good, honest, disinterested advice and service and be subject to regulation and control throughout their careers as members of the legal profession.

To permit the public to be deceived into employing in the field of tax law alleged experts who have given themselves the title "Tax Consultant," or any similar title, thwarts the public protections that exist in respect to legal advice.

In New York its highest public court[1] has enjoined a certified public accountant from calling himself a "Tax Consultant," "Tax Counsel" or from using any similar designation likely to deceive the public. The American Institute of Accountants has recommended that certified public accountants discontinue the use of the title "Tax Consultant" to avoid any suggestion that the accountant is prepared to give advice on legal questions as well as accounting questions which may arise in tax practice.[2]

Many a taxpayer may be competent to prepare his own tax return, but when in its preparation he reaches the point where technical assistance is needed, he is entitled to be expertly advised as to whatever law may affect his situation including, of course, as well, the tax law, its judicial interpretation, rules and regulations. Any determination of applicable law and all advice based thereon must be applied to his problems before anyone can compute his probable tax liability and apply the principles of accountancy in relation thereto.

It has long been recognized by both the legal and accounting professions that professional men should not advertise. As to lawyers, it has been declared unprofessional conduct for them to insert their names in any directory under any title other than as a "lawyer."

If misrepresentations as to alleged expertness in any professional field by unqualified and unauthorized persons were permitted, all of the existing public protections in respect to such service can be evaded. Advertising the title of "Tax Consultant" or any similar title by unauthorized persons, whether in a Classified Telephone Directory or otherwise, tends to bring about such result in the field of tax law.

---

[1] In the Bercu Case, 273 App. Div. 524, 78 N.Y. Supp. (2nd) 209; 9 ALR (2nd) 787 aff'd 299. N.Y. 728. See also: *Gardner* v. *Conway*, Minn. Second Judicial Court, Ramsey County Par. 72, 390, P.H. Fed. 1950; *Lowell Bar Association* v. *Loeb*, 315 Mass. at 18252 N.E. (2nd) 27.

[2] *Journal of Accountancy*, July, 1950, Volume 90, Number 1, p. 5.

Your Committee has come to the following conclusions:

1. The listing of "Tax Consultant" referred to aids and makes possible the unauthorized practice of law because such a conglomerate grouping of lawyers, certified public accountants and others inevitably leads the public to believe that all of those listed are equally competent in the tax law field, results in

the performance of legal services, encourages the giving of legal advice and the rendition of legal services by persons unauthorized to do so.

2. Lawyers who permit their names to be used in such a listing should be apprised of Canon 47[3] which expressly forbids the use of a lawyer's name to aid or make possible unauthorized practice of law by others.

3. Persons listed who are not lawyers may be subject to the penalties provided by the laws which seek to protect the public from the danger inherent in the representation by unauthorized persons that they are qualified to practice law or give legal advice or service.

This Committee expresses the desire that publishers of these directories cooperate with the legal and accounting professions in the public interest, to do away with the classification which, aside from deceiving the public, is manifestly unfair to the thousands of reputable persons who are appropriately listed in the directories under their correct designations, to wit, "Accountants," "Certified Public Accountants" and "Lawyers."

Dated: Washington, D.C.
September 16, 1950
STANDING COMMITTEE ON
UNAUTHORIZED PRACTICE OF LAW
By John D. Randall, Chairman
Thomas J. Boodell, Secretary
Warren H. Resh
Cuthbert S. Baldwin
A. J. Casner
E. N. Eisenhower
Edwin M. Otterbourg[103]

---

[3]Canon 47, Opinion 53, American Bar Association Committee on Professional Ethics and Grievances.

Common Interest of Lawyers and C.P.A.'s

The lawyer and the Certified Public Accountant combine their respective knowledge in countless situations with which modern business is confronted. It is significant that the trouble arose mainly in the field of federal income taxation, where the skills of lawyers

---

[103]Official Decisions and Releases, "Use of Term 'Tax Consultant' Opposed by American Bar Association Standing Committee on Unauthorized Practice of Law," *The Journal of Accountancy*, XCI (February, 1951), 307.

and certified public accountants come together in closer relation, perhaps, than in any other field. But it is also significant that the protagonists in the conflict were not generally the lawyers and Certified Public Accountants who specialized in taxation. The most violent and extreme positions, generally speaking, were taken by spokesmen of the two professions and techniques of tax practice.

It is generally recognized that there is a place in tax practice for both the lawyer and the C.P.A. The National Conference of Lawyers and Certified Public Accountants has subscribed to this view.[104]

SUMMARY

The public accountant, a little over 100 years ago, in 1854, was given professional status by the creation of the designation "Chartered Accountant," first in Scotland and soon after in England. This happened simultaneously with the recognition that the independent auditors accepted a personal responsibility separate from that of the persons who employed and paid them. This responsibility is due not only to the client but also to third parties who may place reliance on the financial statements, which are given a greater credibility by the professional accountant's examination and opinion.

About 70 percent of the new entrants to C.P.A. ranks are college graduates. Advanced degrees in accounting, including masters and doctorates, are now available at many universities.

Forty years ago the American Institute of Certified Public Accountants began the development of a code of ethics which has now evolved into nineteen major rules supplemented by published opinions of the Committee on Ethics and Resolutions of the governing Council.

Alvin R. Jennings mentions the following as typical business situations in which the C.P.A. and the lawyer come together: estate planning, pension or profit-sharing plans, voluntary extension of credit, insurance losses, labor negotiations.

The decade of the 1950's began with the conflict between the lawyers and certified public accountants in litigation and ended

---

[104]Alvin R. Jennings, "Common Interests of Lawyers and Certified Public Accountants," *Lybrand Journal*, XL (1959), 7.

with the problem still unsettled. Yet the public accounting profession made great progress toward national and international recognition. Evidence of this recognition is found in the growth of the large and small public accounting firms and in increased demands for services from certified public accountants.

The management services area in public practice was one of the major developments in the decade. However, the Securities and Exchange Commission continued to exercise great influence over the public accountant and his actions. Finally, future developments in the public accounting profession can be expected to lie in the areas of collegiate education, the Accounting Principles Board, and restrictive legislation. C.P.A.'s have moved ahead rapidly on all fronts: standards are being clarified, services expanded, training improved, and public recognition steadily attained.

CHAPTER IX

Summary

The evolution of bookkeeping into accounting and the improved accounting techniques have, to a certain extent, developed as business has developed. Any nation that has attained a high degree of economic development has carried on extensive commerce. Commercial and industrial development probably could not have been so rapid without corresponding improvements in the system of accounting. Accountancy then is the mirror of the past in which the world's commercial history is reflected. In reading histories of commerce and industry it becomes evident that the higher the stage of culture and commercial development in a community, the more advanced its methods of accounting. The cause and effect are not so readily observed.

The antecedents of American public accounting are to be found in Scotland and England. In these countries the profession developed rapidly during the nineteenth century, receiving impetus from laws enacted by Parliament. The first major legislation, the Companies Acts of 1862 and 1869, required annual audits of regulated firms. At first these auditors were the stockholders in the companies. An auditing committee was appointed by the stockholders. They were not necessarily qualified for the undertaking, nor were they likely to be.

When these company committees recognized the problems involved in the auditing of the records, outside accountants were consulted. Perhaps that is why A. C. Littleton says these Companies Acts have been called the friend of the public accounting profession.

With greatly increased demand for accountants, some unqualified persons began to represent themselves as public accountants. In an effort to protect their profession, the English accountants followed the lead of their Scottish neighbors in forming organizations for mutual benefit, and groups in Scotland, Ireland and England subsequently concluded a working arrangement for the building of uniform professional requirements.

Because of the close economic ties between the British Isles and the United States during the last half of the nineteenth century and the first quarter of the twentieth century, many accountants were sent to the United States to check on English and Scottish investments in the brewery industry and in railroads. Public accounting offices manned by American accountants soon opened in this country.

The first of these local firms was established in New York in 1882 by Barrow, Wade, Guthrie and Company. Prior to 1880, there were scattered references to public accountants and the performance of their functions during the eighteenth and nineteenth centuries. However, accountancy was not a full-time occupation until the late nineteenth century.

The number of firms increased rapidly in the 1890's as a result of increased business activity in the United States. Mergers of railroads and industrial enterprises during the last decade of the nineteenth century gave additional impetus to the development of the profession.

Accountants began to organize almost as soon as they began to practice as public accountants. The Institute of Accountants and Bookkeepers was the first of these organizations. There are few records of the Institute of Accountants and Bookkeepers, but it did play a significant part in the drafting of C.P.A. legislation.

The major accounting organization formed during the 1880's was the American Association of Public Accountants in 1886. The American Association of Public Accountants did not reach any real prominence outside the state of New York, but it, along with the Institute of Accountants and Bookkeepers, was responsible for the drafting of the first C.P.A. bill, which was defeated by the New York legislature because of a restrictive provision.

In the last quarter of the nineteenth century the literature of the profession and its educational facilities alike began to grow. These earliest schools were private ones devoted to bookkeeping. American textbooks began to replace British. These changes typify the increasing interest in education evinced by accountants. Those in New York attempted to set up a school in New York City under the New York State Board of Regents but sponsored by the profession.

In the following period, 1896-1913, the profession received its first legal recognition when the New York legislature enacted the first C.P.A. law. The act was the same as the bill that had been sponsored by both the Institute of Accountants and the American Association except that the restrictive provisions were omitted.

A board of examiners was appointed by the Regents and the first examination was given in December, 1896. According to the records of the American Institute of Accountants, however, the first certificates issued on examination were dated 1898. In that same year the first violator of the C.P.A. law was fined for using "Certified Public Accountant" in an advertisement offering his services.

Accounting firms began to open branch offices to facilitate the services given their clients. It was more satisfactory for the public accounting firms to have a branch office conduct the audit of branch offices of clients than it was to have another firm act as agent.

Industrial consolidations in the early 1900's gave impetus to the development of the public accounting profession. The most notable of the industrial mergers was the formation of the United States Steel Corporation. The stockholders of the United States Steel Corporation elected the auditors for their company in 1902. This election was probably the first instance of a practice that is now a part of accepted corporate procedure.

With public accounting firms and branches beginning to develop and operate over much of the eastern half of the United States, as well to have scattered engagements throughout the country, more attention was given to getting trained assistants.

Professional organizations sponsored educational institutions and guaranteed them against losses. The first department of accountancy, as such, was founded at the University of New York in 1900. In 1902 the Pennsylvania Institute established an accounting department which was turned over to the Wharton School of Accounts and Finance in 1904.

The practitioners also recognized the need for a professional periodical in the accounting field. *The Journal of Accountancy* was established to meet professional needs of accountants. But it was not until 1912—seven years later—that the profession assumed editorial control of the Journal.

When the first C.P.A. law was enacted in 1896, some ten years after the American Association of Public Accountants was organized, there were only forty-five members of that organization. Three years later, an organization called the National Society of Certified Public Accountants was created, but it merged with the American Association in 1899. In 1902 another accounting organization, the Federation of Societies of Public Accountants in the United States, was formed, but it too was absorbed by the American Association after the first International Congress of Accountants at St. Louis in 1904. From a very early date it seems that there was a strong desire within the profession for one national organization.

The auditing reports issued during the first decade of the twentieth century exemplify the standards of that period. The significant items in the auditors' certificates were the statements that the inventories had been verified by an official of the company, that provisions for bad debts had been made, and that adequate depreciation and all ascertainable liabilities had been recorded. Then the auditors certified that the statements were true or were correctly taken from the accounts and books of the company. Thus, the emphasis during the first decade of the twentieth century as far as auditing was concerned was on valuation.

Provisions of the 1909 franchise tax on the income (cash receipts minus the cash disbursements) of a corporation were largely ignored, in that practitioners disregarded the basis for measuring the taxable income and continued to operate on the regular accrual basis. Due to accountants' lack of complaints about the 1909 tax law, the passage of the sixteenth amendment and the 1913 income tax law was facilitated. The stepped-up rates and the excess profits tax of the 1917 act brought more work to public accountants.

During World War I the public accountant was called in by foreign governments to determine the proper cost of war goods purchased in the United States. Among others, J. P. Morgan and Company, which was acting as purchasing agent for England and France, was audited by an American firm. The early engagements on cost determination led to others for the American firms.

By 1924 all states and territories had enacted some law giving legal recognition to the C.P.A. In that year, however, several sections of the Oklahoma law were declared unconstitutional because of the restrictive provision limiting practice to public accountants who had been licensed by the state.

The American Association was reorganized in 1917, when the

name was changed to the Institute of Accountants in the United States of America, later shortened to the American Institute of Accountants. A more satisfactory charter was obtained under the laws of the District of Columbia and the new organization was designed in such a way as to avoid the frequent criticism that it was dominated by New York accountants.

Peace in the national organization lasted only four short years. In 1921 the National Association of Certified Public Accountants, a private corporation, was organized to give examinations and issue C.P.A. certificates. Actually the organization sold certificates—some three thousand in three years. In 1923, an injunction was issued against the organization, restraining it from issuing any more. This decision by the Court of Appeals in the District of Columbia confirmed the states' rights to license Certified Public Accountants and regulate their activities.

The injunction against the National Association of Certified Public Accountants did not settle the problems of the public accounting profession. The American Institute of Accountants did not take as strong action against the National Association, a private organization, as many members felt it should. In 1921, some of the members of the American Institute of Accountants withdrew and formed the American Society of Certified Public Accountants, with the purpose of protecting and fostering the professional designation C.P.A.

Beginning in 1917, the American Institute of Accountants gave its own examinations to prospective members. The Institute disapproved of certain state C.P.A. tests, as excluding qualified public accountants from practicing as C.P.A.'s.

The federal government, through established agencies, gave recognition to the profession in two instances. First, the Federal Trade Commission requested that the members of the American Institute of Accountants prepare a statement on uniform accounting, subsequently issued as *Approved Methods for the Preparation of Balance Sheet Statements,* which was later revised and published under the title *Verification of Financial Statements,* outlining auditing procedures. Second, the Tax Board of Appeals ruled in 1924 that only C.P.A.'s and lawyers could practice before the Board.

Then the Ultramares case, settled in the late twenties, set up a principle regarding the responsibilities of an auditor. The decision confirmed the common law that third parties could not hold auditors liable unless fraud was involved, but extended the concept of fraud almost to the borders of gross negligence.

The demand for more adequate reporting of financial information developed out of the depression in the early 1930's and affected the accounting profession greatly. Most important were the Stock Exchange rulings and the enactment of the Securities Acts of 1933 and 1934. The Securities Acts defined the liability of the auditor to third parties and set minimum reporting standards. Although applied only to those corporations filing registration statements under the Acts, the standards set and the reporting requirements have tended to govern accounting practices throughout business. Auditors no longer could allow the client to dictate what would be included in the certificate. The Securities Acts thus gave support to the professional accountant in establishing professional standards in the requirements of practice before the Securities and Exchange Commission as well as in his other auditing engagements.

Another influential factor has been the American Institute of Accountants' series of research and auditing bulletins that began in 1940. The accounting profession had taken the lead in reviewing auditing procedures and standards before the McKesson & Robbins case was settled, but it was that case which caused the profession to act.

The renegotiation of government contracts after the World Wars and the increasing number of reports required by the federal government gave rise to problems which the profession had to solve. State societies and the American Institute of Accountants were the organs through which accountants obtained information about the government's requirements. Finally, after World War II, the accounting and legal professions found themselves in conflict over the preparation of income tax returns, a conflict which came out into the open in the Bercu case. The full effect of the Bercu decision has not yet been felt by the profession, nor does the question seem to be settled.

The tax practice conflict extended, in the 1950's, from the New York State Bercu case, to Minnesota, with its Conway case, and to California's Agron case. The strained relations between the legal profession and that of the public accountant have not yet been restored. However, the 1951 statement of the joint committee of the American Bar Association and the American Institute has established areas for future agreement.

Reliance on the independent auditor's opinion on financial statements of many non-profit and regulated segments of the economy has significantly increased in recent years. The American Institute of Certified Public Accountants recognized the expanding areas of services to the public accountant by establishing committees dealing with the following: relations with bankers, accounting for non-profit organizations, the special problems of audits of insurance companies, and (at the suggestion of Phillip L. West, Vice President of the New York Stock Exchange) relations with the Interstate Commerce Commission. These committee appointments and their subsequent activities are major examples of the growing acceptance of the certified public accountant's responsibility in all segments of American society. Another example is the A.F.L.-C.I.O. code, which calls for virtually all affiliated unions to have independent audits.

A significant development in recent years in the practice of the public accounting profession has been the growth in the management services offered their clients. The magnitude of the development of the new field has been such that the American Institute issued a pamphlet on management services by CPA's indicating areas of possible service. The intimate knowledge which the C.P.A. gains from close association with his clients is one of the important reasons why he can be expected to offer useful counsel and guidance to management on various phases of business problems.

The national and international demands on various public accounting firms brought about mergers within the profession and the opening of offices throughout the world. The size of domestic clients and the variety of their operating localities contributed to the need for multiple locations of the public accounting firms. Also, the large capital investments overseas stimulated the international operations of many of the national public accounting firms.

Because of the national and international recognition of certified public accountants, the American Institute adopted an official policy supporting regulatory C.P.A. legislation. Under the new policy, the Institute will support state laws providing for the registration of all accountants in public practice, either as C.P.A.'s or P.A.'s. After an appropriate cutoff date for registration of all individuals already in practice, admission to the practice of public accountancy will be limited to those who pass the C.P.A. examination.

The Commission on Standards of Education and Experience created in 1952 recognized the importance of uniformity for entrance into the public accounting profession. The first step toward uniformity—establishing of a standard C.P.A. examination—has been taken; all fifty states now use the uniform examination. The next step, agreement upon education and experience requirements, is necessary before it will become feasible for C.P.A. certificates to be readily issued on a reciprocal basis. The commission recommended that the C.P.A. examination be given at the conclusion of the training acquired through the formal educational process. Thus the practical experience would follow rather than precede admission to the examination of the accountant who has completed the recommended educational program. However, the Commission clearly stated that the accountant who has been designated a C.P.A. on the basis of prescribed educational preparation and satisfactory completion of the C.P.A. examination is not an experienced practitioner.

A Special Committee on Research, approved by the Council of the American Institute, specifically proposed in its report that the organization carrying out the new accounting research program consist of an Accounting Principles Board and an accounting research staff. This group would be the sole group in the Institute having authority to make pronouncements on accounting principles. The Accounting Principles Board would succeed the committees on accounting procedures and on terminology.

The Sixth and Seventh International Congresses on Accounting were held in 1950, the former in England and the latter in the Netherlands. The American George O. May, C.P.A., was the only one present at the Sixth International Congress who had taken an active part in the First International Congress held at St. Louis in 1904.

Three public utility companies which had been plaintiffs in the case against the American Institute had obtained a series of temporary injunctions preventing issuance of a letter interpreting Accounting Research Bulletin Number 44 (Revised) which had been approved by eighteen of the twenty-one members of the accounting procedures committee. The plaintiffs did not challenge the right of the Institute or its committee to issue opinions in the field of accounting. Instead, they protested that the committee had not submitted an "exposure draft" of its opinion to other interested organizations. The right of the Institute to issue research bulletins was affirmed by the United States Supreme Court. This was a welcome decision in that it came on the heels of the establishment of the Accounting Principles Board.

The continuing influence of the Securities and Exchange Commission is found in Haskins and Sells' Thomascolor case, O'Connell and Company's Coastal Finance case, and Touche, Niven, Bailey & Smart's Seaboard case. Also, a significant decision has been rendered on the liability to third parties of all public accountants in the C.I.T. case.

The work of the present-day public accountant is far different from that in the beginning when accountants performed the arduous bookkeeping tasks of "untangling" accounts and checking the work of bookkeepers. Today the services of public accountants are sought in most forms of business and governmental operations on matters ranging from taxation reports and auditing to business policy. The fact that public accountants have risen to the status of business consultants demonstrates the level to which the accountancy profession has risen in the United States during the last half century.

The profession of accounting has become established even though it is still in a developmental stage. Corresponding to the rapid development of the accounting profession is the intellectual interest which is indicated by the new books appearing on the subject of accounting and the appearance of numerous accounting journals whose articles on different phases of accounting are contributed by the top men in the field.

Accounting studies have been included in the institutions of higher learning of the nation, and accounting has become a recognized department in practically every college and university in the United States. Graduate schools of business administration have been established which provide intensive professional study in accounting. An understanding of the fundamentals of accounting is now almost indispensable for the lawyer, banker, or engineer: in fact, for all who deal with business affairs, governmental operations, and activities of public control.

308

Bibliography

Books

American Institute of Accountants. *Fiftieth Anniversary Celebration.* New York: The American Institute of Accountants, 1937.

—. *How to Improve Accounting and Tax Service to American Business.* New York: The American Institute of Accountants, 1950.

—. *Public Relations and Legislative Control of the Accounting Profession.* New York: The American Institute of Accountants, 1951.

—. *Yearbook, 1913, 1917, 1918, 1921.* New York: The American Institute of Accountants.

Brown, Richard. *A History of Accounting and Accountants.* Edinburgh and London: T. C. and E. C. Jack, 1905.

Buss, Lydus Henry. *C. P. A. Examination Requirements.* Urbana, Illinois: The University of Illinois (American Accounting Association) College of Commerce and Business Administration, 1951.

Cambridge Modern History. New York: Macmillan and Company, 1908, Vol. 5; 1909, Vol. 6.

DeMond, C. W. *Price, Waterhouse and Company in America.* New York: The Comet Press, Inc., 1951.

Eyre, George E. and William Spottiswoode. *Statutes of the United Kingdom of Great Britain and Ireland, 25th and 26th Victoria.* Authors, 1862.

Green, Wilmer L. *History and Survey of Accounting.* Brooklyn, New York: Standard Text Press, 1930.

Hanson, Arthur W. *Problems in Auditing,* 2nd Edition. New York: McGraw-Hill Book Company, Inc., 1935.

Haskins, C. W. *Business Education and Accountancy.* New York: Harper and Brothers, 1904.

Klein, Joseph J. *Federal Income Taxation.* New York: John Wiley and Sons, Inc., 1929.

Littleton, A. C. *Accounting Evolution to 1900.* New York: American Institute Publishing Company, Inc., 1933.

Lybrand, William M., Ross, Adam A., Ross, Edward T., and Montgomery, Robert H. *Fiftieth Anniversary.* Privately Printed, 1948.

May, George O. *Twenty-five Years of Accounting Responsibility.* New York: American Institute Publishing Company, Inc., c. 1936. Vols. 1 and 2 bound together.

Montgomery, Robert H. *Fifty Years of Accountancy*. New York: Ronald Press Company, 1939.

New Jersey Society of Certified Public Accountants. *Fifty Years of Service, 1898-1948*. Newark, New Jersey: New Jersey Society of Certified Public Accountants, 1948.

New York State Society of Certified Public Accountants. *The New York State Society of Certified Public Accountants—Fiftieth Anniversary*. New York: New York State Society of Certified Public Accountants, 1947.

Official Record of the Proceedings of the Congress of Accountants Held at the World's Fair, St. Louis, 1904.

Peragallo, Edward. *Origin and Evolution of Double-Entry Bookkeeping*. New York: American Institute Publishing Company, Inc., 1938.

Public General Statutes, The. Passed in the 32nd and 33rd Years of the Reign of Her Majesty, Queen Victoria. London: G. E. Eyres and William Spottiswoode, 1869.

Rich, Wiley Daniel. *Legal Responsibilities and Rights of Public Accountant*. New York: American Institute Publishing Company, Inc., 1935.

Richards, George K. *Statutes of the United Kingdom and Ireland*, 25th and 26th Victoria. London: Geo. E. Eyres and William Spottiswoode, 1862.

Smith, C. Aubrey. *Internal Audit Control*. Austin, Texas: The University Co-Operative Society, 1933.

Standards of Education and Experience for Certified Public Accountants, Published for the Commission by the Bureau of Business Research, University of Michigan, 1956.

Woolf, Arthur H. *A Short History of Accountants and Accounting*. London: Gee and Company, 1912.

Bulletins and Pamphlets

Accounting Research Bulletins, Nos. 13, 15, and 17. New York: American Institute of Accountants, 1942.

Anyon, James T. *Recollection of the Early Days of Accounting*. New York: Author, 1925.

Bentley, H. C. *A Brief Treatise on the History and Development of Accounting*. Boston: Bentley School of Accounting and Finance, 1929.

—. Committee on Management Services, Management Services by C.P.A.'s, American Institute of Certified Public Accountants, 1957, pp. 10.

Clader, Will-A. *Is Public Accounting a Profession?* June 2, 1950.

—. *The Three-Class Public Accounting Law*. January, 1947.

—. *The Two-Class Accounting Law and Its Code of Ethics*. December, 1946.

Haskins, Charles W. *Accountancy—Its Past and Its Present*. An address delivered before the American Institute of Accountants, January 25, 1900.

Haskins, C. W., and Sells, E. W. *The First Fifty Years, 1895-1945*. New York: Privately Printed, 1947.

Littleton, A. C. *Directory of Early American Public Accountants.* Urbana, Illinois: The University of Illinois, 1942.
New York Stock Exchange Yearbook, The. New York: New York Stock Exchange, 1951.
Rules of Professional Conduct. New York: American Institute of Certified Public Accountants, January, 1959, pp. 19.
Statement of Touche, Niven, Bailey and Smart. With respect to the design of the Securities and Exchange Commission in the Seaboard Commercial Corporation Proceedings, 1958, pp. 20.
Young, Arthur. *Arthur Young and the Business He Founded.* New York: Privately Printed, 1948.

Periodical Articles

"Accountancy in New York State," *The Accountant,* XXVII (September, 1901), 983-984.
"Accountancy in the States," *The Accountant,* XXII (June, 1896), 504; XXII (September, 1896), 744-745; XXII (November, 1896), 951-952; XXIII (January, 1897), 52-55; XXIII (January, 1897); 99; XXIII (September, 1897), 857-858; XXIV (April, 1898), 349-350 and 376-377; XXV (April, 1899), 367-369; XXV (August, 1899), 889; XXIX (November, 1903), 1392; XXXVIII (June, 1908), 824-825; LV (September, 1916), 397-399 and 189; LV (November, 1916), 397-399; LVI (January, 1917), 81.
"Accountants as Directors," *The Journal of Accountancy,* LXIX (March, 1940), 165.
"Accountants Found Negligent," *The Journal of Accountancy,* CI, (April, 1956), 5.
"Accountants in England from the Nineteenth Century," *The Accountant,* XLVI (January, 1912), 259-261.
"Accountant Not Liable to Third Parties," *The Journal of Accountancy,* XLVIII (August, 1929), 124-125.
"Accountants and the New York Stock Exchange," *The Journal of Accountancy,* LV (April, 1933), 241-242.
"Accountants Necessary in Tax Practice," *The Journal of Accountancy,* XLI (March, 1926), 202.
"Accounting and the Securities and Exchange Commission," *The Journal of Accountancy,* LXIII (May, 1937), 323-324.
"Accounting Errors in Corporation Tax Bill," *The Journal of Accountancy,* VIII (July, 1909), 212-213.
"Accounting Firm Upheld," *The Journal of Accountancy,* XCVII (May, 1954), 520.
"Accounting for Special Reserves Arising Out of the War," *Accounting Research Bulletin,* XIII (January, 1942), 111-118.

"Accounting for Terminated War Contracts," *Accounting Research Bulletin,* XXV (April, 1945), 203-214.

"Accounting for the Use of Special War Reserves," *Accounting Research Bulletin,* XXVI (October, 1946), 215-222.

"Accounting Organizations Oppose Administrative Practitioners Bill," *The Journal of Accountancy,* LXXXV (March, 1948), 187-188.

"Accounting Research and Accounting Principles," *The Journal of Accountancy,* CVI (December, 1958), 27-28.

"Accounting under Cost-Plus-Fixed-Fee Contracts," *Accounting Research Bulletin,* XIX (December, 1942), 155-162.

"Administration of Federal Securities Act," *The Journal of Accountancy,* LVI (July, 1933), 7.

"AFL-CIO Code of Union Financial Practices—Official Text," *The Journal of Accountancy,* CIV (July, 1957), 50-54.

"After Hearings, the S. E. C. Dismisses 11 (e) Proceedings Against Barrow, Wade, Guthrie and Company Growing out of Drayer-Hanson Case," *The Journal of Accountancy,* LXXXVII (June, 1949), 507-516.

"Agran Case in Perspective, The," *The Journal of Accountancy,* CII (December, 1956), 29-31.

"Agran in Wonderland," *The Journal of Accountancy,* C (August, 1955), 29-30.

"AIA Name Change Rejected," *The Journal of Accountancy,* CI (February, 1956), 7.

Allen, C. E. "The Growth of Accounting Instruction since 1900," *The Accounting Review,* II (June, 1927), 150-166.

"Amalgamation of American Societies of Accountants," *The Accountant,* XXV (June, 1899), 660.

"Amalgamation in America," *The Accountant,* XCVI (March, 1937), 372.

"American Accountants," *The Accountant,* XVII (May, 1891), 329.

"American Accountants and the New York Stock Exchange," *The Accountant,* LXXXVIII (May, 1933), 627-628.

"American Accountants and the War," *The Accountant,* LVI (May, 1917), 429-430.

"American Association of University Instructors in Accounting," *The Journal of Accountancy,* XXV (February, 1918), 155-156.

"American Bar Association Committee Lists Seven Tax Activities It Considers to be Practice of Law," *The Journal of Accountancy,* XCI (February, 1951), 307.

"American Institute and Audit Procedure, The," *The Accountant,* C (February, 1939), 263-267.

"American Institute's Fiftieth Anniversary, The," *The Accountant,* XCVI (March, 1937), 372.

"American Institute of Accountants," *The Accountant,* LVI (April, 1917), 410; LVII (December, 1917), 454-456; XC (February, 1934), 197-202.

"American Institute of Accountants Board of Examiners," *The Journal of Accountancy,* XXIV (July, 1917), 1-20.

"American Society and the American Institute, The," *The Certified Public Accountant,* III (October, 1924), 242-247.

"American Stock Exchange and Financial Statements," *The Accountant,* LXXXVIII (June, 1933), 771.

"American War Taxes," *The Accountant,* LVI (May, 1917), 479.

Andersen, Arthur. "Thirtieth Anniversary Report," *The Arthur Andersen Chronicle,* IV (December, 1943), 1-130.

Anderson, W. R. "The Surety Bond," *The C.P.A. Bulletin,* IV (October, 1925), 4-5.

Angus, Butterworth. "Some Early Episodes in the History of Accountancy," *The Accountant,* CXVII (December, 1947), 388-389.

"Another Chapter of the History," *The Journal of Accountancy,* XLVII (May, 1929), 359-360.

Anyon, James T. "Early Days of American Accountancy," *The Journal of Accountancy,* XXXIX (January, 1925), 1-8; XXXIX (February, 1925), 81-92; XXXIX (March, 1925), 161-169.

"Background, The," *The Journal of Accountancy,* XLVII (May, 1929), 356-357.

Banks, Alexander S. "Problems Now Confronting the Public Accounting Profession," *The Certified Public Accountant,* III (January, 1924), 17-20.

"Basis for Agreement between the Legal and Accounting Professions," *The Journal of Accountancy,* LXXXIX (June, 1950), 461-462.

Belser, F. C. "How the Universities Can Aid the Accounting Profession," *The Accounting Review,* II (March, 1927), 37-42.

"Bercu Case on Tax Practice Upheld in New York Court of Appeals," *The Journal of Accountancy,* LXXXVIII (August, 1949), 93.

"Bercu Decision Reversed," *The Journal of Accountancy,* LXXXV (June, 1948), 452.

Blacklock, Frank. "The Profession of Accountancy, Viewed from an American Standpoint," *The Accountant,* XXVI (January, 1900), 13; XXVI (February, 1900), 143 and 194; XXVI (March, 1900), 253.

Blough, Carmon G. "The Relationship of the Securities and Exchange Commission to the Accountant," *The Journal of Accountancy,* LXIII (January, 1937), 23-39.

"Board of Tax Appeals," *The Journal of Accountancy,* XXXVIII (November, 1924), 205.

Boursy, Alfred V. "The Name of Paciolo," *The Accounting Review,* XVIII (July, 1943), 205-209.

Bowden, J. C. "Is It Regulative or Is It Restrictive?," *The National Public Accountant,* I (November, 1946), 27-29.

"Branch Office Ethics," *The Journal of Accountancy,* XXVIII (September, 1919), 212-216.

"Bright Prospects of Accountancy," *The Journal of Accountancy*, XVI (December, 1913), 459-460.

Brown, Richard. "Recent Proposed Legislation Relating to the Profession," *The Accountant*, XX (July, 1894), 669-672.

Brundage, Percival F. "The Bercu Case," *The New York Certified Public Accountant*, XVII (May, 1947), 277-279.

"Bureau of Research, A," *The Journal of Accountancy*, XLI (May, 1926), 354.

Byrnes, Thomas W. "Reading—Permanent and Temporary," *The New York Certified Public Accountant*, XVI (March, 1946), 150-151.

Carey, John L. "One Man's View of the Sixth International Congress on Accounting," *The Journal of Accountancy*, XCIV (September, 1952), 306-310.

—. "The Place of the CPA in Contemporary Society," *The Journal of Accountancy*, CVI (September, 1958), 27-32.

—. "Relationship of Accountants and Lawyers in Tax Practice," *The Accounting Review*, XXVI (October, 1951), 449-455.

—. "The Seventh International Accounting Congress," *The Journal of Accountancy*, CIV (December, 1957), 34-38.

Cardozo, Benjamin N. "Text of the Ultramares Opinion," *The American Accountant*, XVIII (February, 1931), 54-56.

"Century of Professional Accountancy," *The Accountant*, XCI (February, 1934), 267-272; XCVI (April, 1937), 521-529.

"Certificate of Incorporation of the National Association of Certified Public Accountants," *The C.P.A. Bulletin*, II (December, 1923), 3-5.

"Chartered Accountants," *The Accountant*, XVII (August, 1891), 585-586.

Chase, W. Arthur. "University Education of Accountant Students in United States," *The Accountant*, LVII (September, 1917), 179-180.

"Chicago Stock Exchange Requires Certified Statements," *The Journal of Accountancy*, LV (May, 1933), 321-322.

"Choice of a Profession, The," *The Journal of Accountancy*, XIII (April, 1912), 291-293.

Coates, Charles F. "State Legislation Relative to the Practice of Accountancy," *The Journal of Accountancy*, LXXXII (September, 1946), 221-229.

"College Degree as C.P.A. Prerequisite," *The Journal of Accountancy*, LXIII (May, 1937), 321-323.

"College of Accountants—Petition for It Sent to the University Regents, A," *The Accountant*, XVIII (June, 1892), 520.

"Comment Released by Haskins and Sells," *The Journal of Accountancy*, XCV (January, 1953), 84-85.

Committee on Terminology, "Terminology," *Accounting Research Bulletin*, VII (November, 1940), 51-66; IX (May, 1941), 67-85.

"Conclusion of the Atlas Plywood Story," *The Journal of Accountancy*, CVI (November, 1958), 32-34.

"Congress of Accountants at St. Louis, The," *The Accountant*, XXXI (December, 1904), 704-706 and 761-764.

"Consolidation, The," *The Certified Public Accountant*, XVI (September, 1936), 516-517.

"Constitution and By-Laws of the American Society of Certified Public Accountants," *The Certified Public Accountant*, II (August, 1923), 213-215.

"Conway Decision, The," *The Journal of Accountancy*, XCII (September, 1951), 289-290.

Cooper, Ernest. "Fifty-seven Years in an Accountant's Office," *The Accountant*, LXV (October, 1921), 553-563.

"Cooperation Between Accountants and Bankers," *The Journal of Accountancy*, XCVIII (November, 1954), 597-598.

"Cooperaton between Securities and Exchange Commission and Public Accountants," *The Journal of Accountancy*, LXXVI (August, 1943), 155-158.

"Corporation Tax Correspondence, The," *The Journal of Accountancy*, VIII (August, 1909), 300-303.

"Council, The," *The Journal of Accountancy*, XCII (December, 1951), 656.

"Court Decisions Affecting Accountancy," *The Journal of Accountancy*, XXXVII (March, 1924), 214-215.

"C.P.A. Denied Designation of Tax Consultant," *The Journal of Accountancy*, LXXXVI (November, 1948), 354.

"CPA Examiners Meet," *The Journal of Accountancy*, CIV (December, 1957), 10.

"CPA's' Tax Practice Seriously Threatened," *The Journal of Accountancy*, XCVIII (August, 1954), 161-163.

Cranstoun, William D. "Restrictive Legislation," *New Jersey C.P.A. Journal*, XXII (November, 1951), 1-3.

Davies, W. Sanders. "Genesis, Growth and Aims of the Institute," *The Journal of Accountancy*, XLII (August, 1926), 105-111.

"Debate on HR 3214 Making Tax Court a Court of Record," *The Journal of Accountancy*, LXXXIV (September, 1947), 249-261.

"Decision in Conway Appeal Holds Tax Consultant Practiced Law," *The Journal of Accountancy*, XCII (August, 1951), 135.

"Defects of Title 2 of the Federal Revenue Act of October 3, 1917," *The Journal of Accountancy*, XXV (February, 1918), 81-90.

de Roover, Raymond. "Characteristics of Bookkeeping before Pacioli," *The Accounting Review*, XIII (June, 1948), 144.

—. "Lingering Influences of Medieval Practice," *The Accounting Review*, XVIII (April, 1943), 148-151.

—. "Paciolo or Pacioli?," *The Accounting Review*, XIX (January, 1944), 68-69.

Dickinson, Arthur L. "The Profession of the Public Accountant," *The Accountant*, XXXII (May, 1905), 650-658.

Dickinson, Arthur Lowes. "The American Association of Public Accountants," *The Accountant*, LXXIII (November, 1925), 845-846.

Dieterle, D. Lyle. "An Analysis of Certified Public Accountants Examinations," *The Journal of Accountancy*, LXXII (August, 1941), 159-166.

"Dramatizing the Accounting Profession," *The Journal of Accountancy,* CVIII (December, 1959), 28-29.

"Early Days of Accountancy," *The Journal of Accountancy,* XVI (October, 1913). 310-311.

"Education," *The Accountant,* XXVI (April, 1901), 735-736.

"Education and Experience for CPAs," *The Journal of Accountancy,* CVIII (June, 1959), 67-71.

"Education—Graduate School in Accounting," *The Journal of Accountancy,* CI (May, 1956), 12-14.

"Educational Program of the American Institute," *The Journal of Accountancy,* LXXIX (March, 1945), 226-234.

"Education of English and American Accountants, The," *The Accountant,* XXVI (April, 1907), 764-765.

"Eighteenth Century Audit, An," *The Journal of Accountancy,* XXXVI (October, 1923), 282-283.

"Employment of Lawyers by Accounting Firms," *The Journal of Accountancy,* CIV (September, 1957), 28-30.

"Enforcement of Rules of Conduct," *The Journal of Accountancy,* XXXVIII (September, 1924), 204.

Esenoff, Carl M. "Shall We Have Restrictive Legislation?," *The California Certified Public Accountant,* XII (January, 1945), 3-6.

"Exemption for Accountants," *The Journal of Accountancy,* XXVI (August, 1918), 212-215.

"Expanding Fields for Auditing," *The Journal of Accountancy,* CIV (July, 1957), 23-24.

"Extensions of Auditing Procedure," *The Accountant,* C (June, 1939), 850-854.

"Federal Income Tax, A," *The Journal of Accountancy,* XV (January, 1913). 58-61.

"Federal Incorporation of the Institute," *The Journal of Accountancy,* XXXIII (April, 1922), 286-288.

"Fifty Years of Progress," *The Journal of Accountancy,* LXIII (March, 1937), 175-176.

"Financial Statements for Stock Exchange," *The Journal of Accountancy,* XLII (July, 1926), 37.

"For Federal Incorporation," *The Journal of Accountancy,* XXXIII (January, 1922), 37-39.

Goldberg, Louis. "A Plague on Both Their Houses: The Accountant-Lawyer Difference over Tax Practice," *The Journal of Accountancy,* LXXXIV (September, 1947), 188-195.

Gordon, Spencer. "Accountants and the Securities Act," *The Journal of Accountancy,* LVI (December, 1933), 438-451.

    "Liability of Accountants under Securities Exchange Act of 1934," *The Journal of Accountancy,* LVIII (October, 1934), 251-257.

"Greatest Opportunity of All, The," *The Journal of Accountancy,* LV (May, 1933), 326-327.
"Great Responsibility and Great Opportunity," *The Journal of Accountancy,* LV (February, 1933), 82-83.
"Growth of Accountancy," *The Accountant,* LVII (August, 1917), 134-135.
"Growth of Accountancy," *The Journal of Accountancy,* XXIII (April, 1917), 283-286.
Haskins, C. W. "History of Accountancy," *The Accountant,* XXVII (June, 1901), 699-705.
"History of Accountants and Accountancy," *The Accountant,* XLV (July, 1911), 560-562, 597-600, 640-642, 670-671, 712-714, 748-750, 780-782, 823-824, 855-857, and 901-903. XLVI (January, 1912), 6-8, 44-46, 80-82, 124-126, 200-201, 259-261, 308-311, 340-342, 379-382.
"History of the Accountancy Profession, A," *The Accountant,* XXI (April, 1895), 375-376.
"Holding the Accountant Responsible," *The Journal of Accountancy,* XXVIII (July, 1919), 39-42.
Hope, J. William. "Restriction Would Strengthen the Profession," *The Accounting Review,* XX (April, 1945), 194-198.
"House Passes Bill Making Tax Court a Court of Record," *The Journal of Accountancy,* LXXXIV (September, 1947), 180.
"How the Text Was Published," *The Journal of Accountancy,* XLVII (May, 1929), 358-359.
"Hundred Years of Accountancy, A," *The Accountant,* XXVII (January, 1901), 37-40.
"Improvement in Relation between Accountants and Lawyers," *The Journal of Accountancy,* LXXXIX (February, 1950), 96-97.
"Income Tax, The," *The Journal of Accountancy,* XV (March, 1913), 185-187; XVI (October, 1913), 307-309.
"Income Tax Amendment," *The Journal of Accountancy,* XIX (April, 1915), 292-294.
"Income Tax Experts," *The Journal of Accountancy,* XXVII (February, 1919), 134-136.
"Income Tax in the United States," *The Accountant,* XLIX (December, 1913), 861.
"Independent Audits in America," *The Accountant,* CII (April, 1940), 370-372.
"Injunction against National Association of Certified Public Accountants," *The Journal of Accountancy,* XXXVI (July, 1923), 30-31.
"Institute Dallas Meeting," *The Certified Public Accountant,* XVI (October, 1936), 626-628.
"Institute Examinations," *The Journal of Accountancy,* XXIII (February, 1917), 132-133.

"Institute of Accountants in the United States, The," *The Accountant,* LV (November, 1916), 438-442, 444-445.

"Institute Rejects an Amendment, The," *The Journal of Accountancy,* XL (November, 1925), 355.

"Institute Wins Court Case," *The Journal of Accountancy,* CVIII (August, 1959), 7.

"Institute's Annual Meeting," *The Journal of Accountancy,* LXII (September, 1936), 164.

"Institute's Right to Issue Accounting Opinions Upheld by Courts," *The Journal of Accountancy,* CVIII (August, 1959), 23-24.

"Instructions for Verification of Financial Statements," *The Journal of Accountancy,* XLVII (May, 1929), 355-356.

"Interpretation of the Bercu Case, An" *The Journal of Accountancy,* LXXX-VIII (September, 1949), 255-256.

"Interstate Practice," *The Journal of Accountancy,* LXIX (March, 1940), 165-166.

Jay, Harry M. "Consolidation—Now What?," *The Certified Public Accountant,* XVI (October, 1936), 569-570.

Jackson, J. Hugh. "Accounting as a Profession," *The Journal of Accountancy,* XL (September, 1925), 161-172.

Jeal, E. F. "Some Reflections on the Evolution of the Professional Practice in Great Britain," *The Accountant,* XCVI (April, 1937), 521-529.

Jennings, Alvin R. "Common Interests of Lawyers and Certified Public Accountants," *Lybrand Journal,* XL (1959), 3-17.

Johnson, Harlan. "New York Stock Exchange Questionnaire," *The Journal of Accountancy,* XLVIII (July, 1929), 18-26.

"Joint Report of Special Committee on Professional Relations of American Bar Association and Committee on Relations with the Bar of American Institute of Accountants," *The Journal of Accountancy,* CIII (January, 1957), 53-54.

Jones, Charles W. "A Chronological Outline of the Development of the Firm," *The Arthur Andersen Chronicle,* IV (December, 1943), 9-16.

Joplin, J. Porter. "Growing Responsibilities of the Public Accountant," *The Journal of Accountancy,* XXVIII (July, 1919), 9-15.

Jordon, William P. "Accountancy and Law," *The Journal of Accountancy,* LXXXIII (February, 1947), 161-162.

"*Journal* and The American Association of Public Accountants, The," *The Journal of Accountancy,* XXXII (November, 1921), 538-539.

"*Journal of Accountancy* Has A Birthday, The," *The Journal of Accountancy,* C (November, 1955), 29-30.

"Jubilee of *The Accountant,* The," *The Accountant,* LXXI (October, 1924), 497-502.

Kats, P. "A Surmise Regarding the Origin of Bookkeeping by Double Entry," *The Accounting Review,* V (December, 1930), 311-316.

—. "Early History of Bookkeeping by Double Entry," *The Journal of Accountancy*, XLVII (March, 1929), 203-210; XLVII (April, 1929), 275-290.

"Kingston Cotton Mill Company, Lim., The," *The Accountant Law Reports*, Supplement to *The Accountant*, XXII (November, 1895), 201-202, 213-214; XXIII (December, 1895), 225-232.

"Kingston Cotton Mill Company [Court of Appeal], In re," *The Accountant Law Reports*, Supplement to *The Accountant*, XXIII (May, 1896), 77-78.

Kostelanetz, Boris. "Auditor's Responsibilities and the Law," *The New York Certified Public Accountant*, XIX (February, 1949), 91-97.

Lane, Chester T. "Cooperation with the Securities and Exchange Commission," *The New York Certified Public Accountant*, VIII (April, 1938), 5-11.

"Lawyer-C.P.A. Cooperation," *The Journal of Accountancy*, CVII (March, 1959), 27-28.

"Lawyers and Accountants," *The Journal of Accountancy*, LXXVII (April, 1944), 268; LXXVII (June, 1944), 429; LXXVII (June, 1944), 511-512; LXXXI (February, 1946), 90-91; XCI (June, 1951), 869.

"Lawyers Testify on Administrative Practitioners Bill," *The Journal of Accountancy*, LXXXIV (September, 1947), 178-180.

"Lawyers View of Accountants Practice before Tax Court," *The Journal of Accountancy*, LXXXV (May, 1948), 428-434.

"Legislation for Accountants in the States," *The Accountant*, XXII (May, 1896), 427, 504, 763.

"Legislation Regulating Professions," *The Journal of Accountancy*, CIX (January, 1960), 27-28.

Leland, Thomas W. "Educational Program of the American Institute of Accountants," *The Journal of Accountancy*, LXXIX (March, 1945), 226-234.

Lenhart, Norman J. "Development in Auditing Procedures since the Extension of Such Procedures in 1939," *The New York Certified Public Accountant*, XVI (September, 1947), 565-567.

Levy, Saul "The C.I.T. Case," *The Journal of Accountancy*, C (October, 1955), 31-42.

"Liability in Question," *The Journal of Accountancy*, L (August, 1930), 81-85.

"Library of The Institute, The," *The Accountant*, XIX (December, 1893), 956-958.

Lilly, Lewis. "Restrictive Legislation and Its Concomitants," *The California Certified Public Accountant*, XII (January, 1945), 7-9.

Littleton, A. C. "Auditor Independence," *The Journal of Accountancy*, LIX (April, 1935), 283-291.

—. "Evolution of the Ledger Account," *The Accounting Review*, I (December, 1926), 12-23.

—. "Italian Double Entry in Early England," *The Accounting Review*, I (June, 1926), 60-71.

—. "Social Origins of Modern Accountancy," *The Journal of Accountancy*, LVI (October, 1933), 261-270.

—. "The Antecedents of Double Entry," *The Accounting Review*, II (June, 1927), 140-149.

—. "The Development of Accounting Literature," *Publication of the American Association of University Instructors in Accounting*, IX (April, 1925), 7-17.

—. "The Evolution of the Journal Entry," *The Accounting Review*, III (December, 1928), 383-396.

Lockwood, Jeremiah. "Early University Education in Accounting," *The Accounting Review*, XIII (June, 1938), 131-144.

"Long-Range Objectives of the Accounting Profession," *The Journal of Accountancy*, CVII (May, 1959), 71-73.

McCrea, Roswell C., and Kester, Roy B. "A School of Professional Accountancy," *The Journal of Accountancy*, LXI (February, 1936), 106-117.

McLaren, Norman L. "The Influence of Federal Taxation upon Accountancy," *The Journal of Accountancy*, LXIV (December, 1937), 426-439.

"Many Accounting Practices Have Been Merged in Recent Months," *The Journal of Accountancy*, XCI (January, 1951), 68-69.

Masters, J. E. "The Accounting Profession in the United States," *The Journal of Accountancy*, XIX (January, 1915), 349-355; XX (November, 1915), 349-355.

—. "The Accounting Profession in the United States," *The Accountant*, LIII (December, 1915), 724-726.

Maxwell, David F., and Charles, William. "National Conference of Lawyers and Certified Public Accountants," *The Journal of Accountancy*, LXXXI (February, 1946), 120-126.

May, George O. "Accounting and Regulation," *The Journal of Accountancy*, LXXVI (October, 1943), 295-301.

—. "Influence of the Depression on the Practice of Accountancy," *The Journal of Accountancy*, LIV (November, 1932), 336-350.

—. "The Position of Accountants under the Securities Act," *The Journal of Accountancy*, LVII (January, 1934), 9-23.

Meade, Edward S. "Established Preliminary Examinations in Law and Economics," *The Journal of Accountancy*, III (January, 1907), 193-195.

Miller, Henry J. "The American Society and The American Institute," *The Certified Public Accountant*, V (December, 1925), 157-162.

"Momentous Decision, A," *The Journal of Accountancy*, XLVIII (August, 1929), 125-127.

"'Monopoly' Charge Against Certified Public Accountants, The," *The Journal of Accountancy*, LXXXVI (November, 1948), 355.

"More Professional Education," *The Journal of Accountancy*, CVI (June, 1958), 25-26.

Murphy, Mary E. "An Accountant in the Eighties," *The Accountant*, CXVII (July, 1947), 53-54; CXVII (August, 1947), 67-68, 85-86.

—. "Notes on Accounting History," *Accounting Research,* I (January, 1950), 275-280.

—. "The Profession of Accountancy in England: The Client and the Investor," *The Accounting Review,* XV (June, 1940), 241-260.

—. "The Profession of Accountancy in England: The Public, the Government, the Profession," *The Accounting Review,* XV (September, 1940), 328-343.

—. "The Rise of Accountancy in England," *The Accounting Review,* XV (March, 1940), 62-73.

Musaus, William P. "What Is a C.P.A.?," *The Journal of Accountancy,* XX (December, 1915), 438-450.

"Name Change Approved," *The Journal of Accountancy,* CIII (January, 1957), 8.

"National Aspects of Public Accounting," *The Journal of Accountancy,* XIX (January, 1914), 46-50.

"National Conference of Lawyers and Certified Public Accountants," *The Journal of Accountancy,* XCI (June, 1951), 869-871.

Nau, Carl H. "The Aims of the Institute," *The Journal of Accountancy,* XXXI (May, 1921), 321-328.

—. "The American Institute of Accountants," *The Journal of Accountancy,* XXXI (February, 1921), 103-109.

Neiven, John B. "Income Tax Department," *The Journal of Accountancy,* XVI (November, 1913), 384-407.

"New Department, A," *The Journal of Accountancy,* XVI (November, 1913), 373-374.

"New Solutions for New Problems," *The Journal of Accountancy,* CV (March, 1958), 29-30.

"New York County Lawyers Association Answers a Question on Ethics," *The Journal of Accountancy,* LXXXIX (January, 1950), 71-72.

"Official Summary of SEC Accounting Series Release Number 78 and Statements of Touche, Niven, Bailey and Smart," *The Journal of Accountancy,* CIV (June, 1957), 60-64.

"Oklahoma C.P.A. Law," *The Journal of Accountancy,* XXIII (May, 1917), 368-369.

"One National Organization, *"Bulletin of the American Institute of Accountants,* CLI (November, 1936), 3-8; CLII (December, 1936), 3.

Payne, Robert E. "The Effect of Recent Laws on Accountancy," *The Accounting Review,* X (March, 1935), 84-95.

Peloubet, Maurice E. "Professional Societies and Professional Men," *The Journal of Accountancy,* LXXII (October, 1941), 323.

Peragallo, Edward. "Origin of the Trial Balance," *The Journal of Accountancy,* LXXII (November, 1941), 448-454.

Phillips, Jay. "A Summary of State Legislation during the 1946-1947 Season Affecting Accountants," *The Journal of Accountancy,* LXXXIV (August, 1947), 131-137.

"Post-War Refund of Excess-Profits Tax," *Accounting Research Bulletin,* XVII (December, 1942), 147-150.

"Practice before Government Agencies," *The Journal of Accountancy,* LXXX-III (June, 1947), 533-535.

"Practice before the Tax Board," *The Journal of Accountancy,* XXXVIII (November, 1924), 205-206.

"Practice before Treasury Department," *The Journal of Accountancy,* LXVIII (July, 1939), 1-2; LXVIII (August, 1939), 79.

"Practice before Treasury Department Clarified," *The Journal of Accountancy,* CI (April, 1956), 29-30.

"Preparation of Tax Returns," *The Journal of Accountancy,* XXV (June, 1918), 447-451.

"Present Status of the Profession," *The Journal of Accountancy,* I (November, 1905), 1.

"Profession in Scotland, the Corporation of Accountants dim., and the Scottish Societies of Chartered Accountants, the Use of the Initials M.C.A.," *"The Accountant,* XXIX (November, 1903), 1433-1448 and 1475-1476.

"Profession in the States, The," *The Accountant,* XVII (November, 1891), 782.

"Professional-New Institute Research Program," *The Journal of Accountancy,* CVIII (June, 1959), 7.

"Proposed Amendments to By-Laws," *The Certified Public Accountant,* XVII (February, 1937), 10.

"Public Accountant in Chicago, The," *The Accountant,* XXV (April, 1899), 349-350 and 395.

"Public Accountant's Work," *The Accountant,* XVII (June, 1891), 430.

"Public Accountants and Accounting Legislation," *The Journal of Accountancy,* LXXXIX (February, 1950), 97-98.

"Public Accountants and the Institute's Legislative Policy," *The Journal of Accountancy,* CVII (January, 1959), 25-26.

"Public Accountants and Regulatory Legislation," *The Journal of Accountancy,* LXXXII (November, 1946), 361-362; LXXXIII (January, 1947), 6-7.

"Public Accountants and Regulatory Legislation, The," *Massachusetts Society of C.P.A., Inc.,* XX (January, 1947), 19-21.

"Public Interest in Regulatory Accounting Legislation, The," *The Journal of Accountancy,* LXXXIII (April, 1947), 275.

"Purposes of Accounting," *The Journal of Accountancy,* XXXII (August, 1938), 74-76.

"Questions of Constitutionality," *The Journal of Accountancy,* XLI (June, 1926), 444-445.

"Railroad Accounting," *The Journal of Accountancy,* CIII (May, 1957), 25-26.

"Railroad Accounting Committee," *The Journal of Accountancy,* CII (August, 1956), 7.

"Railroad Accounting Procedures," *The Journal of Accountancy,* CIV (November, 1957), 69-79.

Rand, Waldron H. "Growth of the Profession," *The Journal of Accountancy*, XXVII (June, 1919), 412-419.

Reckitt, Ernest. "History of Accountancy in the State of Illinois," *The Journal of Accountancy*, LXIX (May, 1940), 376-380.

"Recollections of an Old Accountant," *The Accountant*, LI (September, 1914), 72.

"Record of The American Institute of Accountants, The," *The Accountant*, LVII (December, 1917), 453-454.

"Regulatory Accountancy Legislation," *The Journal of Accountancy*, LXXVIII (December, 1944), 443-444.

Reimerth, C. H. "Historical Review of Accounting," *The Certified Public Accountant*, VI (May, 1926), 138-140.

"Reminiscences of the Profession in Pre Institute Days," *The Accountant*, LI (November, 1914), 521-524.

"Renegotiation of War Contracts, The," *Accounting Research Bulletin*, XV (September, 1942), 123-134.

"Renegotiation of War Contracts," *Accounting Research Bulletin*, XXI (December, 1943), 171-177.

"Report to Council of the Special Committee on Research Program," *The Journal of Accountancy*, CVI (December, 1958), 62-68.

"Restrictive Act Upheld," *The Journal of Accountancy*, LXIII (January, 1937), 10.

Rose, Bernard. "Responsibility of Auditors," *The Journal of Accountancy*, XXXV (May, 1923), 335.

Ross, F. A. "Growth and Effect of Branch Offices," *The Journal of Accountancy*, XXX (October, 1920), 252-261.

Ross, T. Edward. "Random Recollections of an Eventful Half Century," *The Journal of Accountancy*, LXIV (October, 1937), 256-278.

Sanders, T. H. "Corporate Information Required by Federal Security Legislation," *The New York Certified Public Accountant*, V (April, 1935), 9-22.

—. "Recent Accounting Developments in the United States," *The Accountant*, C (April, 1939), 535-544.

"S.E.C. Accounting Series Release No. 73: The Thomascolor Case," *The Journal of Accountancy*, XCV (January, 1953), 83-84.

"SEC Criticizes CPA's Report," *The Journal of Accountancy*, CIV (June, 1957), 10-14.

"Securities and Exchange Commission," *The New York Certified Public Accountant*, XI (January, 1941), 274-277.

"Securities and Exchange Commission Release on Independence of Public Accountants," *The Journal of Accountancy*, LXXVII (March, 1944), 179-181.

Sells, C. W. "The Accountant of 1917," *The Journal of Accountancy*, III (February, 1907), 297-299.

Sells, Elijah W. "The Accounting Profession—Its Demands and Its Future," *The Journal of Accountancy*, XX (November, 1915), 325-333.

"Significance of an Accountant's Certificate," *The Journal of Accountancy*, XLI (January, 1926), 33-34.

"Single National Organization, A," *The Certified Public Accountant*, XV (October, 1935), 604-610.

Smith, C. Aubrey. "Accounting Practice under the Securities and Exchange Commission," *The Accounting Review*, X (December, 1935), 325-332.

—. "Education for the Professional Accountant," *The Accounting Review*, XX (January, 1945), 17-23.

Smith, Frank P. "Accounting Requirements of Stock Exchanges," *The Accounting Review*, XII (June, 1937), 145-153.

Smith, T. Savage. "The Education of Accountants: What They Ought to Learn, and How They Are to Learn It," *The Accountant*, XXI (December, 1894), 201-204.

Snell, Frank L. "Coordinating Professional Services of the Lawyer and the Accountant," *The Journal of Accountancy*, LXXIX (April, 1945), 291-294.

"Solicitors Acting as Accountants," *The Accountant*, XVII (October, 1891), 709.

"Some Notes on the Profession of Accountancy," *The Accountant*, XXII (October, 1896), 841-849.

" 'Something for Nothing' Accounting Legislation," *The Journal of Accountancy*, LXXXVII (January, 1949), 2-3.

"Spread of Accountancy Legislation, The," *The Journal of Accountancy*, XVI (July, 1913), 64.

Springer, D. W. "Institute-Society-Institute," *The Certified Public Accountant*, XVI (December, 1936), 743-751.

—. "Regulatory Legislation," *The Certified Public Accountant*, XVI (September, 1936), 522-531.

"St. Louis Congress of Accountants, The," *The Accountant*, XXXI (December, 1904), 737-741.

Starkey, Rodney F. "Practice under the Securities Act of 1933 and the Securities Exchange Act of 1934," *The Journal of Accountancy*, LVIII (December, 1934), 431-447.

"State Society Anniversaries," *The Journal of Accountancy*, CIII (March, 1957), 14.

Stempf, Victor H. "The Securities and Exchange Commission and the Accountant," *The New York Certified Public Accountant*, VIII (April, 1938), 12-16.

Sterrett, Joseph E. "Progress in the Accounting Profession," *The Journal of Accountancy*, VIII (November, 1909), 11-16.

—. "The Development of Accountancy as a Profession," *The Journal of Accountancy*, VII (February, 1909), 265-273.

Stewart, Andrew. "Accountancy and Regulation Bodies in the United States," *The Journal of Accountancy*, LXV (January, 1938), 33-60.

"Stock Exchange Demands Audits of Listed Companies," *The Journal of Accountancy*, LV (February, 1933), 81-82.

Suffern, Edward L. "Twenty-five Years of Accountancy," *The Journal of Accountancy*, XXXIV (September, 1922), 174-181.

"Supreme Court Review Requested," *The Journal of Accountancy*, CVIII (November, 1959), 7.

"Survey of Women CPAs," *The Journal of Accountancy*, CIII (February, 1957), 16-17.

"Suspension of Accountants by SEC–A Dangerous Precedent," *The Journal of Accountancy*, XCV (January, 1953), 33-34.

"Tax Practice in Kentucky," *The Journal of Accountancy*, CIII (March, 1957), 8-9.

"Tax Practice and the Practice of Law," *The Journal of Accountancy*, LXXXII (December, 1946), 452-453.

Taylor, R. Emmett. "Pacioli," *The Accounting Review*, X (June, 1935), 168-173.

—. "The Name of Pacioli," *The Accounting Review*, XIX (January, 1944), 69-76.

"Ten Years of Securities and Exchange Commission," *The Journal of Accountancy*, LXXIX (June, 1945), 427-428.

"Testimony of Expert Witnesses at S.E.C. Hearings," *The New York Certified Public Accountant*, IX (April, 1939), 313-336.

"Testimony on Administrative Practitioners Bill," *The Journal of Accountancy*, LXXXIV (September, 1947), 261-264.

"Text of the Bercu Case," *The Journal of Accountancy*, LXXXIII (April, 1947), 342-348.

"Text of Court Order Reversing Supreme Court in Bercu Case," *The Journal of Accountancy*, LXXXVI (November, 1948), 428.

"Text of the Decision of the Municipal Court of Los Angeles in the Agran Tax Practice Case," *The Journal of Accountancy*, C (July, 1955), 72-75.

"Text of Opinion in Conway Case: Minnesota Supreme Court Upholds Conviction of 'Tax Expert' for Unauthorized Practice of Law," *The Journal of Accountancy*, XCII (September, 1951), 331-337.

"Thirty Thousand Members," *The Journal of Accountancy*, CIV (October, 1957), 30.

"The Top News Stories of 1956," *The Journal of Accountancy*, CIII (January, 1957), 5-16.

"Toward One Accounting World," *The Journal of Accountancy*, XCIV (August, 1952), 163-164.

"Treasury Practice Rules Eased," *The Journal of Accountancy*, CVI (December, 1958), 7.

"Trend of Modern Accountancy," *The Journal of Accountancy*, XLI (January, 1926), 1-8.

"United States Income Tax," *The Accountant*, XLIX (August, 1913), 152.

"University Education of Accountant Students in the United States," *The Accountant*, LVII (September, 1917), 179-180.

"Use of Designation 'Tax Consultant' Is Challenged," *The Journal of Accountancy*, XC (July, 1950), 5-6.

"Use of Term 'Tax Consultant' Opposed by American Bar Association Studying Committee on Unauthorized Practice of Law," *The Journal of Accountancy*, XCI (February, 1951), 306-307.

"Verification of Financial Statements," *The Accountant*, LXXXI (July, 1929), 115-124.

Walton, Seymour. "Relation of the Commercial Lawyer to the C.P.A.," *The Journal of Accountancy*, VII (January, 1909), 205-213.

Watson, Albert J. "Practice under the Securities Exchange Act," *The Journal of Accountancy*, LIX (June, 1935), 434-445.

Webster, Norman E. "College Education as a Requirement for Certified Public Accountants—The New York Experience," *The Accounting Review*, XXI (October, 1946), 445-450.

—. "Congress of Accountants," *The Journal of Accountancy*, LXXVIII (December, 1944), 513-514.

—. "Early Movements for Accountancy Education," *The Journal of Accountancy*, LXXI (May, 1941), 441-450.

—. "Planned Examinations," *The Journal of Accountancy*, LXXV (April, 1943), 348-352.

—. "The Meaning of 'Public Accountant,'" *The Accounting Review*, XIX (October, 1944), 366-376.

Weidenhammer, Robert. "The Accountant and the Securities Act," *The Accounting Review*, VIII (December, 1933), 272-278.

"What Does the Bercu Decision Mean?," *The Journal of Accountancy*, LXXXVIII (September, 1949), 185-187.

"What's In a Name?," *The Journal of Accountancy*, CIV (June, 1957), 30.

"Why the Original Text Was Written," *The Journal of Accountancy*, XLVII (May, 1929), 357.

Wilcox, E. B. "The Pros and Cons of Regulatory Legislation," *The Indiana Certified Public Accountant*, III (May, 1948), 3-4.

Wildman, J. R. "Early Instruction in Accounting," *The Accounting Review*, I (March, 1926), 105-107.

Wilkinson, George. "Organization of the Profession in Pennsylvania," *The Journal of Accountancy*, XLIV (September, 1927), 161-169.

—. "The Accounting Profession in the United States," *The Journal of Accountancy*, X (September, 1910), 339-347.

—. "The Genesis of the C.P.A. Movement," *The Certified Public Accountant*, VIII (September, 1928), 261-266; VIII (October, 1928), 297-300.

Winn, William R. "The Case against Regulatory Accountancy Legislation,"
    The South Carolina Certified Public Accountant, V (October, 1947), 5-10.
—. "The Case against Regulatory Accountancy Legislation," *The Journal of
    Accountancy,* LXXXV (February, 1948), 151-154.

Laws and Legal Decisions

National Surety Corp. v. *Lybrand,* 256 App. Div. 226, 9 B. Y. 52d 554 (1939).
New York Laws, 1896, Ch. 312.
Securities Act of 1933, An Act of May 27, 1933, 48 Stat. 74.
Securities Exchange Act of 1934, An Act of June 6, 1934, 48 Stat. 881.
State v. *Riedell,* 109 Okla. 35, 233 Paci. 685 (1924).
State Street Trust Co. v. *Alwin C. Ernst,* 278 N. Y. 101 (1938).
Ultramares Corp. v. *Touche,* 255 N. Y. 170, 174 N.E. 441, 442 (1931).
William R. Craig v. *James T. Anyon,* 242 N. Y. 569 (1926).

Unpublished Material

Board of Regents of The University of Texas, Minutes, May 13, 1917.
Letter from Donald H. Cramer, Partner in Touche, Ross, Bailey & Smart, to
    James D. Edwards, dated January 14, 1960.
Letter from C. W. DeMond, Partner in Price, Waterhouse and Company, to
    James D. Edwards, dated May 6, 1952.
Letter from L. S. Dunham, Personnel Manager of Arthur Young & Company, to
    James D. Edwards, dated January 21, 1960.
Letter from Firman H. Hass, Resident Partner in Ernst & Ernst, to James D.
    Edwards, dated January 19, 1960.
Letter from Robert Kane, Educational Director of the American Institute of
    Accountants, to James D. Edwards, dated June 2, 1952.
Letter from J. A. Lindquist, Partner in Ernst and Ernst, to James D. Edwards,
    dated May 21, 1952.
Letter from Carl A. Newlin, Jr., Manager of Peat, Marwick, Mitchell & Com-
    pany, to James D. Edwards, dated February 18, 1960.
Letter from Frank P. Smith, Director of Education & Personnel of Lybrand,
    Ross Bros. & Montgomery, to James D. Edwards, dated January 22, 1960.
Letter from E. V. Thompson, Partner in Price, Waterhouse & Company, to
    James D. Edwards, dated February 8, 1960.
Letter from Norman E. Webster, Chairman of the History Committee of the
    American Institute of Accountants, to James D. Edwards, dated October 16,
    1951.

Letter from Paul D. Williams, Arthur Andersen & Company, to James D. Edwards, dated January 13, 1960.

Lovette, James B. "History of Accounting in the United States." Unpublished. 14 typewritten pages.

McLaren, Norman. "Evaluation of American Accountancy." Unpublished. 8 typewritten pages.

Appendix A

FIRST C.P.A. EXAMINATION GIVEN IN THE UNITED STATES

The following is a list of questions given to Certified Public Accountant Candidates by the University of the State of New York under these regulations:

The examination for public accountants required by the Act of Congress recently passed was held on the 15th of and 16th of December, 1896. There were four papers to be answered by the candidates for the degree C.P.A. (Certified Public Accountant). As the Accountancy subjects will be of interest to our readers, we reprint them:—

University of the State of New York. Examination Department.

1st ACCOUNTANT EXAMINATION

Theory of Accounts.

Tuesday, December 15th, 1896—9:15 A.M. to 12:15 P.M. Only.

"The Regents of the University shall make rules for the examination of persons applying for certificates under this act, and may appoint a board of three examiners for the purpose. . . ." Laws of 1896, Ch. 312, s.2.

One Hundred credits; necessary to pass, seventy-five. Answer questions 1, 2, 4, 8, 13, and five of the others, but no more. If more than five of these other questions are answered, only the first five of these answers will be considered. Each complete answer will receive ten credits. Do not repeat questions, but write answers only, designating by number, as in question paper.

Check the number ($\sqrt{}$) of each one of the questions you have answered. Use one side of sheet only.

1. State the essential principles of double entry bookkeeping, and show wherein it differs from single entry bookkeeping.

2. Describe the following, and show wherein they differ: (a) Trial Balance. (b) Balance Sheet. (c) Statement of Affairs. (d) Realization and Liquidation Account.

3. In devising a system of accounts for a business, what are the main subjects for consideration, and in what order should they have attention?

4. Describe the following, and show wherein they differ: (a) Revenue Account, (b) Trading Account, (c) Profit and Loss Account, (d) Deficiency Account.

5. State the purpose for which series of perpendicular columns are employed in books of original entry, and how these purposes may be accomplished relative to the following conditions: (a) several Ledgers comprehended in one system of accounts, (b) several departments comprehended in one business, (c) several accounts comprehended in income and expenditure.

6. Describe the following and show wherein they differ: (a) statement of income and expenditure, (b) statement of receipts and payments.

7. Describe a method of keeping accounts so that the aggregate sums due from customers and due to creditors can be known without preparing a schedule of the accounts of such customers and creditors, and so that an independent balance of the Ledger, containing only the real, nominal, special and controlling accounts, exclusive of the individual accounts of customers and of trade creditors, may be taken.

8. Define and differentiate: (a) capital and revenue, (b) capital receipts and revenue receipts, (c) capital expenditure and revenue expenditure.

9. How may the accounts in a Trial Balance be best arranged to facilitate the preparation of a business and financial statement?

10. Define and differentiate: (a) fixed assets and cash assets, (b) fixed liability and floating indebtedness, (c) fixed charges and operating expense.

11. Describe the following kinds of accounts: (a) personal, (b) impersonal, (c) real, (d) nominal, (e) current, (f) summary.

12. Describe the process and state some of the purposes of analysing a Ledger.

13. Describe the nature of the following accounts: (a) sinking fund, (b) reserve fund, (c) redemption fund, (d) depreciation fund, (e) contingent fund, (f) investment fund.

14. Define the following: (a) stock, (b) capital, (c) surplus, (d) deficiency, (e) capital stock, (f) preferred stock, (g) common stock, (h) share capital, (i) loan capital.

15. Describe the nature of the following accounts: (a) merchandise, (b) construction, (c) consignment, (d) joint, (e) subscription, (f) expense, (g) maintenance, (h) venture, (i) suspense, (j) dividend.

Practical Accounting

Tuesday, December 15th, 1896—1:15 to 4:15 P.M. Only.

One hundred credits; necessary to pass, seventy-five.

Answer questions one and two and two of the others, but no more. If more than two of these other questions are answered, only the first two of these answers will be considered. Each complete answer will receive twenty-five credits. Do not repeat questions but write answers only. Check the number ($\sqrt{}$) of each one of the questions you have answered. Use one side of sheet only.

1. Jones and Robinson, merchants, are unable to meet their obligations. From their books and the testimony of the insolvent debtors the following statement of their condition is ascertained:

Cash on hand	$ 5,500.00
Debtors: $1,000 good; $600 doubtful; but estimated to produce $200; $1,000 bad	2,600.00
Property, estimated to produce $9,000	14,000.00
Bills receivable, good	4,250.00
Other securities: $3,000 pledged with partially secured creditors; remainder held by the fully secured creditors	28,000.00
Jones, drawings	9,000.00
Robinson, drawings	8,400.00
Sundry losses	13,500.00
Trade Expenses	7,400.00
Creditors, unsecured	25,000.00
Creditors, partially secured	23,900.00
Creditors, fully secured	17,000.00
Preferential claims: wages, salaries and taxes	700.00
Jones, Capital	10,000.00
Robinson, Capital	16,050.00

Prepare a statement of affairs, showing the liabilities and the assets, with respect to their realisation and liquidation; also a Deficiency Account, showing such of the above stated particulars as would account for the deficiency shown by the statement of affairs.

2. A., B. and C. enter into partnership, January 1st, 1895. A. contributes $8,500, B. $5,500 and C. $4,500. The profits and losses are to be divided in the same proportion. December 31st, 1895, the partners agree that, before dividing profits and losses, there shall be charged, as an expense of the business, and placed to their individual credits, salaries as follows: A., $800, B., $700, C., $600.

December 31st, 1895, the Trial Balance of their books showed the following:

Capital, A		$ 8,500.00
Capital, B		5,500.00
Capital, C		4,500.00
Cash on hand and in bank	$ 1,900.48	
Stock, January 1, 1895	11,550.00	
Purchases	51,666.70	
Sales		25,650.80
Plant and fixtures	2,068.92	
Book accounts receivable including consignments	20,745.83	
Consignments		33,822.70
Trade creditors		14,855.66
Loan Account		6,250.00
Loan interest		125.00
Salaries	1,257.00	
Wages	2,025.00	
Trading expenses	1,052.65	
Interest and discount	1,273.45	
Losses on exchange	2,108.00	
Commissions		3,510.20
Drawings, A. (includes $800 salary allowance)	2,750.25	
Drawings, B. (includes $700 salary allowance)	2,345.65	
Drawings, C. (includes $600 salary allowance)	1,970.43	
	$102,714.36	$102,714.36

Their inventory of stock on hand, December 31st, 1895, amounted to $11,337.50. Unexpired insurance premiums, $91. December 31st, 1895, $300 was paid for January (1896) rent in advance.

Prepare a Trading Account (cost as against proceeds), a Profit and Loss account, and a Balance Sheet; also partners' capital Accounts as of December

31st, 1895, allowing 6 per cent interest on capital and reserving 2½ per cent for losses on consignments.

3. A. buys a gas business at receiver's sale, taking over the entire plant, subject to a bonded indebtedness of $9,500. A. sells the same to the B. gas company incorporated under the laws of the State of New York, for the purpose of acquiring this property from him, and having an authorized capital of $30,000, divided into 300 shares of $100 each. C., D., and E. subscribe each for one share of the capital stock of the company, and the company purchases the property from A. for 297 shares and assumes the bonded indebtedness stated.

On making and appraising an inventory of the property for the purpose of distribution to proper accounts, the following conservative values, exclusive of good-will, franchise rights, etc., are ascertained:

Land	$ 2,000.00
Buildings	6,000.00
Coal-gas plant, machinery and fittings	3,800.00
Water-gas plant, machinery and fittings	6,000.00
Mains	27,000.00
Meters	1,200.00
Supplies	1,500.00
Office furniture and fixtures	300.00
Sundry and other items	1,200.00
	$49,000.00

Frame the necessary entries to open the company's books and show the capital stock and the fixed assets on the face of the ledger. Prepare a balance sheet.

4. Three partners invest capital as follows: A. $100,000, B. $60,000, C. $40,000. On this basis of capital investment, which is to remain intact, they share profits and losses in the proportion of A. 47½ per cent., B. 27½ per cent., C. 25 per cent., in addition to specified salaries.

At the end of the year the partnership terminates with a loss of $10,000, which includes the salaries drawn by the partners. It appears that C. had drawn against prospective profits to the amount of $5,000, and thereby impaired his capital investment by said amount. They discontinue business and proceed to liquidate and distribute the surplus assets monthly as realized. C. engages in other business, leaving A. and B. to attend to the realization and liquidation of the firm's affairs. A. and B. jointly are to charge C. 5 per cent. for collecting and paying to him his share in the surplus assets.

The amounts collected monthly, less liabilities liquidated and expenses and losses on realisation (exclusive of the 5 per cent. collection charged to C., the amount of which is to be equally divided between A. and B.), are as follows:

First month	$20,250.50	
Second month	30,490.75	
Third month	60,890.25	
Fourth month	58,725.10	
Fifth month	6,717.68	
Last month	4,425.72	$181,500.50

Prepare partners' accounts showing the amounts payable monthly to each without prejudice to the rights or individual interests of the others.

5. On January 15, 1896, A. of New York sent to B. of London, account sales showing net proceeds due February 15th, 1896, $17,550, and remitted 60-day sight exchange at $4.82 for balance of account.

A. had, on November 15, 1895, invested $5,000 in a demand draft, exchange at $4.85, which he remitted to B., and on December 15th, 1895, he had further remitted to B. a 30-day date draft for £1,759 16s. 8d., exchange at $4.83, drawn on C. of London, who owed A. $9,000.00 on open account. Interest to be calculated at 6 per cent. (360 day basis), London date 12 days subsequent to New York date.

Prepare account current as rendered by A. to B.; also the accounts of B. and C. as they appear in A.'s Ledger.

6. A., B., and C. agree to purchase and sell coffee for their joint account. They purchase 3,000 bags of coffee for $58,500, and one month thereafter sell the same at 16 cents per pound (say 130 pounds to the bag). The warehouse charges, labour, cartage, weighing, brokerage, etc., amount to $600.

A. contributes cash			$20,000.00
B. contributes note			
at 4 months	$19,000.00		
discount at 6			
per cent on same	?		?
C. contributes cash		$18,900.00	
C. contributes note			
at 3 months	2,500.00		
discount at 6			
per cent on same	?	?	?
			$59,982.50

It was arranged that each should contribute equally to the requisite purchase money, in default of which interest at 6 per cent. per annum for the month covering the transaction was to be calculated between them, to equalise their respective contributions.

Prepare an account of the venture; also separate accounts of A., B., C., showing the share of each in the final net proceeds.

Auditing

Wednesday, Dec. 16th, 1896—9:15 A.M. to 12:15 P.M., only.

One hundred credits; necessary to pass, seventy-five.

Answer questions 1, 8, 10, 14, 15, and five of the others, but no more. If more than five of these other questions are answered only the first five of these answers will be considered. Each complete answer will receive ten credits. Do not repeat questions, but write answers only, designating by number as in question paper. Check the number ($\sqrt{}$) of each one of the questions you have answered. Use one side of sheet only.

1. Give a brief outline of the duties of an auditor, and of his responsibilities.

2. Explain the principal points to which an auditor should direct his attention in conducting the audit of the accounts of an incorporated company.

3. If the actual cash on hand at the date of the Balance Sheet had not been verified by the auditor on the day of balancing, what method should be employed to prove its correctness before signing the accounts?

4. In an audit where an exhaustive detailed examination of the books is not stipulated, or not practicable, what examination is essential to insure their general correctness?

5. What means should be employed to detect the willful omission to enter in the books under audit, sales made or cash received?

6. State what should be required of a company or firm by one who is to make an audit of its books?

7. What evidence should be required as to the correctness of values of assets (other than customers' accounts) entered in the books?

8. State what is necessary in auditing cash payments, and how to prevent the reproduction and passing of vouchers a second time.

9. State what examination should be made of the receivable Book Accounts of a firm or company to ascertain what accounts, if any, should be written off as bad.

10. How may it be determined whether certain expenditures of a manufacturing business were of the nature of maintenance and repairs or constitutes an actual betterment of the plant? State how in each case they should be dealt with in the Balance Sheet and in the Profit and Loss Account.

11. In auditing the accounts of a business for the first time what books should be produced? What would be the first duty of the auditor respecting these books?

12. In auditing the accounts at the conclusion of the first fiscal year of a corporation formed to acquire an established business, what documents and records should be examined in addition to the ordinary books and subjects of an audit?

13. To what extent should an auditor hold himself responsible for the correctness of (a) inventories, (b) pay-rolls, (c) depreciation and discounts?

14. In an audit stipulating for the examination of all vouchers of every description, what would be proper vouchers for the following: purchases, returned purchases, sales, returned sales, cash receipts, cash payments, journal entries?

15. On what basis should the following assets be valued in the preparation of a Balance Sheet: (a) manufactured goods, (b) partially manufactured goods, (c) raw material, (d) open Book Accounts receivable, (e) stocks, bonds, and other investments, (f) bills receivable?[1]

---

[1]"Accountancy in the States," *The Accountant*, XXIII (January, 1897), 52-56.

Appendix B

ORIGINAL CPA CERTIFICATES ISSUED

Year	ALABAMA			ALASKA			ARIZONA			ARKANSAS		
	E	W	R	E	W	R	E	W	R	E	W	R
1899												
1900												
1901												
1902												
1903												
1904												
1905												
1906												
1907												
1908												
1909												
1910												
1911												
1912												
1913												
1914												
1915										16	6	
1916											4	
1917												
1918												
1919	28						1	4	1	1		2
1920	3	2						1	1	1		
1921	3	2					1			1		3
1922	1									2		3
1923	2	4								2		3
1924	5	1								3		1
1925	2						1			4		
1926	4									9		2
1927	2	1					2	2		1		
1928	5							1		1		2
1929	1							1		2		
1930										6		9

Year	ALABAMA			ALASKA			ARIZONA			ARKANSAS		
	E	W	R	E	W	R	E	W	R	E	W	R
1931	4						1		1			2
1932	4						2			8		1
1933	1							23	2	6		
1934		1					2	1	1	15		2
1935	2	1					1	4	1	5		
1936		5					1		1			1
1937	1	2		3		2	5			9		2
1938	1	3					7		1	4		2
1939		1					5		1	3		
1940	1						2			19		6
1941	2	3				1	2			9		1
1942	3	7		1			4			2		5
1943				1		1	4		1	1		
1944	7	2					3	4	1	3		3
1945	5	2		1			6		3	4		3
1946	13	3					9		7	9		7
1947	3	2		1		3	3		3	6		15
1948	8	3					13		4	14		13
1949	21	1		1		4	15	1	11	12		9
1950	18			1		5	22	2	3	17		20
1951	34	1		1		2	18		5	21		10
1952	30	1				4	17		7	9		5
1953	30	2				3	15		11	14		12
1954	26					4	11	1	15	11		18
1955	26	1		1			16	1	11	10		3
1956	20	2		2		1	11		14	12		7
1957	16	1		2		5	14		10	6		9
1958	21	1		3		2	14		19	19		15
Total	353	55		18		37	228	42	139	297	10	196

(Note: E=Examination, W=Waiver, R=Reciprocity)

ORIGINAL CPA CERTIFICATES ISSUED

Year	CALIFORNIA			COLORADO			CONNECTICUT			DELAWARE		
	E	W	R	E	W	R	E	W	R	E	W	R
1899												
1900												
1901		20										
1902		23										
1903		6										
1904	8	1										
1905	5	2										
1906												
1907	4			1	25							
1908	14				1		28					
1909	4			1			1	1				
1910	8			1	1		4					
1911				4	3							
1912	9			4								
1913	3			4			2				8	
1914	1			9	1			1				
1915	3				1	2	3	1				
1916	5			1			3	1	1	1		
1917	3		4	4		2	8					
1918	11			1			3					
1919	20			3			15	3				
1920	32		6	15		4	14	3				
1921	22		12	7		1	8					
1922	31		14	14		1	27	3		2		1
1923	28		25	15		1	13	2				
1924	50		29	13		4	10				1	
1925	88		41	9			14	2				
1926	29		12	4		1	11	1		1		
1927	63		20	8		1	11			2		
1928	57		23	5			10			1		
1929	64		33				9	5				
1930	50		37	3		3	5					
1931	55		16	4		2	9			1		
1932	46		12	4		1	2	1				
1933	42		14	7			12	2		1		1
1934	46		13	3		1	8	4		1		
1935	39		20	1		3	7	1				
1936	30		12	1			10	3		3		
1937	21		17	4		5	1	8		1		1

Year	CALIFORNIA E	W	R	COLORADO E	W	R	CONNECTICUT E	W	R	DELAWARE E	W	R
1938	41		27	5			6	2	1	1		2
1939	51		19	7			7					1
1940	47		20	6		1	16		1	3		6
1941	44		38	18		1	9		5	1		2
1942	54		24	8		2	20		3	3		1
1943	56		18	2		3	2		2	1		1
1944	31		33	7			13		2	1		1
1945	62		46	9		2	3		1	1		1
1946	127		140	26		12	24		5	2		1
1947	181		111	27		11	11		8	3		
1948	323		138	37		5	20		4	2		5
1949	343		82	31		8	55		5	3		2
1950	436		76	23		1	13		3	6		
1951	438		79	37		7	28		5	6		2
1952	417		61	30		8	51		10	3		
1953	309		56	34		12	52		7	3		1
1954	393		93	41		15	33		5	5		2
1955	358		58	29		21	15		11	5		1
1956	295		86	31		16	37		30	6		3
1957	344		112	27		12	55		17	3		1
1958	368		123	41		18	46		7	2		
Total	5,609	52	1,800	626	27	192	736	31	174	75	8	36

(Note: E=Examination, W=Waiver, R=Reciprocity)

ORIGINAL CPA CERTIFICATES ISSUED

Year	DISTRICT OF COLUMBIA			FLORIDA			GEORGIA			HAWAII		
	E	W	R	E	W	R	E	W	R	E	W	R
1899												
1900												
1901												
1902												
1903												
1904												
1905												
1906					6							
1907												
1908								15				
1909				1			2	6				
1910							2					
1911				1			1					
1912							2					
1913							2					
1914							6					
1915							5					
1916				3			10					
1917				1			12					
1918							13					
1919				1			4					
1920							2					
1921				3			4					
1922				3			7					
1923		13	31	3			12			3	4	
1924	5	3		4			10					
1925	2			3			22					1
1926	5			7			26					2
1927	9	3	3	56	3	4	23			1		
1928	6	1	1	7	4	11	27					
1929	7		8	7	1	1	53			1		
1930	8		3				27			1		2
1931	9		2				30			1		
1932	8		5	10	9	7	8			1		1
1933	12		2	4	1	3	12			6		1
1934	11		4	3	1	1	17			1		
1935	23		2	3		1	9	4				1
1936	10		5	1			4			2		

Year	D.C. E	D.C. W	D.C. R	FLORIDA E	FLORIDA W	FLORIDA R	GEORGIA E	GEORGIA W	GEORGIA R	HAWAII E	HAWAII W	HAWAII R
1937	13		1	5		1	7					
1938	26	4		3			3					
1939	10	5		3	3		8					2
1940	24	2		7	2		4	1		1		
1941	24		1	15	7	2	6			1		
1942	7			7			13					
1943	22			12			7					1
1944	9			12			14					
1945	17			5	1	3	3	9				2
1946	48		6	33		6	17	7		5		3
1947	25		8	21	57	8	14	6		4		3
1948	90		7	55	13	11	31	6		3		
1949	62		3	43		7	48	6		8		1
1950	68		3	58		6	35	2		18		
1951	85		1	56			47	6		8	2	
1952	87		5	61			68	4		8	2	
1953	75		10	59			48	6		7	2	
1954	63		1	65			58	8		7	3	
1955	65		4	52			53	4		14		3
1956	71		12	70			50	3		8		3
1957	77		15	76			43	2		5		4
1958	74		17	84			40	12		7		6
Total	1,157	20	171	923	103	77	969	21	86	118	12	40

(Note: E=Examination, W=Waiver, R=Reciprocity)

ORIGINAL CPA CERTIFICATES ISSUED

Year	IDAHO E	W	R	ILLINOIS E	W	R	INDIANA E	W	R	IOWA E	W	R
1899												
1900												
1901												
1902												
1903				37	6							
1904				42	1							
1905				6								
1906				10								
1907				12								
1908				8	1							
1909				6	1							
1910				5								
1911				5								
1912				3	1							
1913				9								
1914				2								
1915				14			207		5	24		10
1916				6					17	3		1
1917		16		14	1		31		4			
1918		5		13			11		19			2
1919		1		39					3			
1920				31			26		1			
1921	1			36			34		17	2		
1922	2	1		75			67		9			
1923				87			30		17	3		3
1924				101			78		37	6		2
1925	1			94			30		36			
1926				29			44		4	2		9
1927	2		1	68			52		2	3		1
1928	1			45			7		12			8
1929				78			13		1	16		13
1930	1			46			8		2	8		27
1931			1	74			8		4	3		18
1932	1		1	64			8		1	2		8
1933				37			14		4	4		10
1934	2		1	38			6		8	3		8
1935	3			74			15		6	12		12
1936	1		1	75			10		2	6		6
1937	2			69		1	21		6	5		7

Year	IDAHO			ILLINOIS			INDIANA			IOWA		
	E	W	R	E	W	R	E	W	R	E	W	R
1938	5			152		1	21		13	9		7
1939	1			88			13		3	4		14
1940	1			120			9		2	2		21
1941	2			123			19			3		16
1942	2			120			17		7	14		5
1943				249			14		12	9		5
1944	2		1	447		1	3		7			30
1945			2	170		29	20		18	9		7
1946	4		1	177		88	17		16	8		29
1947	3		2	393		44	12		19	9		33
1948	7		4	263	7	62	41		38	24		41
1949	19		2	269	10	89	43		24	21		16
1950	4		1	239	9	72	49		22	34		26
1951	9		3	301		83	64		24	28		23
1952	12		1	115		85	47		29	63		42
1953	15		2	252		86	43		12	13		14
1954	16		4	209		71	40		14	23		25
1955	9		1	167		85	52		14	26		31
1956	4		2	163		134	43		24	25		33
1957	12		1	249		100	38		13	21		40
1958	4			247		64	53		26	21		25
Total	148	23	32	5,865	37	1,095	1,378		554	468		628

(Note: E=Examination, W=Waiver, R=Reciprocity)

ORIGINAL CPA CERTIFICATES ISSUED

Year	KANSAS			KENTUCKY			LOUISIANA			MAINE		
	E	W	R	E	W	R	E	W	R	E	W	R
1899												
1900												
1901												
1902												
1903												
1904												
1905												
1906												
1907												
1908							3	113				
1909							8	42				
1910												
1911							1					
1912												
1913							3			2		
1914							1	1		3		
1915	8						3	1		5		
1916				11			5	1		3		1
1917				3	1		3			18		1
1918	1									5		1
1919	1						1	1		5		1
1920	1			7				7				
1921				14			5	1		1		1
1922	3	4		15	1		11	3		1		3
1923	7	6		9	4		9	2		3		
1924	4	2		12	2		10	8				9
1925	3	1		22			18	10				
1926	1	2		12	3		14	4		1		
1927	4	1		9	4		17	6		4		
1928	6	3			1		19	10				
1929		2			11		6	16				
1930	1						11	17				
1931	4			8	1		11	10				
1932				6	1		14	9		2		
1933	4			9	1		6	3		5		
1934	7	3		7			8	10		1		1
1935	9	1		5	2		5	9				
1936	3	3		5	1		7	1		1		1
1937	1	1		6			27	7		2		2

Year	KANSAS E	W	R	KENTUCKY E	W	R	LOUISIANA E	W	R	MAINE E	W	R
1938	2		1	4		4	14		13			
1939	13	5		14		7	25		14	1		
1940	8			10			17		12	1		
1941	8	3		7			21		18			1
1942	16			10		4	17		9			1
1943	14	1		10		3	22		5			
1944	5	5		13		7	10		19			1
1945	9	7		13		17	16		20	1		1
1946	4	6		21		47	46		11			
1947	12	6		20		17	19		8	1		
1948	16	8		22		9	50		20	9		3
1949	33	5		9		3	28		27	1		1
1950	45	8		66		4	45		19	14		1
1951	37	2		14		6	38		3	2		6
1952	36	12		26		5	41		21	4		1
1953	33	13		36		2	25		21	2		3
1954	40	9		24		6	33		36	5		2
1955	27	4		27		5	28		43	2		4
1956	28	4		23		4	25		28	2		5
1957	37	11		13		9	23		29	3		1
1958	50	9		18		8	28		50	5		1
Total	541	148		560	200		797	155	563	115		53

(Note: E=Examination, W=Waiver, R=Reciprocity)

ORIGINAL CPA CERTIFICATES ISSUED

Year	MARYLAND E	W	R	MASSACHUSETTS E	W	R	MICHIGAN E	W	R	MINNESOTA E	W	R
1899												
1900		25										
1901	1	1										
1902	6											
1903	3											
1904												
1905												
1906	2						18					
1907	1						3					
1908	4						3					
1909	3						3					
1910				78	6		4			4	14	3
1911	3			26							10	
1912	2			4			3			2	7	
1913				7			5					
1914				1			11			5	1	1
1915	1		1	17			7			1	5	
1916	1			18			4	3		5		
1917	7			19			7	2				
1918	1			16			6	10		3	1	
1919	2			31			5	7		1		
1920				26			10	12		1		1
1921	12	2		23			13	5		5		2
1922				45			23	12		6		6
1923	5			64			11	6		5		2
1924	24		5	66			24	5		14		2
1925			2	75			72	91		5		2
1926	36			52			27	6		3		3
1927	29			88			9	3		10		1
1928	5			57			36	20		8		5
1929	40			37			20	8		6		1
1930	23			17		1	29	15				
1931	29		1	25		1	21	15		20		3
1932	15			15			43	5		6		
1933	24			9		2	40	2		15		
1934				17		1	30	8		14		
1935	28	3		25		4	23	3		4		6
1936	47	1		15		2	19	5		4		2
1937	26	1		17			42	6		4		7

Year	MARYLAND			MASSACHUSETTS			MICHIGAN			MINNESOTA		
	E	W	R	E	W	R	E	W	R	E	W	R
1938	10		2	22		1	31		2	5		
1939	37	1		25		3	23		7	13		2
1940	47	1		32			28		10	11		3
1941	59			36			29		2	11		3
1942	40	3		32			41		35	14		3
1943	35	1		25			21		2	6		
1944	32			28			51		6	5		6
1945	26	3		34			30		16	13		27
1946	32	5		48		2	46		24	10		1
1947	58	3		64		9	26		12	29		19
1948	83	3		49		8	58		15	23		34
1949	119	1		77		4	97	70	35	31		5
1950	76	8		138		2	134		20	18		15
1951	90	6		101		3	126		26	51		17
1952	119	8		89		2	137		27	41		25
1953	87	3		93		0	137		42	19		13
1954	64	11		119		2	128		13	36		9
1955	52	7		112			123		47	39		20
1956	98	3		94			143		24	33		21
1957	99	1		85			112		38	40		45
1958	78	4		91		1	167		33	28		11
Total	1,721	26	90	2,284	6	48	2,259	70	685	627	83	328

(Note: E=Examination, W=Waiver, R=Reciprocity)

ORIGINAL CPA CERTIFICATES ISSUED

Year	MISSISSIPPI			MISSOURI			MONTANA			NEBRASKA		
	E	W	R	E	W	R	E	W	R	E	W	R
1899	–	–	–	–	–	–	–	–	–	–	–	–
1900												
1901												
1902												
1903												
1904												
1905												
1906												
1907												
1908												
1909					16			14			14	
1910				9	50							
1911				1	4					1		
1912				3	1			1		2		
1913				2	4							
1914				1	4					1		
1915				4	5		1			1		
1916				1			1					
1917				3	3		2			2		
1918				6						1		
1919					1			19	1	1		
1920	3	70		7	6							
1921	13			12	2					1		
1922	3			15	8		4			5		
1923	10			17	10					5		
1924	3	1	13	17	6		1		1	5		
1925	2		5	17	5					6		
1926	2		5	8	10				1	3		
1927			1	20	5					4		
1928	13		2	25	4							
1929	5		3	7	2							
1930	3		17	10	1					3		
1931	2			15	8		1			1		
1932	2		17	10	2					2		
1933	8		14	19	3		1			3		
1934	2		4	14	8					4		
1935	1		3	9	3			21				
1936	2		3	16	4		1	4				
1937	3			13	8		1	13		1		

Year	MISSISSIPPI			MISSOURI			MONTANA			NEBRASKA		
	E	W	R	E	W	R	E	W	R	E	W	R
1938	4		1	21		14	1			9		
1939			1	13		23	5			7		
1940	3		8	8		8	1			5		3
1941	3		3	17		5	9			5		
1942			2	38		7	3			4		
1943	4		7	24		8	4			5		
1944	3		5	17		6	1		1	4		1
1945	3		13	71		18	7					
1946	13		10	66		8	6		4	8		2
1947	7		17	62		21	4			11		3
1948	16		15	127		20	9		2	22		1
1949	24		15	120		12	14		2	24		
1950	35		11	80		19	15			43		
1951	32		5	63		19	15		1	40		
1952	24		12	87		26	9		4	39		2
1953	22		15	65		28	8			32		4
1954	14		5	49		32	14		1	26		
1955	17		14	68		24	11		3	37		1
1956	17		6	61		28	7			28		
1957	25		5	39		35	5		1	25		
1958	10		2	44		21	11		2	28		16
Total	353	71	259	1,420	67	499	172	72	24	454	14	33

(Note: E=Examination, W=Waiver, R=Reciprocity)

History of Public Accounting

ORIGINAL CPA CERTIFICATES ISSUED

Year	NEVADA			NEW HAMPSHIRE			NEW JERSEY			NEW MEXICO		
	E	W	R	E	W	R	E	W	R	E	W	R
1899												
1900												
1901												
1902												
1903												
1904							27					
1905							16					
1906							2	1				
1907							2					
1908							5					
1909							5					
1910												
1911							4					
1912							2					
1913							1					
1914	1	3					2					
1915	2						4					
1916	5						13					
1917				5	2		7					
1918				19	12		6					
1919				53	21		9					
1920	1			120	8		18					
1921				58	15		38			6		
1922	2			9	13		20					
1923				5	13		31					
1924				1	13		28	13				
1925		1		1	7		18	20				
1926		2		1	2		31	11				
1927	1				2		25	13		3		
1928		2		2	2		20	17		1		
1929	1	1			1		33	18		1		
1930					3		39	20				
1931				1	1		28	20		7		
1932					1		34	12		2		
1933	1	1		3	2		40	12		1		
1934				2	3		46	16		6		
1935		1		2	4		34	13				
1936		1			2		22	1				5
1937		1			1		30	8		3		

Year	NEVADA E	W	R	NEW HAMPSHIRE E	W	R	NEW JERSEY E	W	R	NEW MEXICO E	W	R
1938				1		1	33		15			3
1939							18			1		
1940			1	1		1	50		27			
1941	1		2	1			19		13	2		1
1942			4	1			74			1		2
1943							35					
1944	2	1		2			58					2
1945			2	1			28		18			2
1946			3	1			44		40			7
1947	1		2	2		3	103		31	20		9
1948	3	1		2		4	88		13			
1949	1					1	101		20	16		7
1950	3		1	1		2	142		37	9		1
1951	3		2	1		1	147		32	3		1
1952	3		4	3			149		29	10		15
1953	3		5	2		2	141		32	4		12
1954	1		7	2		3	134		35	5		30
1955	3		3	3		4	124		34	9		8
1956	6	1		5		4	159		28	6		85
1957	8		5			2	127		33	9		17
1958	2		2	1		9	110		26	6		65
Total	54	3	56	315		162	2,481	44	657	125	6	272

(Note: E=Examination, W=Waiver, R=Reciprocity)

ORIGINAL CPA CERTIFICATES ISSUED

Year	NEW YORK			NORTH CAROLINA			NORTH DAKOTA			OHIO		
	E	W	R	E	W	R	E	W	R	E	W	R
1896		56										
1897		70										
1898	6	1										
1899	9	2										
1900	6											
1901	13	49										
1902	30	1										
1903	15	2										
1904	15	2										
1905	24	2										
1906	15											
1907	31											
1908	8										72	
1909	48									22		3
1910	48									13		4
1911	57									10		1
1912	48									2		1
1913	28	3		1	14					5		1
1914	37	4					1	3		12		3
1915	23			6				1		8		2
1916	60			5			2			9		2
1917	41			5	2					10		4
1918	44			4			1			6		1
1919	63			36			2			7		9
1920	45	1		50						34		10
1921	142			27	1					18		3
1922	189		1	76	4		1			19		7
1923	140		1	23	1				4	63		11
1924	156		13	11					1	14		3
1925	207		9	13	1					30		6
1926	327		14	19	33		2			78		5
1927	264		8	17	10		6			15		10
1928	283		30	7	4		2			21		
1929	92		3	8	2					8		1
1930	325		105	4	1		1		1	22		7
1931	303	2	115	9	7		1		1	28		5
1932	368	36		15	8					30		1
1933	237	49		12	5		1			54		3

Year	NEW YORK			NORTH CAROLINA			NORTH DAKOTA			OHIO		
	E	W	R	E	W	R	E	W	R	E	W	R
1934	295	39		10		7				13		4
1935	375	25	5	11		6				52		4
1936	491	43	1	13		1				15		2
1937	629	25		3			1			50		7
1938	924	29	11	30		5				22		
1939	661		13	11		1				44		23
1940	785	2	2	11		3	1			60		4
1941	548	1	2	10			1			80		7
1942	644		4	15		1	2			61		3
1943	499		1	12			2			31		3
1944	323		4	9						43		11
1945	356			16		9	1			49		6
1946	470	14	5	21		6	2		2	87		16
1947	655	8	1	21		5	3			117		10
1948	719	44	19	68		5				159		13
1949	659	156	1	64		23	3		2	66		19
1950	477	26		65		4	7		4	119		19
1951	652			75		9	9			116		6
1952	283		4	52		14	6			137		32
1953	411	3	14	37		16	6		3	114		14
1954	483		33	48		17	6		2	110		28
1955	520			50		19	6		4	122		14
1956	424		32	56		13	12			117		18
1957	377		42	39		54	10		8	92		41
1958	404		38	54		6	9		2	115		15
Total	16,811	695	531	1,149	14	303	107	4	34	2,529	72	422

(Note: E=Examination, W=Waiver, R=Reciprocity)

ORIGINAL CPA CERTIFICATES ISSUED

Year	OKLAHOMA			OREGON			PENNSYLVANIA			PUERTO RICO		
	E	W	R	E	W	R	E	W	R	E	W	R
1896												
1897												
1898												
1899								33				
1900							10					
1901							1					
1902							1					
1903							3					
1904							2					
1905							1					
1906							4					
1907							6		11			
1908							8		3			
1909							7		1			
1910							13					
1911							2		2			
1912							10					
1913					43		10		3			
1914												
1915				5			22		2			
1916				6			16					
1917	1	1		8			8		2			
1918	35		4				31		2			
1919	13		16									
1920	6		9	1			33					
1921	20		2	4		1	30		7			
1922	23			6		6			7			
1923	21		3	11		6	25					
1924	12		4	3		1	43		12			
1925	17			7		2	135		4			
1926	15			4		4	79		8			
1927				10		5	63		9			
1928	3		1	11		1	77		5			
1929			4	9		3	56		13			
1930				5		1	56		8			
1931	2		2	5		1	46		6			
1932	9		5	2		2	60		6			
1933	1		31	3		4	31		7			

Year	OKLAHOMA			OREGON			PENNSYLVANIA			PUERTO RICO		
	E	W	R	E	W	R	E	W	R	E	W	R
1934	3		7	5		1	44		7			
1935	10		3	4		1	43		11			
1936	2		5	6		2	37		11			
1937	10		2	17		4	38		17			
1938	3		8	11			2		30			
1939	5		6	8			102		16			
1940	19		3	21		1	75		12			
1941	12			7			66		6			
1942	40			16		3	70		17			
1943	10		8	16		4	70		9			
1944	23			11		3			10			
1945	5		7	15		7	42		26			
1946	26		8	26		5	97		25			
1947	17		9	23		14	138		41			
1948	53		18	57		6	178		18			
1949	58		4	17		2	250		17			
1950	90		9	85		23	332		25			
1951	25		6	48		39	306		19	3	38	
1952	69		20	44		8	293		10	1	35	
1953	42		14	31		6	181		10	7	11	8
1954	68		12	28		10	106		8	4	46	4
1955	75		9	51		5	167		4	1	15	
1956	47		24	40		10	206		4			
1957	42		18	37		4	107		14			
1958	54		14	46		4	175		14	1		
Total	986	1	295	770	43	199	4,014	33	499	17	145	12

(Note: E=Examination, W=Waiver, R=Reciprocity)

ORIGINAL CPA CERTIFICATES ISSUED

Year	RHODE ISLAND			SOUTH CAROLINA			SOUTH DAKOTA			TENNESSEE		
	E	W	R	E	W	R	E	W	R	E	W	R
1896												
1897												
1898												
1899												
1900												
1901												
1902												
1903												
1904												
1905												
1906	1	13										
1907	1	2										
1908												
1909	1	1										
1910	1		1									
1911			1									
1912												
1913											47	
1914	1		1							2		
1915				2	27							
1916				5								
1917	2			3								
1918							1					
1919			1				2			1		1
1920			3	2		1	1			5		1
1921	2		3	1								
1922				4			1			1		
1923	5		6	2						8	23	9
1924	9			4			1			7	3	3
1925	3		2	1			1			3	100	5
1926	2		1	4						10		20
1927			1	3			1			1		6
1928	3			6	1					16		10
1929	1			4						4	2	17
1930	3			3	2				1	3	3	4
1931					2		1			3	3	5
1932	3									9	2	4
1933	4			1						9		4

Year	RHODE ISLAND E	W	R	SOUTH CAROLINA E	W	R	SOUTH DAKOTA E	W	R	TENNESSEE E	W	R
1934	2			2						4		2
1935	4									10		4
1936	1	2		1	1		2			5		7
1937				1			2			24		5
1938	1	1								18		3
1939	7	2		4	1		1			15	21	5
1940	1				3		1			14		3
1941	3			5			1			21		2
1942	7			1	1		1			14		4
1943	1			1	1					6		1
1944	6			3	1		1			18		10
1945	1			3						22		11
1946	4	1		3	2		1			19		10
1947	9	2		7	2					26		19
1948	4			6						51		11
1949	5	5		4	2					34		24
1950	17	12		12	5		1			70		5
1951	6	7		11	1					73		5
1952	7	2		14	3		2			22		30
1953	3	9		8	4		4			47		12
1954	12	5		11	3		1			50		9
1955	8	4		10	4		3			50		16
1956	6	10		9	1		3			37		13
1957	9	7		10	1		3			46		10
1958	17	20		10	1		4			37		25
Total	183	16	109	181	28	42	40		1	815	204	335

(Note: E=Examination, W=Waiver, R=Reciprocity)

ORIGINAL CPA CERTIFICATES ISSUED

Year	TEXAS E	W	R	UTAH E	W	R	VERMONT E	W	R	VIRGINIA E	W	R
1896												
1897												
1898												
1899												
1900												
1901												
1902												
1903												
1904												
1905												
1906					1							
1907				1	1							
1908				1								
1909												
1910				1						3	16	
1911										2	1	
1912				4						2		
1913								1		2		
1914				4				1		2		
1915	2	24								1		
1916	1	25	7							2		
1917	1		2							6		
1918	2	1	4	2			1		1	2		
1919	1	2	3	4			1		1	2		
1920	7		15	2					1	1		
1921	9		3						2	9		
1922	22		3	2						2		
1923	10			4	1		1			6		
1924	37		12	6	5					6		
1925	16		12	1	3		1			13		
1926	7		7	1	2		2			11		5
1927	27		6	3	1					9		1
1928	42			4	1					11		9
1929	12		1	2			3			20		1
1930	25		1	7			1			18		4
1931	14		4	4						17		1
1932	29		7	5			2			8		
1933	36		15	5			2			4		1
1934	27		7	5			1			10		

Year	TEXAS			UTAH			VERMONT			VIRGINIA		
	E	W	R	E	W	R	E	W	R	E	W	R
1935	33		6	6			2			8		1
1936	15		10			1	1	1		6		
1937	50		31	6						1		7
1938	68		18	6			1			9		
1939	55		12	2	1		1	1		9		
1940	34		9	4	1		1	1		5		
1941	63		11	3						18		1
1942	52		16	9			3	1		28		
1943	43		22	5						19		
1944	37		24	5			1			16		4
1945	78		28	1	6		1			12		2
1946	121		59	15	6			1		16		7
1947	65		32	15	4			1		31		8
1948	210		58	12	10		2	2		18		28
1949	190		43	17	13		1	2		33		8
1950	302		45	20	5		2	1		31		5
1951	249		27	20	5		1			19		13
1952	224		81	20	5		2			55		10
1953	172		35	27	10		4			34		25
1954	201		49	17	7		4	1		22		72
1955	222		34	14	6		1	1		20		18
1956	184		51	22	2		1	1		39		22
1957	218		39	24	18			1		33		9
1958	250		52	34	10		1			38		38
Total	3,463	52	901	372	2	123	45	22		689	17	300

(Note: E═Examination, W═Waiver, R═Reciprocity)

ORIGINAL CPA CERTIFICATES ISSUED

Year	WASHINGTON			WEST VIRGINIA			WISCONSIN			WYOMING		
	E	W	R	E	W	R	E	W	R	E	W	R
1896												
1897												
1898												
1899												
1900												
1901												
1902												
1903	27											
1904												
1905												
1906	5											
1907												
1908	2											
1909	3											
1910	7											
1911	5			18						17		
1912	6											
1913	3							24	7			
1914	5						12	1	7	2		
1915	4				3		12	10	6			
1916	7						1	3	2			
1917	6			9			5	2				
1918							3	1				
1919	17			1			8	1	6			
1920	18			2			7	1	3			
1921	20						8	1	14			
1922	12			1			16	1	11	6		
1923	8			1			7	3	7			
1924	13			2			32		2	1		
1925	6			3			22		2	1		2
1926	7						18	11		1		
1927	20	1		3			21		18	9		1
1928	17	2		5			1		5	2		
1929	19	2		1			40		28	5		1
1930	4	1					17		13			
1931	14	1					44	5	14	3		
1932	18			5			52	11	3			
1933	11			2					10			
1934	15	1		3		2	43	14	3	5		

Year	WASHINGTON E	W	R	WEST VIRGINIA E	W	R	WISCONSIN E	W	R	WYOMING E	W	R
1935	20		2	8		1	38	5	4			
1936	16					2	47					
1937	21					1	80		3	1		
1938	22			2		1	23		9			
1939	29			1		1	33		5	2		
1940	38						51	7	1			
1941	50			2		4	38	5		1		1
1942	36					1	52			3		
1943	30			5			36					
1944	31						32	21		3		
1945	44	6		2			31		3	1		1
1946	51	2		5		1	34		13	1		
1947	98	3		1			40		32	4		
1948	59	8		5		1	55		33	1		
1949	69	27		13		4	74	11		5		1
1950	73	52		8		5	89		25	7		2
1951	107	19		9		5	109		18	2		2
1952	102	20		10		6	92	9	14	2		3
1953	68	13		11		9	72	26		6		
1954	79	19		8		6	30	4	15	5		
1955	61	18		15		1	40		10	3		4
1956	64	24		15		1	63		9	3		4
1957	94	25		6		4	60		41	6		2
1958	68	9		10		5	69		38	5		1
Total	1,602	27	255	174	21	61	1,657	187	424	96	17	25

(Note: E=Examination, W=Waiver, R=Reciprocity)

ORIGINAL CPA CERTIFICATES ISSUED

Year	E	TOTAL W	R	GRAND TOTAL
1896		56		56
1897		70		70
1898	6	1		7
1899	9	35		44
1900	16	25		41
1901	15	70		85
1902	37	24		61
1903	58	41		99
1904	67	31		98
1905	36	20		56
1906	58	20		78
1907	62	28	11	101
1908	56	229	4	289
1909	115	108	8	231
1910	201	117	8	326
1911	122	47	11	180
1912	108	9	2	119
1913	89	139	16	244
1914	122	7	25	154
1915	411	77	35	523
1916	213	33	35	281
1917	254	20	29	303
1918	248	8	56	312
1919	379	27	78	484
1920	532	73	94	699
1921	607	7	99	713
1922	774	2	120	896
1923	724	29	182	935
1924	851	7	210	1,068
1925	988	100	273	1,361
1926	949	11	179	1,139
1927	999	6	147	1,152
1928	875	5	193	1,073
1929	692	3	200	895
1930	793	3	306	1,102
1931	866	10	270	1,146
1932	934	58	121	1,113
1933	759	83	149	991
1934	801	55	139	995

Year	TOTAL E	TOTAL W	R	GRAND TOTAL
1935	963	55	152	1,170
1936	954	48	113	1,115
1937	1,277	38	172	1,487
1938	1,583	31	204	1,818
1939	1,385	21	199	1,605
1940	1,605	9	179	1,793
1941	1,435	13	155	1,603
1942	1,620		175	1,795
1943	1,369		122	1,491
1944	1,345	25	208	1,578
1945	1,247	1	384	1,632
1946	1,863	14	670	2,547
1947	2,425	65	619	3,109
1948	3,165	64	727	3,956
1949	3,251	248	605	4,104
1950	3,712	37	634	4,383
1951	3,784	40	562	4,386
1952	3,272	46	717	4,035
1953	2,963	42	631	3,636
1954	2,988	54	776	3,818
1955	3,019	16	640	3,675
1956	2,931		850	3,781
1957	2,851		912	3,763
1958	3,122	43	887	4,052
Total	68,955	2,604	14,293	85,852

(Note: E=Examination, W=Waiver, R=Reciprocity)

Index

Conway case, 275-276
objectionable tax activities (A.B.A.),
   284
practice before Treasury
   Department, 281-283
statement of principles relating to
   federal income tax practice, 284-
   285
Teele, Arthur W., 108, 131
The Accountant, 6, 30, 51, 167-168
The Accountant's Magazine, 30
The Journal of Accountancy, 75, 81, 103,
   131, 140, 161, 203, 211, 229, 231, 273,
   276, 279
*The Matter of Ramsey County Bar Asso-
   ciation* v. *Conway*, 275-276
The Office, 34
The Public Accountant, 35
The State ex rel. *Short, Attorney General
   et al.* v. *Riedell*, 174
Thomascolor case, 263-264
Touche, George A., 214
Touche, Niven and Company, 141-145, 213
Touche, Niven, Bailey & Smart, 213, 214,
   269-272
Treasury Department, practice before,
   186-187, 281-283

Trial Board, 256

ULTRAMARES CORPORATION v. TOUCHE et
   al, 141-145

VERIFICATION OF FINANCIAL STATEMENTS,
   149, 153, 159
Veysey and Veysey, 48
Veysey, Walter H. P., 48, 55-57
Veysey, William H., 56-57

WANGERIN ET AL v. WISCONSIN STATE BOARD
   OF ACCOUNTANCY, ET AL., 174
War contracts, 106-107
War Profits Control Act, 170
Watson, George, 18, 25
Wharton, Joseph, 61
Wilkinson, George, 36, 49, 84-88
Wilmot, H. W., 86
Women C.P.A.'s, 231
World War I, public accounting influ-
   enced by, 104-109
World War II, public accounting influ-
   enced by, 170-172

YALDEN, JAMES, 49, 55-57, 61, 63, 69
Young, Arthur, 50, 92